Invasions

Manchester University Press

Series editors: Anna Barton, Andrew Smith

Editorial board: David Amigoni, Isobel Armstrong, Philip Holden, Jerome McGann, Joanne Wilkes, Julia M. Wright

Interventions: Rethinking the Nineteenth Century seeks to make a significant intervention into the critical narratives that dominate conventional and established understandings of nineteenth-century literature. Informed by the latest developments in criticism and theory the series provides a focus for how texts from the long nineteenth century, and more recent adaptations of them, revitalise our knowledge of and engagement with the period. It explores the radical possibilities offered by new methods, unexplored contexts and neglected authors and texts to re-map the literary-cultural landscape of the period and rigorously re-imagine its geographical and historical parameters. The series includes monographs, edited collections, and scholarly sourcebooks.

To buy or to find out more about the books currently available in this series, please go to: https://manchesteruniversitypress.co.uk/series/interventions-rethinking-the-nineteenth-century/

Invasions

Fears and fantasies of imagined wars in Britain, 1871–1918

Christian K. Melby

MANCHESTER UNIVERSITY PRESS

Copyright © Christian K. Melby, 2025

The right of Christian K. Melby to be identified as the author of this work has been asserted in accordance with the Copyright, Designs and Patents Act 1988.

Published by Manchester University Press
Oxford Road, Manchester, M13 9PL

www.manchesteruniversitypress.co.uk

British Library Cataloguing-in-Publication Data
A catalogue record for this book is available from the British Library

ISBN 978 1 5261 6885 6 hardback

First published 2025

The publisher has no responsibility for the persistence or accuracy of URLs for any external or third-party internet websites referred to in this book, and does not guarantee that any content on such websites is, or will remain, accurate or appropriate.

EU authorised representative for GPSR:
Easy Access System Europe, Mustamäe tee 50, 10621 Tallinn, Estonia
gpsr.requests@easproject.com

Typeset by Newgen Publishing UK

For Clotilde

Contents

List of figures	*page* ix
Abbreviations	x
Note on spelling	xi
Acknowledgements	xii

Introduction	1

Part I: Beginnings

1 The Battles of Dorking	21

Part II: Expertise, public opinion and invasion-scare fiction, 1870s to 1914

2 After Dorking: expertise, service authors and 1870s future-war fiction	55
3 Public appeals and fiction, c. 1880–1894	83
4 Expert opinion and public pressure: from the 1890s to 1914	117

Part III: Authors and readers

5 Fiction and society: the British public in invasion-scare fiction, 1871–1914	153
6 Readers and receptions: the British public as audience and consumers, from the 1870s to the Edwardian high point	189

viii *Contents*

Part IV: Fiction goes to war

7 Invasion-scare literature and the First World War 231

Conclusion 263

Bibliography 274
Index 310

List of figures

1.1 George Tomkyns Chesney, *The Battle of Dorking: Reminiscences of a Volunteer* (Edinburgh and London: William Blackwood and Sons, 1871). Source: Author's own collection   *page* 33

1.2 George Tomkyns Chesney, *Slaget vid Dorking: En Skarpskytts Minnen* (Fahlun: Carl Nordins Förlag, 1872). Source: Author's own collection   40

4.1 Postcard from the play *An Englishman's Home* (1909). Source: Author's own collection   126

4.2 Postcard from the play *An Englishman's Home* (1909). Source: Author's own collection   126

6.1 Advertisement for William Le Queux, *The Invasion of 1910* (1906), in *The Times*, 13 March 1906, 11. Source: DMG Media, reproduced with permission   207

7.1 George Tomkyns Chesney, *The Battle of Dorking, with an Introduction by G.H. Powell* (London: Grant Richards Ltd., 1914). Source: Author's own collection   233

7.2 'Is your home worth fighting for?', 1915 Irish poster. Source: Imperial War Museum, reproduced with permission   246

7.3 Postcard, postmarked August 1918. Source: Author's own collection   247

Abbreviations

I use the following abbreviations in the footnotes:

BL   The British Library, London
HC   House of Commons
HL   House of Lords
HPD   Hansard Parliamentary Debates
NAM   National Army Museum, London
NLS   National Library of Scotland, Edinburgh
ODNB   Oxford Dictionary of National Biography
        (online edition)

Note on spelling

The titles of pamphlets and books are listed in italics throughout the text, while stories and articles published in newspapers, journals, etc. are listed in quotation marks. For the sake of consistency, if a story was first printed in a journal, and later reprinted as a book or a pamphlet, I have listed the story in italics. Events in fictional accounts will be referred to in the present tense; this is to separate fictional events from historical ones.

Acknowledgements

No book is written and created in a vacuum, springing forth fully formed from the pen (or keyboard, I suppose) of a solitary author. This one most certainly did not.

The book arguably has its genesis in an essay I wrote during my MA studies at King's College London, which triggered a wider interest in the topic. A huge thanks is due to Paul Readman, who I first met when I took his module on Patriotism and National Identities in Britain, c.1870–1918, many years ago. The Modern British History Reading Group, convened by Paul, has been a most conducive environment to exchange research ideas and get feedback on written material. All members of this group have a claim in the book, but a special thanks goes to Oliver Carter-Wakefield, Laura Forster, Michael Humphries, Hélène Maloigne, Martin Spychal, Ian Stewart, Brian Wallace and Matthew White. Ian and Laura are owed an extra nod for their help with the book; Ian has probably read through more of my article and chapter drafts than I have, in addition to serving as a sort of life coach for me through the years – thanks, buddy. Thanks are also due to David Edgerton; and to Jan Rüger and Adrian Gregory for their insightful comments and suggestions. I would also like to thank the members of the Invasion Network, and for all the organisers of conferences and seminars I have attended over the years.

Tuva Nodeland has been a helpful sparring partner for many of the ideas in this book, ever since they first emerged in essay form many years ago. I am very grateful to all colleagues, past and present, for conversations and discussions. Thank you to everyone at Manchester University Press for their help with the book, and a

Acknowledgements xiii

special thank you to the very generous and helpful comments I got from the anonymous reader: all remaining errors and mistakes are (probably) my own.

Finally, a big thanks to my family, to my parents and sister, and an absolutely enormous thanks to Anaïs Waag. Just as I was finishing work on this book, little Clotilde came along. It seems only fitting to dedicate the book to her: I am looking forward to the day when she can read it.

Introduction

The question of how Britain would provide enough food for its growing population in the event of a war breaking out was discussed at a sparsely attended session in the House of Commons in May 1914. The topic was not new – a 1905 Royal Commission on Supply of Food and Raw Material in Time of War had considered it at length and made several suggestions, solutions and criticisms – but the issue had never been settled properly. This lackadaisical attitude could be explained partly as the result of a lack of public pressure, according to one of the MPs who rose to speak that May evening, the Conservative Ellis Hume-Williams. People, he complained, did not understand that the way wars were fought had changed:

> There are wireless telegraphy, submarines and the increased power of explosives, and all of these add a hundred-fold to the dangers of transport. When I was a boy one used to read the stories of Jules Verne about people who dived under the sea and men who fought in the air. We looked upon him as an agreeable teller of fairy stories. But the picture of yesterday is the fact of to-day, and the dreams of now are the events of the future.

He added: 'It is very difficult to make the man in the street, the ordinary man who does not take the trouble to read and understand, apprehend that the danger is immediate'.[1]

Hume-Williams' remarks in the Commons that day are interesting both for what he left out, as well as for what he included. While Jules Verne's stories were popular reading material in Britain, the country had its own homegrown literature of future wars and imaginary battles. In fact, in the years between 1871 and 1914,

2 *Invasions*

Britain not only invented but perfected the wider literary trope of invasion and future war, and made it into a new form of literature. As Britons were subjected to war, revolution and blockade on the pages of fiction in pamphlets, journals, newspapers and books – and even on the stage and on film – the idea of invasion and future war itself became a part of the political and cultural landscape of modern Britain. The small British Expeditionary Force that sailed off to the continent in 1914 did so with an extensive army of authors behind it, an army which had fought and refought varieties of the Great War for decades before that conflict finally arrived. These sharpened pens had operated inside and outside official circles, military and naval commands, and newspaper offices across Britain and indeed the globe in the period leading up to the outbreak of war, and soldiers and civilians alike would continue to engage with imagined wars and invasions through the 1914–1918 conflict. And, as Hume-Williams hinted at, the effect this literature had on 'the man in the street' was unclear at best.

This book is an investigation of such literature. Specifically, it looks at invasion-scare fiction, broadly defined – stories imagining a British military setback and possible invasion – in the period between 1871 and 1918, and how these stories were written, read, experienced and interpreted. Beyond abstract ideas of how a future war and a potential invasion might play out, the stories presented readers with wide-ranging ideas about British society and the numerous challenges facing it. What follows is therefore a cultural history of the language of invasion-scare fiction, a social history of its promotors and audience, and a political history of its influence.

Images or fantasies of invasions were not an invention of the Victorians. According to Herodotus, in the early fifth century BCE the people of Athens fined the playwright Phrynicus after he staged a play about the Persian sack of Miletus, and decreed that the play should never be performed again.[2] While the stated rationale behind the ban was the sorrow the Athenians felt over the loss, it is easy to imagine that the real reason was their fear at the prospect of a similar fate befalling the inhabitants of their own *polis*, making this arguably the earliest invasion-scare story in Europe. In modern history, the prospect of invasion during the struggle with France at the turn of the nineteenth century fuelled not only the rise of the fiscal-military state in Britain, but also the careers of Samuel Coleridge,

Introduction

who wrote *Fears in Solitude* 'in 1798, during the alarm of an invasion';[3] and the caricaturist James Gillray, who visually depicted the 'Promis'd Horrors of the French Invasion' in 1796.[4] The threat of cross-channel invasion was suitably commodified, as Mark Philp notes, with Napoleon becoming 'good business for many printers, print sellers and publishers', as he took on the role of bogeyman by 1803–1805.[5] As Alexandra Franklin notes, such caricatures were particularly popular during the 1798 and 1803 invasion scares, though their meaning was at times ambiguous, and they could often be read in different ways.[6]

In the early nineteenth century, Britons were certainly no strangers to invasion agitation, or the idea of an 'invasion panic', from Napoleonic fears to Richard Cobden's descriptions of the 'puerile ... attempts to frighten the country' with visions of French naval-building plans mid-century.[7] 'Every age has its peculiar folly', wrote Charles MacKay at the beginning of Victoria's reign; 'some scheme, project, or phantasy into which it plunges'.[8] Numerous historians have placed the fear of invasion among the fantasies Victorians indulged in most eagerly. Ian Beckett, for example, surmises that Britain in the 1840s and 1850s was 'a society peculiarly susceptible to the phenomena of the "invasion panic"'; it was against this background that the Volunteer movement was established.[9]

However, attempts to, in Richard Cobden's analysis, elicit more money from parliament through 'appeals to the fears and resentment' of the nation[10] were unsteadily aimed, being directed against an abstract idea of a 'public opinion' that was in the process of changing. While the Duke of Wellington, the Napoleonic war hero, former prime minister and Commander-in-Chief, unwittingly created an invasion scare in 1847–1848 (the first of Cobden's 'three panics' of this period) it was never meant to be an appeal to a wide audience.[11] The scare was initiated by a leaked letter to the press;[12] the Duke never intended, or was much inclined, to inform or appeal to public opinion, no matter how narrowly defined. In contrast, a prominent 'professional "alarmist"' like Admiral Sir Charles Napier spent much energy trying to do the opposite: actively sounding the alarm several times during the 1840s and 1850s over perceived British weaknesses, with the intent to force the government to spend more on defence.[13] Before 'the people' gradually started becoming a meaningful political entity in a modern sense from the

4 *Invasions*

1860s onwards, due to an expanded franchise and an increased readership, this was arguably an abstract, not to say quixotic exercise. Early modern Britain serves as a 'model case' for Jürgen Habermas' idea of the development of a rational and political 'public sphere' – where, at the turn of the eighteenth century, '[f]orces endeavouring to influence the decisions of state authority appealed to the critical public in order to legitimate demands before this new forum' – but this public sphere, as Habermas also argues, was going through a process of change by the period leading up to the First World War.[14] Historians need to treat the mid- and late Victorian public as a different, not to say bigger, political animal than its forebears.

Panics, as Joanna Bourke points out, belong to the crowd; and in the late Victorian and Edwardian eras, 'people were more obsessed by fears about the crowd than at any time since the French Revolution'.[15] The end of the nineteenth century signalled what Gustave Le Bon termed the 'era of the crowds': 'To-day it is the traditions which used to obtain in politics, and the individual tendencies and rivalries of rulers which do not count; while, on the contrary, the voice of the masses has become preponderant'.[16] Between the 1860s and the time Europe's lamps went out in August 1914, 'the masses' were increasingly difficult to ignore for policymakers in Britain.[17] One key reason for this was the extension of the parliamentary franchise in 1867 and again in 1884, which did much to fashion a politics that contemporary observers described, by the Edwardian era, as 'democratic'.[18] By the 1890s and 1900s, approximately two-thirds of adult men had the vote.[19] With a more representative parliament and the birth of a 'respectable' electorate in 1867, what constituted 'public opinion' expanded as well: Walter Bagehot's proverbial average man had stepped out of the omnibus by the 1890s, and public opinion could now be found by asking 'the man in the street'.[20]

Added to this development was the expansion of the written word. The decade prior to the passing of the Second Reform Act in 1867 had seen the foundations being laid for a mass press in Britain. Beginning in 1853, the tax on advertisements was abolished, followed by the abolition of the newspaper tax itself in 1855, and the abolition of the duty on paper in 1861. In Stephen

Introduction 5

Koss' words, this meant that 'newspapers came into their own as moulders of public opinion'.[21] As the 1884 Reform Act expanded the franchise even further, the latter part of the nineteenth century was not only the era of Le Bon, but also of the newspaper baron Alfred Harmsworth, as Asa Briggs notes.[22] Illiteracy was declining; the daily newspaper became more widespread.[23] The period between 1870 and 1914 can thus be characterised as a time of burgeoning mass readership alongside electoral expansion. The public, in short, gradually started to matter more than it had done before, and as a consequence, attempts were made to manipulate, mould, and direct it. In G.R. Searle's words, '[t]he "man in the street" (to use the abstraction so favoured by the Edwardians) must at times have felt bewildered at the quantity and variety of the good advice he was receiving'.[24] The problem was that democracy – both a political phenomenon and a social category, meaning the newly enfranchised parts of society – was often perceived as unable to deal with questions of national defence in a rational and satisfactory way.

What was new about the invasion-scare fiction that emerged in the wake of George Tomkyns Chesney's story *The Battle of Dorking* (1871) was its engagement with a mass readership. Initially this audience was reached accidentally, and stories in the 1870s tended to decry rather than appeal to the masses. But this changed towards the end of the century, resulting in narratives aimed at a wide and varied audience from the 1890s onwards. In this period, as the idea of public opinion was changing, political agitators adopted the tools of advertising and the market. 'Our curse is the parochial politician in Parliament and the ineptitude of our Foreign Office ... and ill-informed democracy!' as the outspoken Admiral John Fisher wrote to Arnold White in July 1900. 'Is not a league of preaching friars required for a new crusade! ... You must keep on telling the people the same thing, and of course this is the secret of advertisement – Pears' Soap, etc!'[25] What followed in the wake of the first hesitant steps of democracy was therefore the gradual democratisation – or commodification, in the same manner as one would sell a commercial product, if Fisher's jibe is taken at face value – of invasion 'panics' in fictional form.[26] This development, and its result, is the subject of this book.

6   *Invasions*

Invasion, future wars and the British public

Much ink has been spilt over the question of how Britons perceived the outside world, and by extension themselves in the period leading up to 1914 and into the war years. Linda Colley's seminal study *Britons: Forging the Nation* remains the most famous, and arguably the most influential, though interest in Britain's relationship with its neighbours before 1914 has never really died down.[27] Curiously, however, few previous studies have attempted to adequately investigate and trace the influence that invasion scares generally, and invasion-scare fiction specifically, had on opinion in Britain. Despite more recent studies moderating earlier theories about a general 'war enthusiasm' in 1914,[28] the sentiments of pre-war society remain more of a mystery, and established opinions about Edwardian anxieties are rarely challenged. For military planners, the prospect of invasion was a feature of pre-1914 defence planning, but also marked an instance when the public seemed to have a direct influence over policy. As David Morgan-Owen's study of how the invasion question influenced military planning within both services prior to the First World War observes, 'the spectre of invasion excited the passions of the public on a regular basis – obliging politicians to take an active, if episodic interest in the armed forces' readiness to repulse a foreign attack'.[29] But what about the literature of invasion itself, the texts that existed in the grey area between official planning, public debate and the market? The aim of the following chapters is partly to challenge the assumption, expressed often enough, that the popularity of invasion-scare fiction is evidence that invasion constituted 'a national obsession' for the pre-1914 generation.[30] It certainly was for some, but invasion, and the literature of invasion, meant different things to different people at different times.

I.F. Clarke's *Voices Prophesying War*, the first edition of which was published in 1966, remains the pre-eminent study of what Clarke described as the 'literature of the imaginary wars of the future'.[31] Wary of describing such stories as 'science fiction', Clarke's preferred term 'future wars' was firmly established by the time the second edition of *Voices* was published in 1992.[32] In the wake of Clarke, who was more of a compiler and bibliographer, science fiction scholars have analysed future-war and invasion-scare

Introduction

fiction from various angles, though with a similar tendency to be wary of categorisation: the literary theorist Darko Suvin has noted that 'except for the purely political aspect of who wars with whom with what final redrawing of boundaries, ["future war" tales] do not contain any further S-F [science fiction] novum, such as a significantly different technology employed during or social organization arising out of the future war'.[33] However, as Kingsley Amis noted, science fiction itself is difficult to categorise in general, and '[a] definition of science fiction, though attempted with enormous and significant frequency by commentators inside the field, is bound to be cumbersome rather than memorable'.[34]

In this book I use the term 'invasion-scare fiction', to describe such texts where the British Isles are threatened with military invasion or a military setback in a recognisable (i.e., not too distant or too outlandish) future. The term owes much to A. Michael Matin, one of the foremost scholars on this type of literature, who classifies 'invasion-scare fiction' as 'a subtype of the future-war narratives'. 'This subtype, in turn, divides into and overlaps with various other sub-genres, such as espionage, terrorism, and naval blockade fictions', in addition to fictions describing attacks on imperial possessions.[35] Other literary studies, such as by Ailise Bulfin, have included various invasion texts in a wider category of gothic fiction.[36] In short, the invasion genre was multifaceted, ranging 'in sophistication and intent',[37] and encompassed a wide variety of stories and tropes: naturally, some were more anchored in reality than others.

The links between the political and the cultural, between the way invasion-scare and future-war fiction in the nineteenth and twentieth centuries were read and understood, have received thorough treatment from literary scholars as well as historians.[38] Limiting himself to Edwardian Britain – or England, to be specific – Samuel Hynes interprets the invasion literature as a sign of national anxiety; the stories verbalised Tory fears of the increasing power of the lower classes, and of the weakened ability to stave off hostile invasion as a consequence of this.[39] A conservative, reactionary mentality went alongside the national anxiety of the immediate pre-war years, according to Hynes. Other scholars have agreed with this focus on anxiety and political conservatism, rather than on technological innovation, as the driving force of the stories. Daniel Pick, questioning Clarke's assertion that invasion literature remained

8   *Invasions*

unchanged throughout the nineteenth century, sees anxiety directed at modernity in *fin-de-siècle* stories.[40] Matin, on the other hand, has used risk-perception theory to gauge the potential influence the author William Le Queux had on his readers, an approach than can help us understand how Le Queux's *oeuvre* was understood in its own time. While such approaches can be useful, they also miss the different ways the literature was read and discussed in its own time, and can therefore obfuscate rather than illuminate the context in which it was read.[41]

The structure of the book

The following chapters build on – alternatively, stand on the shoulders of – these existing studies and several others, but present a different reading of invasion-scare fiction: one that sees the literature as a complex, many-sided aspect of British culture. This entails reading the stories both as cultural products, and yet also as something less than clear political statements. The prospect of invasion, and the image of invasion in fiction, could serve different purposes and have different meanings depending on how it was presented or used. While there is much truth to Joep Leersen's point that literature and language – what people said and wrote – can tell us a lot about a period, I am less convinced by the idea that 'imaginative fiction (in England) prepared the nation for the trenches'.[42] In fact, British invasion-scare fiction pointed in different directions, and presented its audiences with different ideas and interpretations. Rather than taking sides in an argument over whether British *fin-de-siècle* society was one of 'optimism' or 'pessimism' – such ideas could coexist; societies are not monolithic entities – the book argues that invasion-scare fiction needs to be read in context with other developments. Peter Mandler's analysis of how the cultural historian 'must have a mental map of the *entire field of representation* in which their texts sit' springs to mind here.[43] Texts need to be contextualised; their meaning is found not only through an in-depth reading of the texts themselves, but by situating them in a societal and cultural framework.

Consequently, the book situates invasion-scare fiction within Victorian and Edwardian debates about the nature of 'the public' – a

Introduction 9

term that encompassed a varied group of people – and in particular how the public featured in defence debates. In his study of Victorian and Edwardian notions of 'public opinion', James Thompson has shown how the concept was contested throughout the period.[44] In 1867 John Morley asserted that the Second Reform Act had transferred power 'from a class to the nation',[45] but class has remained important in studies of readership and also of public opinion, not least because the Victorians and Edwardians themselves were very much in favour of seeing their society as one consisting of different classes.[46] Several studies have increased our understanding of Victorian readers – Jonathan Rose begins his book *The Intellectual Life of the British Working Classes* by stating that he 'proposes to enter the minds of ordinary readers in history'.[47] Underneath the surface of all this book's seven chapters lies the question of class, of belonging, of national and of imperial identity; of 'the public' both as an abstract idea and as a concrete category of readers, voters, and consumers. The following chapters therefore see the British readership as a political category as well as a socio-cultural one – that is, a group that was both talked about and talked to, through the medium of fiction.

The book combines specific case studies with a more general discussion of developments in publishing, in political and military debates, and in British culture to illustrate how the literature was received and what it can tell us about British society. The study argues that invasion-scare fiction needs to be read as politically less significant than previously thought, while still retaining its cultural influence. In the first couple of decades of the genre's existence, its engagement with a wide audience was limited. When the stories became a massively popular phenomenon in the early 1890s, they were reinvented, with spectacle at their centre and their political arguments toned down for a general audience. In addition, the stories were always open for reinterpretation, comments, praise and criticism – the genre, in short, needs to be read within the complex society in which the stories were written and disseminated. By the First World War, the genre could only with difficulty be mobilised as propaganda, partly because its meaning and ideology remained contested and open.

The book is divided into four parts, and seven chapters. Part I, covering chapter 1, serves as a prologue to the rest of the book, and shows how George Chesney's *The Battle of Dorking* laid the foundation for the invasion-scare genre for the rest of the century, and also how the literature of invasion would be received: as a politically contested, mocked, admired and flexible form of literature, where readers applied their own interpretation to the story. Part II, covering chapters 2, 3 and 4, provide a chronological overview of the development of invasion-scare fiction from the 1870s to the Edwardian era. These chapters examine the role of service writers and the idea of expertise in fiction and military planning, and shows how the stories developed in tandem with discussions over national and imperial defence. Part III, chapters 5 and 6, are thematic, providing an overview of how the British public featured as subjects in (chapter 5) and as readers of (chapter 6) invasion-scare literature between 1871 and 1914. Finally, in part IV, chapter 7 serves as the book's epilogue, showing how invasion-scare fiction could comment on and be used as war propaganda when the real 'Great War' broke out in 1914. The trend that had been in evidence ever since the publication of *The Battle of Dorking* in 1871 – that fiction could be used, reimagined, reinvented and repurposed – was cemented by the 1914–1918 war, bringing the genre, in a sense, full circle as Chesney's story was republished as war propaganda.

The focus in all of the chapters is on the British Isles, and the discussion only touches upon the rest of the world as it was seen from this vantage point at the edge of Western Europe. In a sense, of course, this spatial limitation, as the book's temporal limits, is arbitrary. The study could have included other periods, and other countries – invasion-scare literature did not die in the trenches on the Western Front; nor was it exclusively a British product – but there was something very British about the genre itself, and the way it was directly linked to the country in which its modern incarnation was born. Invasion-scare fiction illustrates the tensions between a burgeoning democratic system, the men who sought to govern it and the masses who composed it. Rather than being about the threats of an external world, the stories presented their authors' ideas of the British self to a readership who had their own visions of British insularity. This, therefore, is a study of pre-Great War Britons' ideas of themselves.

Introduction   11

The book ends in 1918, with a British mass-army mobilised and deployed to Western Europe. Its starting point is elsewhere, however, on a warm summer's day, and its location is more specific. It begins in an otherwise quiet, drowsy corner of Surrey, on a warm August afternoon in the 1870s.

Notes

1 Hansard Parliamentary Debates [hereafter HPD] House of Commons Debates [hereafter HC Deb] 13 May 1914 vol. 62 cc1233 and 1235.
2 George Rawlinson (ed.), *History of Herodotus*, 4 vols. (London: John Murray, 1875), III, 418: book six, 21.
3 Samuel Taylor Coleridge, *Fears in Solitude* (London: J. Johnson, 1798).
4 Held at the British Museum, London, museum number 1851,0901.823: www.britishmuseum.org/collection/object/P_1851-0901-823
5 Mark Philp, 'Introduction: The British Response to the Threat of Invasion, 1797-1815', in Mark Philp (ed.), *Resisting Napoleon: The British Response to the Threat of Invasion, 1797–1815* (Aldershot: Ashgate, 2006), 8.
6 Alexandra Franklin, 'John Bull in a Dream: Fear and Fantasy in the Visual Satires of 1803', in Philp (ed.), *Resisting Napoleon*, 125–139.
7 Richard Cobden, *The Three Panics: An Historical Episode*, 3rd edition (London: Ward & Co., 1862), 4.
8 Charles MacKay, *Memoirs of Extraordinary Popular Delusions and the Madness of Crowds*, 3rd edition, 2 vols. (London: G. Routledge & Co., 1856), II, 1.
9 Ian F.W. Beckett, *Riflemen Form: A Study of the Rifle Volunteer Movement 1859–1908* (Barnsley: Pen & Sword, 2007), 9.
10 Cobden, *Three Panics*, 8.
11 The second panic was in 1851–1853, and the third in 1859–1861. All three were Francophobic, and centred on the perceived threat of the French navy.
12 Cobden, *Three Panics*, 9.
13 Michael Steven Partridge, *Military Planning for the Defence of the United Kingdom, 1814–1870* (Westport: Praeger, 1989), 9, 14.
14 Jürgen Habermas, *The Structural Transformation of the Public Sphere: An Inquiry into a Category of Bourgeois Society*, transl. Thomas Burger and Frederick Lawrence (Cambridge: Polity, 1992), 57. Craig Calhoun writes that the principle of an inclusive public

sphere meant that it was open to '[a]nyone with access to cultural products – books, plays, journals': 'Introduction: Habermas and the Public Sphere', in Craig Calhoun (ed.), *Habermas and the Public Sphere* (Cambridge, MA & London: MIT Press, 1992), 13. An expanded readership and changes in consumer culture also changed the nature of the public sphere – to its detriment, according to Habermas.

15 Joanna Bourke, *Fear: A Cultural History* (London: Virago, 2006), 54.

16 Gustave Le Bon, *The Crowd: A Study of the Popular Mind* (London: T. Fisher Unwin, 1903), 15.

17 As Angus Hawkins points out, the modern 'two-party system', where parties compete for legitimacy through appeals to a mass electorate, was a product of the 1870s: ' "Parliamentary Government" and Victorian Political Parties, c.1830-c.1880', *The English Historical Review*, 104 (1989), 643.

18 See Graham Wallas, *Human Nature in Politics* (London: Archibald Constable & Co., 1908). Though Victorians were often wary of describing their political system as *democratic*, and indeed few claimed that it ever was or should be, they could at least see their system as representative. See Martin Pugh, *The Making of Modern British Politics, 1867–1945*, 3rd edition (Oxford: Blackwell Publishing, 2002), 4. The term 'democracy' is problematic in this period, since the word did not mean the same to Victorians as it means today. Hawkins notes that it 'was an elastic, ill-defined, illiberal, and potentially repressive concept fraught with danger – not least in threatening the swamping of intelligence by the ill-educated masses'. By the 1860s and 1870s the term lost some of its earlier negative connotations and moved towards a more positive and inclusive definition, but the exact meaning of the term remained unclear: Angus Hawkins, *Victorian Political Culture: 'Habits of Heart and Mind'* (Oxford: Oxford University Press, 2015), 13–14, 269–270.

19 See Neal Blewett, 'The Franchise in the United Kingdom 1885–1918', *Past & Present*, 32 (1965), 27–56.

20 See Hawkins, *Victorian Political Culture*, 270; and James Thompson, *British Political Culture and the Idea of 'Public Opinion', 1867–1914* (Cambridge: Cambridge University Press, 2013), 35ff.

21 Stephen Koss, *The Rise and Fall of the Political Press in Britain* (Chatham: Fontana Press, 1990), 1–2.

22 Asa Briggs, 'The Language of "Mass" and "Masses" in Nineteenth-Century England', in David E. Martin and David Rubinstein (eds), *Ideology and the Labour Movement: Essays Presented to John Saville* (London: Croom Helm, 1979), 71.

23 G.R. Searle, *A New England? Peace and War 1886–1918* (Oxford: Clarendon Press, 2004), 110.

Introduction 13

24 G.R. Searle, *The Quest for National Efficiency: A Study in British Politics and Political Thought, 1899–1914* (London: Ashfield Press, 1990), 51.

25 Quoted in *Fear God and Dread Nought: The Correspondence of Admiral of the Fleet Lord Fisher of Kilverstone*, Arthur J. Marder (ed.), 3 vols. (London: Jonathan Cape, 1952–1959), I, 157.

26 The word 'commodification' entails not only the wish to spread the message of invasion scares, but an insistence on the marketability and sales of them. The use of advertising, and publishers' wish to sell invasion-scare narratives meant that scares were part of a wider Victorian 'commodity culture', a term used by Thomas Richards, *The Commodity Culture of Victorian England: Advertising and Spectacle, 1851–1914* (London: Verso, 1991).

27 Linda Colley, 'Britishness and Otherness: An Argument', *Journal of British Studies*, 31 (1992), 309–329; also Colley, *Britons: Forging the Nation 1707–1837* (London: Pimlico, 1994). On Englishness, see Robert Colls and Philip Dodd (eds), *Englishness: Politics and Culture 1880–1920*, 2nd edition (London: Bloomsbury Academic, 2014); Krishan Kumar, *The Making of English National Identity* (Cambridge: Cambridge University Press, 2003); Kumar, *The Idea of Englishness: English Culture, National Identity and Social Thought* (Farnham: Ashgate, 2015); Peter Mandler, *The English National Character: The History of an Idea from Edmund Burke to Tony Blair* (New Haven and London: Yale University Press, 2006), to name a few. On Britain's relationship with Germany, Paul M. Kennedy, *The Rise of the Anglo-German Antagonism 1860–1914* (London: George Allen & Unwin, 1980) is still influential, but scholars have continued to publish on the relationship between the two countries: Jan Rüger's two books, *The Great Naval Game: Britain and Germany in the Age of Empire* (Cambridge: Cambridge University Press, 2009); and *Heligoland: Britain, Germany, and the Struggle for the North Sea* (Oxford: Oxford University Press, 2017); and article, 'Revisiting the Anglo-German Antagonism', *Journal of Modern History*, 83 (2011), 579–617, are good examples of comparative studies of the two countries in this period. On the Anglo-German pre-1914 'newspaper wars', see Dominik Geppert, *Pressekriege: Öffentlichkeit und Diplomatie in den deutsch-britischen Beziehungen (1896–1912)* (Munich: Oldebourg, 2007), esp. 307–319 for a discussion of invasion-scare literature. See also Richard Scully, *British Images of Germany: Admiration, Antagonism & Ambivalence, 1860–1914* (Basingstoke: Palgrave Macmillan, 2012).

28 Adrian Gregory, 'British "War Enthusiasm" in 1914: A Reassessment', in Gail Braybon (ed.), *Evidence, History and the Great War: Historians*

14 *Invasions*

and the Impact of 1914–18 (New York and Oxford: Berghahn, 2003), 67–85; Adrian Gregory, *The Last Great War: British Society and the First World War* (Cambridge: Cambridge University Press, 2008), 9–39; Catriona Pennell, '"The Germans have Landed!" Invasion Fears in the South-East of England, August to December 1914', in Heather Jones, Jennifer O'Brien and Cristoph Schmidt-Supprian (eds), *Untold War: New Perspectives in First World War Studies* (Leiden and Boston: Brill, 2008), 95–116; and Catriona Pennell, *A Kingdom United: Popular Responses to the Outbreak of the First World War in Britain and Ireland* (Oxford: Oxford University Press, 2012). A similar view is expressed in Douglas Newton, *The Darkest Days: The Truth Behind Britain's Rush to War, 1914* (London and New York: Verso, 2014). See also Alexander Watson, *Enduring the Great War: Combat, Morale and Collapse in the German and British Armies, 1914–1918* (Cambridge: Cambridge University Press, 2008), esp. 44–56; and Niall Ferguson, *The Pity of War* (London: Allen Lane, 1998), 174–211. Ferguson argues that the popularity of Edwardian future-war stories was not necessarily an indication that people expected, or wished for, a Great War: 1–15.

29 David G. Morgan-Owen, The Fear of Invasion: Strategy, Politics, and British War Planning, 1880–1914 (Oxford: Oxford University Press, 2017), 12. For a critical discussion of the links between invasion scares and official strategy, see Morgan-Owen, 'Scares, Panics, and Strategy: The Politics of Security and British Invasion Scares before 1914', *Diplomacy & Statecraft*, 33 (2022), 442–473. In an earlier study, John Gooch noted that Britain was at times obsessed with the fear of being invaded. However, this claim, like Morgan-Owen's monograph, focuses on the defence apparatus – the services and their members – not British society as such: *The Prospect of War: Studies in British Defence Policy 1847–1942* (London: Frank Cass, 1981), 1. See also W. Michael Ryan, 'The Invasion Controversy of 1906–1908: Lieutenant-Colonel Charles à Court Repington and British Perceptions of the German Menace', *Military Affairs*, 44 (1980), 8–12. Ryan sees invasion scares, served up in press and fiction, as 'induc[ing] a state of near paranoia' in late nineteenth- and early twentieth-century Britain, helping to push the country towards war in 1914. However, Ryan is more concerned with the inner workings of the defence establishment, rather than public perceptions.

30 The quote is from Howard Roy Moon, 'The Invasion of the United Kingdom: Public Controversy and Official Planning 1888–1918' (University of London, Ph.D. thesis, 1968), 652. A similar conclusion has been reached by, among others, Catriona Pennel,

A Kingdom United, 20. In his social history of the Volunteer force, a body originally set up in the wake of questions raised over British vulnerability earlier in the century, Hugh Cunningham opens with the statement that 'Victorian Britain was afflicted by a chronic anxiety about invasion': Hugh Cunningham, *The Volunteer Force: A Social and Political History 1859–1908* (London: Croom Helm, 1975), 5. See also Beckett, Riflemen Form. Claims like this are found in other literature not dealing specifically with invasion scares. Worth mentioning here is John Ramsden's work on German–British relations after 1890, which states that stories of German invasion influenced British public opinion to a degree that made a war with Germany go from 'utterly fantastic' in 1890 to 'inescapable' in 1914: *Don't Mention the War: The British and the Germans since 1890* (London: Abacus, 2007), 58, 71, 77. For Andreas Rose, 'England trembled at least until 1910 almost daily at warnings of an imminent invasion, presented all too credibly': *Between Empire and Continent: British Foreign Policy before the First World War*, transl. Rona Johnston (New York & Oxford: Berghahn, 2019), 43. Rose also argues that writers both directly and indirectly influenced policymakers in Britain.

31 I.F. Clarke, *Voices Prophesying War, 1763–1984* (London: Oxford University Press, 1966), 4.

32 I.F. Clarke, *Voices Prophesying War: Future Wars 1763–3749*, 2nd edition (Oxford: Oxford University Press, 1992). Unless otherwise specified, I will be referring to this second edition throughout the book. See also I.F. Clarke, *The Tale of the Future, from the Beginning to the Present Day*, 3rd edition (London: The Library Association, 1978); *The Pattern of Expectation, 1644–2001* (London: Jonathan Cape, 1979); 'The Battle of Dorking', *Victorian Studies*, 8 (1965), 309–328; 'Forecasts of Warfare in Fiction 1803–1914', *Comparative Studies in Society and History*, 10 (1967), 1–25; 'The Origins of Future War Fiction', *Science Fiction Studies*, 23 (1996), 546–548; 'Before and after "The Battle of Dorking"', *Science Fiction Studies*, 24 (1997), 33–46; 'Future-War Fiction: The First Main Phase 1871–1900', *Science Fiction Studies*, 24 (1997), 387–412; 'Trigger-Happy: An Evolutionary Study of the Origins and Development of Future-War Fiction, 1763–1914', *Journal of Social and Evolutionary Systems*, 20 (1997), 117–136; 'The Battle of Dorking: Second Thoughts', *Extrapolation*, 40 (1999), 277–283. Clarke also edited two volumes of future-war stories: *The Tale of the Next Great War, 1871–1914: Fictions of Future Warfare and of Battles still-to-come* (Liverpool: Liverpool University Press, 1995); *The Great War with Germany, 1890–1914: Fictions*

16   *Invasions*

and Fantasies of the War-to-come (Liverpool: Liverpool University Press, 1997).

33 Darko Suvin, *Victorian Science Fiction in the UK: The Discourses of Knowledge and of Power* (Boston: G.K. Hall & Co., 1983), 4–5. See also Suvin, *Metamorphoses of Science Fiction: On the Poetics and History of a Literary Genre* (New Haven and London: Yale University Press, 1979).

34 Kingsley Amis, *New Maps of Hell: A Survey of Science Fiction* (London: Penguin Books, 2012), 3. Science fiction can be defined here as fictional imaginings of future events. The term is helpful, but still problematic, for the pre-1930 era, as clear publishing categories had yet to emerge: see Edward James, 'Science Fiction by Gaslight: An Introduction to English-Language Science Fiction in the Nineteenth Century', in David Seed (ed.), *Anticipations: Essays on Early Science Fiction and its Precursors* (Syracuse: Syracuse University Press, 1995), 27. H. Bruce Franklin does not attempt to define science fiction, but states that although the phrase may not have been used until the twentieth century, this can be explained by 'the earlier taboo against using nouns to modify nouns', and he hints that science fiction's depth is more vast than many imagines: *Future Perfect: American Science Fiction of the Nineteenth Century* (New York: Oxford University Press, 1966), x, xii. Victorian and Edwardian proto-science fiction is often referred to as 'scientific romance', a term preferred by some scholars: see Brian Stableford, *Scientific Romance in Britain, 1890–1950* (London: Fourth Estate, 1985); and Roger Luckhurst, 'Scientific Romance, Fantasy and the Supernatural', in Michael Saler (ed.), *The Fin-De-Siècle World* (London: Routledge, 2015), 677–690. H.G. Wells, in the preface to a later edition of his 1908 novel *The War in the Air*, noted of those stories he had written 'which are usually spoken of as "scientific romances" or "futurist romances"', that a better term would be 'fantasias of possibility': *The War in the Air: And Particularly How Mr. Bert Smallways Fared While It Lasted* (Harmondsworth: Penguin Books, 1941), 7.

35 A. Michael Matin, 'The Creativity of War Planners: Armed Forces Professionals and the Pre-1914 British Invasion Scare Genre', *English Literary History*, 78 (2011), 802. On espionage fiction and 'spy fever' see David A.T. Stafford, 'Spies and Gentlemen: 'The Birth of the British Spy Novel, 1893–1914', *Victorian Studies*, 24 (1981), 489–509; and David French, 'Spy Fever in Britain, 1900–1915', *The Historical Journal*, 21 (1978), 355–370. Matin, more specifically, also argues that invasion-scare stories, in their essence, consist of ten literary motifs, though this is more an illustration of the generic use of clichés in the genre than a way of separating the various sub-genres from

Introduction 17

one another ('Creativity of War Planners', 804). See also A. Michael Matin, '"We Aren't German Slaves Here, Thank God": Conrad's Transposed Nationalism and British Literature of Espionage and Invasion', *Journal of Modern Literature*, 21 (1997–1998), 251–280; Matin, ' "The Hun is at the Gate!"': Historicising Kipling's Militaristic Rhetoric, From the Imperial Periphery to the National Center: Part One: The Russian Threat to Imperial India', *Studies in the Novel*, 31 (1999), 317–356; Matin, ' "The Hun is at the Gate!"': Historicising Kipling's Militaristic Rhetoric, From the Imperial Periphery to the National Center: Part Two: The French, Russian, and German Threats to Great Britain', *Studies in the Novel*, 31 (1999), 432–470; Matin, 'Scrutinizing *The Battle of Dorking*: The Royal United Service Institution and the Mid-Victorian Invasion Controversy', *Victorian Literature and Culture*, 39 (2011), 385–407.

36 See Ailise Bulfin, ' "To Arms!"': Invasion Narratives and Late-Victorian Literature', *Literature Compass*, 12 (2015), 482–496; Bulfin, *Gothic Invasions: Imperialism, War and Fin-de-Siècle Popular Fiction* (Cardiff: University of Wales Press, 2018); and Bulfin, ' "Fast lapsing back into barbarism": Social Evolution, the Myth of Progress and the Gothic Past in Late-Victorian Invasion and Catastrophe Fiction', *Victorian Popular Fictions*, 5 (2023), 37–57.

37 Michael Hughes and Harry Wood, 'Crimson Nightmares: Tales of Invasion and Fears of Revolution in Early 20th Century Britain', *Contemporary British History*, 28 (2014), 298.

38 See, for example, Michael Paris, *Warrior Nation: Images of War in British Popular Culture, 1850–2000* (London: Reaktion, 2000). The third chapter of the book deals with future-war stories, 83–109. See also Cecil D. Eby, *The Road to Armageddon: The Martial Spirit in English Popular Literature, 1870–1914* (Durham and London: Duke University Press, 1987).

39 Samuel Hynes, *The Edwardian Turn of Mind* (Princeton: Princeton University Press, 1968), 34. See also Matthew Beaumont, 'Cacotopianism, the Paris Commune, and England's Anti-Communist Imaginary, 1870–1900', *English Literary History*, 73 (2006), 465–487. Joseph S. Meisel uses similar arguments to Hynes, seeing pre-1914 British invasion as revealing 'contemporary questions and fears', though without specifically singling out class antagonisms: 'The Germans are Coming! British Fiction of a German Invasion, 1871–1913' in *War, Literature and the Arts*, 2 (1990), 41–79.

40 Daniel Pick, *War Machine: The Rationalisation of Slaughter in the Modern Age* (New Haven and London: Yale University Press, 1993), 118. See also 115–135.

18   *Invasions*

41 A. Michael Matin, 'Gauging the Propagandist's Talents: William le Queux's Dubious Place in Literary History: Part One', *Critical Survey*, 32 (2020), 79–98; Matin, Gauging the Propagandist's Talents: William le Queux's Dubious Place in Literary History: Part Two', *Critical Survey*, 32 (2020), 193–218. Matin's discussion of Le Queux's relationship with official propaganda during the First World War is, however, very insightful.
42 Joep Leersen, 'Enmity, Identity, Discourse: Imagology and the State', in Katharina Edstadler, Sandra Folie and Gianna Zocco (eds), *New Perspectives on Imagology* (Leiden and Boston: Brill, 2022), 56.
43 Peter Mandler, 'The Problem with Cultural History', *Cultural and Social History*, 1 (2004), 97. Original emphasis.
44 Thompson, *British Political Culture*. A.J.A. Morris observes that 'it is apparent that what was supposed to constitute public opinion depended upon who was defining the term and for what purpose': *The Scaremongers: The Advocacy of War and Rearmament, 1896–1914* (London: Routledge & Kegan Paul, 1984), 377.
45 Quoted in Briggs, ' "Mass" and "Masses" ', 70.
46 Suvin, *Victorian Science Fiction*, 264. As David Cannadine notes, 'most Victorians believed that theirs was a viable hierarchical society': *Class in Britain* (New Haven and London: Yale University Press, 1998), 104.
47 Jonathan Rose, *The Intellectual Life of the British Working Classes*, 2nd edition (New Haven and London: Yale University Press, 2001), 1. See also Philip Waller, *Writers, Readers and Reputations: Literary Life in Britain 1870–1918* (Oxford: Oxford University Press, 2006).

Part I

Beginnings

1

The Battles of Dorking

What if the case of either combatant was ours? ... could we do what is now being done by the Germans? Could we imitate the conduct of the French? What if Kent and Sussex were in possession of the invader – what if foreign cavalry were levying contributions in Lewes and Tunbridge Wells – that London was threatened by a conquering army?[1]

Happily, with an Empire on which the sun never sets, we ought never to be without an occasion for alarm. When the fit of panic is subsiding and the fit of parsimony is coming on, there is always an abundant reserve of wars and rumors of wars, of invasions, and conquests, and other terrible contingencies ...[2]

Dorking is a sleepy southern English town, located amidst green hills in the county of Surrey, about an hour's train ride from London. *Baedeker,* in its first edition guide to Great Britain, described it as 'delightfully situated ... amid some of the most pleasing scenery in England'. Nearby Box Hill, now in the possession of the National Trust, 'commands a charming view' according to the guide book. Keats wrote *Endymion,* a poem that also praises the area as peacefully pastoral, near the hill.[3] *Baedeker* also noted that the town of Dorking itself might be familiar for its own piece of literature: 'Others will know the name from the "Battle of Dorking", a clever little book by Col. Chesney, who depicts the imaginary overthrow here of the British forces by the invading Teuton'.[4] This 'clever little book' is the subject of this chapter.

The short distance from the capital, along with the lush English scenery of the surrounding countryside, made Dorking a fitting location for George Tomkyns Chesney to place an invading German army. Chesney was an engineer in the Indian Army, first commissioned to

22   *Beginnings*

the Bengal Engineers in 1848; by 1871 he was a brevet lieutenant-colonel and principal at the Royal Indian Civil Engineering College at Coopers Hill.[5] In Chesney's tale, presented as a warning from the future, Dorking is the scene of a destructive battle between poorly trained and equipped British Volunteers and their efficient German opponents. The latter routs the unprepared British troops and proceeds to conquer Britain and dismantle its empire.

Stating that he planned to 'invade' Guildford, Chesney first sketched out the idea in a letter to John Blackwood, of the Edinburgh-based *Blackwood's Magazine*, in February 1871. He argued that a story of a successful invasion of the British Isles would be 'a useful way of bringing home to the country the necessity for thorough reorganisation'.[6] The resulting *Battle of Dorking*, published anonymously in the May issue of *Blackwood's Magazine*, was therefore a highly politicised text, throwing heavy punches against the Liberal government, the organisation of the army and British short-sightedness in general.

By April 1872 Chesney's reprinted story had sold 108,252 copies in pamphlet form alone, according to *Blackwood*'s own statistics.[7] Foreigners also took an interest, and gaps in the company's correspondence along with a suspicion that a number of translations were pirated could mean that the final number of printed versions of the tale might be substantially higher than we know, according to I.F. Clarke, the foremost authority on the story.[8] For John Blackwood and his circle, 1871, or 'the year of the "Battle of Dorking"' in their own parlance,[9] saw a universal and spontaneous response to the story, described in a letter from Blackwood to his nephew, where he claims to have been told that 'nobody can take it up for five minutes without a waiter coming to ask if he is done with it'.[10] A later history of the publishing firm retold this interpretation, quoting the same letter,[11] and Clarke repeated the claim.[12] The publisher's interpretation of the story's readership and reception has become accepted history: Clarke described *Dorking* as having 'alarmed the nation, amazed a continent, and annoyed the Prime Minister'.[13] Clearly, Chesney's narrative was a publishing success, reaching a large number of readers. But its cultural and political influence was ambiguous, and even its author's intent in writing it remains not entirely clear. These are the subjects of this chapter, which looks at 1871 – the year of *The Battle of Dorking*.

The Battles of Dorking

The *Dorking* narrative

The Battle of Dorking was in its essence an anti-Gladstone tale, and *Blackwood's Magazine* – a publication leaning heavily towards the Conservatives – was thus a fitting place to publish it. Previous 1871 issues of the magazine had featured a series of articles attacking the Liberal Prime Minister William Gladstone's first ministry (1868–1874) in general and the – in *Blackwood's* eyes – failed Cardwell army reforms in particular. As Secretary of State for War, Edward Cardwell oversaw a number of administrative and organisational reforms of the British army, including the attempt to create a reserve of trained men through the introduction of short service, and the abolition of the purchase system. Victorian army officers had up until the reforms purchased their commissions, a state of affairs with several obvious drawbacks. However, Cardwell's reform attempts met with opposition, and the Secretary of State had to contend with criticism from several different sources.[14] Contributors to *Blackwood's Magazine* were among the unimpressed. The February issue, for example, published the same month that the Treaty of Versailles finally put an end to the Franco-Prussian war, included several scathing comments on the state of British military preparedness. One article took stock of the lessons learned from the war about effective army organisation, noting that '[t]he French army [...] is democratic to the core. [...] The Prussian army, on the contrary, is thoroughly aristocratic'.[15] Another piece observed of the military unpreparedness of the Liberal governments that 'Continental Europe has been a huge camp for not far short of twenty years, without, as it would seem, giving an hour's serious uneasiness to the Liberal Governments which have in this country succeeded one another'.[16] The edition also included a poem, ominously titled 'Wake, England Wake!', that summed up the mood of the magazine:

> Above, around, and east and west,
> The storm-clouds muster swift and dark;
> Think *we* the flood of fire to breast,
> Safe in our isle as in the ark?[17]

Chesney, however, along with some other contributors to *Blackwood's*, was not a blinkered anti-reformist; his objections to Cardwell and Liberal policies were not based on any ingrained unwillingness to

24   *Beginnings*

contemplate change in Britain's military organisation. Rather, the problem was that the reforms were not far-reaching enough.

Opening with a lament over the lost riches of England, *The Battle of Dorking*'s narrator, a former Volunteer speaking fifty years into the future, tells his grandchildren how the country was lost to the invaders because of political short-sightedness: 'in our folly' he notes, 'we were too careless even to insure our prosperity'. The German victory over France should have provided a lesson, but, the narrator sighs, 'our Government had come into office on a cry of retrenchment, and could not bring themselves to eat their own pledges'.[18] He continues:

> This party always decried military establishments as part of a fixed policy for reducing the influence of the Crown and the aristocracy. They could not understand that the times had altogether changed, that the Crown had really no power, and that the Government merely existed at the pleasure of the House of Commons, and that even Parliament-rule was beginning to give way to mob-law.[19]

The narrator, and by extension Chesney, then takes aim at the Gladstone administration's failure to reform the army: 'the ministry were only too glad of this excuse to give up all the strong points of a scheme they were not really in earnest about'. This has led to untrained militia and Volunteers, 'because to call them out for drill would "interfere with the industry of the country"'.[20] When these untrained part-time soldiers meet the Germans in the climactic battle, the result is defeat and humiliation. In *Dorking*, British pluck is not frowned upon; Chesney simply relates how planning and training are needed to accompany such martial vigour.

Not bothering too much with describing international affairs, except a note on the overstretched resources of the army and navy,[21] Chesney summed up the outline of the story in a letter to John Blackwood in March:

> We have the quarrel with America and Russia, dispersion of all our forces, followed by rising in India. Sudden appearance of Germany on the scene. Sentimental platitudes of Messrs. Gladstone & Co., trim[m]ing leaders in the "Times". Destruction of our "Field Line" by new torpedoes. Arrival of 100,000 Sanscrit-speaking Junkers [in the end, Chesney decided to double that number[22]] brimming over with "Geist" and strategy.[23]

The Battles of Dorking 25

From the beginning, Blackwood was supportive of Chesney's suggestion of an invasion story to 'awaken people': 'I like uncommonly your idea ... of a supposed successful invasion of England' he wrote to him in February.[24]

The story itself is a richly detailed portrayal of the ensuing battles, though even contemporaries commented on the archaic mode of fighting. An American critic, presumably with his own country's civil war experience fresh in his memories, scoffed at the lack of trenches and other prepared defences: 'Have European nations never yet heard of the shovel and the temporary earthwork as important protections for young troops against the modern arms of precision?'[25] Yet Chesney was not attempting to provide a thorough description of modern warfare; his story depicts the *consequences* of such warfare.

The Battle of Dorking's sympathies lie with an idealised version of a rural, English nation: naïve, failing but definitively worth fighting for. London is initially the scene of panic and consternation,[26] while by contrast the city on the night before the German landing is described in pastoral terms, and therefore with more sympathy:

> The whole town was quite still – the lull before the storm; ... I could not but contrast the peacefulness of the morning – no sound breaking the silence but the singing of birds in the garden – with the passionate remorse and indignation that would break out with the day.[27]

Even the narrator's arrival at the would-be battlefield, before the Volunteers are redirected to Dorking, is described in fond, rural terms:

> At last we reached the top of Leith Hill. It is a striking spot, being the highest point in the south of England. The view from it was splendid, and most lovely did the country look this summer day, although the grass was brown from the long drought.[28]

The scene at Dorking is similarly lovingly portrayed, described as 'one of the most beautiful scenes in England': 'what, as I remember, most impressed me', the narrator continues,

> was the peaceful beauty of the scene – the little town with outline of the houses obscured by a blue mist, the massive crispness of the foliage, the outlines of the great trees, lighted up by the sun, and relieved by deep blue shade.[29]

26 *Beginnings*

The scene is thus set: fighting and dying in such a location makes the British defeat all the more disturbing. Retreating back on Kingston after being mauled by the German advance at Dorking, the Volunteers take up position on another hill, which has a view over the Thames, 'glistening like a silver field in the bright sunshine'.[30] This is the English landscape that the narrator and the other Volunteers have fought for, and lost: 'To most of us the scene could not but call up their associations of happy days of peace – days now ended and peace destroyed through national infatuation'.[31] Chesney ends his description of the defeats suffered by the Volunteers, with the battle raging in the gardens and homes of his middle-class readership: 'that straggling line of houses and gardens must surely be broken through at some point'.[32]

And broken through it is, as the war reaches the women and children in their villas, outside London.[33] Here the narrative ends, and the final pages instead turn to the Volunteer's interpretation of the reasons behind the collapse:

> There, across the narrow Straits, was the writing on the wall; but we would not choose to read it. The warnings of the few were drowned in the voice of the multitude. Power was then passing away from the class which had been used to rule, and to face political dangers, and which had brought the nation with honour unsullied through former struggles, into the hands of the lower classes, uneducated, untrained to the use of political rights, and swayed by demagogues ... Politics had become a mere bidding for Radical votes, and those who should have led the nation stooped rather to pander to the selfishness of the day, and humoured the popular cry which denounced those who would secure the defence of the nation by enforced arming of its manhood, as interfering with the liberties of the people.[34]

To Clarke, the story was perfectly suited to capture the anxiety of the period: he assumed that the success of the tale was partly due to the timing of its publication, since, for Britain, 'the year 1871 was passed in a mood of foreboding and anxiety for the future'.[35] This echoes a contemporary understanding: *The Morning Post* attributed its success to the feeling in the country:

> Without wishing to depreciate the literary merits of "The Battle of Dorking," we are disposed to attribute its extraordinary circulation

The Battles of Dorking

and popularity mainly to the circumstance of its having hit the right nail on the head and struck a responsive chord by giving expression to a widespread feeling of insecurity and distrust.[36]

Such a statement is not surprising coming from *The Morning Post*, however; the paper was as critical of Gladstone as the story. Indeed, *Dorking*'s seemingly Conservative-leaning arguments meant that it was discussed more on the Tory end of the political spectrum than on the Liberal. *Punch* correctly identified this schism when it mocked that 'Ebony's [*Blackwood*'s] Article-writer might have shifted colours and figures – have given England the Lion's part and Germany that of the Mouse ... had he but hailed from Gladstone's instead of Dizzy's [Conservative leader Benjamin Disraeli's] side of the House'.[37] Liberal feelings were perhaps best summed up by *The Evening Gazette*'s judgement on *Blackwood*'s story. It was, the paper noted, 'a sarcastic invective on the Government policy in general, and Mr Cardwell's Army Reorganisation Bill in particular'. The paper concluded that '[i]f England is in danger, it is not the Tories, as at present led or organised, who will save her'.[38] Thus, whereas the Conservative *Pall Mall Gazette* could praise Chesney for having described 'scenes imagined for England without one violation of the laws of probability',[39] the Liberal *Liverpool Mercury* instead lambasted the invasion argument by stating that neither Chesney's story, nor a bellicose counterblast in *The Times*, had any 'tangible plea for their possibility'.[40] *The Times*, which Chesney had derided in his story – though without mentioning the paper by name – somewhat unsuccessfully tried to occupy the moral high ground, publishing the abovementioned answer to *Blackwood*'s story on 22 June, in which the imagined invaders are defeated by staunch resistance on the landing beaches and the timely appearance of the Royal Navy.[41] The Liberal-oriented, or perhaps more accurately, establishment-leaning newspaper concluded, perhaps understandably, that it was completely safe to continue with business as usual: 'Alarms, we suppose, will never cease, till every alarmist has had his own conceits fully satisfied'. The paper added, however, that 'we may bring these alarms within limits, and reduce facts to their true dimensions'.[42]

28 *Beginnings*

The 'panics' of 1870–1871

As these examples show, while Chesney's story was certainly widely read, it did not thereby instigate a panic, or an 'invasion scare'. Nor did it necessarily take advantage of an already widespread feeling of apprehension. The language of scares and panics in this period was complex and protean. Commenting on the story's reception, A. Michael Matin observes that the 'quantity of public anxiety' is hardly an easy thing to calculate: 'whether one detects a "panic" to be occurring at any given moment in history is largely a function of where one takes one's readings'.[43]

Interestingly, however, most commentators at the time assumed that there had, in fact, been an invasion panic in one form or another in Britain in 1870–1871. This was true even of those who were critical of an invasion being possible, such as *The Times*. The word 'panic', though, was loosely defined; it was never made clear who had panicked, and what this entailed. In the summer of 1870, at the outbreak of hostilities between France and Prussia, the word was used to describe scenes of consternation on the stock exchange,[44] implying that the panic was unrelated to an invasion fear as such. However, there were also comments on a broader panic, described in more general terms. In May 1871, the same month that *The Battle of Dorking* made its appearance, the historian Edward Freeman observed in *Macmillan's Magazine* that the country seemed to be going through 'one of those curious fits of panic, which seem ever and anon to seize upon the English nation'. Seeing himself as detached from the general fear of a German menace – Freeman noted that it was 'always my lot to be on the unfashionable side' – the historian nevertheless argued that in the nation at large 'the great cry of all is the cry of no men, no rifles, no powder'.[45] A month earlier, Chesney's own brother, Charles, himself an army officer, wrote in *Macmillan's* that panics were not only widespread, but had an obvious explanation:

> The causes of our panics are simply these. All Englishmen, save an inappreciable percentage of enthusiasts, know and feel that there are certain possible complications which would bring us, at short notice, to open issue with one or more of the great military Powers. They are further aware that, as a balance to our maritime supremacy, we should almost certainly be threatened with an invasion of

The Battles of Dorking

land-forces ... they have an uneasy feeling that ... we might prove miserably unequal to the contest for the integrity of our own territory which would follow ...

Panics, Charles Chesney concluded, had become 'a chronic disease, for the simple reason that their cause remains untouched'.[46] Even outside observers, like the aforementioned American reviewer of *The Battle of Dorking*, surmised that Britain was embroiled in some form of panic: 'the Briton periodically indulges in a paroxysm of alarm over some vividly pictured invasion, which he solemnly, and to the great amusement his neighbors, succeeds in persuading himself is imminent'. The reviewer had an equally detached view as Freeman on this spectacle: 'A collection of English invasion-panic literature would make a rare addition to our [American] public libraries'.[47] A few years later, the future Liberal leader William Vernon Harcourt would echo the claim that the United States was not prone to panics, which seemed to be a peculiarly British phenomenon, and an unfounded one at that.[48]

Chesney's narrative was not the only text in 1870–1871 dealing with Britain's relations with the outside world. Before the publication of *Dorking*, a much-discussed pamphlet was already in circulation, arguing that Britain was losing its position as international arbiter, through its non-interference in the Franco-Prussian struggle. Although insecurity over Britain's military abilities are, as in *Dorking*, expressed here, the consequences are different. *Dorking* described the fall of British defences, and the occupation of the Home Counties, whereas the earlier pamphlet, *Dame Europa's School*, portrayed British unwillingness to assert itself in foreign affairs.[49] However, there were also numerous direct fictional responses to Chesney which presented a more optimistic vision of how Britain could meet an invader.

One of these responses, *What Happened after the Battle of Dorking*, describes how the nation rises to the invasion challenge. As with *Dorking*, the story relishes in specifically pastoral scenes of rural Kent – 'one of the gardens of England'[50] – even managing to shoehorn a love story into the narrative. By contrast, London is less glowingly portrayed:

Certainly we could have witnessed the demolition of many of the public edifices and streets of London without overwhelming regret,

30 *Beginnings*

as regards their loss as architectural monuments; but we considered the feelings of the metropolitan ratepayers, and abstained.[51]

Even though the story presented a nation prepared for invasion – 'the discipline of the invaders had succumbed to the courage and energy of the new English levies, leavened as they were by a considerable sprinkling of old soldiers'[52] – the author, Charles Stone, was in full agreement with Chesney in having no love lost for the Liberals. Writing that 'a very large party in the nation, especially amongst the trading classes, counselled submission', the narrator is quick, however, to assure his listeners that 'the old party in the country was the stronger' – and it is decided that resistance against the invader will be the course of action.[53]

In *The Times,* 'The Second Armada' – the aforementioned answer to Chesney's story – portrayed a nation that could put aside its differences in an emergency, while also hinting that in times of peace the country was indeed somewhat disorganised:

> although we are constantly running into extremes, although we are by turns profuse from groundless alarm and niggardly from undue confidence, although representative institutions are by no means favourable to the production of good administrators, we are not altogether wanting in an emergency ...[54]

'The Second Armada' was quick to underline that the Liberal Cardwell reforms had, in fact, made the army better – 'well officered under the new system of selection'. However, *The Times'* story was also rather keen to highlight the blue-blooded contingents on both sides: after the enemy is defeated, 'Princes, Archdukes, and Dukes were made prisoners by the score'. On the British side, the Heir Apparent, at the head of a Hussar regiment, is held back in reserve close to the landing beaches.[55] The abolition of purchase could be praised in principle, but the armies on both sides in the story are still led by royalty and aristocrats. A week after 'The Second Armada' was published in *The Times* the Prince of Wales was reported to himself have read and at least in part endorsed Chesney's *The Battle of Dorking.* The *Pall Mall Gazette* wrote that the prince, at a speech in a dinner party, had said that the tale had been written 'to give a broad hint to all of us that we must not be found napping'.[56]

In stories like 'The Second Armada' and *What Happened after the Battle of Dorking* the timeless Englishness desecrated in

The Battles of Dorking   31

Chesney's story proves able to cope with invasion. They can be read as comforting assurances that, though it may seem otherwise, Chesney's mob rule is as fictional as his invasion. The prospect of uncivilised public violence, as perceived in the Paris Commune, would, the stories assure their readers, be a foreign idea in Britain. As a colonel in *What Happened after the Battle of Dorking* notes, even the German troops who end up besieged in the British capital would be unlikely to 'resort to the uncivilized expedients of burning and destroying, like the Communists of Paris'.[57] The British troops are facing a disciplined enemy army, not a riotous mob.

Whether presenting Britain as unable or unwilling to take part in European affairs, or as being in danger of invasion by a foreign host, the real or imagined panic of 1870–1871 was therefore a military, political and social issue. Britain was seen as either militarily weak and internally divided, or as spuriously panicking over a non-issue. It has been argued that the publication of *The Battle of Dorking* 'struck a mighty blow at English complacency'.[58] The English, of course, needed no such blow. There were voices aplenty in the run-up to May 1871 and beyond, that were ready, willing and articulate enough to argue that the nation was indeed frightened; that it had panicked, and that the panic had something to do with its perceived inadequate military capabilities. What was special about the 1870–1871 agitation was precisely its popular nature. The public held the leading role – after all, Chesney had noted that the story was written with a public audience in mind. Others saw the introduction of a public debate as problematic, rather than useful. As the nominally Liberal writer William Rathbone Greg argued in late 1870, the uninformed public – with its short attention span – controlled politics, to the detriment of informed debate. Writing on the subject of professional versus popular armies in the *Contemporary Review*, Greg wrote a biting *'J'Accuse'* aimed at this public:

> Such as it is, however, the twenty-four hours' decision goes forth in leading articles and large type; it is adopted by what the general public "is pleased to call its mind;" is swallowed whole at the breakfast-table with the breakfast; passes from hand to hand, or rather from mouth to mouth, as the day ripens; and before a week is over has been consolidated into that vague, inexplicable, often unfounded, but always mighty influence called public opinion.[59]

32   *Beginnings*

Such comments on the public mind aside, it is difficult to pinpoint the exact influence *The Battle of Dorking* had on its readership. John Gooch argues that the impact of Chesney's tale has probably been over-emphasised, noting that 'the years from 1868 to 1872 were disastrous for Volunteer recruiting, despite Chesney's efforts', a conclusion also reached by Ian Beckett.[60] Even Clarke is sober in his appraisal of the actual effect the story had, writing that, despite his success, Chesney 'had not won a military victory, since there is no evidence that the story had any influence on the reorganization of the Army'.[61] According to Clarke the 'panic' caused by the story lasted until the September manoeuvres seemed to prove that the army was up to the task of defending Britain.[62]

Statements like these are, however, missing the point. Gooch and Beckett misread Chesney's narrative in believing that increased recruitment to the Volunteers was the author's goal. It would indeed be eccentric to believe that many would want to join up as a Volunteer after reading about the organisation's lack of plans, training and provisions in *The Battle of Dorking*. As such, the lacklustre recruitment numbers for the Volunteers may even be an indication of the success of the story. What Chesney really wanted his readers to take away from the tale is slightly convoluted, however. Clarke thought that Chesney's central argument was the necessity for Britain to introduce conscription, going so far as to state that '[h]ad the British accepted [Chesney's] argument for conscription in 1871, the offensive power of a vastly enlarged British Expeditionary Force might well have prevented the outbreak of war in 1914'.[63] The second part of this comment is problematic, but there is some truth to the first bit: Chesney's narrator-Volunteer wants, as the final lament states, the 'enforced arming of [Britain's] manhood', and better organisation and preparation at the top; not more cannon fodder in the form of untrained Volunteers. But if conscription was indeed what he initially wanted to promote through the story, Chesney would soon change his mind. Writing anonymously to the *Spectator* in June 1871, he argued that, while organisation was lacking and the War Office was over-centralised, he was convinced that 'the present rate of military expenditure is sufficient ... and that larger establishments are not wanted'.[64] He had made the same claims in a letter to William Blackwood in late May – lack of organisation was the problem, not the small size of the army.[65]

Figure 1.1 George Tomkyns Chesney, *The Battle of Dorking: Reminiscences of a Volunteer* (Edinburgh and London: William Blackwood and Sons, 1871). Source: Author's own collection

34 *Beginnings*

The Battle of Dorking in culture

The story was certainly successful on at least one level: over the summer of 1871 'The Battle of Dorking' entered the vocabulary as a byword for invasion, as in *Punch's* question on the possible sale of Heligoland to Germany being 'their first step to The Battle of Dorking?'[66] The phrase could even be used to describe past invasion attempts: in May *The Times* wrote in an 'obituary' of the Paris Vendôme Column, dismantled by the Communards, that it displayed Napoleon I's armies planning to fight a 'Battle of Dorking'.[67] Its readers were presumed to understand what this meant – the invasion of Britain – even in a paper that was critical of the story.

This trend is all the more marked when one looks at the Radical *Reynold's Newspaper* where, initially, the story was treated contemptuously, if mentioned at all. Hardly remarked on over the summer of 1871, the paper printed a comment on *Dorking* after Gladstone's reported repudiation of the story in a speech at Whitby in September. The paper added its own critique to that of Gladstone, and noted that the tale was an 'absurdly overpraised literary performance'. It finished by imagining a sober British public reaction in comparison to that of foreign editions of the story: 'we trust the public will take Mr. Gladstone's energetic repudiation of "alarmism" to heart' it noted, 'and refuse to be befooled by the trash which may find more credulous readers abroad'.[68] Phlegmatic stoicism would evidently be the proper British response. *Reynold's*, however, soon also came to adopt the term 'Battle of Dorking' as a simile for invasion, and here the paper was clearly not alone. In January 1873, a full year-and-a-half after the story was first published, *Reynold's* reported a speech held by William Vernon Harcourt at a dinner in Oxford, where he spoke of the American immunity from panics:

> I wonder that the panicmongers are not a race which the United States breeds ... Why, with an army of 24,000 men, are they not in daily and nightly dread of invasion? ... Why are they not afraid we shall fight a battle of Dorking a few miles from New York? (Hear, hear, and a laugh.) It would be a very fine stroke of foreign policy. When this is suggested every one will see the absurdity of it.[69]

Dorking slowly but surely acquired a cultural significance even among those who were opposed to it. Harcourt's invocation of it

The Battles of Dorking 35

to an audience clearly unsympathetic to increased armaments indicates that the story had become a common reference point, shared by Radicals as well as those who could be condemned as 'panic-mongers'. As stories of invasion and defeat proliferated during the remaining decades of the nineteenth century, *Dorking* took on a more exalted role, even in the columns of *Reynold's Newspaper*. By 1878 it had earned the description 'the celebrated pamphlet, the "Battle of Dorking" ',[70] and by 1885, with the publication of a story called *The Siege of London*, Chesney's narrative was favourably contrasted to the 'silly' premise of 'this Jingo author of this Jingo book'.[71] By the mid-1880s at the latest, therefore, *The Battle of Dorking* had been accepted even by *Reynold's* as the proper template of how a credible invasion narrative should be told. Chesney had been 'thoroughly *au fait* with the subject he was discussing', in contrast to the later pretender.[72]

Even earlier than this, the story had been reworked and reinterpreted, both in literary form and as a dramatic piece. In August 1871 the Alhambra theatre in London, 'the favourite resort of the over-taxed – mentally and physically – workers in this busy hive of commerce',[73] staged a production called *About the Battle of Dorking; or My Grandmother*. The two authors, F.C. Burnand and Arthur Sketchley, were professional satirists. Francis Cowley Burnand made a career out of satirising popular works, and would later, in 1880, become editor of *Punch*;[74] Arthur Sketchley, a pseudonym for George Rose, was the author of a successful series of stories about 'Mrs. Brown' – a heavily-accented housewife, who made patriotic, John Bull-like, and more or less perceptive remarks about the world around her.[75] In the play, Sergeant Blower and Cheeks the Marine, two cowardly and dishonest veterans from the land-battle and – in a curious suspension of disbelief – sea-battle at Dorking, impersonate one another to get hold of an inheritance. The play ends with the revelation that the battle of Dorking never took place, but with the two protagonists agreeing to write an account of it anyway, to make money.[76] The play was only tentatively connected to Chesney's narrative, and did not convince the critics: both the *Pall Mall Gazette*, who had praised the original story, and the more critical *Reynold's Newspaper,* found the play tedious and the premise strained. The *Pall Mall Gazette* believed that the authors, by using *Battle of Dorking* in the title, had 'excited expectations they were unable to gratify'.[77] Evidently, the mere words were expected to increase ticket sales, illustrating how the story had moved beyond politics into pure commercialism – indeed, this was not the only stage adaptation that capitalised on the early success of *Dorking*.[78] The unfavourable response from the audience indicates that, despite their 'over-taxed' minds, the entertainment-seeking consumers still wanted the play they paid for to meet their expectations.

George Rose engaged with *Blackwood*'s story more faithfully in one of his *Mrs. Brown* pamphlets, titled *On the Battle of Dorking*. The readers were clearly expected to have intimate knowledge of the original tale, and there are running references to specific pages and sentences from Chesney's story throughout the text.[79] Here Mrs. Trimley, a friend of Mrs. Brown, has read *The Battle of Dorking*, believing it to describe true events in real time, though her understanding of the narrative is clearly limited.[80] Although she is sceptical about Britons ever being defeated, as Mrs. Brown reads the pamphlet she becomes wary of the possibility of an invasion, not calming down until her husband, himself a Volunteer, brings home another pamphlet a week later, written by 'Mr Cheeks, the Marine' and 'Sarjint Blower'. The pamphlet is described as 'a little yaller book with two noble pictures of milingtary men outside on it'.[81] The yellow pamphlet Mrs. Brown took comfort in was indeed in circulation at the time. Though anonymously published, it was probably written by either Burnand or Rose, or possibly both. Purporting to refute several factual errors in the original *Dorking* account, the pamphlet – tongue firmly in cheek – was titled *Our Hero!! Or, Who Wrote 'The Battle of Dorking?'*.[82] Like *Mrs. Brown on the Battle of Dorking*, the humour in this pamphlet was based on the assumption that its readers had read Chesney's story, and frequent references are made to specific pages in the pamphlet version of *The Battle of Dorking* throughout the text. The pamphlet also pokes fun at the anonymous narrator in Chesney's story, claiming that he uses Americanisms to hide his real nationality.[83] No one, except perhaps Mrs. Brown, could have suspected this text to be meant seriously – in the story John Bright, an outspoken critic of wars, is Commander-in-Chief, and the invading forces are singlehandedly defeated by Blower, while Cheeks takes care of the enemy fleet. The two heroes also disclose that there really was

The Battles of Dorking 37

no battle: as in the music-hall play it had all been an invention.[84] Burnand and Rose carved out their own universe from the *Dorking* controversy, referring to their creations throughout the different parodies they made: Mrs. Brown learns that Cheeks and Blower are in fact friends of her husband;[85] Cheeks' retelling of events in *Our Hero!!* is addressed to his grandmother,[86] the same from whom Cheeks and Blower try to get an inheritance in the Alhambra play.[87]

For Burnand and Rose, mocking *The Battle of Dorking* was a means to an end: not for one moment did they take the ideas or political arguments in the story seriously, but merely used it as a way to air their own jokes. Some of these jokes might indeed have worked better in a different setting, as the reviews of the Alhambra play hinted at, but the point was to latch on to the attention created by Chesney's story, using it as a promotional vehicle. That Chesney's *The Battle of Dorking* was worthy of attention for its literary qualities, outside of any political criticisms or military prognostications, was explicitly stated by the magazine *Fun*, which commented that 'Everybody should read it, for it is clever and amusing; and we can afford to laugh at its dark forebodings!'[88] What Chesney had discovered was a recipe for a narrative that, above all, *sold*.

This reuse of the story happened outside of the control of author and publisher, much to Chesney's chagrin. 'Have you seen the "battle of Berlin"' he asked in a letter to John Blackwood, presumably referring to a pamphlet written by 'Motly Ranke McCauley';[89] 'it seemed to be in the worst possible taste'.[90] Blackwood's reply must have been only marginally comforting: 'all these imitations are sure to be rot as no real man will try to tack himself on to another man's work'.[91] The summer and autumn of 1871 would, however, provide an abundance of such men. Two musical pieces, one titled simply *The Battle of Dorking*, and another, *The Battle of Berlin*, were also part of the burgeoning *Dorking* industry of 1871. The first dealt with the 'dream' that was the invasion – confidently exclaiming 'England invaded, What a strange idea!'[92] – while the second simply depicted the invasion in reverse, as Britain captures Berlin after a war over Heligoland. This latter piece was presumably based on the pamphlet by 'Motley Ranke McCauley'.[93] Frank Green, who wrote the words for both musical pieces, was credited with also writing lyrics to another piece, titled *The Row in Dame Europa's School*. This was probably based on the pamphlet with a

38 *Beginnings*

similar title – illustrating how a veritable cottage industry grew up in the wake of the pamphlet war of 1870–1871.

The politics of *Dorking*

Blackwood's story of internal decay was a paradoxical political argument. Presenting Britain as a nation in moral decline that has forgotten its old greatness, Chesney decried modernity, and simultaneously warned about what a lack of awareness of modern weapons could mean for the country. He expected his audience to share his vision of a country led by an elite, where foresight ruled and the green hills of Surrey were left unspoiled by foreign invaders and domestic industry alike. The tale was an appeal to a reading and thinking audience, but its language also insulted the same audience by claiming that they knew little of war and were too preoccupied with making money.

According to Darko Suvin, *The Battle of Dorking* was specifically aimed at the Liberal bourgeoisie. It was an attempt to convince them of Britain's present state of unpreparedness, and to wean them 'away from antiaristocratic prejudices and brought under a new political consensus'.[94] The idea of an intended Liberal audience is tenuous, although others have gone so far as to argue that its author was himself a staunch Liberal, whose only goal was the reorganisation of the army, not criticism of Gladstone.[95] Chesney would enter parliament in 1892 on a Conservative ticket, somewhat belying that theory; though he claimed that his seat – the city of Oxford – was won due to the support he received from Liberal Unionists.[96] In his slightly riled letter to the *Spectator* in early June 1871, signed 'THE WRITER OF THE TALE IN "BLACKWOOD"', Chesney exclaimed that he was 'nothing if not a Liberal'. However, the letter also claimed that the story was not intended as political 'in any sense'.[97] The eponymous hero of his 1873 story *A True Reformer* – a thinly disguised version of Chesney himself – had similar ideas: the protagonist seeks to reform the army without recourse to troublesome partisan politics.[98] This was, of course, hardly a Liberal position to hold. David Finkelstein is probably correct in stating that the letter was an 'attempt at damage limitation', as Chesney tried to steer his readers' interpretation of the story.[99]

The Battles of Dorking   39

Whatever his intentions, Chesney rapidly lost control of his own narrative. He had taken the opportunity to change parts of the story when it was published in pamphlet form, toning down hints that could be interpreted as calling for an increased army budget.[100] The reference to the government as pursuing a policy of retrenchment – a clear dig at Gladstone – was taken out, and the pamphlet instead directed its ire at both political parties, arguing that the army reforms had been a party matter rather than a national one.[101] The *Pall Mall Gazette* saw this renewed focus on reform and unpreparedness as a clear sign that the still-unknown author was not a 'Tory alarmist'.[102] This did not stop the more raucous *John Bull* from gleefully proclaiming that '[i]t is reported that the PRIME MINISTER, on reading "The Battle of Dorking," said that either he or the writer should be shot'.[103] The story lived its own life, each reader able to insert their own meanings into the text. Among the stories published in the wake of *Dorking*'s success could be found texts promoting a wide array of different ideas covering differing political standpoints, in addition to satires such as those of Burnand and Rose. This may explain the success of the story: it became a focal point for different ideas, rather than a piece of clearly understood propaganda. This is evidenced by the story's enthusiastic reception abroad, and its long afterlife. The translator of the Swedish edition of the story perceptively noted that Chesney's story had something to tell everyone, not just English readers.[104]

Few, however, seem to have understood this at first, least of all the author or the publisher. The house of Blackwood was initially unprepared for the success of Chesney's invasion narrative, and was taken completely by surprise at the increased demand for reprints of the story.[105] *Blackwood*'s first attempts at anticipating the public mood was uncertain and careful. John Blackwood's nephew William initially wrote of the plans for a sixpenny pamphlet that, 'the returns from which, unless we sell thousands, is very small'.[106]

By September, William Blackwood had been following the pamphlet sales closely for a while, providing detailed reports on the progress to his uncle. Gladstone's speech in Whitby that month was 'contemptible, but it will do the Dorking good, and introduce it to quite a new class of people'. William toyed with the idea of making the story available to an even larger audience, noting that 'we will soon have to think of a people's ed[itio]n I think at 1d or 2d'.[107]

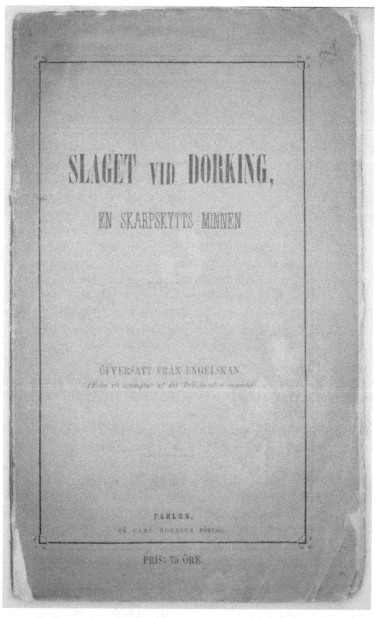

Figure 1.2 George Tomkyns Chesney, *Slaget vid Dorking: En Skarpskytts Minnen* (Fahlun: Carl Nordins Förlag, 1872).
Source: Author's own collection

The Battles of Dorking 41

By this stage, the mass appeal of the story was clear. 'The Battle rages on furiously', as William described the sales in late June.[108] In Finkelstein's words, John Blackwood looked at a literary text as something to be used commercially: 'working' it as one would ' "work" a horse in the fields or on the roads to gain the most from it'.[109] Although the initial success of the narrative was a surprise to the publisher, Blackwood quickly capitalised on the reception, initiating an advertorial offensive to promote it, which included the use of sandwich-board men for publicity.[110] The success of *Dorking* was therefore in many respects due to 'calculated publishing and marketing decisions'.[111]

However, neither the publishers nor the author truly controlled the story's reception or readership. William Blackwood was well aware of this. When there were rumours that *The Times'* story 'The Second Armada' was to be republished, he noted that 'I do not think it will do us any harm'.[112] Reports that the Prince of Wales and Duke of Cambridge had read *Dorking* were also seen as a good sign, as William hoped it would boost sales.[113] Even the public revelation that Chesney had authored the story was assessed in terms of its influence on pamphlet sales. The younger Blackwood was unimpressed: 'I am terribly disgusted with the author of the Battle letting out the secret. That accounts for the falling off of the sales'.[114] It is easy to see cynicism in William Blackwood's remarks; it is more difficult to see a stated intent to either foment a panic through the dissemination of the story, or an understanding that the tale itself was representative of an existing popular panic.

Audience

The story's intended audience is, in many ways, less interesting than the audience that appropriated it. Whereas the writers on *Blackwood's* 'military staff' had written fairly complex arguments on army reorganisation, the sensationalism of *Dorking* meant that it could be marketed to a wider audience than those interested merely in army reform, or indeed in party politics. As *Blackwood's* sought to capitalise on the initial success of the story, the marketing machinery that sprang into action went beyond the normal advertising strategies preferred by the Edinburgh publisher.[115] Railway

42   *Beginnings*

stalls and platforms were particularly targeted, and the ensuing arguments and counter-arguments played out in cheap pamphlets in glaring colours – 'in violent yellow, red, lavender, magenta and blue' – promoted and sold in large part at these transport hubs.[116]

This link between the modern means of communication and transport is interesting for a number of reasons. When the *Hampshire Advertiser* wrote that the reprinting of *Dorking* in pamphlet form would mean that 'its influence on the public mind [would], probably, be very great', it did not specify what this 'public mind' was or who it involved, or indeed what the influence would be.[117] The Victorians did, however, have an inkling as to who constituted 'the public', illustrated by the clichéd 'the man on the omnibus', a term that implied not only the middle-class credentials of its subject, but also hinted at motion and urbanism.[118] Train stations, no less than omnibuses, were scenes of modernity and urbanism, and trains, as Walter Benjamin argued, were the first means of transport that also formed masses of people.[119] Train stations were therefore fitting places to market a pamphlet of *The Battle of Dorking*'s character, with its mass appeal and flexible message.[120] Mrs. Trimley, in George Rose's fictional account, got hold of her copy while waiting at a train station, after seeing an advertisement for it. Before rushing off to tell Mrs. Brown, she reads through parts of the invasion story in the station waiting room.[121] We even know the supposed date, for in Rose's story, Mrs. Trimley is also shocked to hear of 'The Second Armada', from *The Times*, on 22 June: 'I 'eard a gent a-talkin' at the station, as said as the "Times" were full on it this werry mornin', as 'ad give notice as a reg'lar Harmader, jest for all the world like Queen Lizzybeth, were come to inwade us'.[122]

Trimley and Brown were naturally fictional characters, the products of George Rose's imagination, but the story is still an interesting comment on how *Dorking* was disseminated. In this case it was bought by an intrigued reader on a train platform, and read alongside a group of other people, whose conversations informed and expanded on the narrative. Similarly, while both Mrs. Trimley and Mrs. Brown misunderstand and misread *The Battle of Dorking* to comical effect, they are not passively adopting the idea of a vulnerable Britain. Mrs. Brown is calmed by reading Cheeks' and Blowers' frankly ridiculous account.[123] She is also reassured after buying an old copy of *The Times*, from the battle of Waterloo: 'it did my 'art

The Battles of Dorking 43

good to read about the way as them noble fellers as was Princes and Dooks laid down their lives and limbs'.[124]

There is obviously a gendered aspect to the *Mrs. Brown* story. Brown herself is clearly partial to the sovereign, the army and the British nation, holding strongly argued and vaguely understood ideas about British supremacy. It is clear to the reader that both she and Mrs. Trimley are frightened because they lack proper understanding of the themes being discussed in the pamphlet, in *The Times* and by Mrs. Trimley's fellow travellers at the train station. George Rose mocked those who were frightened by the *Dorking* narrative by showing two such scared people: old, hysterical and slightly silly women. It takes a Volunteer and a man, Mr. Brown, to calm the waters, by introducing the parodic Cheeks and Blower story. Still, even though – or, perhaps more accurately, because – they approached the invasion narrative with a feeble understanding of political and military affairs, Mrs. Brown and Mrs. Trimley filtered the argument through their own perceptions of the world around them. In the end, Mrs. Brown finds renewed faith in Queen and country after reading a pamphlet that, since she does not understand its irony, confirms her own world view. Readers had agency, at least insofar as they could seek out and take comfort in those pamphlets they agreed with; whether their doing so was mocked or not is beside the point. Rose's joking portrayal of fictional characters was a comment on real readers of Chesney's story.

The Battle of Dorking was certainly widely read and commented upon, but that does not mean that its arguments were taken at face value. It is hardly surprising that Gladstone would dismiss the idea of an invasion succeeding – '[m]ay our fortifications prove as difficult to capture as our officers', he jokingly wrote to Cardwell, '& we are safe enough'.[125] It was also natural that Chesney's invasion story would receive attention within the military and naval establishment.[126] The story was mentioned in the House of Commons proceedings throughout the summer of 1871, but not as often as might perhaps have been expected, and more as a way of attacking the government than as a serious prospect. Francis Charteris, Lord Elcho, exclaimed, for instance, that it was 'better to have a Battle of Dorking in time of peace than in time of war'.[127] The Liberal Financial Secretary at the War Office, Captain Vivian, politely but persistently pointed out to the same Lord Elcho in the House in

44 *Beginnings*

June 1871 that the Lord, in invoking the tale, seemed to know little of military matters.[128]

The Battle of Dorking certainly touched a nerve. Its quality of writing and its shock-effect arguably brought the idea of a hostile invasion to life for a mass audience for the first time. This was Chesney's first and best venture into fiction; his other attempts fell flat simply because he was not a very good storyteller,[129] while *Dorking* succeeded largely because the story told itself. The country was the main character, the story's narrator merely there to relate what happened to it. But the political arguments in the story – its anti-democratic bias and its anti-Liberal overtones – were not matched by any clearly defined solution to the problem Chesney raised: how to keep a foreign invader from marching across English soil and occupying English homes. The story was received and read with different views in mind: as F.D. Tredrey understood when he wrote the history of *Blackwood's*, the pamphlet war in the wake of *Dorking* took place '[i]n a clamour of laughter and anger' – two contrasting responses.[130]

Notes

1 Standard, 22 August 1870, 4.
2 *Daily News*, 9 June 1871, 5.
3 K. Baedeker [J.F. Muirhead], *Great Britain, England, Wales and Scotland as far as Loch Maree and the Cromarty Firth: Handbook for Travellers* (London: Karl Baedeker, 1887), 50.
4 Baedeker, Great Britain, 51.
5 Roger T. Stearn, 'Chesney, Sir George Tomkyns (1830–1895)', Oxford Dictionary of National Biography [hereafter ODNB]. See also Stearn, 'General Sir George Chesney', *Journal of the Society for Army Historical Research*, 75 (1997), 106–118. Though a civilian college, Chesney largely staffed Coopers Hill with Royal Engineer officers.
6 Quoted in Mrs. Gerald Porter, *Annals of a Publishing House: John Blackwood. The Third Volume of William Blackwood and his Sons: Their Magazine and Friends* (Edinburgh and London: William Blackwood and Sons, 1898), 299.

The Battles of Dorking

45

7 David Finkelstein, *The House of Blackwood: Author-Publisher Relations in the Victorian Era* (University Park: Pennsylvania State University Press, 2002), 161.

8 I.F. Clarke, 'Before and After *The Battle of Dorking*', *Science Fiction Studies*, 24 (1997), 46.

9 Porter, *John Blackwood*, 298.

10 Porter, *John Blackwood*, 302.

11 F.D. Tredrey, *The House of Blackwood, 1804–1954: The History of a Publishing Firm* (Edinburgh: William Blackwood and Sons, 1954), 140.

12 I.F. Clarke, *Voices Prophesying War: Future Wars 1763–3749* (Oxford: Oxford University Press, 1992), 35.

13 Clarke, *Voices*, 34. The story does indeed seem to have caused some annoyance to William Gladstone, the Liberal Prime Minister. Gathorne Hardy, a Conservative MP, noted with glee in his diary on 26 May 1871, in reference to the parliamentary proceedings the day before: 'Gladstone's inability to attend the House and consequent postponement of business ... [sic] It is said that the Battle of Dorking gave him dysentery!'. *The Diary of Gathorne Hardy, Later Lord Cranbrook, 1866–1892: Political Selections*, ed. Nancy E. Johnson (Oxford: Clarendon Press, 1981), 137.

14 Edward M. Spiers, *The Late Victorian Army, 1868–1902* (Manchester: Manchester University Press, 1992), 1–28.

15 'What We May Learn', *Blackwood's Magazine* (February 1871), 133.

16 'Position of the Government', *Blackwood's Magazine* (February 1871), 268.

17 'Wake, England Wake!', *Blackwood's Magazine* (February 1871), 257–258.

18 [George Tomkyns Chesney,] 'The Battle of Dorking: Reminiscences of a Volunteer', *Blackwood's Magazine* (May 1871), 540–541. References in this chapter, unless otherwise specified, will be to the original story as published in *Blackwood's*. Later chapters will refer to the pamphlet version. For the sake of consistency, the title will be italicised in the main text throughout the book.

19 'Dorking', 541.

20 'Dorking', 541. Criticising the Volunteers was something of an open goal in 1871. In April, the satirical magazine *Fun* printed a poem titled 'My Volunteer', which ended with the following verse (*Fun*, 15 April 1871, 157):

Yet were invasion on us thrust,
    Before one hostile shot was fired
My volunteer would – as I trust –

46 *Beginnings*

> From active service have retired!
> His own domestic hearth to screen,
>> To guard his wife and children dear,
> These are his tactics, so I glean.
>>>> My Volunteer!

21 'Dorking', 541.

22 'Dorking', 543.

23 Quoted in Porter, *John Blackwood*, 300.

24 National Library of Scotland [hereafter NLS], Blackwood's Papers, MS. 30363 ff. 403–404, John Blackwood to Col. Chesney, 7 February 1871.

25 Anon., 'The Fall of England! The Battle of Dorking: Reminiscences of a Volunteer by a Contributor to "Blackwood", *North American Review*, 113 (1871), 476. Clarke asks, rhetorically, if the reviewer had not misread Chesney here: 'Had he not seen that the Volunteers had to appear incompetent and unprepared, so that there would be no mistake about the lesson of their defeat?' (I.F. Clarke, 'Trigger-Happy: An Evolutionary Study of the Origins and Development of Future-War Fiction, 1763–1914', *Journal of Social and Evolutionary Systems*, 20 (1997), 129). Clarke overestimated the clarity of Chesney's argument: the anonymous reviewer would not be the only one to misread *The Battle of Dorking*, of which more later.

26 'Dorking', 545.

27 'Dorking', 544.

28 'Dorking', 549.

29 'Dorking', 553.

30 'Dorking', 565.

31 'Dorking', 565.

32 'Dorking', 567.

33 'Dorking', 567–569.

34 'Dorking', 571.

35 Clarke, *Voices*, 28. In an earlier article he argues that 'The nation was a ready victim for a tale of terror, for most of 1871 was a time of chronic anxiety': Clarke, 'The Battle of Dorking, 1871–1914', *Victorian Studies*, 8 (1965), 316.

36 *Morning Post*, 29 June 1871, 5.

37 *Punch*, 20 May 1871, 207.

38 *Evening Gazette* [Middlesbrough, Stockton and District], 8 May 1871, 3.

39 *Pall Mall Gazette*, 3 May 1871, 4.

40 *Liverpool Mercury*, 23 June 1871, 6.

41 *The Times*, 22 June 1871, 5.

The Battles of Dorking 47

42 *The Times*, 24 June 1871, 9.

43 A. Michael Matin, 'Scrutinizing *The Battle of Dorking*: The Royal United Service Institution and the Mid-Victorian Invasion Controversy', *Victorian Literature and Culture*, 39 (2011), 389–390.

44 For example, *Morning Post*, 26 July 1870, 4.

45 Edward A. Freeman, 'The Panic and its Lessons', *Macmillan's Magazine* (May 1871), 1–12.

46 Lieut.-Col. C.C. Chesney, R.E., 'Our Panics and Their Remedy', *Macmillan's Magazine* (April 1871), 452, 457.

47 Anon., 'The Fall of England!', 473.

48 See below. Harcourt was the target of considerable ire from armed forces professionals in the debates following in the wake of *Dorking*, and for years after. See Matin, 'Scrutinizing'.

49 [Henry William Pullen], *The Fight at Dame Europa's School: Shewing how the German Boy Thrashed the French Boy; and how the English Boy Looked On* (London: Simpkin, Marshall and Co., [1870]). As with *Dorking*, the popularity of this story was reportedly a surprise to its author: writing 25 years later, Joseph Shaylor at the publisher Simpkin, Marshall and Co., put the final print of the pamphlet at 200,000 copies, and mused that the demand had been driven by press reports: J. Shaylor, 'On the Selling of Books', *The Nineteenth Century* (December 1896), 941.

50 [Charles Stone], *What Happened after the Battle of Dorking; or, the Victory at Tunbridge Wells* (London: George Routledge and Sons, [1871]), 55.

51 [Stone], *After Dorking*, 57–58.

52 [Stone], *After Dorking*, 56.

53 [Stone], *After Dorking*, 4.

54 *The Times*, 22 June 1871, 5. Clarke lists the author as Abraham Hayward: *Voices*, 225.

55 *The Times*, 22 June 1871, 5.

56 *Pall Mall Gazette*, 29 June 1871, 7.

57 [Stone], *After Dorking*, 49.

58 Cecil D. Eby, *The Road to Armageddon: The Martial Spirit in English Popular Literature, 1870–1914* (Durham and London: Duke University Press, 1987), 15.

59 W.R. Greg, 'Popular Versus Professional Armies', *Contemporary Review* (December 1870), 352. Greg's position within the Victorian Liberal tradition is somewhat difficult to place, but his comments above fit well with his views on 'scientific' governance and the importance of rational ways of organising a state. As Alex Middleton notes, Greg can be classified as 'a leading spokesman for the rationalistic,

48 *Beginnings*

antidemocratic strand within mid-Victorian Liberalism'. See Alex Middleton, 'William Rathbone Greg, Scientific Liberalism, and the Second Empire', *Modern Intellectual History*, 19 (2022), 683.

60 John Gooch, *The Prospect of War: Studies in British Defence Policy 1847–1942* (London: Frank Cass, 1981), 5; Ian F. W. Beckett, *Riflemen Form: A Study of the Rifle Volunteer Movement 1859–1908* (Barnsley: Pen & Sword, 2007), 105.

61 Clarke, *Voices*, 37.

62 Clarke, *Voices*, 36. One study has argued that the 'genesis' of the 1871 autumn manoeuvres can be found in *Dorking*, and has hinted of a link between Chesney's story and the later construction of defensive lines in the Dorking area, but this link is somewhat tenuous. See Patrick M. Kirkwood, 'The Impact of Fiction on Public Debate in Late Victorian Britain: The Battle of Dorking and the "Lost Career" of Sir George Tomkyns Chesney', *Graduate History Review*, 4 (2012), 1–16.

63 I.F. Clarke, 'Before and After "The Battle of Dorking"', *Science Fiction Studies*, 24 (1997), 42, 45.

64 *Spectator*, 3 June 1871, 15.

65 NLS MS. 4273 ff. 35–36, George Chesney to William Blackwood, 27 May 1871. David Finkelstein reaches a similar conclusion; Chesney wanted reorganisation, not a larger army: 'From Textuality to Orality – the Reception of *The Battle of Dorking*', in John Thompson (ed.), *Books and Bibliography: Essays in Commemoration of Don McKenzie* (Wellington: Victoria University Press, 2002), 94. Chesney reiterated that he in no way wanted to promote a large army – or, in his words, 'bloated armaments' – nor conscription, in a speech he made at the Royal United Service Institution in 1874: George Chesney, 'The English Genius and Army Organization', *Journal of the Royal United Service Institution*, 44 (1900), 53–64. More on this speech in chapter 2.

66 *Punch*, 24 June 1871, 262.

67 *The Times*, 17 May 1871, 5.

68 *Reynold's Newspaper,* 10 September 1871, 6.

69 *Reynold's Newspaper,* 5 January 1873, 5. Harcourt had made a similar remark at a discussion on the topic of invasion at the Royal United Service Institution (RUSI) in June 1872. Raising the issue of why the United States was not worried about being invaded by Britain, Harcourt had noted that 'America is not in dread of invasion by a country which possesses an army at least three times as numerous as its own, i.e., Britain'. See 'Adjourned Discussion of Mr. Vernon Harcourt's Paper', *Journal of the Royal United Service Institution*, 16 (1872), 628. More on this in chapter 2.

The Battles of Dorking 49

70 *Reynold's Newspaper*, 27 January 1878, 5.

71 *Reynold's Newspaper*, 18 January 1885, 2. The story in question was 'Posteritas' [pseud.], *The Siege of London* (London: Wyman & Sons, 1885).

72 *Reynold's Newspaper*, 18 January 1885, 2.

73 [William White], *The Illustrated Handbook of the Royal Alhambra Palace, Leicester Square* (London: Nicholls Brothers, [1869]), 4.

74 Jane W. Stedman, 'Burnand, Sir Francis Cowley (1836–1917)', ODNB.

75 Emma Plaskitt, 'Rose, George (1817–1882)', ODNB.

76 British Library [hereafter BL] Add. MS 53099 A: 'About the Battle of Dorking, [F.1:] Alhambra Theatre. F.C. Burnand and Arthur Sketchley. London August 4th 1871. License sent August 7'.

77 *Pall Mall Gazette*, 9 August 1871, 11–12; *Reynold's Newspaper*, 13 August 1871, 8.

78 From Boxing Day 1871 the Royal Polytechnic staged, as part of a wider set of entertainments, 'Professor Pepper's ... Story of THE BATTLE OF DORKING ANSWERED by the AUTUMN MANÆUVRES, with martial music and patriotic songs, by Miss Alice Barth'. See advert in, among other papers, the [*London*] *City Press*, 16 December 1871, 1.

79 Arthur Sketchley [George Rose], *Mrs. Brown on The Battle of Dorking* (London: George Routledge and Sons, [1871]).

80 Sketchley, *Mrs. Brown*, 9–12.

81 Sketchley, *Mrs. Brown*, 44.

82 'Sergt. Blower' and 'Cheeks the Marine' [pseud.], *Our Hero!! Or; Who Wrote 'The Battle of Dorking?' A Military and Naval Review of the Now Celebrated Pamphlet* (London: Bradbury, Evans & Co., 1871).

83 'Blower' and 'Cheeks', *Our Hero!!*, 16.

84 'Blower' and 'Cheeks', *Our Hero!!*, 25, 30.

85 Sketchley, *Mrs. Brown*, 58.

86 'Blower' and 'Cheeks', *Our Hero!!*, 38.

87 BL Add. MS 53099 A: 'About the Battle of Dorking'.

88 *Fun*, 17 June 1871, 247.

89 'Motly Ranke McCauley' [pseud.], *The Battle of Berlin (Die Slacht von Königsberg)* 5th edition (London: Tinsley Brothers, 1890 [1871]). The 1890 date on the title page may be an invention; the first edition was from 1871, and it is unclear if the pamphlet was reprinted.

90 NLS MS. 4714 ff. 200–203v, George Chesney to John Blackwood, [n.d.].

91 NLS MS. 30364 ff. 51–53, John Blackwood to George Chesney, 31 October 1871.

92 Frank W. Green and Carl Bernstein, *The Battle of Dorking: A Dream of John Bull's* (London: C. Sheard, [1871]).

50 *Beginnings*

93 Frank W. Green and Carl Bernstein, *The Battle of Berlin* (London: C. Sheard, [1871]).

94 Darko Suvin, *Victorian Science Fiction in the UK: The Discourses of Knowledge and of Power* (Boston: G.K. Hall & Co., 1983), 342.

95 Finkelstein, 'Textuality', 94.

96 See Stearn, 'Chesney', ODNB.

97 *Spectator,* 3 June 1871, 15.

98 As the reformer states, 'there are no Conservatives now, nor any Liberals; we all belong now to the Great United Party': [George Tomkyns Chesney], *A True Reformer,* 3 vols. (Edinburgh and London: William Blackwood and Sons, 1873), III, 154.

99 Finkelstein, 'Textuality', 95.

100 Finkelstein, 'Textuality', 91–92.

101 [George Tomkyns Chesney], *The Battle of Dorking: Reminiscences of a Volunteer* (Edinburgh and London: William Blackwood and Sons, 1871), 6.

102 *Pall Mall Gazette*, 12 June 1871, 4–5.

103 *John Bull*, 22 July 1871, 504.

104 [George Tomkyns Chesney], *Slaget vid Dorking: En Skarpskytts Minnen* (Fahlun: Carl Nordins Förlag, 1872), 3: see figure 1.2. A more radical example of how the story could be reused is the 1940 German edition, printed for a German audience and portraying Chesney's vision as much as a current possibility as a cultural artefact from another century: Will-Erich Peuckert/Chesney, *Was England Erwartet: Ein Zukunftsroman von 1871* (Berlin: August Groß Verlag, 1940).

105 Finkelstein, 'Textuality', 90.

106 NLS MS. 4271, ff. 33–34, William Blackwood to John Blackwood, 22 May 1871.

107 NLS MS. 4271, ff. 136–137, William Blackwood to John Blackwood, 5 September 1871.

108 NLS MS. 4271, ff. 55–56, William Blackwood to John Blackwood, 29 June 1871.

109 Finkelstein, *Blackwood*, 25.

110 Robert L. Patten and David Finkelstein, 'Editing *Blackwood's*; or, What Do Editors Do?', in David Finkelstein (ed.), *Print Culture and the Blackwood Tradition, 1805–1930* (Toronto: University of Toronto Press, 2006), 175.

111 Finkelstein, 'Textuality', 88.

112 NLS MS. 4271, ff. 51–52, William Blackwood to John Blackwood, 27 June 1871.

The Battles of Dorking 51

113 NLS MS. 4271, ff. 55–56, William Blackwood to John Blackwood, 29 June 1871; ff. 57–58, William Blackwood to John Blackwood, 30 June 1871.

114 NLS MS. 4271, ff. 91–92, William Blackwood to John Blackwood, 21 July 1871.

115 Finkelstein, 'Textuality', 91–92.

116 Tredrey, *House of Blackwood*, 140.

117 *Hampshire Advertiser*, 10 June 1871, 7.

118 James Thompson, *British Political Culture and the Idea of 'Public Opinion', 1867–1914* (Cambridge: Cambridge University Press, 2013), 36.

119 Walter Benjamin, *The Arcades Project*, Rolf Tiedemann (ed.), transl. Howard Eiland and Kevin McLaughlin (Cambridge, MA and London: The Belknap Press, 2002), 602.

120 The *Daily Mail* would later write of the popular late Victorian and Edwardian invasion-scare author William Le Queux that '[t]here is no better companion on a railway journey': quoted in Roger T. Stearn, 'The Mysterious Mr Le Queux: War Novelist, Defence Publicist and Counterspy', *Soldiers of the Queen*, 70 (1992), 9. Invasion-scare literature, like similar forms of suspense fiction, were read on the move.

121 Sketchley, *Mrs. Brown*, 11–12

122 Sketchley, *Mrs. Brown*, 15.

123 Sketchley, *Mrs. Brown*, 44–45.

124 Sketchley, *Mrs. Brown*, 48. Note the reference to blue-blooded sacrifice, a trope mentioned above. A similar rallying around the lords and princes of the land can be seen in, for example, McCauley, *Battle of Berlin*, 9–10.

125 Letter to Cardwell, 27 May 1871, quoted in *The Gladstone Diaries*, H.C.G. Matthew (ed.), 14 vols. (Oxford: Clarendon Press, 1968–1994), III, 501.

126 See Matin, 'Scrutinizing'. More on this in chapter 2.

127 HPD HC Deb 10 August 1871 vol. 208 c1358.

128 HPD HC Deb 30 June 1871 vol. 207 cc918–919.

129 'The Battle of Dorking was a great coup, but does not make it clear that you will be a successful novelist': NLS MS. 30364 ff. 85–86, John Blackwood to George Chesney, 15 January 1872.

130 Tredrey, *House of Blackwood*, 140.

Part II

Expertise, public opinion and
invasion-scare fiction, 1870s to 1914

2

After Dorking: expertise, service authors and 1870s future-war fiction

The majority never has right on its side. Never, I say! That is one
of the social lies that a free, thinking man is bound to rebel against.
Who make up the majority in any given country? Is it the wise men
or the fools? I think we must agree that the fools are in a terrible,
overwhelming majority, all the wide world over. But how in the dev-
il's name can it ever be right for the fools to rule over the wise men?
- Dr Stockmann, in Henrik Ibsen's *An Enemy of the People,*
Act IV, 1882.[1]

The publication of, and subsequent attention surrounding, *The
Battle of Dorking* made George Tomkyns Chesney something of
a household name in Britain. However, if anyone hoped Chesney
would use his newfound fame to promote the dangers of invasion,
they would be sorely disappointed. Chesney's first public lecture
after *Dorking*, held at the Royal United Service Institution (RUSI) in
London on 27 March 1874, was concerned with issues far removed
from the question of invasion. In the lecture, Chesney even made
a throwaway remark regarding the feasibility of a foreign invader
landing in Britain: 'For defensive purposes', he said,

> our position has no doubt been vastly strengthened of late years, and
> I for one venture to believe that as we now stand, a successful invasion
> of England has been placed beyond the category of possible events.[2]

Instead of concerning itself with invasion threats, Chesney's RUSI lecture focused on a proposal he had arrived at, for reorganising the army
into a mounted unit – a somewhat quixotic issue and one that does
not seem to have received much traction among his audience.[3] But
Chesney also spent much of the lecture discussing the links between
the British political system and the question of how to prepare for a

56   *Expertise, opinion and invasion-scare fiction*

future war – and this was a subject that certainly provoked a good deal of interest among the armed forces in the years after 1871. In fact, much of the debate surrounding the publication of *Dorking* centred on the armed forces, as well as the political system the army and navy operated in, rather than on invasion as such. In turn, much of this debate was itself driven by service members, and discussed within service fora, such as RUSI. These debates, which included numerous fictional treatments of invasion and future wars, continued for the next decade and indeed up until the First World War and beyond. In these discussions, service members used fiction to highlight perceived failings in the British machinery for war and its system of government.

The next three chapters look at how invasion-scare fiction developed alongside debates about the role public opinion should have in shaping defence policy. Fictional arguments must be seen in context with other forms of public engagement; authors of future-war stories, like George Chesney, put their pens to use in different ways after *Dorking*. The genre developed alongside, reflected, and was influenced by, the various defence questions discussed in public in the decades after 1871. While the expert/amateur division is relevant here, there is also a dividing line between the halls of power – where politicians, civilian theorists and professionals mingled – and the outside world. Sometimes these two worlds met and interacted, but often the political-military establishment tried to exclude the public from its deliberations, rather than include them.

This was not a straightforward development, and the question of how professional institutions could be combined with a democratic society was common in pre-First World War Britain. The question of how much power and influence bureaucrats, the civil service, soldiers and sailors had over politicians in the years before 1914 has been discussed by scholars for decades.[4] After the Boer War, the search for national efficiency led Edwardians to tinker with ideas of a rationally organised society and empire, one where the expert would have a clear role in government.[5] This chapter looks at attempts to combine parliamentary decisions on war and peace with the democratic developments that had been initiated after 1867. The chapter links these discussions with the changes in invasion-scare fiction in the same period.

While service authors were initially quick to replicate the premise of *Dorking*, they did not create the same popular waves as Chesney's publication. The 1870s was a comparatively quiet period for

After Dorking   57

publications of invasion-scare and future-war fiction. Yet Chesney's formula – imagining foreign invaders or the outlines of future conflicts – was used by service writers to discuss and criticise the ways in which popular government limited the soldiers' and sailors' influence over war. Criticism of politicians, the British political system and the public alike, were part and parcel of these discussions.

After a brief outline of how the concept of 'expertise' was discussed and understood in Victorian Britain, the chapter gives a more in-depth analysis of how war, fiction and future-war was presented and discussed in the service journals and among members of the armed services in the 1870s. The chapter ends with an overview and a brief discussion of the limited set of future-war fiction published in Britain between 1871 and 1880.

Communication, the public and the Victorian idea of expertise

Henrik Ibsen's plays were almost invariably a mystery to the reviewers when they were staged in late Victorian Britain. *An Enemy of the People*, a quote from which opened this chapter, was a notable exception. It was performed in London over the summer of 1893 – over a decade after it had been written. 'Happily,' the *Morning Post* concluded, 'in this drama there are none of the repulsive theories which have made some of the Norwegian dramatist's plays so objectionable'; instead, it was a play 'in which keen satire and knowledge of human nature are equally to be admired'.[6] There are hints here of some of the earlier 'pruderies and philistinism of much of the British public' in their encounters with Ibsen's dramas.[7] That newspapers and the public should be more favourably inclined towards a play that attacks the press and where the protagonist, Dr Stockmann, heaps scorn on 'public opinion, and the compact majority, and all that sort of devilry'[8] may seem a bit surprising. Part of the explanation lies in its otherness: as T. Carlo Matos notes, English critics were not too troubled by theatrical characters located far away – in 'not just Norway but provincial Norway'.[9] The sharp satire, it seemed, was aimed at someone else.

More perceptive critics, like George Bernard Shaw, had long seen Ibsen's plays as more universal – or, indeed, directly applicable to Britain.[10] This was true in particular of *An Enemy of the People*, which describes a situation that 'though it has an intensely local

58   *Expertise, opinion and invasion-scare fiction*

Norwegian air, will be at once recognized as typical in England', in Shaw's estimation.[11] Ibsen's tale of an expert, an educated man of principles battling against the 'compact majority' of press, public and vested interests, should indeed have seemed like a familiar trope to Britons in the 1890s. There were many Doctor Stockmanns in late Victorian society, and their attempts to alternately invoke or do battle with public opinion made them – no less than the fictional doctor – see themselves as part of an intellectual vanguard.

The Victorian idea of 'expertise' was complex and is not easily dissected.[12] There was no agreed-upon definition of what it meant to be an expert, and the mantle was often claimed by politicians and various authors and thinkers. The term is used loosely in the following three chapters, but primarily in the context of how professional soldiers and sailors and, to a certain extent, some military theorists, defined themselves as distinct from the public or 'the man in the street'. The distinction between 'expert' and 'others' in discussions of military defence was always blurry.[13] And when it came to invasion-scare fiction, the important dividing line was not necessarily between service authors and civilian writers, as some have argued.[14] A simplified division like this can be unhelpful, as it creates a dichotomy between two groups who tended to overlap. It is also problematic to distinguish between imaginative civilian authors and uninspired professionals, as Antulio Echevarria has done, arguing that military thinkers before the First World War 'tend to fall into the category of failing in imagination', while 'it was non-specialists, amateurs, who were considered more imaginative, and who thus had a better sense of what the next war would bring'.[15] Not all military writers, taking the known technology of the time as a starting point for their analyses, were unable to see that the conduct of war was a thing in constant flux. This, as David Edgerton has noted in relation to how aircraft were first adopted, is a common misconception when it comes to military personnel: there is, he writes, 'an influential assumption that soldiers and sailors are stupid, or at least less intelligent than engineers ... But these stories should not be taken seriously'.[16] Nor were all, or even most, amateur authors capable of accurately envisioning what the next war would be like.

The Cardwell reforms may or may not have laid the groundwork for a distinct, professional officer identity in Britain; either way, the army would continue to recruit its officers from the landed aristocracy.[17] That said, rapid technological change in the nineteenth century put demands on the competency of officers. As Michael Crawshaw writes, this development 'called for a new breed of military men – the "educated soldiers" ';[18] though the demands on sailors were at least as pressing.[19] In the background loomed the perpetual question of what officers should learn and how they should learn it. Within European armed forces there has for a long time been a tension between theory and practice, and between a view of soldiering or sailing as composed of practical skills versus the idea that warfare could be learned in the classroom or from books.[20] What type of knowledge could be said to be requisite for a late Victorian officer was a question with different answers, and there were of course distinctions both of expertise and professionalism within the armed forces: artillerymen and engineers, like Chesney, belonged to highly specialised branches of the army, requiring a large degree of technical competency and expertise. Even prior to 1871, the purchase of commissions had not applied to the artillery or to the engineers.[21]

The engineering and artillery education at the Royal Military Academy, Woolwich, accepted cadets through open competition and was initially more academically oriented (primarily towards mathematics) than Sandhurst, its counterpart for the cavalry and infantry.[22] A Staff College (though not yet a general staff) on a European model was set up, after some back-and-forth, at Camberley in the wake of Crimea. While it had initially suffered from a bad reputation within the army, by the later Victorian era the college had more credibility and prestige, with an increasing number of officers attending.[23] The navy, albeit with some setbacks, also saw the development of more advanced officer training and education, including through studies at the Royal Naval College, in the decades after the Crimean War.[24]

In the two decades prior to 1870, it looked as if the expert was coming to the forefront in governing the country, leading A. Wyatt-Tilby, in his biography of Lord John Russell, to describe the period of his subject as a time when '[t]he day of the expert and technician had arrived': 'There was', he wrote, 'no need to argue for the demonstration proved itself, and public opinion was of no consequence one way or another'.[25] Chesney, as shown in chapter 1, was more ambivalent about public opinion and its role in government, lamenting that 'Parliament-rule was beginning to give way to mob-law'.[26] As an

60   *Expertise, opinion and invasion-scare fiction*

engineer, Chesney was part of a profession that in Victorian Britain could be presented as politically disinterested public servants, a valuable source of expert knowledge and advice – not for nothing has the period up until the end of the century been termed the 'Reign of the Engineer'.[27] The decades between the publication of *The Battle of Dorking* and the First World War saw the simultaneous cementing of the role of experts as well as the increased importance of the public in matters of governance – what Chesney had derisorily termed 'moblaw'. There was a disjuncture between these two developments. The expansion of the press had frustrated Edward Bruce Hamley in 1856, having seen from the front lines in Crimea the influence journalists had on parliament and, ultimately, the army. Hamley, later professor of military history at the Staff College, saw danger in an ill-informed public, taking its opinions from journalist amateur-soldiers.[28] Little seemed to have changed a half-century later. Writing in the *Fortnightly Review* in 1903, an anonymous author – presumably a service writer, judging from the soliloquies on military strategy, or otherwise a civilian devoid of any sense of irony – presented an invasion-scare narrative in which public opinion forces the hand of the professionals, with predictable results. At one point, a dying journalist deliriously deprecates the military authorities' unwillingness to listen to the press:

> I watched him anxiously. Every now and then he would sit up suddenly in bed, and in half coherent sentences exclaim; "If only Lord Roberts had done what we told him on page six column nine of our issue of April 1st;" "Those who have at least the ear of the public;" "A citizen army," and other phrases I could not catch, about the folly of the artillery in not listening to the instructions of the *Weekly Infallible.*[29]

Writing in the *Journal of the Royal United Service Institution* in 1894, 'F.N.M.' noted that the professionals had already lost the battle against ignorance: 'The initiative has now passed out of our hands, the spell of our power is broken, the issues of peace or war now rest in the hands of misinformed voters, instructed by a still misinformed press'.[30] One writer in the February 1896 issue of the *United Service Magazine*, under the pseudonym 'Hibernicus', despaired of how '[s]elf-styled "experts" contribute to the daily press letters in which sometimes pitiful ignorance and sometimes petty spite predominate', and complained of how the army and navy lacked a literature of their own:

Of what does our literature consist? Lives of generals and admirals, rather wearisome accounts of campaigns, dull dissertations upon tactics, a few *brôchures* – such as "In the [sic] Conning Tower," "The Battle of Dorking," "The Last Great Naval War," etc., and dreary textbooks – little else. There is apparently a feeling that to popularise our craft would be to vulgarise it.[31]

The April issue of the same magazine was less enthused about the positive effects of popularising war writings. Citing William Le Queux's invasion-scare narrative *The Great War in England in 1897* (1894) as an example, A. Hilliard Atteridge claimed that the effect of such popular works was to exaggerate the vulnerability of Britain, and potentially create a panic if a war broke out in the future. The public needed calm reassurance, not hysteric fictions like Le Queux's – and to let the professionals get on with their work.[32]

In one sense the public was seen as an impediment to good governance – how could the experts give advice when the mob could countermand them? But, as Wyatt-Tilby's phrase above suggests, there was also a more positive way of seeing the public role of expertise: if experts could prove the feasibility of something, who were the public to argue against them? In matters of national defence, some took it even further: the public would have to become experts of their own; only then would they be able to promote the correct policies. In 1876, Captain H.M. Hozier expressed this view in a two-volume discussion of past and possible future invasions of Britain:

> If we were willing boldly to sacrifice ourselves to the guidance of a despotic government, which would relieve us of all care and of all thought, we might also plead justly, we were thus relieved of all responsibility. Such is not the case in England. Every man can make himself heard, and it is the duty of every man to have a care for his national security ...[33]

'Every man' gradually expanded into meaning something more than just the upper and upper-middle class. There were dangers, however, in giving power to those uneducated in its use. Gladstone was quick to criticise the aggressive foreign policy of Benjamin Disraeli, seeing in the latter's policy a 'sham-Caesarism', pandering to a mob.[34] This feeling was of course not limited to the leader of the Liberals; the public could be an ally as well as an opponent for those who governed.

62 *Expertise, opinion and invasion-scare fiction*

The British mass reading public was created by the nineteenth-century education acts: 'The difference between the nineteenth-century mob and the twentieth-century mass', John Carey observes, 'is literacy. For the first time, a huge literate public had come into being'.[35] The role of education was controversial, and not met with universal praise. W.E. Forster framed the 1870 Education Bill in terms of educating the newly enfranchised public, leading Valerie E. Chancellor to comment that,

> Such remarks have given rise to suspicions that the growth of the state system of education in England was closely connected with the desire to mould working-class opinions into non-revolutionary and 'respectable' patterns which would leave the upper classes free to govern and maintain their position in society in a supposedly democratic era.[36]

Above all, this indicates an uncertainty regarding how the reading masses should be included in decision-making processes. Though often critical of the public, experts did directly invoke public opinion in their campaigns. Despite all his issues with the press, Hamley was not averse to engaging with the public, in attempts to educate them on the dangers Britain faced. He wrote articles on the issue of national defence, and as a Conservative MP promoted the Volunteers in the 1880s and early 1890s.[37] And while intellectuals – a term no less woolly than 'expert'[38] – may have scoffed at popular newspapers, national defence experts (both those in uniform and civilian writers who took an interest in matters of war and peace) occasionally attempted to make use of the medium.

Ibsen's Dr Stockmann, for all his one-mindedness and zeal, never quite understood how to use the 'compact majority' of a democratic society to his advantage. The men in this and the next two chapters, though often more perceptive than the Norwegian doctor, struggled with the exact same problem.

Service writers and *Dorking*

As outlined in chapter 1, *The Battle of Dorking* itself and the reactions to it were more focused on the domestic rather than foreign aspect of the story; the narrative and those who commented on it were mostly interested in Britain itself, rather than the supposed

After Dorking 63

external enemy. The German invaders, after all, were never explicitly identified as such – though they did speak German, and few would have doubted their nationality. Chesney's story had instead aimed particularly harsh criticism at the British political system and the planning for future war. This had led to accusations of partisanship, even though his invasion story had been flexible enough to find a home among readers across the political spectrum.

In the service journals, Chesney's tale divided opinion. One rather angry correspondent to the *Broad Arrow*, a 'paper for the services', was not overly impressed with the merits of Chesney's imagined invasion. 'I have waited patiently to see what smart and intelligent officer would answer the ridiculous "Battle of Dorking", the letter opened, before the writer complained in earnest: 'The idiot who wrote that *brochure*', the letter continued,

> should be reminded that it is a "dirty bird which fouls its own nest," and that no two powers combined would have the slightest chance against the millions of Anglo-Saxons who would like magic be mustered by sea and land from our Fatherland, and all our vast colonies around the globe.[39]

As with the general reaction to the story, quite a few of those who submitted letters about *Dorking* to service fora such as the *Broad Arrow*, were mostly concerned with the domestic political issues they identified in the story. In September 1871, *Colburn's United Service Magazine* printed a letter from a reader (presumably a retired army officer) who, while he admitted that *The Battle of Dorking* seemed to be 'without much foundation' and made the invaders' path to conquering and occupying the country rather easy, also found some merit in what he considered the main argument of the story. 'The grand feature', the letter noted,

> which is supposed to lead to our national disgrace and ruin, ... is, however, quite correct, viz. the committing [of] all military command and arrangements, the defence of England, of all that is dear to us, to a lot of civilians (not possessed even of the "warrior prestige" of noble or gentle blood), but mere mercantile men.

The letter writer was not without solutions, however: 'Let an old soldier venture to propose', continued the anonymous reviewer, 'that in the event of the "invasion threat" suddenly becoming a matter of

64   *Expertise, opinion and invasion-scare fiction*

fact ... both Houses of Parliament ... should pass an instantaneous vote by acclamation, placing England, as regards her coming struggle for life or death, under martial law, with our most experienced and cleverest general officer at her head'. Alternatively, the letter writer concluded, a military council of three – 'say the Duke of Cambridge, Lord Strathnairn and Lord Sandhurst' – could jointly take the helm.[40]

In his 1874 speech at RUSI, Chesney was more optimistic about the British political and military system, finding that 'Englishmen are distinguished by their love of freedom, their aptitude for self-government, their energetic temperament, their readiness of resource, and their faculty of invention'.[41] Surely, a major war might have tested this assessment, but throughout his career – and despite his comments in *Dorking* – Chesney hoped that the British political system would and could adapt to changes and provide rational and well-thought out plans for army and navy organisation.[42]

Not everyone was as sanguine as Chesney. Many of the same arguments that could be found in the anonymous letter to *Colburn's United Service Magazine* in September 1871 – a distrust of civilian authority running alongside a belief in the general capabilities of British arms – were put forward in the two fictional answers to *Dorking* that appeared in the journal in the latter half of that year.

The first of these, 'Fifty Years Ago', was published in the August and September issues, during the height of the *Dorking* agitation in Britain.[43] The story, which did not appear under any author's name, took its cues from Chesney's tale, and ostensibly belonged to the same timeline or reality. But instead of presenting a story of defeat and the dismemberment of the British empire, 'Fifty Years Ago' outlines a more optimistic version of the events described by Chesney's Volunteer. As such, the story belongs to the large category of fiction that responded to *Dorking* in 1871 by offering narratives of success in the face of invasion, while retaining the structure and setting of the original invasion text. Among these stories can be counted 'The Second Armada' and *What Happened after the Battle of Dorking*, both discussed in more detail in chapter 1. The main difference from these two other stories is that 'Fifty Years Ago' was written primarily for a professional audience of soldiers and sailors; it was probably also written by an officer.

'Fifty Years Ago' does not shy away from criticising British society and politics in much harsher terms than Chesney did. Criticism

After Dorking   65

is levied at the way the Volunteers have been organised and trained, and how the armed forces have been funded. In the story, the author purports to offer a 'correction' to the narrative presented in *The Battle of Dorking*. Its opening paragraph lobbies an invective against the underlying domestic issues which can be blamed for the invasion and defeat as described in *Dorking*:

> We were too confident in our strength, too fond of money-grubbing, too unobservant of the signs of the times, too yielding to democracy and political immorality to see our nakedness and preclude an attempt at invasion, much more the success of such an effort.

Luckily, all this changes in the wake of the invasion: 'The pandering to *vox populi* had had its day, the rottenness of communism, and its co-partner universal suffrage … was estimated at its real value'.[44] After these criticisms, the story picks up where the narrator in Chesney's story left off, and the tale describes in detail the battles and retreats that follow the initial defeat at Dorking.

In the second part of the story, the narrative takes a slight left turn, and we are informed that the invaders are not Germans at all, but a 'continental combination' consisting of France, Russia and a group of minor nations.[45] After checking a Russian advance on India and a fleet attack on Australia, and after beating back the invaders on British soil, a peace is signed and British supremacy restored. The story ends with the narrator outlining a happier vision of the future than Chesney's narrator: 'Great Britain with India, Australia and huge colonial possessions,' fifty years after the invasion, 'is friendly with the German Empire on the Continent, and these, acting in concert with the Republic of America, have made peace to be universally maintained and respected'.[46]

This rather fantastical ending is indicative of some of the flexibility of Chesney's story, and also in intra-service debates on war and war planning. Even in a story that explicitly framed itself as a continuation of *The Battle of Dorking*, the author saw no problem in changing the unspoken but obvious enemy for another group of hostiles. The point of 'Fifty Years Ago' was not to comment on international developments, though fears over Russian threats to India were, of course, not uncommon in Britain throughout the later nineteenth century. Instead, the story followed the general trend of many other Dorking imitators and commentary, directing its ire towards

66   *Expertise, opinion and invasion-scare fiction*

the British political system, the country's defence organisation and what the author deemed a general lack of planning and preparation.

External enemies were interchangeable in this and stories like it; the domestic issues were what mattered, and what the story's author – and other commentators – set out to address. The utopian dream of a world order organised according to British principles and in conjunction with Germany and the United States, is contingent on an initial reorganisation of the domestic political order in Britain. Therefore, victory is only achieved after old political divisions have been healed, and Britons are able to work towards a common goal: 'Party spirit was forgotten', we are told, 'and none suspecting could not suspect his political opponent of dishonesty, or want of patriotism'.[47] This entails a utopian ideal of how the imagined invasion could function as a catalyst for inner regeneration and national unity, a topic discussed in more detail in chapter 5.

The domestic focus also means that the story directs most of its ire towards civilian society rather than towards the perfidy of the invaders. Scoffing at civilian experts, the author of 'Fifty Years Ago' was scathing in their description of journalists or other, self-described experts: 'Certainly, one did not see the *Times* on the breakfast-table', the narrator observes, as the British counter-offensive is well under way,

> nor did you read wonderfully grammatical leaders in "Head-Quarter" papers, shewing how everybody, except the writer of that particular article, was nearly a fool, and totally incapable of understanding the question of the day ...[48]

As 'Fifty Years Ago' was published anonymously, it is difficult to ascertain who the author was and their relationship to the armed forces. The service journals reached a wider readership than their limited subject field might indicate, and the idea of expertise was, as noted above, always contested, even in such fora as *Colburn's*. As noted by Albert Tucker, in discussing the readership of early Victorian military journals, 'professional' readers meant more than men in uniform: 'In the military journals, therefore, assumptions could be made about a literate, specialized reading public that was also integrated into all the social norms of the middle and upper classes'. Tucker also observes that publishers like Henry Colburn, the eponymous publisher behind *Colburn's United Service Magazine*,

After Dorking 67

had 'no official or formal ties to the services'.[49] Civilians could, and indeed did, publish in *Colburn's*, and the magazine offered its readers a heterogenous selection of literature, including fiction dealing with matters other than invasion, translations from foreign journals, letters, historical studies and articles on current events.

That said, the discussion that took place within service journals and in other venues in the wake of *Dorking* was based on a division between those – whether in uniform or without – who were perceived as more informed about modern warfare, and those civilians who, as the argument went, knew little of such things. The latter were deprecated, and seen as a hindrance rather than as potential converts to the cause of bettering Britain's defences. This tension, between the ignorance of civilian authority and those who were in the know, was at the centre of the other fictional response to *The Battle of Dorking* published in the August 1871 issue of *Colburn's*. In 'The Defeat of the Navy at the "Battle of Dorking"', the narrator explains that the naval defeat, as described in Chesney's story, can be blamed on the civilian authority rather than the navy itself: 'The officers were enthusiastic and behaved nobly; the men fought like lions, and shewed no lack of either knowledge or pluck'. Instead, the Admiralty, the navy's political leadership, is to blame: 'But from first to last, the Administration was defective'.[50]

Arguments like these were certainly not uncommon in Britain throughout the Victorian era. In particular, the question of how much influence the British public and parliament had over matters of war permeated many debates over British war planning.[51] A large part of these discussions centred on the issue of what constituted proper expertise and expert opinion. In the 1850s the Crimean War had focused the British public's attention on perceived failures in the organisation of the army. Less than a year before the publication of *Dorking*, the court martial into the sinking of the Royal Navy warship HMS *Captain* found that construction of the ship had gone ahead, despite several design flaws, 'in deference to public opinion'.[52] While this was only half the truth – the construction had been the result of a tug of war between different ideas of how the Royal Navy's warships of the future should be designed – the loss of the *Captain* drew much public attention in Britain, and was profoundly embarrassing for the Admiralty. More than this, it highlighted the tension between the two different forms of expertise that were involved in the construction of

68   *Expertise, opinion and invasion-scare fiction*

the Royal Navy's ships: the purportedly scientific approach of engineers and naval architects, and the experience of serving officers. Over these forms of expertise hung the influence of press, public and parliament, which had led to the design being approved.[53]

The publication of *Dorking* had taken place during a time of heightened discussion over the future of the army, and the effects the proposed Cardwell reforms might have on the service. Within service publications and at the Royal United Service Institution, such concerns, rather than the issue of foreign threats, continued to dominate the debate over both *Dorking* and the prospect of invasion in 1871 and 1872. In other words, the fiction of invasion fitted neatly into existing discussions, rather than fuelling any new or heightened sense of Britain being threatened by a particular external enemy; indeed, who the enemy was did not really seem to matter.

When the issue of invasion was discussed at the RUSI in May and June 1872, the debate ultimately centred on the division between rational war planning and the deficiencies in Britain's current armed forces and military system. On this occasion, the Liberal MP William Vernon Harcourt had been invited to speak to RUSI members on the issue of 'Our naval and military establishments regarded with reference to the dangers of invasion'.[54] According to A. Michael Matin, the debate at RUSI 'constituted the professional equivalent of the public quarrel over the story', and the lecture itself was 'specifically designed as a response to the controversy stirred up over the publication of *The Battle of Dorking*'.[55] This is partly true – Harcourt did mention *Dorking* in his lecture, and in a follow-up letter to *The Times* later in May[56] – but the lecture discussed invasion and the needs of the army and navy more broadly, and the question of invasion and military organisation – not least the effects of the Cardwell reforms – had been a topic of much debate before Chesney's story was published in May of that year. *The Battle of Dorking* was therefore part of a larger picture, and was mentioned as such in the lecture and the following discussion at RUSI.

Harcourt's lecture at RUSI was a meeting between two cultures – and was understood as such both by Harcourt and his audience. '[W]hen I accepted the invitation', Harcourt stated at the beginning of his lecture, 'it was strictly in my professional capacity, because the business of a lawyer is not so much to know anything himself as to endeavour to extract information from others'.[57] While

After Dorking 69

the lecture and the following discussion focused on technical issues regarding the feasibility of Britain being invaded, its overarching theme was the meeting between expert knowledge and civilian power – whether represented by parliament or by the public that voted for members of parliament. 'I think we owe [Harcourt] a deep debt of thanks for giving the whole country by its voice in the press the opportunity of stating straightforwardly what is the public mind upon this subject [i.e. invasion]', commented George Chesney's older brother, Charles, who was present at the RUSI meeting and an active participant in the discussion that followed.[58] As such, the debate followed the same logic as the fictional treatments in *Colburn's*, as well as *The Battle of Dorking* itself: control of the armed forces, the argument went, was in the hands of a public and a parliament that was uninformed, and this had repercussions for the way Britain's defences were organised.

This clash of cultures – between what was seen as an uninformed wider public, and those who saw themselves as being in the know – shaped both the form and function of much British invasion-scare fiction up to the 1870s. While many stories discussed various schemes and the merits or demerits of invasion from a naval or a military perspective, the stories were often scathing in their criticism of civilian authority. As external enemies changed with rapid frequency in such stories, this criticism of wider British society was constant in many of the stories that were mainly written by and for service personnel in the 1870s.

Future-war literature in the 1870s

The development of future-war and invasion-scare fiction needs to be seen in a context of increasingly irate discussions over politics, public interference in military planning, and the perceived influence irrational civilians seemed to have over defence planning and politics. It is, for example, striking how unwilling authors of the comparatively few invasion-scare fiction stories published in the 1870s were to treat more than a small section of British society as rational. It would take some years before stories aimed at a mass readership emerged; not only were there more texts describing fictional invasions from the 1890s onwards, but there were more readers as well. Apart from the

70 *Expertise, opinion and invasion-scare fiction*

accidental commercial success of *Dorking* in 1871, it was not until the end of the century that invasion-scare fiction started evolving into a viable commercial genre in its own right.[59] This development is traced in subsequent chapters; for now, I want briefly to explore the fiction published in the decade following 1871.[60]

The first major wave of invasion-scare fiction in 1871 was largely self-contained, with stories commenting on each other – and mostly on Chesney's *Dorking* – rather than promoting specific issues. In contrast to the deluge of stories published in 1871, the rest of the decade was not a fruitful period for invasion literature: I.F. Clarke lists a total of 23 works related to *Dorking* published in Britain in 1871, but only 11 British future-war stories for the rest of the 1870s.[61] In September 1878 *Blackwood's Magazine* surmised that the replacement of Gladstone with Disraeli was the reason behind the calm:

> During Mr Gladstone's tenure of power we were the butt and laughing stock of the world … Those were the days when men wrote of 'Battles of Dorking' and of English humiliation and defeat. Now it is Russia that shrinks from the mere scabbard of England's sword, whilst Prince Bismarck speaks of the magnificent triumph England has achieved.[62]

This comment was, of course, made while the complexities of the Eastern Question – the European Great Powers' relations with the crumbling Ottoman Empire – were hanging over British politics. Lord Beaconsfield had recently returned successfully from the Congress of Berlin, where war had been avoided.[63] Satisfaction with Disraelian political manoeuvres in Europe may possibly explain the lack of invasion-scare texts in this period. A more credible explanation for the lull is that the genre lost its newsworthiness, or that interest dropped off after the initial burst of creativity unleashed by *Dorking*. Supporting this view is the low number of stories published between 1872 and 1874, when Gladstone was still in power. Those that were published later in the decade tended to owe many of their tropes to Chesney's original story, with few innovations in terms of writing or ideas. Illustrative of this is Chesney's 1878 future-war story *The New Ordeal;* a bland satire rather than a serious diatribe.[64] The genre was not as dead as *Blackwood's* assumed in 1878, however: Clarke lists 37 stories of 'imaginary wars' published in Britain between 1880 and 1890.[65]

After Dorking 71

Most fictional forecasts both in the 1870s and later in the 1880s were written and published under various pseudonyms, making it difficult to establish the authors' identities. However, at least some officers in the armed services turned their minds to fiction. At the time, the front was hardening between those who argued for strengthening the navy, and those who favoured bolstering the army as the best way to ensure the safety of Britain. The 'Bolt from the Blue' school claimed that an invasion could happen without a prior declaration of war; the invaders could, conceivably, land on British soil unannounced one day, having in one way or another defeated or evaded the Royal Navy. A strong army, therefore, was the only guarantee of stopping them.[66] Navalists in the 'Blue Water' school, on the other hand, pointed out that the country was safe so long as the navy was supreme. With the navy sunk or chased off the enemy would not need to invade; the threat of starvation would instead force the island nation to surrender.[67] Historians should be wary of seeing the period prior to 1914 as an all-out tug of war between the two services and their respective 'schools'; tensions between army and navy in this period can be, and have been, overstated.[68] Army officers, like Lieutenant-Colonel Alan H. Burgoyne, were not averse to writing on naval issues, and many showed a marked interest in both services: the National Service League, promoting conscription in the immediate pre-war years, counted several admirals among its members, as well as the secretary of the Navy League.[69] Defence policy was never a zero-sum game, with the army losing out every time a new battleship was launched. However, the tension outlined above at least offers a helpful way of thinking about defence debates at a time when questions were often raised over the allocation of resources or the deployment of forces.

International developments were commonly touched upon in the stories written both in the 1870s and later in the 1880s. The Eastern Question was a common topic in the 1870s, with several stories touching either directly on the issue, or discussing the prospect of war with Russia more generally. *The Carving of Turkey* (1874), written by the pseudonymous 'Clarendon Macaulay', describes a war with Germany and Russia that eventually leads to an unsuccessful invasion of Britain.[70] Germany and Russia are also enemies in the anonymously published stories *The Invasion of 1883* (1876), *Fifty Years Hence* (1877), and *Gortschakoff and*

72   *Expertise, opinion and invasion-scare fiction*

Bismarck: or, Europe in 1940 (1878), though Britain, or more accurately Scotland, is only invaded – unsuccessfully – in the first of these three.[71] Future-war fiction of the later 1870s seemed mostly untroubled with the idea that Britain itself could be suddenly and unexpectedly invaded. Stories more often portrayed the country being dragged into a European conflict over the fate of the Ottoman Empire, and suffering defeat abroad, rather than on home ground. *The Invasion of 1883* and *The Carving of Turkey* – where invaders do land – are optimistic in their descriptions of Britain's ability to isolate and defeat an invading force. Writing in 1872, 'An Octogenarian' envisioned an invasion of Britain which eventually leads to the establishment of a British Federal Empire in a Liberal, utopian vision of the future.[72] One story that portrayed a future occupation of the country did so as a way of satirising Britain's unwillingness to assist the Balkan peoples in their struggles against the Ottoman Empire. *A Parallel Case* (1876) presents a version of the 'Decline and Fall of the British Empire' chapter from 'future history' that would be a common trope in the following decades. In this story, Britain has been invaded and subjugated by the 'Ashantees'.[73] The pamphlet is interspersed with citations and references to Arthur J. Evans' *Through Bosnia and the Herzegóvina on Foot* – a travel book that described parts of the European Ottoman Empire that were in revolt against the Sultan – just to make sure the readers understood where the story was aimed.[74]

Colburn's United Service Magazine did not publish much more in the way of invasion-scare fiction or tales of future war for the rest of the 1870s. In 1872 the magazine printed a summary of, and commentary to, a future-war story that had appeared in France under the title of 'The Battle of Berlin in 1875'. While the story, according to *Colburn's*, 'cannot be said to bear comparison either in interest or in graphic power of description to the celebrated "Battle of Dorking", it was still worth commenting on, 'as an example of the species of literature now popular in France'.[75] In the story, Germany finally meet its end at the hands of a European coalition, including France, Russia, Sweden, Denmark and Britain.

The trends evident in the 1870s – fiction written often by and for a specific target audience – would continue into the 1880s. *Colburn's* published a short, unremarkable fictional tale of the

After Dorking 73

'Battle of Wilton' in 1880 – where a battle takes place sometime after an undisclosed enemy invasion in the near future.[76] The story was mostly concerned with descriptions of the fighting itself, and had in many ways less in common with Chesney's story – with its melodrama and pathos – than with such technical discussions of the autumn army manoeuvres as could be found in the same journals and magazines.[77] Aside from this example, there were no future-war stories published in the journal for the remainder of the 1880s, even as *Colburn's* continued to show a mild interest in such literature throughout the decade, including stories appearing in other countries, such as an 1882 US story, *The War of 1886,* describing a near-future war between Britain and the United States.[78] A review in *Colburn's* observed that the short story constituted 'a Trans-Atlantic example of a form of political satire, which, for the last twelve years, has every now and then appeared among ourselves [in Britain]'.[79] Clearly, military libraries were starting to be filled up with stories of imaginary future wars and the prospect of invasion.[80] Still, this was not yet a mass literature, fiction for a wide audience. However, the 1880s also gave hints that stories of future war and invasion could, at some point, again reach the same level of popularity as *Dorking* had, and that the history of imaginary invasions is tied in with attempts to engage with an expanded body politic on questions of war and war planning. This is the subject of the next chapter, which covers the period between 1880 and 1894.

Notes

1 *The Collected Works of Henrik Ibsen,* with introductions by William Archer, 11 vols. (London: W. Heinemann, 1907), 'An Enemy of the People', VIII, 134.

2 George Chesney, 'The English Genius and Army Organization', *Journal of the Royal United Service Institution,* 44 (1900), 57. This remark was met with cheers, according to the correspondent from the *Morning Post* (28 March 1874, 6).

3 One correspondent noted that the audience uttered 'remarks of incredulity and disappointment' at the end of the lecture, as there had been much initial excitement in hearing the author of *The Battle of Dorking* deliver his first public address (*The Scotsman,* 28 March 1874, 7). The lecture had originally been delivered at the Institution

74 *Expertise, opinion and invasion-scare fiction*

on 27 March 1874, and was reprinted in the RUSI journal 'by special request' – for some reason, it was not printed in the 1874 editions of the journal. Renewed interest in the subject, and subsequent 'reprinting' of the lecture in 1900, was perhaps understandable, as mounted troops presumably made much sense in light of the army's experiences fighting highly mobile mounted Boer troops in South Africa.

4 See Roy MacLeod (ed.), *Government and Expertise: Specialists, Administrators and Professionals, 1860–1919* (Cambridge: Cambridge University Press, 1988); Peter Gowan, 'The Origins of the Administrative Elite', *New Left Review*, 162 (March-April 1987), 4–34; for the military, see, for example, W.S. Hamer, *The British Army: Civil-Military Relations 1885–1905* (Oxford: Clarendon Press, 1970). Of interest here is also Harold Perkin's study of post-1880 England – a society, he claimed, with a 'vertical career hierarchy rather than the horizontal connection of class': *The Rise of Professional Society: England since 1880* (London and New York: Routledge, 2001), 9.

5 See Bernard Semmel, *Imperialism and Social Reform: English Social-Imperial Thought, 1895–1914* (Cambridge, MA: Harvard University Press, 1960); and G.R. Searle, *The Quest for National Efficiency: A Study of British Politics and Political Thought, 1899–1914* (London: Ashfield Press, 1990).

6 *Morning Post*, 22 July 1893, 5.

7 Aaron Matz, *Satire in an Age of Realism* (Cambridge: Cambridge University Press, 2010), 105.

8 'An Enemy of the People', 184.

9 T. Carlo Matos, *Ibsen's Foreign Contagion: Henrik Ibsen, Arthur Wing Pinero, and Modernism on the London Stage, 1890–1900* (Bethesda: Academica Press, 2012), 83.

10 Matz, *Satire*, 107–109.

11 George Bernard Shaw, *The Quintessence of Ibsenism*, 3rd edition (London: Constable and Company, Ltd., 1926), 91.

12 The word itself entered the English language around 1860: Roy MacLeod, 'Introduction', in MacLeod (ed.), *Government and Expertise*, 2. A similarly woolly definition can be applied to the Victorian use of the term 'scientific'. As Alex Middleton writes, writers like William Rathbone Greg used 'science' and 'scientific' to describe the 'systematic study of general principles', more than a method. See Alex Middleton, 'William Rathbone Greg, Scientific Liberalism, and the Second Empire' *Modern Intellectual History*, 19 (2022), 688.

13 The unclear nature of 'expertise', even in modern times, is illustrated by David Kennedy, *A World of Struggle: How Power, Law and Expertise Shape Global Political Economy* (Princeton: Princeton

After Dorking   75

University Press, 2016). Tor Krever notes of the book that, 'crucially for Kennedy's argument, expertise is not the exclusive province of professionals. We ought not to speak of experts or expertise, he suggests, but of an "expertise effect": the ability to convince others to yield to one's status as an expert'. See 'Spectral Expertise', *New Left Review* (July–August 2017), 106, 152. As Kennedy himself observes, it is a fantasy to believe that 'expertise' is somehow separate from politics: *World of Struggle*, 3. This perceptive analysis can just as well be applied to late Victorian discourse. On the close links between scientists and warfare in the twentieth century, see David Edgerton, 'British Scientific Intellectuals and the Relations of Science, Technology and War', in Paul Forman and José M. Sánchez-Ron (eds), *National Military Establishments and the Advancement of Science and Technology* (Dordrecht: Kluwer Academic, 1996), 1–35.

14 For example, A. Michael Matin, 'The Creativity of War Planners: Armed Forces Professionals and the Pre-1914 British Invasion Scare Genre', *English Literary History*, 78 (2011), 801–831.

15 Antulio J. Echevarria II, *Imagining Future War: The West's Technological Revolution and Visions of Wars to Come, 1880–1914* (Westport and London: Praeger Security International, 2007), xiv.

16 David Edgerton, *England and the Aeroplane: Militarism, Modernity and Machines* (London: Penguin Books, 2013), 14–15.

17 The classic definition of a professional officer corps is the one offered by Samuel Huntington, where a common understanding of expertise, as well as meritocratic selection can be said to constitute core components (see Samuel Huntington, *The Soldier and the State: The Theory and Politics of Civil-Military Relations* (New York: Vintage Books, 1957), 8–10, 30–31). As Edward M. Spiers notes, the purchase system 'hindered the development of professional attitudes within the army', yet while abolition may have altered this it did not in itself do much to change the social composition of the army: Edward M. Spiers, *The Late Victorian Army, 1868–1902* (Manchester: Manchester University Press, 1992), 12, 93–94. Also Brian Bond, *The Victorian Army and the Staff College, 1854–1914* (London: Eyre Methuen, 1972), 122–123.

18 Michael Crawshaw, 'The Impact of Technology on the BEF and its Commander', in Brian Bond and Nigel Cave (eds), *Haig: A Reappraisal 70 Years on* (Barnsley: Leo Cooper, 1999), 156–157.

19 Arguably more so than the demands on the army, according to Ian F. Beckett, *A British Profession of Arms: The Politics of Command in the Late Victorian Army* (Norman, OK: University of Oklahoma Press, 2018), 14.

76   *Expertise, opinion and invasion-scare fiction*

20 See John B. Hattendorf, 'The Conundrum of Military Education in Historical Perspective', in Gregory C. Kennedy and Keith Neilson (eds), *Military Education: Past, Present, and Future* (Westport, CT: Praeger, 2002), 1–12.

21 Beckett, *Profession of Arms,* 38.

22 Spiers, *Late Victorian Army,* 99–102.

23 Spiers, *Late Victorian Army,* 109–112. Of the officers attending before 1900 none, as Bond notes, were from the navy, nor any from the dominions: Bond, *Staff College,* 168. Bond's book offers a general overview of the Staff College's history in this period, and its place within the Victorian army and military thinking.

24 On the development of naval officer education, see Andrew Lambert, 'Education in the Royal Navy: 1854–1914', in Geoffrey Till (ed.), *The Development of British Naval Thinking: Essays in Memory of Bryan McLaren Ranft* (London: Routledge, 2006), 34–59. Lambert, however, deems the educational developments in the Royal Navy in the decades before the First World War as not systematic enough to have had an impact on the development of strategy.

25 Quoted in MacLeod, 'Introduction', 9.

26 [George Tomkyns Chesney], *The Battle of Dorking: Reminiscences of a Volunteer* (Edinburgh and London: William Blackwood and Sons, 1871), 6.

27 MacLeod, 'Introduction', 10–11. Royal Engineers also provided services to civilian society: Beckett, *Profession of Arms,* 16. On the engineering profession in the nineteenth century, see R.A. Buchanan, 'Engineers and Government in Nineteenth-Century Britain', in MacLeod (ed.), *Government and Expertise,* 41–58. Railway inspectors, in particular, often had background from the Royal Engineers (Buchanan, 'Engineers', 49–50). Coopers Hill, where Chesney was principal, was a civilian college.

28 [Edward Bruce Hamley], 'Lessons from the War', *Blackwood's Magazine* (February 1856), 232–242; Jay Luvaas, *The Education of an Army: British Military Thought, 1815–1940* (London: Cassell, 1965), 133. This was a common complaint among professional soldiers. By the late Victorian era, John Frederic Maurice, the 'second pen of Sir Garnet', agreed with Sir Arthur Wellesley's old statement that 'the English public never formed "an accurate estimate of the difficulties attending *any* military enterprise they undertake"', but this problem had been amplified by the increased pressure of public opinion on governments. See Luvaas, *Education of an Army,* 186.

29 'Vates' [pseud.], 'The Revenge for Fashoda', *Fortnightly Review,* 73 (May 1903), 804.

After Dorking 77

30 F.N.M., 'Notices of Books: The Great Alternative: A plea for a National Policy. By Spencer [sic] Wilkinson', *Journal of the Royal United Service Institution*, 38 (June 1894), 683.

31 'Hibernicus' [pseud.], 'The Services and Civilians', *United Service Magazine*, 807 (February 1896), 541, 545. The author is listed as 'Amicus' on the contents page, but the text is signed 'Hibernicus'.

32 A. Hilliard Atteridge, 'National Defence: Some Neglected Conditions', *United Service Magazine*, 809 (April 1896), 1–13.

33 Captain H.M. Hozier, *The Invasions of England: A History of the Past, with Lessons for the Future*, 2 vols. (London: Macmillan and Co., 1876), II, 390–391.

34 Jonathan Parry, *The Politics of Patriotism: English Liberalism, National Identity and Europe, 1830–1886* (Cambridge: Cambridge University Press, 2006), 338–339.

35 John Carey, *The Intellectuals and the Masses: Pride and Prejudice among the Literary Intelligentsia, 1880–1939* (London: Faber and Faber, 1992), 5.

36 Valerie E. Chancellor, *History for their Masters: Opinion in the English History Textbook: 1800–1914* (Bath: Adams & Dart, 1970), 7–8.

37 Luvaas, *Education of an Army*, 159–161.

38 For two different discussions of 'intellectuals' and society in this period, see Carey (*Intellectuals and Masses*) who argues that the intelligentsia excluded the newly literate masses from their domain; and Stefan Collini, who sees the period's intellectuals as 'public moralists': *Public Moralists: Political Thought and Intellectual Life in Britain 1850–1930* (Oxford: Clarendon Press, 1991).

39 *Broad Arrow*, 15 July 1871, 76, 'Letters to the Editor'.

40 *Colburn's United Service Magazine* (September 1871), 126.

41 Chesney, 'English Genius and Army Organization', 59.

42 On this, see chapter 3.

43 Anon., 'Fifty Years Ago', *Colburn's United Service Magazine* (August 1871), 475–493 [Part I], and (September 1871), 75–89 [Part II].

44 Anon., 'Fifty Years Ago', [I], 475–476.

45 Anon., 'Fifty years Ago', [II], 77–78.

46 Anon., 'Fifty years Ago', [II], 89.

47 Anon., 'Fifty years Ago', [II], 86.

48 Anon., 'Fifty years Ago', [II], 86.

49 Albert Tucker, 'Military', in J. Don Vann and Rosemary T. VanArsdel (eds), *Victorian Periodicals and Victorian Society* (Toronto: University of Toronto Press, 1995), 62, 65. The *United Service Magazine* and *Colburn's United Service Magazine* both refer to the same journal: between 1842 and 1890 it was usually referred to as *Colburn's*

78   *Expertise, opinion and invasion-scare fiction*

United Service Magazine, and this was the name given on its masthead and the title under which it can usually be found in libraries. From 1890 it was referred to as the *United Service Magazine.* Tucker, 'Military', 79.

50 Anon., 'The Defeat of the Navy in the "Battle of Dorking"', *Colburn's United Service Magazine* (August 1871), 562. In this story, unlike in *Dorking,* the invaders are explicitly identified as Germans – but as in 'Fifty Years Ago' Britain is clearly facing more than one opponent, with Germany getting 'important and valuable aid from an ally' (557).

51 On this, see David Morgan-Owen, 'Strategy, Rationality, and the Idea of Public Opinion in Britain, 1870–1914', *Historical Research, 94* (2021), 397–418; and Christian K. Melby, 'War, Public Opinion and the British Constitution, c.1867–1914', *Journal of Modern European History,* 21 (2023), 441–457.

52 For example, the *Army and Navy Gazette,* 15 October 1870, 1.

53 The *Captain* affair and the question of expertise is discussed in Don Leggett, *Shaping the Royal Navy: Technology, Authority and Naval Architecture, c.1830–1906* (Manchester: Manchester University Press, 2015), 126–164.

54 The lecture was held at RUSI on 15 May 1872: W. Vernon Harcourt, 'Our naval and military establishments regarded with reference to the dangers of invasion', *Journal of the Royal United Service Institution,* 16 (1872), 575–607. A discussion followed the presentation, and the following debate had to eventually be adjourned to another meeting on 5 June: 'Adjourned Discussion of Mr. Vernon Harcourt's Paper', *Journal of the Royal United Service Institution,* 16 (1872), 607–632.

55 A. Michael Matin, 'Scrutinizing *The Battle of Dorking*: The Royal United Service Institution and the Mid-Victorian Invasion Controversy', *Victorian Literature and Culture,* 39 (2011), 390–392.

56 See *The Times,* 24 May 1872, 8. For a good overview of the lecture and discussion at RUSI, and the newspaper debate, see Matin, 'Scrutinizing'. One commentator in *Colburn's* surmised that, with a proper army 'we ought to give the French a good thrashing' if a French army decided to land. See Major W.P. Jones, 'The Invasion of England', *Colburn's United Service Magazine,* July 1872, 367.

57 Harcourt, 'naval and military establishments', 576.

58 'Adjourned Discussion'. See also Matin, 'Scrutinizing'.

59 Darko Suvin registers this as a change towards a more approachable format, describing future-war fiction as developing during the 1880s and 1890s into 'a yellow-press subgenre addressed to a mass reader'. See *Victorian Science Fiction in the UK: The Discourses of Knowledge and of Power* (Boston: G.K. Hall & Co., 1983), 403.

After Dorking 79

60 The stories mentioned here and throughout the book, while not an exhaustive list, has been put together with the help of existing bibliographies, mainly I.F. Clarke's own 'Checklist of Imaginary Wars': I.F. Clarke, *Voices Prophesying War: Future Wars 1763–3749* (Oxford: Oxford University Press, 1992), 224–262. This bibliography is flawed, and Clarke does not explain what merits an inclusion or not on the list, or the format or publisher, but at least it gives a tentative indication of the future-war fiction published each year. Other bibliographies have additional information, but suffer from similar issues. Among the best are Everett F. Bleiler, *Science Fiction: The Early Years* (Kent, OH, and London: Kent State University Press, 1990) in which the author also admits that defining and cataloguing 'imaginary war stories' proved to be a headache (viii); and Clarke, *The Tale of the Future, from the Beginning to the Present Day* 3rd edition (London: The Library Association, 1978). The *Encyclopedia of Science Fiction* (www.sf-encyclopedia.com) remains an excellent source for this form of literature, as does the website *The Riddle of the Sands* (www. theriddleofthesands.com), edited by Derek Linney. Suvin includes his own bibliography of future-war fiction in *Victorian Science Fiction*, 82–85. Stories that were printed in periodicals and magazines are often underrepresented in science fiction studies and bibliographies, with stories published as books being more frequently listed and commented on. Bleiler in his *Checklist* explicitly states that he is 'concerned with books and pamphlets, but not with periodicals or serial publications', even though the distinction between serialisations and books was often blurry: *The Checklist of Science-Fiction and Supernatural Fiction* (Glen Rock: Firebell Books, 1979), ii. A glance through I.F. Clarke's checklist of 'imaginary wars' also betrays a certain lack of stories published in magazines and periodicals. The most important work done to date on science fiction in magazines focuses on popular science fiction: Sam Moskowitz (ed.), *Science Fiction by Gaslight: A History and Anthology of Science Fiction in the Popular Magazines, 1891–1911* (Cleveland: World Publishing Co., 1968), is worth mentioning here.

61 Some clarification is needed here. Clarke in the second edition of *Voices*, 225–226, lists 23 works altogether related to *Dorking* in 1871. However, of these, two are duplicates – different editions of the same text (The anonymous *The Suggested Invasion of England by the Germans*, and a story in German purportedly written by J.M. Trutz-Baumwoll); two of the works listed are not fiction (Lieut.-Col. William Hunter, *Army Speech Dedicated to Those Who Have been Frightened by the Battle of Dorking* (London: Simpkin Marshall, 1871); and Sir Baldwyn Leighton, *The Lull before Dorking* (London: Richard

80   *Expertise, opinion and invasion-scare fiction*

Bentley and Son, 1871); and some works are not listed, even though they clearly should have been. These are: Francis Cowley Burnand and Arthur Sketchley's theatre production *About the Battle of Dorking* from 1871; Arthur A. Beckett, 'How the Prussians Invaded Brighton: A Story of the Review', *London Society* (May 1871), 453–460; 'A Wayside Observer' [pseud.], *The Years before the Battle* (London: Elliot Stock, [1871]); and Anon., 'Der Ruhm, or the Wreck of German Unity: The Narrative of a Brandenburger Hauptmann', *Macmillan's Magazine* (July 1871), 230–240. The latter is, however, one of the stories reprinted in Clarke's anthology *The Tale of the Next Great War, 1871–1914: Fictions of Future Warfare and Battles Still-to-come* (Liverpool: Liverpool University Press, 1995), 77–94. In addition, there are such stories as the two printed in *Colburn's United Service Magazine* – 'Fifty Years Ago' and 'The Defeat of the Navy in the Battle of Dorking' – both discussed in more detail above. Taken together, these changes make for a total number of, at the very least, 26 works – though the anonymous satire *The Hens Who Tried to Crow* (London: Robert Hardwicke, 1871), which Clarke lists, is at best tenuously connected to the other works, as it is not primarily concerned with invasions or *The Battle of Dorking*. There are probably other, uncatalogued or tenuously related works that could have been mentioned here as well. The point still stands: a large quantity of fiction was produced in the immediate aftermath of, and directly inspired by, *Dorking*.

62 'Lord Hartington's Resolutions, and the Position of the Opposition', *Blackwood's Magazine* (September 1878), 361.

63 On the Eastern Question, see Richard Millman, *Britain and the Eastern Question, 1875–1878* (Oxford: Clarendon Press, 1979).

64 *The New Ordeal* describes a near-future Europe where weapons have become so deadly that war would be national suicide. When conflict breaks out between Britain and 'Bæotia' 'over the Happygoland question', the conflict is resolved through trial by combat, rather than by mass armies. The story was originally serialised in *Blackwood's Magazine* between October (385–405) and November 1878 (511–535), and later reissued as a pamphlet (Edinburgh and London: Blackwood and Sons, 1879).

65 Clarke *Voices*, 226–228. This number is flawed, as Clarke had a broad understanding of what constituted an 'imaginary war' story, but it gives an indication of the overall increase in published stories from the previous decade, 1871 excluded.

66 The history of wars breaking out without warning was outlined by Brevet-Lieutenant Colonel J.F. Maurice in *Hostilities without the Declaration of War: An Historical Abstract of the Cases in Which*

After Dorking 81

Hostilities Have Occurred Between Civilized Powers Prior to Declaration or Warning. From 1700 to 1870 (London: Clowes and Sons, 1883). The book was often pointed to by officers eager to bolster home defences, to the exasperation of critics who pointed out that while an attack on Britain might take place without an official declaration of war, it would be unlikely to happen without some form of prior warning – a bolt would hardly come from a perfectly blue, cloudless sky. See Howard Roy Moon, 'The Invasion of the United Kingdom: Public Controversy and Official Planning 1888–1918' (University of London, Ph.D. thesis, 1968), 296.

67 For a concise summary of these two competing schools, see John Gooch, *The Prospect of War: Studies in British Defence Policy 1847–1942* (London: Frank Cass, 1981), 3–5; and Arthur J. Marder, *British Naval Policy 1880–1905: The Anatomy of British Sea Power* (London: Putnam & Co., [1940]), 65–83. See also Searle, *New England?* 245. The term 'navalists' is used here in the same limited sense as does Marder (*British Naval Policy*, ix): to describe proponents of a large navy. Matthew Johnson claims that the term should be understood as more than strategic calculations, and that pre-war 'Navalism' was indeed ideological, with the navy linked to national prestige. See Matthew Johnson, 'The Liberal Party and the Navy League in Britain before the Great War', *Twentieth Century British History*, 22 (2011), 140. On the navy's relationship with national identity, see Jan Rüger, *The Great Naval Game: Britain and Germany in the Age of Empire* (Cambridge: Cambridge University Press, 2009).

68 See David G. Morgan-Owen, *The Fear of Invasion: Strategy, Politics, and British War Planning, 1880–1914* (Oxford: Oxford University Press, 2017), 4.

69 An early member was the outspoken Lord Charles Beresford. Roger T. Stearn, '"The Last Glorious Campaign": Lord Roberts, the National Service League and Compulsory Military Training, 1902–1914', *Journal of the Society for Army Historical Research*, 87 (2009), 314, 324. The National Service League and Navy League are discussed in more detail in chapter 4.

70 'Clarendon Macaulay' [pseud.], *The Carving of Turkey: A Chapter of European History, from Sources hitherto unpublished* (London: Mead and Co., 1894 [1874]). Clarke lists the author as Walter Marsham Adams: *Voices*, 226.

71 Anon., *The Invasion of 1883: A Chapter from the Book of Fate* (Glasgow: James Maclehose, 1876); Anon., *Fifty Years Hence: An Old Soldier's Tale of England's Downfall* (London: G.W. Bacon & Co., 1877); Anon., *Gortschakoff and Bismarck, or Europe in 1940. A Dream* (Oxford and London: James Parker and Co., 1878).

82   *Expertise, opinion and invasion-scare fiction*

72 'An Octogenarian' [pseud.], *The British Federal Empire in the Twentieth Century* (London: Charles H. Clarke, [1872]). Charles Dilke's book on the idea of a 'Greater Britain' had been published a few years prior to the pamphlet: *Greater Britain: A Record of Travel in English-Speaking Countries during 1866 and 1867*, 2 vols. (London: MacMillan and Co., 1868). The Victorian hopes and dreams of a federal empire is outlined in Duncan Bell, *The Idea of Greater Britain: Empire and the Future of World Order, 1860–1900* (Princeton and Oxford: Princeton University Press, 2007).

73 Anon., *A Parallel Case; or, the Straits of Dover Question A.D. 2345* (Darlington: Bell, 1876).

74 Arthur J. Evans, *Through Bosnia and the Herzegóvina on Foot during the Insurrection, August and September 1875. With an Historical Review of Bosnia and a Glimpse at the Croats, Slavonians, and the Ancient Republic of Ragusa* (London: Longmans, Green, and Co., 1876).

75 Anon., 'The Battle of Berlin in 1875', *Colburn's United Service Magazine* (August 1872), 533.

76 Anon., 'The Battle of Wilton. By A Survivor', *Colburn's United Service Magazine* (September 1880), 93–97.

77 The autumn manoeuvres in 1872 had taken place in the same area, around Wiltshire, and had been reported on and discussed in detail in *Colburn's*. See Anon., 'The Wiltshire Campaign', *Colburn's United Service Magazine* (October 1872), 226–239 [Part I], and November 1872, 367–387 [Part II].

78 Sam Rockwell Reed, *The War of 1886 between the United States and Great Britain* (Cincinnati: Robert Clarke & Co., 1882).

79 Anon., 'The War of 1886 between the United States and Great Britain' [review], *Colburn's United Service Magazine* (October 1882), 216. Other stories were also reviewed or briefly commented on in the 1880s. In 1887 the journal contained a short review of *The Great Naval War of 1887*, described as a 'naval battle of Dorking': 'Reviews', *Colburn's United Service Magazine* (January 1887), 74. In 1888, *Colburn's* had short reviews of the stories *The 'Russia's Hope'* (March, 266–267); and *The Taking of Dover* (September, 632). The September 1889 issue included a review of Robert Cromie, *For England's Sake* (628–629).

80 By 1921, there were clearly enough such books in the War Office library in Whitehall that one commentator thought a cull might be in order: the library, they noted, 'is weak, where it should be strong, in military history and biography and in military geography; but it contains a few works on theology, on social reform, much fiction of the school of Chesney's "Battle of Dorking," and a vast number of quite worthless books having the recent war [the First World War] for their subject'. See *Civil and Military Gazette* [Lahore, India], 7 July 1921, 11.

3

Public appeals and fiction, c. 1880–1894

On 12 February 1894, the *Standard* reported that the Surrey Brigade of the Metropolitan Volunteers – the same body of part-time soldiers that George Chesney had lambasted in *The Battle of Dorking* two decades previously – were to have their Easter manoeuvres alongside regular troops on Easter Monday, between Guildford and Aldershot.[1] The paper also contained a report of the council of the National Rifle Association – an organisation that, as its president had boasted in 1890, 'may fairly claim to have established rifle shooting as a national pursuit, and to have thus added greatly to the defensive power of Great Britain and the colonies'.[2] The *Standard* thought it 'a matter for regret that an Association like this, which was established to give permanence to Volunteer corps, should not be more liberally supported from the wealth of the country, which would, but for the existence of this force, have to maintain a vastly increased Regular Army'. The paper also had a suggestion for the future:

> When that invading foreigner, who is supposed to be coming some day, has at length succeeded in effecting a landing on our shores, after having blown our ships to pieces, it will be just as well for our riflemen to be able to shoot him as he is dodging from bush to bush, instead of waiting till he stands still to be made a target of. Our Volunteers have very little practice at this kind of work.[3]

Amateur soldiers were still amateurs, and their ability to hold back an invading army was not guaranteed. In the long term, a more coherent, well-planned programme would have to be worked out if Britain wanted to see its defences raised to a satisfactory level. Planning, not improvisation, would save Britain from possible military disaster in the future.

84   *Expertise, opinion and invasion-scare fiction*

That, at least, was the view of three cross-party MPs and a journalist, as they dispatched on that same February Monday an impassioned plea for 'forethought and preparation' beyond the machinations of party politics, in matters of war and defence. The letter was addressed to William Gladstone, then Prime Minister for the fourth and last time; Lord Salisbury, who would take over the Premiership the year after, following Rosebery's short-lived Liberal government; the Duke of Devonshire; Arthur Balfour; and Joseph Chamberlain. The four signatories were Sir Charles Dilke, Spenser Wilkinson, H.O. Arnold-Forster and George Chesney.[4] The letter-signatories, as its recipients, came from different parties: Dilke was a Liberal, Arnold-Forster a Liberal Unionist, and Chesney had by this stage been elected to parliament as a Conservative. Only Wilkinson lacked an official connection to any of the political parties, being a journalist and military historian.

Beyond representing different political parties, all four signatories had shown mixed loyalties to their respective parties in the past. Chesney's distaste for party politics and his wish to see a Great United Party, as articulated in *A True Reformer*, has already been mentioned. Arnold-Forster had become estranged from the Liberal party in the 1880s, among other things due to his experiences in Ireland, as secretary to his adoptive father, W.E. Forster, the Chief Secretary. However, he had always been somewhat ill at ease among the Gladstonians and their imperial policies, and in his wife's opinion it was the Egyptian policy and the 'sacrifice' of General Charles Gordon in 1884–1885 that led to the final break.[5] By 1894 he was a Liberal Unionist MP for West Belfast.[6] As with Chesney, party politics frustrated him: 'I wish the names Liberal and Tory were both at the bottom of the sea, and then we could start afresh, and begin to judge men and policies, not by virtue of the catalogue in which they are placed, but by the light of their conformity with honesty, reason, and common sense'.[7] Wilkinson had made a name for himself as a knowledgeable journalist and military writer. He had worked with Charles Dilke on a book on imperial defence, published a few years previously.[8] Presenting Charles Beresford with a potted autobiography in a letter written in October 1894, Wilkinson described himself as being 'brought up to the belief that the public good ought to be the first object of a man's life, and was therefore from a boy a keen politician',[9] though he was never an

Public appeals and fiction

85

elected member of parliament. Nominally a Liberal, by 1894 he had left the *Manchester Guardian* after C.P. Scott decided to let him go due to his less than stellar Liberal credentials, as the long-serving editor saw it. A year later, he had gravitated even more towards the other party, and was writing for the Conservative *Morning Post*.[10] The last member of the group was also the most famous and arguably the most influential of the four. In Victorian politics, Charles Dilke was a force in his own right, a radical Liberal who was also a baronet, connected with MPs of all political colours and convictions. Dilke was influential enough to have one of his biographers label him 'the lost Prime Minister'.[11] However, he was also controversial: another biographer spent most of his monograph detailing the convoluted divorce case that ultimately ruined Dilke's career.[12]

The Dilke letter, as it will be referred to from now on, reflected two contradictory modes of thought among a vocal group of people occupied with matters of national and imperial defence. On the one hand, there was an expressed wish to see experts take on a larger role in planning and preparation in matters relating to war. The letter, drafted by Wilkinson, stated that the current organisation of army and navy was inefficient. The way the parliamentary system operated, with parties unable to unite behind a coherent defence policy, was detrimental to the security of the empire. Expertise and politics needed to work in tandem, not in opposition: 'It is to the conciliation of these two necessities, that of compatibility with the constitution and that of adaptation to the purpose of war, that our attention has been directed'.[13] Politicians alone were simply not up to the task of deciding the best practice when it came to matters of war: 'The ordinary Cabinet Minister knows nothing whatever about Defence', Arnold-Forster wrote in a letter to Dilke. On the other hand, however, the problem with the existing defence organisation was not necessarily the politicians as such, but the public: 'If the public were really interested in Defence questions', Arnold-Forster noted, 'they would insist upon Ministers understanding them, but the public are not interested'.[14] Bringing experts in as advisers would be meaningless without public pressure insisting that politicians heed expert advice. Public opinion, that ill-defined and unwieldy concept, would have to be mobilised if the experts were to have a role to play at all. The signatories were aware of this problem: Chesney expressed doubts regarding the viability of

86   *Expertise, opinion and invasion-scare fiction*

trying to convince 'the man in the street' with the abstract arguments put forward in the letter, and Dilke did not expect much in the way of response from the party leaders.[15] Although the plan was to make the letter public alongside the politicians' responses,[16] by addressing themselves to party leaders rather than the electorate the signatories seemed to be approaching the problem of national defence from the wrong end.

Building on the issues examined in chapter 2, this chapter looks at a group of people who attempted to inform and use public opinion, and who saw the public as the gateway to changing the political debate on national defence. For them, the expanded franchise and the increased power of public opinion was both a problem and an opportunity. A public led by experts would be a strength to the parliamentary system, and to the defence of Britain; the question was how to convince the seemingly fickle public mind – and indeed the parliament – about the need for such experts. One way was by delivering 'facts' through shocking revelations, and this led to newspaper campaigns that invoked an abstract public. Their cultural influence will be examined later; this chapter focuses on attempts to inform and shape public opinion, in the 1880s and early 1890s. The chapter looks at three interconnected national defence issues that all, in one form or another, involved top-down attempts at engaging with the public through media. Aside from the Dilke letter, these are the channel tunnel debate in the 1880s, and the 1884 naval scare.

The first and last of these are intimately connected and involved some of the same individuals. Taken together, the two events illustrate competing ideas of the public's role in guiding defence policy. The 1884 naval scare, it has been argued, introduced the Royal Navy to the public imagination: along with the later 1888 scare, it led to public opinion taking an 'intelligent interest' in the fleet.[17] After 1884, aggressive self-publicists like Admiral Charles Beresford could utilise newspapers to take their arguments directly to the public – arguably contributing, ultimately, to the two-power standard and the Naval Defence Act of 1889.[18] In the 1890s, writers like John and Philip Colomb – not to mention the American Alfred Mahan – found a ready market for their writings on naval strategy.[19] However, the symbolic importance of 1884 in the popularisation of strategic thinking has as its obverse image the simultaneous development towards a more exclusionary, more professionalised

Public appeals and fiction 87

defence policy, as symbolised by the sentiments expressed in the 1894 Dilke letter.

Rather than giving a detailed outline of how naval and military policy was discussed in the decades leading up to the First World War, the chapter contextualises the role of public opinion in defence debates, and links these discussions with developments in invasion-scare and future-war fiction. By looking at a set of interconnected case studies, the chapter identifies an unresolved conflict in the way the British public featured and were discussed in these debates, in particular after the 1884 franchise expansion.

The 1884 naval scare

Hugh Oakeley Arnold-Forster had attempted a public approach a decade before the Dilke letter, when he was among the initiators of the 1884 naval scare. The rationale behind this episode in British politics was simple: if the government would not listen to reason, perhaps it would listen to the rising power of the press?

It speaks volumes about his idea of not only parliamentary politics, but also of the electorate in general, that Arnold-Forster thought it was more important to convince public opinion than individual politicians. Uneasily straddling traditional Liberalism and – somewhat later – the new Liberal Unionism under Joseph Chamberlain, Arnold-Forster saw politics through Manichean eyes, neatly sub-divided into 'right' or 'wrong'. Philip Gibbs, who had worked as a subordinate to Arnold-Forster at the publisher Cassell, later recalled that of all the men he had met, Arnold-Forster was 'quite the rudest ... to all people of superior rank to himself':

> He treated distinguished admirals, generals and colonels as though they were office-boys, so that they perspired in his presence and were sometimes deeply affronted; but, on the other hand, as a proof of chivalry, he treated office-boys and printer's devils as though they were distinguished admirals and colonels, with a most particular courtesy.[20]

This also illustrates Arnold-Forster's view on expertise – the men in uniform were not necessarily those that should be listened to; facts should speak for themselves, and in Arnold-Forster's mind they did – anyone who took the time to read and inform themselves properly could be made to understand the 'correct' policy

88   *Expertise, opinion and invasion-scare fiction*

on any given issue. Though he could be personally charming, the later Secretary of State for War was never one for the subtle compromises of politics. In a slightly two-sided compliment, Admiral John Fisher called this character trait a perfect quality for a lawyer: 'He has brought into prominence matters of minor importance. Nevertheless, it is most advantageous that he has done so, as it is all in the direction of efficiency'.[21] In their first dealings together however, Fisher was invited to consider a matter that was important to both men: the Royal Navy.

In 1888, Arnold-Forster anonymously wrote a short story for *Murray's Magazine*, where he envisioned a clash between ironclads in a near-future war. 'In a Conning Tower' was written to instruct a general reader on modern means of naval warfare, and was well enough received that it was reprinted as a pamphlet under his full name in 1891.[22] I.F. Clarke comments that the author wrote it 'without any political intentions',[23] which is an erroneous reading of Arnold-Forster's character and motivations. The story was certainly written as entertainment, but also contained criticism of the way the fleet was organised. However, even though it has been claimed that the story launched Arnold-Forster's political career,[24] his election as a Liberal Unionist in West Belfast in 1892 had probably more to do with his fierce criticism of Home Rule than his interest in the Navy; he had already made himself a name as an ardent critic of Irish Nationalists by that time.[25] Either way, no entertaining fiction clouded the message Arnold-Forster wanted to give to the British public in 1884: British sea power was no longer up to the task of defending Britain. This time, the blunt instrument he chose to hammer his point home with was the apostle of popular journalism, W.T. Stead.

As Stead himself told the story, a young Arnold-Forster showed up in Stead's *Pall Mall Gazette* office, brusquely asking the paper's editor when he was planning on 'tak[ing] up the question of the Navy'.[26] The resulting series of articles, beginning on 15 September 1884,[27] and culminating in proposals for increased naval construction by the end of the year, has been described as 'an example of the efficiency of a lobby rather than the power of the press'.[28] It was, of course, both – a political victory for the press, as much as for the lobby in question. The campaign made it seem like journalism could influence public and parliament alike. Stead himself was naturally of the opinion that the articles had had their intended

Public appeals and fiction 89

effect: 'In 1884', he wrote 20 years later, 'the nation was almost in despair about the condition of the navy'.[29]

Arnold-Forster fired the opening salvo in January 1883, from the pages of the *Nineteenth Century*, where he outlined the domestic problems a loss of naval supremacy would lead to: 'Panic, disorder, suffering, starvation among our overcrowded population will bring home to us with painful clearness the error we make in neglecting to maintain a sufficiently powerful, and, above all, sufficiently numerous, navy'.[30] He further wrote a preliminary article, not directly linked to the 'Truth about the Navy', for Stead's *Pall Mall Gazette* on 14 August 1884, under the headline 'More Ships for the Navy'.[31] The first article in the 'Truth about the Navy' series was published in the same paper a month later. 'Not only our Imperial position', it stated, 'but the daily bread of twenty millions out of the thirty millions of our population depends entirely upon our dominion of the sea. If that is lost, or even endangered, our existence is at stake'.[32] Such arguments were not unheard of, but rarely had they been so forcefully made and pressed home to a reading public.

In a number of articles in September and October dedicated to the topic, the *Pall Mall Gazette* continued to question the government on the state of the navy.[33] Fisher, then a Captain, was brought in on the campaign as a technical expert, and Reginald Brett – the Victorian socialite and all-round *éminence grise*, who would later become Lord Esher and at the time was chief assistant to the Secretary of State for War – provided inside information for the campaigners.[34] The first article under the heading 'The Truth about the Navy' directed 12 questions to the Lords of the Admiralty – the first of these questions in essence summed up the following 11: 'Our war risks have enormously increased. Has our navy, which is our national insurance, been correspondingly strengthened?'[35] The paper answered this question in the negative three days later. Comparing investments in 1868 with 1883, an article written by 'One who Knows the Facts'[36] presented the *Pall Mall Gazette*'s readers with gloomy statistics: 'we are', the article stated, 'spending to-day less money on our navy than we spent in 1868'. In dry, factual language, peppered with numbers, names and technical details, the unsatisfactory state of the British navy in comparison to its counterparts was laid bare.[37] The next day the Conservative MP Sir John Hay, a naval campaigner writing in the *Pall Mall Gazette*

90   *Expertise, opinion and invasion-scare fiction*

under his full name, confirmed the inadequate state of the British fleet, adding more numbers and figures to the argument.[38]

Hay was not the only Conservative to support the campaign, but political divisions were toned down on the pages of the *Pall Mall Gazette* in the following days. An anonymous letter by a 'distinguished officer', as the newspaper described him, 'rejoice[d] to see this subject brought forward by a paper of the same general politics as those of the present Government. It leads me to hope that the navy may cease to be sacrificed to party politics'.[39] The *Pall Mall Gazette* naval agitation was above party – the term used in another letter, 'from an officer whose name, could we give it, would deservedly carry much weight', was that the campaign was 'patriotic'.[40] Indeed, the paper had followed this 'patriotic' line since the initial publication of the 'One Who Knows' article, by prefacing it with a statement of intent. The *Pall Mall Gazette* had published the revelations of 'The Truth about the Navy' because, as the preface read, they were 'somewhat impatient with the endless polemic carried on between the two parties over a subject so vital to the national existence as the efficiency of the fleet'.[41] The role of the press was to hammer home the facts, and lift the navy out of the hands of politicians and into those of the wider public. The navy was too important to be a party issue, or to be left solely to the whims of politicians in parliament. This argument was revisited four years later during Beresford's agitation against the Admiralty in the 1888 naval scare, where he strongly hinted that politicians should make way for professional opinion.[42]

A final article by Arnold-Forster was published in the *Nineteenth Century* in November 1884, bringing the campaign full circle.[43] 'Hardly three weeks after the publication of this article', Arnold-Forster's wife and biographer Mary later wrote,

> Parliament, which had been repeatedly told that nothing more was required or would be asked for the Navy, was asked to sanction an expenditure of three and a half millions sterling in addition to the ordinary vote, to make good deficiencies in H.M. Navy.[44]

This request was made by the First Lord, the Earl of Northbrook, in the House of Lords on 2 December 1884. It was, he admitted, the 'general public interest which has been expressed upon questions relating to the Navy' that led him to make a statement about the navy in the autumn session, rather than as part of the estimates. Though

Public appeals and fiction   91

he claimed to be in favour of such public debate, he noted that it was 'somewhat unfortunate' that naval officials in the Admiralty – he used the phrase 'those who are most responsible for the affairs of the Navy, who have most knowledge on the subject' – were not part of that debate.[45] The Admiralty, in short, had not had a chance to have their say. Lord Northbrook still requested £3,100,000 added to the navy,[46] making it seem as if the admirals should perhaps have spoken up sooner – though he was quick to state that Britain held a comfortable lead over its maritime rival France.[47]

Civil lord of the Admiralty, Sir Thomas Brassey, speaking for the government in the Commons, also protested that the navy was not in such a bad shape as his critics would have it. Yet he still made the same request as Northbrook. Brassey hinted at the pressure the government had been put under by the 'Truth about the Navy' campaign – though without mentioning the *Pall Mall Gazette* – in his opening remarks:

> In the present anxiety out-of-doors, it was the obvious duty of the Government to give to the House an opportunity of discussing the subject; ... We [the Admiralty] feel our great responsibility for the maintenance of the naval power of the country and we know that much of the criticism to which we have been subjected is due to imperfect acquaintance on the part of the public both with what we have done and what we propose to do in the future.[48]

Brassey's speech in the Commons that Tuesday was, whether intentional or not, a reply to the challenge put forth by the *Pall Mall Gazette*. The request for more money to the navy followed the logic of the 'Truth about the Navy' article of 18 September: Brassey wanted more torpedo boats, protection of shipping and of harbours and coaling stations, and he assured the assembled MPs that the production of modern guns would keep up with the laying down of new ships.[49] In addition, the prospect of invasion was raised. 'In the First place', the Liberal MP Sir Donald Currie argued, 'these islands must be safe from invasion'.[50] All of this pointed towards an indication that defects pointed out by 'One Who Knows' were also recognised by the Admiralty. It looked as if public opinion – the 'anxiety out-of-doors' – had forced the government's hand.

All was not what it seemed, however. First, the relative weakness of the Royal Navy in relation to its rivals was largely overstated.

92   *Expertise, opinion and invasion-scare fiction*

The navy's efficiency in a Great War would not be tested until 30 years later, and during rather different circumstances, but those who feared a French and Russian naval challenge up until 1905 – when the *Entente Cordiale* and the Russian defeat at Tsushima had changed the political and military outlook – were probably under-estimating the readiness of the Senior Service.[51] In warship tonnage, Britain dwarfed its rivals in the 1880s,[52] though this was not necessarily a good indication of a fleet's effectiveness – a point stressed in the 'Truth about the Navy' articles.[53] Even if, in relative terms, the navy was weakening compared to its rivals,[54] it is still easy in hindsight to dismiss Sir John Hay's assessment of British capabilities in 1884 as so meagre that a French fleet could, at will and without a declaration of war, steam up to Liverpool and hold the city ransom for £100,000,000, or, for good measure, 'burn it and Birkenhead'.[55]

Realities are, however, subject to interpretation. And as long as there was a sense of British maritime inferiority, the realities of a complex issue like naval parity are of minor importance. The naval agitators had, through the pages of the *Pall Mall Gazette*, argued that Britain's defences were underfunded. Those who agreed with this assessment claimed that they had public opinion behind them in clamouring for more naval investments. If the first of these claims was at least somewhat convincing, the second was rather more dubious.

The unintentional scaremongers

For the 'Truth about the Navy' clique, their campaign seemed vindicated by Brassey's speech in the Commons.[56] The last act of the drama had played out in parliament, but the campaign had been fought and won in the press, and had been pursued beyond party boundaries and outside of the established political channels. For Arnold-Forster, this represented a new form of politics – 'it is now painfully evident that the most effectual manner of rousing the Government to a proper performance of their duties is by an appeal to the crowd'.[57] For Stead, writing two years later, the newspaper had superseded parliament as the real power for change in Britain in the 1880s: 'Parliament will continue to meet in the midst

Public appeals and fiction

of a newspaper age, but it will be subordinate. The wielders of real power will be those who are nearest the people'.[58]

The professionally promoted scare narrative had come a long way from Chesney's uncertain venture into the genre over a decade earlier. Eschewing melodrama for statistics and measurable quantities, the naval campaign was a more focused attempt at changing policy. The audience was 'the crowd', the message was clear and unmistakable and the results were tangible. In a sense, the invasion or naval scare narrative had come of age. Later historians have largely agreed with Stead and Arnold-Forster, seeing the newspaper campaign as successfully instigating a panic. Arthur Marder claims that the English in 1884 were led to '[a]lmost instinctively ... inspect their first line of defence, and were shocked to find it inadequate',[59] and Paul Kennedy has noted that the *Pall Mall Gazette* articles 'fell like a bomb upon a public already uneasy at the commercial and colonial threats to Britain's world interests'.[60]

'The crowd' was a nebulous audience, however, and the press was an unwieldy instrument with which to measure public opinion in 1884, as it had been in 1871. Stead himself can be forgiven for thinking that he was witnessing the beginning of a 'government by journalism'; the belief in the power of the press to influence society was common not only among journalists but also advertisers and other stakeholders in the newspaper business in the nineteenth century.[61] 1884 was the year of the Third Reform Act, leading to an extended franchise that, after that year, included around 60 per cent of adult males.[62] Stead's brand of journalism – the New Journalism of the 1880s and 1890s[63] – could be seen as effective, even dangerous, in combination with the newly enfranchised masses; this was a press wielding real power at the ballot boxes. However, though welcomed by Stead, the idea was far from universally acclaimed outside or even within Fleet Street newspaper offices.[64] Democracy loomed as both a blessing and a curse between the lines of 'One who Knows' and the revelatory 18 September article in the *Pall Mall Gazette*:

> In 1869 power passed for the first time into the hands of the Democracy ... Fifteen years of government by the borough have passed since then, and we are now about to take a new departure in a democratic direction by enfranchising the householders of the counties.

94 *Expertise, opinion and invasion-scare fiction*

The fifteen years in question, the article continued, had brought material progress, but no increase in the first line of defence.[65] This was a subtle hint that political freedom meant material gains, but it should also be accompanied by the willingness to make sacrifices to protect this prosperity.

Whether the enfranchised masses were really the intended audience for Stead's exposé is doubtful. For all his faith in an enlightened readership, Stead's *Pall Mall Gazette* reached a specific and limited audience, being a paper 'which came out at tea-time and was much read in the London clubs'.[66] Its audience at the end of 1883, when Stead took over the editorial chair, belonged, for the most part, to the Victorian middle class.[67] 'The Truth about the Navy' was no mass appeal, despite Stead and Arnold-Forster's assertions otherwise. As Brett's involvement, and the cross-party support for increased naval expenditure in the Commons on 2 December illustrate, the issue was not forced upon an unwilling political establishment by public pressure. Indeed, as Steven R.B. Smith notes, pressure from the City of London may have been more important than any public campaign when it came to driving naval expansion in the 1880s.[68] British naval policy from the late nineteenth century was shaped by a multitude of different demands, including the need to protect seaborne trade, as well as the requirements of a global empire.[69]

Sir Donald Currie could point to 'the public mind' when he threw his support behind new naval building plans, and as his measure of public engagement on the topic was presumably the newspapers, he might well have been justified. But, as Paul Kennedy notes, the influence of the press in Victorian Britain could be exaggerated due to its 'intimacy with the political world';[70] the politicians were really agreeing with or arguing among themselves, not with the public mind. Stephen Koss is broadly correct in asserting that, by 1880, 'politicians came to realize, sometimes grudgingly that press opinion and public opinion were not necessarily synonymous';[71] but as illustrated by the 1884 navy campaign and its replies in the Commons, the idea that public and press spoke with one voice could still be articulated and used to underline the importance of certain issues. As with the comments over *The Battle of Dorking* earlier in the century, coming so close after the 1867 Second Reform Act, the 1884 debate was framed as if the British people had been shocked into realising the danger the country was in.

Public appeals and fiction   95

Whereas *Dorking* became a cultural reference rather than a political force, the opposite was arguably true of the 1884 scare: 'The Truth about the Navy' had direct political implications for naval funding, but its actual audience was limited. If this was indeed the beginnings of 'government by journalism', where 'appeals to the crowd' would ensure sound government, it is worth asking who people like Arnold-Forster and Stead understood as constituting this 'crowd', and how appeals related to national defence were to be presented to them. This necessitates another look at the interpretation of public opinion in the intersection of press and parliament.

The elusive public

A general discussion of what constituted the Victorian public is beyond the scope of this chapter. However, as the parliamentary and extra-parliamentary agents in the 1884 naval debate made frequent references to, and claimed to act and speak on behalf of, public opinion, a brief look at the official mind's impression of the people it governed in the year of the Third Reform Act is necessary.

Parliament, of course, was accountable to the people that had elected it; indeed, parliament was, in a sense, the voice of the people. However, as James Thompson points out, this naturally meant that there was also a 'public opinion' that parliament – the Commons in particular – was supposed to represent.[72] José Ortega y Gasset's thesis of 'hyperdemocracy', where 'the mass believes that it has the right to impose and to give force of law to notions born in the café', was still half a century away. British parliamentarians in 1884 might, however, uncomfortably have agreed that they were entering into this 'hyperdemocratic' stage, away from what Gasset saw as normal democracy; one where 'the mass handed over the exercise of [politics] to specialised persons'.[73] Both sides in the 1884 naval scare claimed that specialists or experts were needed to ensure efficiency in national defence. This was not a new notion – the idea that war, as 'An Old Harrovian' commented in 1871, 'should be treated more as an actual science' was not uncommon in the immediate aftermath of the Franco-Prussian war and the debates after the publication of *Dorking*, to take one example.[74] However, the

96   *Expertise, opinion and invasion-scare fiction*

1884 naval scare highlighted how expertise on its own, if not communicated properly, was worthless in an age of democracy. The Third Reform Act, by expanding the political nation, loomed over the naval debate in 1884, though it was largely unmentioned in the actual discussion over ship design and armaments.

It is important to stress that the public, though despaired of as uninformed and uneducated about matters of national defence, was not portrayed as irrational. Arnold-Forster was not alone in thinking that if the people knew the truth, they would ensure that the 'correct' policy was followed, meaning that the 1884 naval scare invoked a political public and not an irrational mob. 'While the crowd' – in a different meaning than Arnold-Forster gave the term – 'could be seen as volatile, or as sullenly inarticulate, the political public was constituted through speaking and writing', notes Thompson.[75] When the papers published statistics and compared navies, and parliament debated expansion of the senior service, this rational public was the intended audience.

Future-war fiction in the 1880s: from naval wars to channel tunnels

With the above developments in mind, it should be noted that service authors dealt only tentatively with defence policy in their excursions into invasion-scare and future-war fiction in the 1880s. Yet, the 'Bolt from the Blue' and 'Blue Water' arguments, as discussed in the previous chapter, were at least in part present here as well. Navalists and other interested parties weighed in on the course of future naval engagements in stories like *The Battle off Worthing*, subtitled *Why the Invaders Never got to Dorking* (1887).[76] The anonymous author – presumably a navy officer – of *The Battle of Port Said* was less optimistic, and imagined Britain losing a naval war in the near future due to mismanagement of the navy,[77] a theme also present in *The Great Naval War of 1887* (1886), written by the journalist and naval expert William Laird Clowes, possibly in cooperation with either Alan H. Burgoyne or Commander Charles Napier Robinson. *The Great Naval War*, a highly technical treatise, ended with a political message on the state of the navy: the British defeat is due to 'years of indifference, mismanagement, and parsimony' – in

Public appeals and fiction 97

short, poor planning and lack of foresight.[78] Arnold-Forster's own *In a Conning Tower* was first published in 1888. Translated work appeared as well: *The 'Russia's Hope'* (1888), for example, was penned by an anonymous Russian navy officer. The story described a successful Russian naval war against Britain, summarised in the evocative subtitle: *Britannia no Longer Rules the Waves. Showing how the Muscovite Bear got at the British Whale*.[79]

In 1883, William F. Butler – army officer and husband of the painter Lady Elizabeth Butler – penned a story titled *The Invasion of England*, under the pseudonym 'An Old Soldier'. Despite the professionalism and experience inherent in Butler's choice of *nom de plume*, the story was less interested in disseminating ideas of warfare than it was in unfavourably contrasting the state of modern Britain with its former glories.[80] In this, the narrative was in line with the general trend in invasion-scare fiction of the period: the stories were principally polemics – against society, or the general state of politics in the era of representative government. The majority of these narratives were also firmly anti-Liberal, blaming Gladstone for the perceived dangers of the franchise expansions of 1867 and 1884, and for the future they envisioned as a consequence. Some texts eagerly criticised the political system itself, rather than siding with one party or other.[81] Gladstone's policy in Ireland became a popular theme with authors in 1886, the year Irish Home Rule was defeated in parliament, permanently splitting the Liberal Party.[82] Darko Suvin categorises stories that dealt with a 'future civil war in Ireland' as a separate sub-genre of Victorian science fiction,[83] and it is useful to approach those stories that rarely involved invasion-threats, but instead imagined Ireland's capability to descend into chaos when left to its own devices, as a distinct category. However, such stories often mentioned Irish-American involvement in Irish affairs, and though they technically do not belong to the invasion-fiction category, they were clearly part of the same wider group of texts.[84]

Irish-American links were not taken completely out of the blue. Charles Stewart Parnell had visited the United States on a fundraising trip in 1879–1880, leading the *Saturday Review* to comment that, while his welcome among Irish settlers could be expected to be warm, '[t]he reception of Mr. Parnell among the real Americans will be watched with more genuine curiosity'.[85]

98   *Expertise, opinion and invasion-scare fiction*

Despite such arguments, as in the 1870s, comparatively few of the invasion-scare and future-war narratives published in Britain in the 1880s were directly concerned with specific – as opposed to more general – issues of national defence, or debates related to it. There were, for instance, no stories in the immediate wake of or clearly inspired by the 'Truth about the Navy' articles – 1884 was a quiet year for future-war and invasion-scare fiction – though the publication of texts, in particular with a naval focus, was more frequent towards the end of the decade, as outlined above.[86] Nor is there an indication that these texts intended to engage with a wide readership: many stories were either highly technical treatises, or they decried the ignorance of the reading masses. If intended as a top-down attempt at influencing public opinion, the invasion-scare literature of the 1870s and 1880s was therefore of limited success. Stories were clearly not written to cater to a popular demand for invasion-scare texts among the public, nor did the future naval war narratives of the 1880s inspire widespread 'spin-off' scares; there was no 'Dorking moment' in the 1880s, equivalent to the many replies to Chesney's story in 1871. The nearest thing to a similar reaction came with the many fictional commentaries in the channel tunnel debate, the focus of the rest of this chapter.

The channel tunnel in the 1880s

The idea that the English Channel could be traversed by a tunnel intrigued as well as infuriated Victorians. A tunnel could be seen as undermining the island fortress, and its opponents therefore presented it as a threat to the country's island identity as well as to national security.[87] By 1882 the issue had reached the floor of the House of Commons, and become a question debated in the press as well as among outspoken service members. The Duke of Cambridge, the intransigent and ageing Commander-in-Chief of the Army, was naturally opposed to the idea, and found a ready ally in general Sir Garnet Wolseley.[88] The Duke thought that a dissemination of their objections would be advisable, 'in the hope that by drawing public attention to the subject this mischievous project may after all be given up'.[89] The result was an appeal to the public in which fear and national identity were key components.

Public appeals and fiction

Wolseley based his opposition to the channel tunnel on two interlinked suppositions: a tunnel would increase the chances of a foreign invasion of Britain succeeding; and the mere possibility of this would lead to panic. In a letter to the Departmental Committee tasked with examining the prospect of a tunnel, he articulated the latter problem in an evocative passage:

> Even now when protected by our "silver streak" we suffer from periodic panics, which are as injurious to trade as they are undignified; this tunnel would render their recurrence much more frequent, thereby increasing the loss they occasion.[90]

The argument was convincing, at least for some: in June 1888 Sir Michael Hicks-Beach, Conservative President of the Board of Trade, used similar words during the second reading of a channel tunnel bill. A tunnel, he told the Commons, would not produce any gains that would not be 'far outweighed by the injury to trade from the anxiety caused by the perpetually recurring panics, and the feeling of insecurity which would arise from the existence of a Tunnel'.[91]

Keith Wilson sees the outline of an 'unholy alliance' in the early months of 1882 against the channel tunnel, including, aside from Wolseley and Admiral Sir Cooper Key, Sir Charles Dilke at the Foreign Office.[92] The latter seems to have kept himself within official channels however, and Wilson presents the ensuing 'manufactured' panic as a product of War Office, rather than Foreign Office circles – primarily Wolseley's and Cambridge's creation, in other words.[93] Wolseley was no stranger to interactions with a reading public, having, among other things, written an anonymous account for *Blackwood's Magazine* of the Red River Expedition he led in 1870; along with Chesney he was part of John Blackwood's 'Military Staff' at the magazine.[94] His anti-channel tunnel campaign, according to Wilson, was manipulation akin to the Jingoism manufactured by Conservatives during 1877–1878, when Britain and Russia had seemed on the verge of war.[95] This implies War Office engagement with public opinion, and a public acceptance of, or at least reaction to, this engagement. Wilson does note that Cambridge and Wolseley were in contact with the *Nineteenth Century*, where Wolseley's views were presented in an article he had initially intended to write himself, but which finally ended up being penned by Lord Dunsany.[96] Wolseley's anonymously presented

100 *Expertise, opinion and invasion-scare fiction*

opinion in this article used suggestive words to capture its readers' imaginations:

> what security have you that our end of the tunnel ... shall not be seized some night suddenly by a couple of thousand men introduced into the place by treachery, or allowed within it by stupidity, or who had forced their way in by escalade or surprise? To land such a body of men any dark night during calm weather in Dover harbour would be an easy operation; or why should they not be sent through the tunnel itself without any warning?[97]

These were words deliberately chosen to evoke an image of insecurity and unease – not calmly to inform.

'Throughout 1882', Wilson writes, 'the channel tunnel was kept very much in the public eye'.[98] A familiar question arises with this assertion: which public? On the policy level, the channel tunnel issue was mainly debated behind closed doors within the corridors of power: in the summer of 1881, the tunnel started its tour of government committees, beginning with a departmental committee, followed by a defence committee, before ending up in a parliamentary joint select committee.[99] A concentrated effort by the *Nineteenth Century* aside, the decision not to go ahead with a channel tunnel in the 1880s was taken without reference to what the public wanted: an exasperated Gladstone claimed in 1890 that the tunnel had the support of 'the sensible population of this country' by which he did not mean 'only the people who agree with me, but the mass of the working population'.[100] The masses wanted a tunnel, Gladstone argued, but they were opposed by the military authorities, presumably of a less 'sensible' calibre. George Potter, the trade unionist and former editor of the *Bee-Hive*, would have agreed with him in his assessment of the workers' as being the 'sensible' part of the population, if that was indeed what Gladstone meant. Writing in 1882, Potter not only slammed opposition to the tunnel as a product of 'political panic, military doubt, or feminine timidity', but also noted that 'the working-men – but another word for the general community' were largely in favour of a tunnel; the problem, Potter argued, was that relevant information was kept away from the public.[101] Edward Watkin, the principal promoter of the channel tunnel in the 1880s, argued in a speech to the Commons in 1888 that opposition to the tunnel in newspapers which had previously

Public appeals and fiction 101

supported the idea was no indication of a lack of public support: 'It may be said there had been a change of opinion,' he observed, 'but he was afraid there had only been a change of editors'.[102]

In 1887, looking back on the debate over the channel tunnel earlier in the decade, and forward to the prospect of one being built at some point in the future, the radical MP Charles Bradlaugh wrote a pamphlet highly critical of the objections put forward by Wolseley. As Bradlaugh saw it, the invasion argument was the only serious objection to the tunnel, and '[t]he war danger is the only cry to which the democracy need pay any attention'.[103] Turning Wolseley's vision of a panicked populace on its head, Bradlaugh denounced how 'the British democracy are in 1887 asked to reject the tunnel scheme because a real or counterfeit fear, in any case begotten of ignorance and prejudice, has seized some of our "great generals" and hysterical journalists'.[104] Wolseley, not the British public, was unreasonably fearful. As Bradlaugh saw it, Wolseley was hiding the weakness of his arguments behind literary flourishes, 'poetry' and 'pathos':

> The strongest military objections to the proposed tunnel are those stated with considerable literary skill, heightened by strong flavor [sic] of romance, in the long Memorandum of Adjutant-General Sir Garnet (now Lord) Wolseley, dated 16 June 1882.[105]

Robert J. Griffiths, author of an 1887 work expressing support for the channel tunnel, held a similar opinion: 'it is idle to criticise a "Battle of Dorking" romance of this nature', he noted of the general's opposition to the project.[106] This was not a far-fetched comparison: as Norman Longmate observes, 'Wolseley was surely a fiction-writer manqué, for his paper had far more in common with *The Battle of Dorking* than the usual military appreciation'.[107] There was no need for him personally to imitate Chesney, however: Wolseley's words inspired authors to create their own vision of a future channel tunnel. An anonymous pamphleteer, 'The Demure One', took his pseudonym from a verbatim retelling of Wolseley's arguments in Dunsany's February 1882 *Nineteenth Century* article: the satirical pamphlet explained its author's pseudonym by quoting 'the "Warning" by Sir Garnet Wolseley and Lord Dunsany in the "Nineteenth Century"', where it said: 'A man of DEMURE EXTERIOR .... [sic] will rise up in France to seize the Channel Tunnel during a time of profound peace'.[108] The initial dire forecast of the pamphlet was somewhat hampered

102   *Expertise, opinion and invasion-scare fiction*

by the ending, where the tunnel proves its worth as a viable invasion route for a British, rather than a French army. 'The one clear thing about the matter was that by three o'clock in the afternoon Boulogne was completely in possession of the English, and a few hours afterwards they were reinforced by some 20,000 fresh soldiers who had come from England through the Tunnel'.[109] 1882 was not lacking in more pessimistic fictional forecasts, however: a curious reader could dive into stories with titles like 'The Seizure of the Channel Tunnel' and *How John Bull lost London; or, the Capture of the Channel Tunnel*.[110] At least two of the fictional works – an earlier 1876 pamphlet and an 1882 story presented in the form of 'secret' dispatches – portrayed Germany as the enemy, with France being as much a victim of German aggression as Britain.[111] As in most invasion-scare fiction, the enemy was of relatively minor importance, and the adversary in one story could easily be replaced by another in a different publication without many changes to the narrative itself.

The claim that military questions trumped other considerations in the channel tunnel debate led Bradlaugh to tone down a perhaps more prescient observation later in his pamphlet. Referring to an exchange between Mr. Eckroyd, MP for Preston, and the Earl of Devon in the joint Committee of Lords and Commons, Bradlaugh noted how the latter had asked Eckroyd about the 'spread of Socialistic or Communistic views from an increased intercourse between the large body of French and English workmen'. Eckroyd had answered that he thought there would indeed be 'an active propaganda of an Atheistic and Socialistic kind'. Bradlaugh's comment on this was perceptive as well as acidic:

> Lord Wolseley and the Duke of Cambridge fear that French soldiers may conquer us bodily, coming for that purpose secretly through the tunnel. The Earl of Devon and Mr. Eckroyd have like fears of French Atheists and Socialists, who would find in the Channel tunnel a convenient conduit-pipe for their propaganda![112]

James Peddie, the author of a vitriolic and anti-Liberal invasion-scare story taking aim at atheists, republicans and socialists could not have agreed more, and envisioned that after building a tunnel Britain would 'become part of the continent', and start 'importing all the sceptical ideas of irreligious France'.[113] Incidentally, the villainous French Prime Minister in 'The Demure One's pamphlet was an atheist, as

Public appeals and fiction 103

well as a republican and 'a man of pleasure', which presumably constituted a very un-English triptych of vices.[114] International cooperation was surely not on the mind of the author behind the pseudonym 'Grip' either, who, in describing a French conquest of Britain through a channel tunnel saw the defeat as the 'triumph of the alien'.[115]

The idea that the channel tunnel in the 1880s was opposed for reasons of national identity as much as for any real sense of military danger has been perceptively commented on by Daniel Pick and Duncan Redford.[116] The important point to underline for the purpose of this chapter is how army officials could appeal to a public mind by pointing out two contradictory points. The public was prone to panics, and the tunnel should not be built because it would lead to undignified anxiety of invasion. Simultaneously, the public *should* fear an invasion, which would be more probable if a tunnel was built. Wolseley's arguments were necessarily colourful precisely because they were so thin and easily refutable. The extent to which the anti-tunnel arguments were an appeal to emotions rather than intellect is demonstrated by the way they inspired invasion tracts describing threats to British identity.

The tunnel-invasion narratives were outside of the control of the original instigator, Wolseley, who seems to have been in two minds about what he really wanted his main point against the tunnel to be. In many ways, this does look a lot like a repetition of *The Battle of Dorking*. Wolseley's use of emotive imagery rather than his expert knowledge as an army officer is therefore a curious contrast to how the author of *Dorking* himself decided to approach national defence policy a decade later. The 1894 Dilke letter, co-signed by Chesney, was an appeal to let expert opinion inform political decisions, supported, but not influenced by public opinion. The letter was addressed to policymakers, bypassing the public altogether.

The 1884 naval scare had seen public opinion figure in the background rather than at the forefront of the debate – the public was talked about in the abstract, rather than talked to. In the channel tunnel debate, Wolseley's leaks to the press had indeed instigated a popular reaction – if nothing else, it proved fruitful territory for writers of speculative fiction – but it had not been on the public stage that the decision not to build the tunnel had been taken. In both cases there had been visions of public outcry and

104   *Expertise, opinion and invasion-scare fiction*

of a panicked population, but the absent-minded scaremongering of the 1880s and 1890s did not set out to actively foment a panic; in fact, the scaremongering was aimed at the political institutions rather than the public. References to public outcry aside, the scares over naval expenditure and of the threats a channel tunnel would pose were part of political debates within parliament and the service departments. Despite Wolseley's emotive language, his 1882 objection to the channel tunnel scheme had more in common with George Chesney's 1894 approach than with *The Battle of Dorking*.

It is in this context that the Dilke letter needs to be seen. Scares as a policy tool could be eliminated if the experts were given direct access to policymakers, nullifying the effect of either direct appeals, or more absent-minded references to the public. Invasion scares, broadly defined, as a tool which experts – politicians, theorists and service personnel, some having more than one of these roles, like Chesney – could use to communicate with and influence the public, seemed to have been gradually purged from the political stage, and left to the cultural sphere where anonymous pamphleteers could still churn out fantasies of decline and conquest.

However, 1895 would prove that the political use of scare narratives was not quite dead yet – and that the link between invasion in fictional form and political arguments was very much alive. The personification of this was Alfred Harmsworth.

Notes

1 *Standard*, 12 February 1894, 3.
2 *The Times*, 5 May 1890, 6.
3 *Standard*, 12 February 1894, 3.
4 Stephen Gwynn and Gertrude M. Tuckwell, *The Life of the Rt. Hon. Sir Charles W. Dilke*, 2 vols. (London: John Murray, 1917), II, 416–419. The letter in its entirety is printed on 417–419.
5 Mary Arnold-Forster, *The Right Honourable Hugh Oakeley Arnold-Forster: A Memoir by His Wife* (London: Edward Arnold, 1910), 37–38, 49.
6 For a discussion of Arnold-Forster's political and familial background, and his attempt to settle soldiers in South Africa after the South African War, see Christian K. Melby, '"Of Paramount Importance to Our

Public appeals and fiction 105

Race": H.O. Arnold-Forster and South African Soldier-Settlement', *History*, 102 (2017), 596–616.

7 Quoted in M. Arnold-Forster, *Hugh Oakeley Arnold-Forster*, 52.

8 Sir Charles Wentworth Dilke and Spenser Wilkinson, *Imperial Defence* (London: MacMillan and Co., 1892).

9 National Army Museum [hereafter NAM], Spenser Wilkinson papers, 1990–11–42, 13/21 [Wilkinson to Charles Beresford], 9 October 1894.

10 A.J.A. Morris, 'Wilkinson, (Henry) Spenser (1853–1937)', ODNB.

11 David Nichols, *The Lost Prime Minister: A Life of Sir Charles Dilke* (London and Rio Grande: The Hambledon Press, 1995).

12 Roy Jenkins, *Sir Charles Dilke: A Victorian Tragedy* (London and Glasgow: Fontana Books, 1968).

13 Gwynn and Tuckwell, *Dilke*, II, 416–417.

14 BL Dilke Papers, vol. XX, Add MS 43893, ff.93–95, H.O. Arnold-Forster to Dilke, 16 January 1894.

15 Frans Coetzee, *For Party or Country: Nationalism and the Dilemmas of Popular Conservatism in Edwardian England* (New York and Oxford: Oxford University Press, 1990), 15.

16 BL Dilke Papers, vol. XX, Add MS 43893, f.148 [Dilke to Spenser Wilkinson], 5 January 1894.

17 Arthur J. Marder, *British Naval Policy 1880–1905: The Anatomy of British Sea Power* (London: Putnam & Co., [1940]), 45.

18 For a discussion of the background to the Naval Defence Act, and the disjuncture between Admiralty planning and popular agitation, see Robert E. Mullins, *The Transformation of British and American Naval Policy in the Pre-Dreadnought Era: Ideas, Culture and Strategy*, ed. John Beeler (Basingstoke: Palgrave Macmillan, 2016). Bradley Cesario uses the term 'directed navalism' to refer to the cooperation between serving naval officers, press, and members of parliament and the more subtle ways in which this form of navalism influenced naval policy from the 1880s, in contrast to the more overt 'cultural navalism' of the same period. See Bradley Cesario, *New Crusade: The Royal Navy and British Navalism, 1884–1914* (Oldenburg: De Gruyter, 2021).

19 See D.M. Schurman, *The Education of a Navy: The Development of British Naval Strategic Thought, 1867–1914* (London: Cassell, 1965); and W. Mark Hamilton, *The Nation and the Navy: Methods and Organization of British Navalist Propaganda, 1889–1914* (New York: Garland Publishing, 1986).

20 Quoted in Simon Nowell-Smith, *The House of Cassell 1848–1958* (London: Cassell and Company, Ltd., 1958), 166.

106   *Expertise, opinion and invasion-scare fiction*

21 J.A. Fisher to Lord Selbourne, 20 November 1901, in *Fear God and Dread Nought: The Correspondence of Admiral of the Fleet Lord Fisher of Kilverstone*, ed. Arthur J. Marder, 3 vols. (London: Jonathan Cape, 1952–1959), I, 214.

22 [H.O. Arnold-Forster], 'In a Conning Tower: How I Took H.M.S. "Majestic" into Action', *Murray's Magazine* (July 1888), 59–78; Arnold-Forster, *In a Conning Tower; or, How I took H.M.S. 'Majestic' Into Action: A Story of Modern Ironclad Warfare* (London: Cassell & Company, Limited, 1891). Arnold-Forster's connections with Cassell, who published the story, may of course also have played a part in the decision to reprint it.

23 I.F. Clarke, *Voices Prophesying War: Future Wars 1763–3749* (Oxford: Oxford University Press, 1992), 58.

24 Duncan Bell, *The Idea of Greater Britain: Empire and the Future of World Order, 1860–1900* (Princeton: Princeton University Press, 2007), 39.

25 M. Arnold-Forster, *Hugh Oakeley Arnold-Forster*, 87–90. The title and signature of H.O. Arnold-Forster's anonymously published pamphlet on the Land League from 1882 bears a striking resemblance to the later articles of the 1884 naval scare: [H.O. Arnold-Forster], *The Truth About the Land League, Its Leaders and Its Teaching, by 'One Who Knows'* (Dublin: The National Press Agency, Limited, 1882). Cassell later published Stead's own similarly titled *The Truth About Russia* in 1888, at a time when Arnold-Forster was associated with the publisher.

26 W.T. Stead, 'The Rebuilding of the British Navy: How a Great Imperial Work was Begun', *Review of Reviews* (July 1897), 77.

27 *Pall Mall Gazette*, 15 September 1884, 1.

28 Lucy Brown, *Victorian News and Newspapers* (Oxford: Clarendon Press, 1985), 189.

29 W.T. Stead, 'Character Sketches: The Three Most Notable Men in the Empire', *Review of Reviews* (January 1904), 24.

30 H.O. Arnold-Forster, 'Our Position as a Naval Power', *Nineteenth Century* (January 1883), 13.

31 *Pall Mall Gazette*, 14 August 1884, 1–2. Characteristically, Arnold-Forster finished the article by stating that 'It is the public upon whom the blow will fall, and it is to the public, therefore, that it is necessary to appeal. They must have the facts brought before them in a way which they can understand'. This was the role Arnold-Forster saw himself in, as an educator of the public. In an earlier letter to *The Times*, Arnold-Forster had also underlined the need for such an education: 'As long as the public is content to rely exclusively upon

official Parliamentary views as to the condition of the Navy I fear there is little chance of improvement' (24 July 1884, 8).

32 *Pall Mall Gazette*, 15 September 1884, 1.

33 Articles were published under the headline, or variations of, 'The Truth about the Navy' on 15, 18, 19, 20 and 23 September 1884. Two articles on 'The Truth about our Coaling Stations' were published on 16 and 17 October.

34 J.O. Baylen, 'Politics and the "New Journalism": Lord Esher's Use of the "Pall Mall Gazette"', *Victorian Periodicals Review*, 20 (1987), 126, 131.

35 *Pall Mall Gazette*, 15 September 1884, 1.

36 Probably written by Stead – that was how he spoke of it himself (Stead, 'The Rebuilding of the British Navy', 78) – but with input from the rest of the group; the article title and the author's pseudonym ('"The Truth about the Navy", by One Who Knows the Facts') hint at Arnold-Forster's influence.

37 *Pall Mall Gazette,* 18 September 1884, 2.

38 *Pall Mall Gazette*, 19 September 1884, 1–2.

39 *Pall Mall Gazette*, 23 September 1884, 2.

40 *Pall Mall Gazette*, 23 September 1884, 2. A letter on the same page, written by Admiral F.L. McClintock and published under full name, opened with a similar line: 'Your patriotic endeavour to awaken popular attention to the true state of the navy is deserving of all praise'.

41 *Pall Mall Gazette*, 18 September 1884, 1.

42 See Mullins, *Transformation of Naval Policy*, 124 – though Beresford's public critique of politicians would always be awkward, seeing as he was himself a Conservative MP.

43 H.O. Arnold-Forster, 'The People of England versus Their Naval Officials', *Nineteenth Century* (November 1884), 702–714.

44 M. Arnold-Forster, *Hugh Oakeley Arnold-Forster*, 56–57.

45 HPD House of Lords [hereafter HL], Deb 02 December 1884 vol. 294 cc395–396.

46 Where Mary Arnold-Forster, and indeed Stead himself (Stead, 'The Rebuilding of the British Navy', 79) got the number £3,500,000 from is a bit unclear. This confusion is perhaps understandable, as navy estimates were notoriously difficult to untangle, and were subject to several sub-votes and sub-sections. In 1888, Admiral Sir R. Spencer Robinson told an audience at the Royal United Service Institution that the 'confused, imperfect, and unintelligible form of the Navy Estimates' was among the causes that had hindered the development of the Royal Navy. See Admiral Sir R. Spencer Robinson, 'Causes Which Have Hindered the Development of the Fleet', *Journal of the*

108   *Expertise, opinion and invasion-scare fiction*

Royal United Service Institution, 32 (1888), 508–509. All in all, Northbrook requested an additional £3,100,000 for ships in the navy estimates; an additional £1,600,000 in the army estimates, for guns; and £825,000 more for the protection of coaling stations, giving a grand total of £5,525,000 on top of the ordinary estimates, spread over a period of five years: HPD HL Deb 02 December 1884 vol. 294 cc463–464. The estimates for 1885–1886 were published in February 1885, showing an increase of £1,210,730 for that year: see House of Commons papers, 1884–1885, vol. 48, no. 46, 'Navy. Explanations of differences. Statement showing the explanations of the differences between the amounts proposed in the navy estimates for 1885–86, and the amounts voted for 1884–85'. 'We are not prepared to say that this increase is by any means adequate to the needs of the service', noted the *Standard*, 'but it is sufficient to redeem the promise given by the Government in December, and must be accepted as a grateful, if grudging, concession to popular feeling' (25 February 1885, 5).

47 HPD HL Deb 02 December 1884 vol. 294 cc395–412.

48 HPD HC Deb 02 December 1884 vol. 294 cc448–449. The *Pall Mall Gazette,* two days after the publication of the article by 'One Who Knows' claimed that '[t]he London daily papers, for obvious reasons, with one exception, are in a conspiracy of silence on the subject, but the provincial journals are speaking out very freely' (20 September 1884, 4). The London paper in question may have been the Conservative *Morning Post,* which had published a verbatim summary of the points in 'The Truth about the Navy' article from 18 September (19 September 1884, 6). More papers took up the call in the months that followed, and looking back on the agitation in 1897, Stead claimed that the press 'with few exceptions' had taken up the subject: 'The Rebuilding of the British Navy', 78. See also Raymond L. Schults, *Crusader in Babylon: W.T. Stead and the Pall Mall Gazette* (Lincoln, NE: University of Nebraska Press, 1972), 94–100 for a description of how the agitation spread to other newspapers.

49 HPD HC Deb 02 December 1884 vol. 294 cc448–463.

50 HPD HC Deb 02 December 1884 vol. 294 cc477–479. That Currie, a wealthy ship-owner, chose to underline the invasion aspect seems to contradict Andrew Porter's surmise that Currie's support of naval expansion in the 1880s was fuelled by the need to protect shipping rather than the needs of foreign policy: *Victorian Shipping, Business and Imperial Policy: Donald Currie, the Castle Line and Southern Africa* (Woodbridge: Boydell, 1986), 85–93, 138. That said, the need to protect shipping was of course a core task for the late Victorian Royal Navy.

Public appeals and fiction   109

51 Paul M. Kennedy, *The Rise and Fall of British Naval Mastery* (London: Penguin Books, 2017), 179. John Beeler convincingly argues that the Liberal government were spending adequate sums on the navy in the early 1880s, and that by 1884 the balance of power between the French and British fleets were much in favour of the latter. In addition, the Royal Navy was outspending its other Great Power rivals by a wide margin, meaning that Stead's articles were based on faulty assumptions. See 'In the Shadow of Briggs: A New Perspective on British Naval Administration and W.T. Stead's 1884 "Truth about the Navy" Campaign', *International Journal of Naval History*, 1 (2002), [1–10], www.ijnhonline.org/issues/volume-1-2002/apr-2002-vol-1-issue-1/. See also Mullins, *Transformation of Naval Policy*, 60.

52 Paul M. Kennedy, *The Rise and Fall of the Great Powers: Economic Change and Military Conflict from 1500 to 2000* (London: Unwin Hyman, 1988), 203, table 20.

53 As 'One Who Knows' noted, '[i]t is only when the ships are contemporary that the comparison of displacement is useful': *Pall Mall Gazette*, 18 September 1884, 2.

54 Marder, *British Naval Policy*, 120.

55 HPD HC Deb 02 December 1884 vol. 294 c488.

56 Baylen, 'Politics and the "New Journalism"'', 132.

57 Quoted in M. Arnold-Forster, *Hugh Oakeley Arnold-Forster*, 60.

58 W.T. Stead, 'Government by Journalism', *Contemporary Review* (May 1886), 657.

59 Marder, *British Naval Policy*, 121.

60 Kennedy, *British Naval Mastery*, 178.

61 Aled Jones, *Powers of the Press: Newspapers, Power and the Public in Nineteenth-Century England* (Aldershot: Scolar Press, 1996), 180.

62 G.R. Searle, *A New England? Peace and War 1886–1918* (Oxford: Clarendon Press, 2004), 133. The new electorate was, however, disproportionately located across the UK and, as Neal Blewett points out, by the time of the 1911 census 70 per cent of the adult population was excluded from the franchise: 'The Franchise in the United Kingdom 1885–1918', *Past & Present*, 32 (1965), 31.

63 The term 'New Journalism' had not been coined by the time of the 1884 naval scare. Its origin has been attributed to Matthew Arnold, who wrote disparagingly of the easily swayed 'new voters' of the extended franchise in an 1887 *Nineteenth Century* article – for him, the new democracy, like the new journalism which influenced it, were both '*feather-brained*': See Alan J. Lee, *The Origins of the Popular Press in England 1855–1914* (London: Croom Helm, 1976), 118. Stead himself used an image that would later find popular usage, of

110   *Expertise, opinion and invasion-scare fiction*

the journalist as a 'muck-raker': 'Bunyan's man with the muck-rake', Stead wrote, 'has many a prototype on the press' (Stead, 'Government by Journalism', 664).

64 Jones, *Powers of the Press*, 132.

65 *Pall Mall Gazette*, 18 September 1884, 2.

66 Brown, *Victorian News*, 180.

67 Schults, *Crusader in Babylon*, 49. 'Of popular panic there was no trace', wrote the admittedly biased F.W. Hirst in 1913, 'but Mr. Stead and his fellow-conspirators managed to produce a feeling of nervous disquietude in high society': *The Six Panics and Other Essays* (London: Methuen & Co., Ltd., 1913), 42.

68 Steven R.B. Smith, 'Public Opinion, the Navy and the City of London: the Drive for British Naval Expansion in the Late Nineteenth Century', *War & Society*, 9 (1991), 29–50.

69 Bryan Ranft, 'Parliamentary Debate, Economic Vulnerability, and British Naval Expansion, 1860–1905', in Lawrence Freedman, Paul Hayes and Robert O'Neill (eds), *War, Strategy, and International Politics: Essays in Honour of Sir Michael Howard* (Oxford: Clarendon Press, 1992), 75–93; Andrew S. Thompson, *Imperial Britain: The Empire in British Politics, c.1880–1932* (Harlow: Pearson Education, 2000), 110–132. Empire and navy were intimately linked. As Steven Smith notes, the two points where businessmen considered their influence over government policy to have been successful in the later nineteenth century were 'the expansion of the British Empire and the increase in the size of the British Navy'. As Smith also points out, the 1884 scare combined these two, as the condition of the navy was brough to City and government attention from three sources in the autumn of that year: the Imperial Federation League conference, centred on imperial defence; an article by Admiral Sir Thomas Symonds in the *Statist* in July; and finally, the 'Truth about the Navy' articles. Arnold-Forster had a finger in all three pies, being the honorary secretary of the Imperial Federation League, as well as the political editor of the *Statist*. See Smith, 'Public Opinion', 30, 31–32, 37.

70 Paul Kennedy, *The Realities behind Diplomacy: Background Influences on British External Policy, 1865–1980* (London: George Allen & Unwin, 1981), 52. Frank Bösch argues that, from the 1880s onwards, the rise of mass media as well as a more polarised political debate led 'political journalists' to focus on revealing scandals in both Britain and Germany. Political scandals in newspapers often formed part of the larger political struggle between parties: 'Transfers and Similarities: Journalists, Politicians and Scandals in Imperial Germany and Britain', in Frank Bösch and Dominik Geppert (eds), *Journalists*

Public appeals and fiction 111

as Political Actors: Transfers and Interactions between Britain and Germany since the late 19th Century (Augsburg: Wissner Verlag, 2008), 16–34.

71 Stephen Koss, *The Rise and Fall of the Political Press in Britain* (Chatham: Fontana Press, 1990), 215–216.

72 James Thompson, *British Political Culture and the Idea of 'Public Opinion', 1867–1914* (Cambridge: Cambridge University Press, 2013), 87.

73 Jose Ortega Y Gasset, *The Revolt of the Masses* (London: George Allen & Unwin, Ltd., 1932), 18.

74 Lieut.-Col. William Hunter, *Army Speech Dedicated to Those Who Have been Frightened by the Battle of Dorking* (London: Simpkin Marshall, 1871), 25.

75 Thompson, *British Political Culture*, 146.

76 'A Captain of the Royal Navy' [pseud.], *The Battle off Worthing: Why the Invaders Never Got to Dorking* (London: The London Literary Society, 1887).

77 Anon., *The Battle of Port Said: A Chapter in the History of the Future* (London: Offices of "Engineering", 1883). The story had originally been published in *Engineering*, a technical journal, between 6 July and 10 August 1883.

78 Anon., [W. Laird Clowes and possibly Alan H. Burgoyne or Commander Charles Napier Robinson], *The Great Naval War of 1887* (London: Hatchards, 1887), 58. The story was first serialised in *St. James's Gazette* between 5 and 10 November 1886; it was published as a pamphlet the following year. I.F. Clarke attributes the story to Clowes and Burgoyne (Clarke, *Voices,* 227), whereas the *Encyclopedia of Science Fiction* attributes it to Clowes and Robinson (www.sf-encyclopedia.com/entry/clowes_w_laird). Bleiler simply lists the story as written by Clowes: Bleiler, *Science Fiction*, 143. Clowes and Burgoyne would later collaborate on *Trafalgar Re-Fought* (London: Thomas Nelson and Sons, [1905]).

79 Anon., *The 'Russia's Hope', Or, Britannia no Longer Rules the Waves*, transl. Charles James Cooke (London: Chapman and Hall, Limited, 1888). See also Spiridion Gopčevik, *The Conquest of Britain in 1888, and the Fights and Battles that Led to It*, transl. Commander F.H.E. Crowe (Portsmouth: Griffin and Co., 1887). This was a more technical pamphlet, reportedly originally published in Germany the year before as *Der Grosse Seekrieg im Jahre 1888*. "*Down with England!*", another story from the same year, purported to be a translation of a French text: Anon., "*Down with England!*" *A French Prophesy* (London: Chapman and Hall, 1888). This latter story found at least

112   *Expertise, opinion and invasion-scare fiction*

one British reply: A.G.F.B., *Plus Encore d'Angleterre; or, Repulse of the French* (Bristol and London: J.W. Arrowsmith, [1888]).

80 'An Old Soldier' [William F. Butler], *The Invasion of England, Told Twenty Years After* (London: Sampson Low, Marston, Searle, & Rivington, 1882). The story was serialised, under the author's full name, in *Merry England* between November 1888 and April 1889.

81 Butler, for example, sombrely described in *The Invasion of England* how 'Whig and Tory, Radical, Liberal and Conservative ... were all overwhelmed for ever beneath the full flood of foreign invasion in one common grave' (12). The author of an 1889 semi-satirical story describing a combined German, French and Russian plan to overwhelm an unprepared British navy portrayed a Conservative government in power, but its criticism was aimed at political quarrels more generally: 'The great seafaring nation of the world, instead of making itself absolutely impregnable by a navy equal to the total of European fleets, was engrossed in wrangling over the pettiest details of domestic legislation': V., *The Swoop of the Eagles: An Episode from the Secret History of Europe* (London: Ward and Downey, 1889), 4.

82 Searle, *New England?* 149. 1886 introduced British readers to several dystopian visions of near-future Ireland: Anon., *In the Year One (A.D. 1888) of Home Rule de Jure* (London: W.H. Allen & Co., [1886]); 'A Landlord' [pseud.], *The Great Irish Rebellion of 1886* (London: Harrison & Sons, 1886); Anon., *Newry Bridge, or Ireland in 1887* (Edinburgh and London: William Blackwood and Sons, 1886); and Edward Lester, *The Siege of Bodike: A Prophecy of Ireland's Future* (London: John Heywood, 1886). All of these were pamphlets (or short books, in Edward Lester's case), though *Newry Bridge* was originally published in the Tory *St James's Gazette* between 3 May and 11 May 1886, before being published in pamphlet form. See also 'Ulidia' [pseud.], *The Battle of Newry; or, the Result of Thirty Years' Liberal Legislation*, 2nd edition (Dublin: Hodges, Figgis, and Co., 1883); and Rev. Alexander Donovan, *The Irish Rebellion of 1898: A Chapter in Future History* (Dublin: Hodges, Figgis, and Co., Ltd., 1893). Not all stories were unfavourable to Home Rule: G.H. Moore offered the readers of his pamphlet *Openings and Proceedings of the Irish Parliament* (London: Reeves & Turner, 1886) two different visions of Ireland: one chaotic and violent and one peaceful. Moore was not necessarily interested in being taken seriously, as the pamphlet included extracts from a few cold judgements on his work – including one by H. James who noted that 'you were an ass to write it' (23), but Moore clearly thought the positive vision more probable. Tom Greer, the author of *A Modern Dædalus* (London: Griffith,

Public appeals and fiction 113

Farran, Okeden & Welsh, 1885), used an Irish civil war as backdrop for his story about an inventor of a flying machine, but prefaced his narrative by stating that he was no enemy of England, and wanted a firm union between the two countries.

83 Darko Suvin, *Victorian Science Fiction in the UK: The Discourses of Knowledge and of Power* (Boston: G.K. Hall & Co., 1983), 5.

84 The anonymous author behind *The Battle of the Moy, or How Ireland gained Her Independence: 1892–1894* (Boston, MA: Lee and Shepard Publishers, 1883), envisioned a German invasion of Ireland that eventually leads to its independence – a fantasy for pro-Irish independence campaigners in the United States, and a nightmare for Home Rule opponents across the Atlantic. The anonymous author of *In the Year One* hinted that there was a possibility of other Great Powers establishing themselves in a free Ireland in the future (28). Donald MacKay, *The Dynamite Ship* (London: Page, Pratt, & Turner, 1888), imagined an international group of freedom fighters, working from the United States, forcing Britain to grant Ireland independence.

85 *Saturday Review*, 10 January 1880, 1.

86 Clarke (*Voices*, 227) lists one future-war story published in Britain in 1884: The pamphlet *The Siege of London* by 'Posteritas'. However, there is no indication that this was published any earlier than 1885. Liberal failure to adequately finance the Royal Navy is mentioned in passing in this story, but is only one of a litany of complaints lobbied against Gladstone and the 'Radicals'. Other stories published in 1885 were the anonymous *The Battle of To-Morrow* (London: Chappell and Company Ltd., 1885) – which does not feature an invasion and might have been intended as a more philosophical discussion of war in general – and the abovementioned Greer, *Modern Dædalus*.

87 Anthony S. Travis, 'Engineering and Politics: The Channel Tunnel in the 1880s', *Technology and Culture*, 32 (1991), 463. Duncan Redford, 'Opposition to the Channel Tunnel, 1882–1975: Identity, Island Status and Security', *History*, 99 (2014), 100–120, specifically looks at how the tunnel impacted on British identity. Keith Wilson, *Channel Tunnel Visions, 1850–1945: Dreams and Nightmares* (London and Rio Grande: The Hambledon Press, 1994), 1–88 provides a good and detailed overview of the development of the channel tunnel idea before the First World War.

88 Wolseley, a largely self-made man and proponent of army reform, would, as adjutant-general from 1882, spend much of the rest of the decade in direct opposition to Cambridge's conservatism. The channel tunnel was one of the few things for which the two could find a mutual loathing. See Ian F.W. Beckett, 'Wolseley, Garnet Joseph, first Viscount Wolseley (1833–1913)', ODNB.

114   *Expertise, opinion and invasion-scare fiction*

89 Quoted in Wilson, *Channel Tunnel Visions*, 37.
90 Quoted in Wilson, *Channel Tunnel Visions*, 26. The letter was dated 10 December 1881.
91 HPD HC Deb 27 June 1888 vol. 327 c1453.
92 Wilson, *Channel Tunnel Visions*, 28–29.
93 Wilson, *Channel Tunnel Visions*, 48.
94 Mrs. Gerald Porter, *Annals of a Publishing House: John Blackwood. The Third Volume of William Blackwood and his Sons: Their Magazine and Friends* (Edinburgh: William Blackwood and Sons, 1898), 266, 295.
95 Wilson, *Channel Tunnel Visions*, 48.
96 Lord Dunsany, 'The Proposed Channel Tunnel', *Nineteenth Century*, 60 (February 1882), 288–304. Dunsany had written on the topic for the *Nineteenth Century* before ('The Silver Streak', *Nineteenth Century*, 51 (May 1881), 737–755). See Wilson, *Channel Tunnel Visions*, 39, 48.
97 Dunsany, 'The Proposed Channel Tunnel', 294–295.
98 Wilson, *Channel Tunnel Visions*, 39.
99 Travis, 'Engineering and Politics', 476.
100 HPD HC Deb 5 June 1890 vol. 345 c46. See also Wilson, *Channel Tunnel Visions*, 48.
101 George Potter, *The Channel Tunnel and International Progress* (London: 14 Fetter Lane, [1882]), 14, 16, 23. Potter specifically wanted the report of the scientific, or defence committee, chaired by Sir Archibald Alison, to be made public.
102 HPD HC Deb 27 June 1888 vol. 327 c1435.
103 Charles Bradlaugh, *The Channel Tunnel: Ought the Democracy to Oppose or Support It?* (London: A. Bonner, 1887), 7.
104 Bradlaugh, *The Channel Tunnel*, 13.
105 Bradlaugh, *The Channel Tunnel*, 16,17.
106 Robert J. Griffiths, *Under the Deep Deep Sea: The Story of the Channel Tunnel* (London: Moffatt & Paige, [1887]), 90.
107 Norman Longmate, *The Island Fortress: The Defence of Great Britain 1603–1945* (London: Grafton, 1993), 359.
108 'The Demure One' [pseud.], *The Battle of Boulogne; Or, How Calais became English Again: Another Version of the Channel Tunnel Affair* (London: C.F. Roworth, 1882), 1. Reference is also made to Wolseley and Dunsany's arguments later in the pamphlet (7, 36). The quote was paraphrased, and largely an exaggeration of Wolseley's words. He had written that 'it is quite possible that the government of France may some day or other pass into the hands of a man of supposed

Public appeals and fiction   115

peaceable proclivities, but beneath whose demure exterior may be hidden an ambition and a thirst for conquest …' (Dunsany, 'The Proposed Channel Tunnel', 296). Interestingly, the narrator in the story, the former French Prime Minister, is inspired to attempt an attack on Britain after acquainting himself with the descriptions of a successful attack in Dunsany's article, and by reading *The Times*, where similar weaknesses are portrayed ('The Demure One', *The Battle of Boulogne*, 7, 19, 36, 51). Here, perhaps, the author was attempting to vindicate those who thought it had been awkward to make public utterances on the weaknesses in Britain's walls. *The Battle of Bolougne* is, however, too tongue-in-cheek to take very seriously as a political tract – it was as much a denunciation of alarmism as it was an alarmist text on its own.

109 'The Demure One', *Battle of Boulogne*, 46.

110 F.A., 'The Seizure of the Channel Tunnel: A Tale of the Twentieth Century', *Time* (April 1882), 91–121; 'Grip' [pseud.], *How John Bull lost London; or, the Capture of the Channel Tunnel*, 4th edition (London: Sampson Low, Marston, Searle, & Rivington, 1882). See also less conventional invasion tracts like the poem by CD.DO, *The Channel Tunnel. A True View of it! Regarded as a Great Whole* (London: Hamilton, Adams, & Co., 1882).

111 'Cassandra' [pseud.], *The Channel Tunnel; or, England's Ruin* (London: Wm. Clowes and Sons, 1876); 'Vindex' [pseud.], *England Crushed; the Secret of the Channel Tunnel Revealed* (London: P.S. King, 1882). Later still, in 1888, H.F. Lester published a pamphlet titled *The Taking of Dover*, where a French and Russian army take Dover Castle through treachery. It was prefaced by warnings from the Duke of Cambridge and Wolseley, and although a channel tunnel does not feature in the story, the plans for it are described as symptomatic of British complacency: *The Taking of Dover* (Bristol: J.W. Arrowsmith, 1888), 4. The pamphlet is written from the perspective of a French officer in 1898, a veteran of the fictitious invasion.

112 Bradlaugh, *The Channel Tunnel*, 19.

113 James Peddie, *The Capture of London* (London: General Publishing Company, [1887]), 6.

114 'The Demure One', *Battle of Boulogne*, 3–4. In this narrative, Bradlaugh is locked up in the Tower.

115 'Grip', *How John Bull lost London*, 15. A tunnel is part of, if not central to, the plot in Anon., *Europa's Fate: or the Coming Struggle. A History Lesson in New Zealand, A.D. 2076* (London: Griffith and Farran, 1875). Here, the invading army is composed of socialists.

116   *Expertise, opinion and invasion-scare fiction*

116 Daniel Pick, *War Machine: The Rationalisation of Slaughter in the Modern Age* (New Haven and London: Yale University Press, 1993), 88–135; Redford, 'Channel Tunnel'. A tunnel was unwelcome as it would imply that Britain gave up its insularity to *become* the continent; and because it would mean tampering with the English landscape – both prospects were viewed with horror in certain circles. See Paul Readman, ' "The Cliffs are not Cliffs": The Cliffs of Dover and National Identities in Britain, c.1750-c.1950', in *History*, 99 (2014), 249–250.

4

Expert opinion and public pressure: from the 1890s to 1914

The Portsmouth *Mail*'s description of its post-general election interview with Alfred Harmsworth on 17 July 1895 as a 'cheery chat' could only partially hide the Conservative candidate's disappointment. The headline was more to the point, announcing to its readers that the column dealt with 'Our Defeat'.[1] It had been a curious kind of defeat, too: nationwide, the 1895 general election was a landslide for the Conservatives and Liberal Unionists. The *Mail,* a Harmsworth-owned daily that had functioned as a mouthpiece for him and his Liberal Unionist colleague Evelyn Ashley throughout the election campaign,[2] reported large gains for the Unionists across Britain. 'A Unionist Majority is Pretty Safe' was the message on 18 July.[3] Portsmouth belonged to the exceptions, returning two Liberals rather than Harmsworth and Ashley. The town even gave the 'Home Rulers' an increased majority compared to the 1892 election.[4] In Ashley's opinion, this was due to 'a dense mass of dockyardmen and dwellers in the northern portion of the town, to whom politics and Imperial considerations, and even their own self-interest, are as nothing compared with their Socialistic and unreasoning hatred of everything which, rightly or wrongly, they consider superior to themselves, either as to position or intelligence'.[5]

Harmsworth was more conciliatory. He thought that the defeat was due to the outgoing Liberal government's hold on the dockyards due to its naval programme: 'which programme, by the way', he added, 'was forced upon them by the Conservatives'.[6] Clearly, the two candidates' claim that the dockyard workers would be better off under a different ministry had not worked. As the argument went, a vote for the Unionists would mean more money in the

118   *Expertise, opinion and invasion-scare fiction*

voters' pockets, and be a sign of sympathy for the 'workers and the poor'. But, more than this, a vote for Unionism had been presented as being in the interest of national and imperial security:

> Because the Radicals and their leaders are notoriously careless of the IMPERIAL INTERESTS OF ENGLAND, and reluctant to spend the money that is needed to keep OUR ARMY AND NAVY strong enough to repel invasion.[7]

The extent to which Harmsworth chose to focus on this latter aspect is illustrated by the publication in the *Mail* of a serialised invasion story, 'The Siege of Portsmouth', between 17 June and polling day, 16 July. The story was anonymously penned by Beccles Wilson, with input from the naval expert William Laird Clowes.[8] In fact, the 1895 general election in Portsmouth marks the first serious attempt to use an invasion-scare story for direct and immediate electoral purposes, which makes the Unionist defeat a stark judgement on the efficacy of the invasion narrative as a political tool. Harmsworth knew how to sell papers, but was not able to transfer sales into votes.

This chapter explores the invasion narrative in politics and culture from the 1890s into the early twentieth century. The chapter argues that by 1914, invasion-scare fiction had moved away from the political sphere to become a cultural trope and a commodity in a market. Part of the chapter is devoted to the developments in the narratives themselves, but this will be discussed in more detail in the following chapter. This chapter instead explores the role of experts within the genre, as the popularisation of invasion-scare and future-war texts meant that stories were endorsed and promoted by famous soldiers and sailors. Yet at the same time, experts' influence over the narratives were limited, and the stories' usefulness in elections and in promoting specific issues was no less restricted in this period than before 1895, despite their increased popularity.

'The Siege of Portsmouth'

It is perhaps not surprising that the brash and impetuous Harmsworth has been seen as acting out of 'circulation-boosting and vote-catching' motivations rather than patriotism when he commissioned 'The Siege of Portsmouth' for the *Mail*.[9] This is

Expert opinion and public pressure 119

unfair: Harmsworth was perfectly capable of combining patriotism and business acumen.[10] 'The Siege of Portsmouth' may have been, as I.F. Clarke described it, a 'nasty compound of commercialism and electioneering',[11] but there is little reason to doubt Harmsworth's sense of patriotism in eliciting votes in this manner. Patriotism, after all, has many guises, and Harmsworth expressed his version 'in a mixture of jingo polemic and vague platitudes about the need for national efficiency'.[12]

What ultimately separated Harmsworth from a man like Arnold-Forster was not their respective motivations, which could sometimes overlap, at least as far as the 1895 election went. Instead, where the young Arnold-Forster had barged into W.T. Stead's newspaper office, demanding that facts about the navy be presented before the public, the newspaperman Harmsworth had commissioned a professional author and hired expert help to intersperse his invasion narrative with trickles of fact. Arnold-Forster had been a prophet in search of a messenger; the latter was a messenger in search of an argument. This may not seem like much of a difference, but it illustrates an important shift in the dynamic between publisher and expert: expert opinion was no longer a driving force behind the scares. The change had been a long time coming. As outlined in chapter 1, Chesney quickly lost control of his *Dorking* story. By the time Harmsworth entered the political stage in Portsmouth, many invasion-scare stories were already being written to entertain, rather than to promote specific political arguments.[13] The channel tunnel controversy, for example, led to several stories unrelated to the Wolseley and Duke of Edinburgh campaign. When *Punch*, always with its finger on the pulse of at least a section of public opinion, mocked naval war stories in 1891 – the same year Arnold-Forster's *In a Conning Tower* was reissued in pamphlet format – there was no room for experts at all:

> Mr. *Punch* may as well state that he has *not* submitted this story to any naval experts. His facts speak for themselves, and require no merely professional approval to enhance their value.[14]

This was of course satire, parodying the many attempts to utilise expert opinion to portray near-future warfare in the later Victorian era. Authors often insisted on the seriousness and verisimilitude of even the most fanciful tales; Max Pemberton was sufficiently eager

120   *Expertise, opinion and invasion-scare fiction*

to underline the factual basis of *The Iron Pirate* (1893) that he wrote a letter to the *Academy* in November 1893 to correct its review of the book. The reviewer had assumed that a ship motor in the story had been powered by oil: 'This is an entire misapprehension', noted Pemberton, invoking expert advice in his reply. 'The ship, whose specification was drawn up for me by one of the foremost marine engineers living, is driven by gas'.[15]

Arnold-Forster's own description of naval conflict contained a preface that specified the author's position as 'amateur student', but one whose role as an expert in the field was proven by the favourable reception the original story had received from naval personnel.[16] However, his comment did also hint that professional approval could be seen as of secondary importance, an afterthought or *ex post facto* application to narratives. Satire tends to be perceptive regarding trends,[17] and *Punch* had, whether intentionally or not, pointed to a trend that would become clear as the decade progressed. Expert opinion mattered – which is why the knowledgeable Arnold-Forster bashfully referred to it. But something else was more important: readability and sales. This was true not just of invasion-scare fiction, but of literature in general. 'Literature nowadays is a trade', Jasper Milvain explains in George Gissing's *New Grub Street*, also first published in 1891; 'your successful man of letters is your skilful tradesman'.[18]

A more in-depth attempt to imagine future warfare was undertaken the following year, with 'The Great War of 1892', printed in *Black and White,* a weekly periodical.[19] Published in book form in 1893, the edited narrative claimed to give its readers as realistic a description of a great war as possible:

> The writers, who are well-known authorities on international politics and strategy, have striven to derive material for their description of the conflict from the best sources, to conceive the most probable campaigns and acts of policy, and generally to give to their work the verisimilitude and actuality of real warfare.[20]

Charles Dilke, interviewed in an appendix for the edited volume of *The Great War of 189-*, was perhaps more astute when he commented that the war in this story 'lent itself to literary and dramatic treatment, instead of the war which might be more natural but less picturesque'.[21] This was a perceptive remark; even though

Expert opinion and public pressure 121

experts – service personnel or various 'educated amateurs' – were still at the forefront of the public debate on issues of war and defence, fictional narratives were being infused with drama meant to entertain as well as inform.

During the last decade of the century, 'the tale of the future became a commodity in the calculations of the managers of the new mass newspapers' – Harmsworth is the premier example.[22] The death of Chesney in 1895 coincides with this shift. But what did this change mean? What were the concrete results of this commodification, and how was the relationship between publishers and authors changing? Even though it was the advent of a truly mass-readership that lured them away from shorter stories and into full-length tales of imaginary future conflict – like *The Great War of 189-*[23] – service writers still found it difficult to get their message across to the public. The increased relevance of amateur authors did not necessarily mean that professionals had given up on the idea of engaging with public opinion, though they at times seemed to have outsourced the job. Charles Beresford, a pugnacious and eager self-publicist, may not have intended it, but when he endorsed 'The Siege of Portsmouth' in a telegram printed in the *Mail* on 17 June, he implicitly handed the responsibility to influence defence politics over to newspapers and away from officers. 'The country owes the Naval Defence Act and late additions to the Fleet to the untiring efforts of the Press', was an admission of the power the press was presumed to have over public opinion.[24] However, since 'The Siege of Portsmouth' failed in its attempt to woo voters, it is worth having a closer look at the story itself, to see how a newspaperman of Harmsworth's ilk handled this power.

Though certainly political – the instalment on 4 July was an extended attack on the Liberal administration[25] – 'The Siege of Portsmouth' dedicated a larger number of its pages to providing a familiar setting for its readers than it did to political statements. True, the first instalment imagined that in a future 1897, when Britain is invaded by Russia and France, the dockyard workers of Portsmouth had 'their lot greatly improved by the Unionist Government'.[26] However, as the narrative unfolded over the next month, most of the columns were dedicated to finding roles for its own readership in the ensuing carnage. The story relished making the narrative seem immediate and real, naming heroes and victims

122   *Expertise, opinion and invasion-scare fiction*

and the manner of their death. When the town hall is partially destroyed by French and Russian bombardment, the lengthy casualty list reads like a *Who's Who* of Portsmouth society:

> Aldermen West, Ellis and Kent, Councillors Power, Cowd, Foster, Bamber, Dunning and Freeman, the Vicar of Portsmouth, the Vicar of St. Agatha's, Mr John Street, Mr. J.W. Boughton, Mr. G.W. Edmonds, Mr. T.H.F. Lapthorn, Mr. Henry Croucher, Mr. A.J. Vinall, Mr. John Dummer, Col. Brunker, Major Bridge, Captain Dathan, R.N., Mr. W.M. Deane, Captain Key, R.N.[27]

What the victims thought about being named like this is not easy to assess – though at least one 'deceased' wrote to the *Mail* to complain. Corporal Elwin Thomas, a Crimean War veteran, thought that his death had been somewhat unglamorous. In the instalment on Thursday 20 June he 'fell down in a fit' while stirring Portsmouth's citizens with stories of past battles and sieges.[28] The Saturday edition of the paper reported that Thomas had expressed in a letter that he would have preferred being dispatched by 'an old-fashioned eighty-pounder' instead.[29] This was light-hearted critique; more substantial reservations, or unease expressed by higher-ranking members of Portsmouth society, were not voiced, at least not within the pages of the *Mail*. Having one's name in the newspaper, being the talk of the town, and having a role to play in the drama – even if that role was to die of a heart attack – must have been part of the appeal of reading the story. Being caught up in the fictional invasion was a spectacle; it was meant to be entertaining. It was presumably much more of an insult not to be mentioned in the narrative than it was to see one's name on the casualty list.

Without going into too much detail about the story itself – as the title suggests, it contains a siege in addition to several stirring battle scenes, a French spy and an eventual British victory in a naval battle – it is difficult to see what makes 'The Siege of Portsmouth' any different from earlier invasion-scare fiction. Clarke sees it as a 'most instructive case study of the tale of imaginary warfare ... It illustrates every device and attitude to be found in this form of fiction'.[30] Northcliffe's 'genius, and in large part the reason for his phenomenal commercial success was that he shared the prejudices of his readers',[31] and a friend described him as having been born 'with an instinct for understanding the great reading public'.[32] In 1895

Expert opinion and public pressure   123

he used a classic invasion-scare narrative – one that only stood out by its more immediate local connection to its intended readership – and failed to convince his readers with it.

Evelyn Ashley's invective against the dockyardmen who had voted against their superiors points towards an out-of-touch and elitist Unionist campaign. But, as Paul Readman points out, the Unionists fought the 1895 general election on an alternative *liberal* platform to the radical liberalism of the Liberal party.[33] The Unionist election campaign in Portsmouth was an appeal to the working man – though conflating 'the workers and the poor' may have been a poor choice of words – and Harmsworth was certainly not averse to casting a wide net in his search for votes. The election result therefore raises questions about the broader electorate's preoccupation with national defence and the threat of invasion in general, and specifically with the press's ability to convey the message. It also raises questions about the efficacy of invasion-scare fiction itself.

A new kind of agitation

The shift from expert to amateur writers is one of the more misunderstood aspects of Victorian invasion-scare fiction. According to Clarke, at the turn of the century 'generals and admirals had retired from the future-war industry,' leaving the field to journalists.[34] In the mid-1890s, in Cecil Eby's opinion, 'amateurs, less concerned with selling defense than books' 'invaded' the genre.[35] This argument is misleading: there was always a strong contingent of 'amateur' authors in the genre, and there was never a lack of officers eager to try their pen at futuristic fiction. The late Victorian and Edwardian periods saw plenty of narratives eager to preach about Britain's internal weaknesses, and the need for panaceas like conscription. However, it is true that the way the stories were written and published changed in the 1890s. What analyses like Clarke's and Eby's miss, however, is the wider context within which this development took place, and how interactions between experts and amateurs continued to influence the genre, even after it had been 'invaded' by the latter.

Harmsworth, soon to be Lord Northcliffe, solicited the assistance of Field-Marshal Lord Roberts when he commissioned William Le

124   *Expertise, opinion and invasion-scare fiction*

Queux – perhaps the most prolific future-war author in the pre-war period – along with the naval writer H.W. Wilson to write another invasion-scare serial for his *Daily Mail* in 1906.[36] Bizarrely, considering the fact that Le Queux had written invasion fiction before, he claimed in his autobiography that it was Lord Roberts who came up with the idea that Le Queux should write a fictional invasion story to wake up the public.[37] This was an example of the author's relaxed relationship with the truth.[38] The idea behind the story, what would become *The Invasion of 1910*, was first presented to Roberts in a letter dated 28 July 1905, where Le Queux asked for comments on an outline of the enemy's operations he had made with the help of Wilson. 'Instead of being a fantastic novel, as was "The Great War [in England in 1897]"' Le Queux noted in the letter, referring to his 1894 story, 'this will be a <u>serious</u> description of an invasion in 1910'.[39] Le Queux, not Roberts, had the idea for the book, and the latter's involvement seems to have been of minor importance to the narrative.

According to legend, Harmsworth demanded that Le Queux should completely ignore Roberts' suggested invasion plan in favour of giving the invaders a circulation-boosting tour across the country.[40] Whether true or not, Roberts – no stranger himself to using the press to create and maintain the image of himself as among Britain's foremost authorities on war – still endorsed the final product, recommending Le Queux's work 'to the perusal of every one who has the welfare of the British Empire at heart'.[41] It seems clear, however, that Le Queux cared less about the verisimilitude of the story, than he did about presenting an action-packed narrative.[42]

When experts were more directly involved in writing invasion fiction, the reception was not always positive among the general readership. After Grant Richards published the anonymous *New Battle of Dorking* in 1900 he received a letter from George Bernard Shaw that simply stated 'Who wrote the New Battle of Dorking? Not Arnold Forster [sic] surely? Only a professional soldier could be so grossly ignorant of warfare'.[43] It was indeed written by an army officer, Colonel Frederic Natusch Maude. Richards noted that he had commissioned the work in the hope that it would be as efficacious as its predecessor and namesake. His conclusion was stoic: 'It did not succeed'.[44]

Expert opinion and public pressure

Experts were certainly involved in the new invasion-scare industry, but they generally took a more passive role in a medium where melodrama was more in demand than realism. Symptomatic of this shift was the way *An Englishman's Home* (1909), written by Major Guy du Maurier, was presented to the theatre-going audience. Du Maurier showed the play to his brother Gerald, an actor-manager who, with the help of J.M. Barrie (of *Peter Pan* fame), gave it a title and – without informing its author – produced it while Guy was in South Africa, serving with the 20th Mounted Rifles.[45] Gerald kept the original premise – Britain is invaded by 'Nearlanders' on Boxing Day, when most of the country is on holiday – but still changed parts of it, 'strengthening the situations and revising here and there the dialogue', in addition to giving the story a happy ending and a British victory. The play was listed as having been written by 'A Patriot', 'yet another of Gerald's shrewd touches'.[46] As the play ran its course, the cast, unknown to Gerald who was preoccupied with another play at the time, changed it even further, improvising and adding to the original script.[47]

Those who had the knowledge and capacity to produce or publish invasion-scare narratives appropriated the ideas of service writers and experts, giving them their own interpretation, and the stories tended to take on a life of their own. Guy du Maurier, the original author of *An Englishman's Home* was among the last to hear of its success. Gerald thought that Guy would 'be the most amazed man in the whole world' when he read about the play in South Africa.[48] For Gerald, 'entirely innocent of political convictions' in his biographer's assessment, the play was staged for its artistic merits, as 'an excellent piece of theatre'.[49]

Seeing *The Invasion of 1910* in relation to Erskine Childers' earlier story *The Riddle of the Sands*, Clarke argues that 'the prediction made by Erskine Childers in 1903 was shown to be true by the events of Le Queux's invasion in 1910'; thus, the two books 'played a part in increasing national anxieties'.[50] *The Riddle of the Sands* takes place around the Frisian Islands in the North Sea, where the two protagonists – Davies and Carruthers – discover a German plan for invading Britain. Written as if based on real events, the book was subtitled 'a Record of Secret Service'.[51] Although Childers himself was no stranger to war, having served in the City Imperial Volunteers in the South African War, and writing a book about his

Figure 4.1 Postcard from the play *An Englishman's Home* (1909).
Source: Author's own collection

Figure 4.2 Postcard from the play *An Englishman's Home* (1909).
Source: Author's own collection

Expert opinion and public pressure 127

experiences,[52] his two protagonists are both amateur spies. The amateur had made a definite entry in the genre, both in wielding the pen and within the pages of invasion-scare fiction. Focusing on the amateur heroics of everyday heroes was the logical extension of earlier narratives, like 'The Siege of Portsmouth', with its naming of as many citizens as possible. In Childers' story, the amateurs are no passive victims: Davies and Carruthers accidentally stumble upon the German invasion plans, trusting to their native English pluck and Davies' seamanship to see them through where Britain's established military and naval authorities have been unsuccessful. Whereas Chesney's half-trained and unprepared Volunteers had failed in the 1871 *Battle of Dorking*, the amateurs – at least Davies; it takes longer for the city-bred Carruthers to adjust himself – were able heroes in their own right by the time Childers wrote *The Riddle of the Sands*. Although Davies argues that Englishmen should undertake a form of national service, preparing themselves for fighting either on land or on the sea,[53] Britain seems to do just fine with men like these in her unofficial secret service. At least, with a poorly organised defence apparatus – Davies has nothing but contempt for the Admiralty, for example[54] – amateurs become the default first and last line of defence. In the preface to a later edition, Childers noted that, although experts were the only ones who currently studied the 'high problems of national defence', 'they should be so studied, to the best of his ability, by every thoughtful citizen'.[55]

Military authorities come across as rather hapless in such stories. The general facing a German landing in James Blyth's 1909 story *The Swoop of the Vulture* hopes for 'a small army of civilians who knew the district where the fighting would take place' – a more valuable contribution to the war effort than 'certain pompous asses from the war office', or 'Admiralty and War Office pedants, and the hysterical screamers of the halfpenny papers'.[56] In *The Invasion of 1910* the Germans land on a drowsy Sunday morning, and one of the first to learn of it (a journalist rather than a military official) finds the War Office closed and has to hunt down the Permanent Under-Secretary who is away for the weekend. Meanwhile, the War Office stands empty – 'its machinery useless' – as does the Admiralty.[57] Unpreparedness due to a bank holiday was a regular trope in invasion stories; it was echoed in the Boxing Day invasion in *An Englishman's Home* as well as other invasion narratives. In the end, a volunteer

128   *Expertise, opinion and invasion-scare fiction*

group calling itself The League of Defenders – along with, and probably inspired by, the Legion of Frontiersmen – is central in defeating the invader, the regular army having failed in its task.[58] Thus, both Le Queux and Childers relegated the men in uniform to secondary roles, with authors as well as their protagonists having little patience with those supposed to defend Britain from invasion.

One might ask what was left for the naval and military experts in this new environment. While warfare was becoming increasingly more complex, experts were often presented as unable to keep up with the changing times. Invasion-scare literature in the immediate pre-war decades often contrasted the inefficiency of the established defence apparatus with the professionalism of the foreign invaders. In *War*, a story published on the eve of the real Great War, the inability of British 'experts' to plan for the proper defence against an enemy landing is decried on the same page as the word 'expertly' is used to describe the efficient workings of the invading troops. Hapless defenders – their training and preparations useless in the face of real opposition – are contrasted with the 'artificial decision and certainty of clockwork' of the enemy: British 'experts' have come up short against this superior form of planning and execution.[59]

There were certainly still roles for old military heroes in these new stories. There was Roberts, of course, present in the background of Le Queux's 1906 invasion narrative – 'They should have listened to Lord Roberts', a character exclaims[60] – and Garnet Wolseley, captured by the enemy and thus whisked away in an inverse *deus ex machina* in the early stages of 'The Siege of Portsmouth'.[61] However, by the turn of the century invasion scares had seemingly been democratised, the heroics now performed by average citizens in Portsmouth, amateur sailors in the North Sea, or a national rising by a League of Defenders. *The War Inevitable*, an invasion story from 1908 written by the officer Alan H. Burgoyne, is more favourable to the officer class, and dreams of Lord Kitchener, as generalissimo, issuing a proclamation that 'abolished, *pro tem.*, Government by Parliament!'[62] Yet even in this story there is room for individual heroics, and for the people of Britain to make their mark. An initial German landing at Worthing, for example, is beaten back, not by the might of the assembled British army, but by a group of eager riflemen, who have learned to shoot at public

Expert opinion and public pressure 129

rifle ranges – a very British form of *levée en masse*: ' "Giddy work, Bill," yelled a sturdy labourer, drawing his bloody [bayonet] blade from a fat Teuton neck'.[63]

Charles E. Gannon points out that Le Queux, in portraying angry crowds outside the empty War Office and Admiralty in *The Invasion of 1910*, suggests that the people of England have mistakenly placed their trust in 'technologically retrograde' officials, unable to understand that war now demands readiness on a scale not seen before.[64] Realising that experts will not save Britain, the crowds are forced to take up arms themselves. Similarly, in *The Enemy in Our Midst* (1906), the nation realises that 'it had been inefficiently protected by its responsible leaders', with a Guards' Colonel described as 'engaged in Bridge, of which his knowledge was admittedly more profound than his acquaintance with either strategy or tactics, or the profession of arms'. An admiral in the story is by his own admission 'crippled by rheumatism, and … a useless hulk'.[65] Such is the state of much of the political, military and naval leadership in this and many similar narratives.

Expertise and planning: the limits of popular appeals

Fiction's representation of the defence establishment as retrograde and inefficient was not necessarily echoed in real life, even after the shocks and setbacks of the South African war at the turn of the century. Soldiers were often idolised, and there were plenty of positive depictions of war and soldiering in late Victorian and Edwardian society.[66]

Walter E. Houghton noted of the early Victorians that their romantic preoccupation with hero worship marked a reversal of the rationalism of the previous century;[67] but Victorians were not averse to have 'rational' heroes as well. The distrust shown towards Britain's professional defence machinery in stories like *The Riddle of the Sands* and *The Invasion of 1910* contrasts with the high esteem in which 'experts' – albeit an abstract term – were generally held in the same period; it is worth remembering that the Fabian George Bernard Shaw's invective against professional soldiers was not an argument against experts as such.[68] By the end of the century, the earlier 'reign of the engineer' had been supplanted by the

130   *Expertise, opinion and invasion-scare fiction*

natural and social sciences, but this was a change in the nature of expert advice, not a move away from it. As Roy MacLeod puts it, specialist advice took the more formal path of 'minutes and forms', instead of 'draft legislation, let alone letters to *The Times*'.[69] Yet this did not mean that there were not tensions between different kinds of experts – broadly defined – and amateurs, especially when it came to matters of war and the role of civilian government. When Henry Campbell-Bannerman, Liberal leader of the opposition, criticised the role of military experts and argued that defence issues should be determined by parliament, his comments were described as 'antediluvian' by Lord Esher.[70]

Campbell-Bannerman's criticism was occasioned by the report from Esher's War Office (Reconstitution) Committee in 1904. This recommended the creation of a secretariat at the Committee of Imperial Defence (CID) thereby creating an effective coordinating body for the two services, inspired at least in part by the 'scientific' nature of German war planning.[71] For Esher, the CID meant a new direction in British defence planning. Previously, 'it ha[d] been left to publicists, without any special knowledge, but dependent upon newspapers and books, to endeavour to inspire Englishmen with the spirit of strategical enquiry'. Balfour's dialectic mind, and the establishment of an expert committee, meant that defence planning could finally be treated in a systematic and scientific way.[72] Esher was on the side of the technocrats: if public opinion could not be manipulated, it could be ignored or bypassed.[73] It was certainly not uncharacteristic that he criticised the 'misconception and jealousy' aroused by the development of the committee 'in the minds of politicians mistrustful of a novel political force, which they do not see their way to control by campaigns in the platform or in the Press'.[74] For Esher, 'the Defence Committee, as constituted by Mr. Balfour, may not be the ideal tribunal as conceivable by a Sieyès or any other constitution monger', but that was not the point either.[75] This is, of course, not to say that Esher eliminated democracy from defence planning. Public opinion still constituted a limitation, and, along with the 'heterogeneous Imperial system', one 'from the trammels of which we cannot at present escape'. Indeed, Esher himself would often and with success mobilise public opinion for the support of his causes. The CID did not hold any executive power, but was instead meant to offer advice to the cabinet. 'Under our

Expert opinion and public pressure 131

constitutional forms of government, and with our well-established Parliamentary traditions, it is certainly the best and most effective method for focussing in war national and Imperial effort, which can at present be devised'.[76] It did, however, aim to limit the effects of public opinion, and as such was indicative of an attempt to create a more closed or structured way of influencing defence policy than Stead's earlier idea of 'government by journalism'.

The CID had its antecedents in a long struggle between military planning and civilian control that stretched back at least to the Cardwell reforms. The 1904 Esher committee argued that Britain needed continuity and forethought in its defence planning: the risk was that a future prime minister, elected by the people, would not know enough about imperial defence to make the right decisions. A permanent committee, consisting of a nucleus of professional naval and military advisors, would mean 'that the Prime Minister shall have at his disposal all the information needed for the due fulfilment of his weighty responsibilities';[77] it would, in short, ensure that he knew more than the 'man in the street'. This argument contrasted with the 1884 'Truth about the Navy' campaign: Stead's *Pall Mall Gazette* had used expert opinion to justify its attacks on naval policy – the paper had made frequent references to the numerous officers who had written to it in anonymous support – but had still formulated its campaign in the language of a popular appeal. Esher's argument in 1904 pointed in a different, less open, direction.

Expert opinion and public pressure: pressure groups

A clear pattern was starting to emerge. While the wider public featured in invasion-scare fiction to a greater extent than before, they were, at least in part, left out of military planning and deliberations. This development is confirmed by the limited influence of pressure groups in the period – mainly the Navy League and National Service League. The Esher committee's recommendation to Balfour regarding the CID echoed the somewhat similar arguments outlined twenty years earlier in the Dilke letter. Perhaps ironically, then, one of the letter writers, Spenser Wilkinson, had in the meantime decided that a pressure group outside of parliament was a more credible way of forcing the elected representatives to care

132   *Expertise, opinion and invasion-scare fiction*

about defence and, more specifically, about the navy. The pressure group's successes, or lack thereof, illustrate the limited usefulness of popular appeals in comparison to the Esher committee proposals, and are worth a closer look.

Established in the wake of the 1884 naval scare, and the two scares which followed in its wake in 1888 and 1893, the Navy League was from its inception balancing awkwardly between expert and public opinion. In a series of articles published in the *Pall Mall Gazette* over the course of September and October 1894, Wilkinson mused on the lack of a coherent naval policy, and on the theme of 'The Command of the Sea' and its importance to Britain.[78] Inspired by these writings, a group of 'Four Average Englishmen' wrote to the paper and suggested the establishment of a Navy League. This was officially formed on 10 January 1895, with Wilkinson as a founding member.[79]

From its inception, there was tension within the League over how best to secure British naval supremacy. In the last of his 'Command of the Sea' articles, Wilkinson argued that Britain's defences were unprepared for war, and what was needed to fix the imperial ramparts was 'a national policy' or, in other words, nonpartisan expertise:

> There is only one way in which you can obtain a sound navy. You must find a man who understands war and understands modern sea fighting, and you must put him, with all the assistance he requires, to design your naval wars and to conduct them when they come.[80]

He expanded on this in a later article: Britain needed a 'Naval Moltke' – a 'professional adviser on the subject of war', subordinate to the Cabinet, but with the authority that came with being an expert on war.[81]

Wilkinson himself was no amateur in this respect – by the time he was called to the bar he, in his own words, knew 'as much about war as could be got from text-books', and also had some practical experience from having held a commission.[82] A commentator in *Journal of the Royal United Service Institution* described him as 'one of the few civilians who has ... successfully grasped, the principles on which the security and welfare of our Empire essentially depend'.[83] In 1909 he became the first Chichele professor of military history at Oxford University.[84] Yet within the Navy League, his campaign for a single responsible professional adviser was seen

Expert opinion and public pressure 133

as 'an unwarranted intrusion by a civilian into military affairs', and 'suggested to a number of observers that indeed the league suffered from the delusions of civilians who presumed in their arrogance to instruct the professionals'.[85] The 'Four Average Englishmen' had instead suggested that the Navy League should focus on informing public opinion, being a public pressure group on a strictly non-partisan line, and certainly not an organisation trying to influence the established naval authorities.[86] This focus on educating and guiding public opinion was specified in the Navy League's constitution, with its emphasis on spreading information about navy and empire, and most of its 'Programme of Action' was dedicated to specifying how the league should publish and distribute information.[87] Wilkinson soon resigned from the organisation he had inspired after realising that only a watered-down version of his aim to provide Britain with a 'Naval Moltke' would be put forward.[88]

The league itself, beset by monetary problems, internal squabbles and lacking a clear vision for what it wanted to achieve, split into two separate wings in January 1908 – the original one and a rogue Imperial Maritime League.[89] Having been approached by both of these, an exasperated Honorary Secretary of the Victoria-Esquimalt branch of the Navy League in British Columbia wrote to Wilkinson to get his opinion on which one the branch should adhere to.[90] In the lengthy reply Wilkinson stated that he had 'much sympathy' with the breakaway league.[91] This should not have been a surprise – the Imperial Maritime League had listed his old vision of creating a strategy department within the Admiralty as one of its 'Specific Aims'.[92] However, his letter also contained a number of lines on the background to and development of the original Navy League, and where, in Wilkinson's opinion, it had gone wrong. Whereas he had wanted the organisation to focus on changes at the Admiralty level, the executive had instead decided on an ' "educational" mission; that is', he wrote, 'they organised lectures about the importance of Sea Power'.[93] But getting money voted for the navy was not the same as seeing that money spent in the best manner possible, and as Wilkinson had earlier argued, 'to administer at the bidding of popular agitation is bad administration, and it is in every way desirable that governments should not follow but lead in regard to their executive action'.[94] Informing the public that the navy was important was hardly the way forward – instead,

134   *Expertise, opinion and invasion-scare fiction*

direct advice to the professional and political leadership would ensure British naval supremacy. As mentioned earlier, several Navy Leaguers were uneasy about this infringement on the professionals' territory, and a popular pressure group was hardly the right medium for Wilkinson's policy anyway.

Perhaps unsurprisingly, therefore, the Navy League was not as influential as its founders had initially hoped it would be. It was, for example, not an effective vote mobiliser for pro-navy candidates. This was illustrated by the Croydon by-election following the departure from the scene of one of the main characters in this as well as the preceding chapter. On the evening of 12 March 1909, after having commented to his wife earlier in the evening that the recent Liberal naval estimates were insufficient, Hugh Oakeley Arnold-Forster died.[95] His health had not been good[96] and by early 1909 he was on the verge of retiring from public life, but at the time of death he was still Unionist MP for Croydon. On the surface, the by-election that followed, where another Unionist candidate, Sir Robert Hermon-Hodge, was returned seemed like a vindication for navalists arguing for a stronger Royal Navy.[97] 'I attribute my defeat to the wholesale working up of the naval scare', the Liberal candidate J.E. Raphael stated. 'This has produced a kind of "mafficking" spirit throughout the constituency'.[98] However, local issues in Croydon probably played a bigger role in the election.[99] Even Raphael had to admit that there were other influences at work beside the navy question, including the presence of a Labour candidate, who, despite not winning many votes 'had the effect of taking heart out of many Liberals in the town and outside'.[100]

1909 was the year of a naval scare that resulted in a four-plus-four Dreadnought building programme, after public agitation against the government – with Fisher, by then First Sea Lord, and the Admiralty all too eager to take advantage of the idea that Germany was outbuilding Britain.[101] The Navy League itself spent 1909 debating how they could reach out to public opinion: its executive committee concluded that 'the league had been "too aristocratic, too far above the level of the crowd"'.[102] If the following year was anything to go by, the league was hardly successful at transforming itself into a broad church and a mass organisation, despite its attempts at non-partisanship, as it was seen as a branch of the Unionist party.[103] Its political influence was limited.[104]

Expert opinion and public pressure 135

The conscription movement had a similar development. It is difficult to know what Lord Roberts hoped to achieve by placing himself at the head of the National Service League in 1905. While Commander-in-Chief he had expressed to Arnold-Forster the opinion that a large-scale invasion of Britain was not to be anticipated: 'Putting himself in the position of a Commanding Officer of an invading force,' Arnold-Forster wrote of Roberts' opinion in his diary, 'he cannot perceive how the difficulties he would have could be overcome'; Arnold-Forster was in full agreement with him on this.[105] In taking up the presidency of the National Service League, a body founded in 1902, the old Field Marshal performed a *volte-face*, threw his weight behind the campaign for conscription, and contributed to successfully forcing the CID into conducting an invasion enquiry in 1907.[106] However, while Roberts personally may have been popular, the League was small – with eighteen branches in 1906, although this had doubled by 1908 – and conscription was decidedly less popular than navalism.[107]

The National Service League under the aegis of Lord Roberts focused on home defence, rather than conscription understood as service overseas – the army would still be based on the volunteer principle. As a letter from Roberts to *The Times* expressed in June 1905, making rifle-shooting a 'national pursuit' would go a long way to secure peace by providing Britain with a reserve of skilled marksmen. While also arguing that legislation should aim to put in place a system of obligatory physical training, the letter took care to convey that rifle-shooting should be a voluntary activity.[108] In a later letter, Roberts specified that the organisation wanted men, upon reaching military age, to undergo a limited period of training with the aim that '[e]very man of sound physique, without distinction of class, shall be legally liable during certain years of his life to be called upon for service in the United Kingdom in case of emergency'.[109]

The terminology around this 'national service' was vague and Archibald Hurd, writing in the *Fortnightly Review* in 1910, perceptively criticised 'the invasion school' for their deliberately opaque nomenclature: 'It is no doubt regarded as diplomatic, at present', Hurd noted, 'to speak of "national training", because the phrase sounds innocuous, but the ultimate aim is – and must be – a form of conscription'.[110] Either way, the campaign for national service was unsuccessful. Anne Summers, though seeing the National

136 Expertise, opinion and invasion-scare fiction

Service League as 'large, vigorous and flourishing', also notes that it 'totally failed in its stated objective'.[111] Spenser Wilkinson was critical of the organisation, concluding that a system of compulsory military service would not be accepted by the British people.[112] Lord Roberts and the National Service League did not succeed as a pressure group for similar reasons to that of the failure of the Navy League: not only were professionals unimpressed by outside influences,[113] but the majority of the public were also not convinced that the pressure groups were necessary.

Experts' top-down engagement with public opinion on the issue of national defence in the period covered in these chapters illustrates a general confusion on what it meant to appeal to the 'man in the street'. In 1888, a retired Royal Navy officer wrote to his fellow officers in *Colburn's United Service Magazine* that 'a game of "Invasion" be popularised':

> to lead <u>civilians</u> to take an interest in the general question of the possibility of the desecration of Old England by the foot of an enemy: then, as a consequence of the realisation of this lamentable <u>possibility</u>, to use their influence, in and out of season, towards the attainment of a clear, simple and intelligent system of defence ...[114]

Experts and professional soldiers and sailors were respected, and they were listened to in Victorian and Edwardian Britain; the navy and the army mattered to people. But there was not necessarily a correlation between the popularisation of any invasion 'game' and the role experts played in the popular imagination. Electors presumably liked and respected heroes of empire like Wolseley and Roberts, and when Charles Beresford, who had endorsed 'The Siege of Portsmouth' in 1895, ran for the same seat as a Unionists in 1910 he was duly elected – lack of invasion-scare fiction in his campaign notwithstanding. Neal Blewett connects this victory with the re-ignited Naval Scare of that year, manifesting itself in Unionist returns in dockyard towns 'always peculiarly sensitive to the jingo scare' – though this is of course debatable.[115] The absence of heroes from popular invasion-scare fictions from the same period – like 'The Siege of Portsmouth' and *The Invasion of 1910* – leaving ordinary people to deal with invading armies, was therefore not in itself an indication of any lack of faith in the army or navy. Readers

Expert opinion and public pressure 137

engaged with the fantasy of invasion fiction, not the perceived reality of it. As a political tool, then, invasion-scare fiction engaged with social anxieties, national and imperial identities and political ideologies; but its wider influence was more limited. National and imperial defence in the years before the First World War was debated within professional and political circles, and was the subject of agitation outside of the two services and of parliament, intended to influence these in one direction or another. Rather than looking at how Britain's defences were organised, or presenting an exhaustive study of professional-amateur relations, the last three chapters have illustrated how the public was invoked by those who organised the defence of Britain. Despite their presence in invasion-scare narratives, and appeals directed to an abstract 'public opinion', the public and the electorate was a vaguely understood entity in the arguments of experts and politicians. However, invasion-scare fiction itself, though still connected with expert opinion throughout the period prior to 1914, was 'democratised', portraying a more inclusive nation as victim of foreign invaders. This aspect, and the stories' readership, is explored in detail in the next two chapters.

Notes

1 *Mail*, 17 July 1895, 2.
2 Harmsworth had ebulliently referred to the paper when asked at a public meeting whether he had anything up his sleeve: *Mail*, 20 June 1895, 2. He had acquired the paper around a month before the election, renaming it from the *Evening Mail* (J. Lee Thompson, *Northcliffe: Press Baron in Politics, 1865–1922* (London: John Murray, 2000), 28). The first edition under new ownership was out on Monday 10 June; Northcliffe judged it 'a big success': BL Northcliffe Papers Add MS 62383, f.27v.
3 *Mail*, 18 July 1895, 2.
4 *Mail*, 17 July 1895, 2. The paper could report a 'Home Rule majority' of 734 votes, compared to 508 in 1892.
5 *Mail*, 17 July 1895, 3.
6 *Mail*, 17 July 1895, 2. Henry Pelling agrees with Harmsworth in his analysis of the election result, noting that 'the accelerated expansion of the Navy under the Spencer administration being the obvious

138 *Expertise, opinion and invasion-scare fiction*

explanation' for the Liberal success: *Social Geography of British Elections, 1885–1910* (Aldershot: Gregg Revivals, 1994), 129.

7 *Mail*, Monday 15 July 1895.

8 I.F. Clarke, *Voices Prophesying War: Future Wars 1763–3749* (Oxford: Oxford University Press, 1992), 109.

9 Norman Longmate, *Island Fortress: The Defence of Great Britain, 1603–1945* (London: Grafton, 1993), 387.

10 J. Lee Thompson sums up Harmsworth's political philosophy as a combination of 'Tory populism, Disraelian imperialism, and a firm belief in the "Anglo-Saxon future"': J. Lee Thompson, *Politicians, the Press, & Propaganda: Lord Northcliffe & the Great War, 1914–1919* (Kent, OH, and London: The Kent State University Press, 1999), 8. His business empire reflected, rather than contradicted this political worldview.

11 Clarke, *Voices*, 109.

12 A.J.A. Morris, *The Scaremongers: The Advocacy of War and Rearmament, 1896–1914* (London: Routledge & Kegan Paul, 1984), 6.

13 There was evidence of this from the late 1880s onwards. Stories like Edward Lester, *The Siege of Bodike: A Prophecy of Ireland's Future* (London: John Heywood, 1886) and Anon., *England's Danger; or, Rifts within the Lute. A Russian Plot* (Portsmouth: Griffin & Co., 1889), were thrilling spy stories, presenting internal and external threats to Britain in a more exciting format than earlier narratives. Robert Cromie's *For England's Sake* (London and New York: Frederick Warne and Co., 1889), an adventure story describing a Russian invasion of India, is another example. Its sequel, *The Next Crusade* (London: Hutchinson & Co., 1896), took the action to Eastern Europe and the Mediterranean.

14 *Punch*, 3 October 1891, 160, 'Mr. Punch's Naval Novel'. There was a none-too-subtle reference to Arnold-Forster's story in the *Punch* parody. The former had invited the reader to imagine the captain of a modern ironclad warship; how he, at the touch of a button, could send the ship forward; how a 'touch, a spark' could discharge the guns, and 'another touch, another signal will liberate the little clips which detain the four Whitehead torpedoes in their tubes'. 'Think', Arnold-Forster wrote, 'what the power confided to one man's hand must be': H.O. Arnold-Forster, *In a Conning Tower; or, How I took H.M.S. 'Majestic' into Action: A Story of Modern Ironclad Warfare* (London: Cassell & Company, Limited, 1891), 15–17. *Punch* was eager to oblige: 'The roaring furnaces, the cylindrical boilers, the prisoned steam, the twin screws, the steel shot that crashes like thunder,

Expert opinion and public pressure 139

the fearful impact of the ram, the blanching terror of the supreme moment, the shattered limbs and scattered heads, – all these were ready, waiting but for the pressure of my finger in the middle button of the boatswain's mess-waistcoat to speed forth upon their deadly work between the illustrated covers of a shilling pamphlet'.

15 *Academy*, 25 November 1893, 466. Not everyone was convinced by such claims: When the *Athenæum*, an establishment journal, reviewed Pemberton's 1898 story *The Phantom Army*, it opened by stating that '[i]t is hard to review seriously a purely fantastic romance', adding that 'one cannot help feeling that the author would have held his readers in a more effective spell if he had been a little less lavish of improbabilities'. See *Athenæum*, 15 October 1898, 524.

16 Arnold-Forster, *In a Conning Tower*, vi-viii.

17 Or, more accurately, satire 'insist[s] upon its historical specificity, its torrential references to the peculiarities of particular individuals in the society that it represents': Brian A. Connery and Kirk Combe, 'Theorizing Satire: A Retrospective and Introduction', in Connery and Combe (eds), *Theorizing Satire: Essays in Literary Criticism* (Basingstoke: Palgrave Macmillan, 1995), 4.

18 George Gissing, *New Grub Street* (Hertfordshire: Wordsworth Editions Limited, 1996), 4.

19 'The Great War of 1892' was serialised between 2 January and 21 May 1892.

20 Rear Admiral P. Colomb, Colonel J.F. Maurice, R.A., Captain F.N. Maude, Archibald Forbes, Charles Lowe, D. Christie Murray, and F. Scudamore, *The Great War of 189-: A Forecast* (London: William Heinemann, 1893), 1.

21 Colomb et al., *The Great War*, 305. Hindsight would prove Dilke's alternative reading of events wrong. He was sceptical of the next great war starting in the Balkans, as the authors of *The Great War of 189-* had described; neither did he think it probable that the British public would force the British government to send troops to Belgium in the event of a Franco-German war (305–307). It is worth remembering, however, that Dilke was asked to comment on a narrative taking place in the 1890s, not in 1914.

22 I.F. Clarke, 'Forecasts of Warfare in Fiction 1803–1914', *Comparative Studies in Society and History*, 10 (1967), 14.

23 See Clarke, *Voices*, 80.

24 *Mail*, 17 June 1895, 2.

25 *Mail*, 4 July 1895, 1.

26 *Mail*, 17 June 1895, 1.

27 *Mail*, 10 July 1895, 1.

140   *Expertise, opinion and invasion-scare fiction*

28 *Mail*, 20 June, 1.
29 *Mail*, 22 June, 3.
30 Clarke, *Voices*, 111.
31 Morris, *Scaremongers*, 8.
32 Max Pemberton, *Lord Northcliffe: A Memoir* (London: Hodder and Stoughton Ltd. [1922]), 41.
33 Paul Readman, 'The 1895 General Election and Political Change in Late Victorian Britain', *The Historical Journal*, 42 (1999), 479.
34 I.F. Clarke, 'Trigger-Happy: An Evolutionary Study of the Origins and Development of Future-War Fiction, 1763–1914', *Journal of Social and Evolutionary Systems*, 20 (1997), 133.
35 Cecil D. Eby, *The Road to Armageddon: The Martial Spirit in English Popular Literature, 1870–1914* (Durham and London: Duke University Press, 1987), 26.
36 Clarke, *Voices*, 122. Le Queux also had the assistance of 'Colonel Cyril Field, R.M.L.I., and Major Matson, both military experts': William Le Queux, *Things I Know about Kings, Celebrities, and Crooks* (London: Eveleigh Nash and Grayson Limited, 1923), 245. Field had illustrated Le Queux's earlier *The Great War in England in 1897* (London: Tower Publishing Company Limited, 1894). *The Invasion of 1910* originally ran in instalments in the *Daily Mail* from Wednesday 14 March 1906 until Wednesday 4 July 1906. It was later reprinted as a book: William Le Queux, *The Invasion of 1910. With a Full Account of the Siege of London* (London: Eveleigh Nash, 1906). Aside from Le Queux and H.W. Wilson, there were several early science fiction, future war and invasion-scare authors in Harmsworth's orbit. In addition to Max Pemberton, his friend and biographer, Harmsworth's immediate circle also included Louis Tracy, who – along with Kennedy Jones – convinced Harmsworth to invest in the *Evening News*. See Pemberton, *Lord Northcliffe*, 56–58.
37 Le Queux, *Things I Know*, 244.
38 Le Queux's autobiography is about as fantastical and unrealistic as his invasion literature. *Things I know of Kings, Celebrities, and Crooks* introduces a world where fact and fiction are mixed, and where the reader is never quite sure what to believe. The memoir is best read as a source to Le Queux's thinking, rather than to his life and times. Alternatively, it is 'best approached as an extension of his [Le Queux's] fictional output': Ailise Bulfin & Harry Wood, 'Introduction', *Critical Survey* 32 (2020), 3. A later, 'official' biography is not much more trustworthy: N. St. Barbe Sladen, *The Real Le Queux: The Official Biography of William Le Queux* (London: Nicholson & Watson, 1938). The best study of Le Queux's

Expert opinion and public pressure 141

life is Roger T. Stearn, 'The Mysterious Mr Le Queux: War Novelist, Defence Publicist and Counterspy', *Soldiers of the Queen*, 70 (1992), 6–27, which is reprinted in *Critical Survey*, 32 (2020), 17–58, as part of a special issue dedicated to Le Queux. See also Chris Patrick and Stephen Baister, *William Le Queux: Master of Mystery* (Purley: Chris Patrick & Stephen Baister, [2007]).

39 NAM, Roberts papers, 7101/23/47, William Le Queux to Lord Roberts, 28 July 1905, underlines in the original. There is no indication in the letters Le Queux sent to Roberts that the two men were on particularly friendly terms; Le Queux is business-like and deferential in the correspondence. Aside from the 28 July letter, the Roberts papers includes another one from Le Queux dated 27 January 1906, also related to *The Invasion of 1910*; and one dated 27 October 1912, where Le Queux reminds Roberts of the 'kind help and advice' he gave with *The Invasion*, and asks if he could again ask for his help in making 'a series of pictures depicting the attack upon us by Germany', which Le Queux and the Gaumont Cinematograph Company was undertaking. On this, see chapter 7.

40 Clarke, *Voices*, 122. The episode is also mentioned in Samuel Hynes, *The Edwardian Turn of Mind* (Princeton: Princeton University Press, 1968), 40. The story may be apocryphal. Hynes gives no reference, but may have read about it in Clarke; Clarke, in turn, refers to Bernard Falk, *Bouquets for Fleet Street: Memories and Musings over fifty years* (London: Hutchinson & Co., 1951), 65. Le Queux does not refer to any such exchange in his autobiography, where he notes that the four-month quest to map out a viable invasion route ended up costing Harmsworth £3,000 (*Things I Know*, 245). Neither is there any mention of Harmsworth's veto in the preface to the book edition. In 1915, after Roberts' death, Le Queux would continue to claim that the invasion plan had been the brainchild of Roberts. 'When writing my forecast "The Invasion of England," [sic] in 1905', Le Queux stated, 'I received the greatest advice and kind assistance from the late Lord Roberts, who spent many hours with me and who personally revised and elaborated the German plan of campaign which I had supposed': William Le Queux, *Britain's Deadly Peril: Are We Told the Truth?* (London: Stanley Paul & Co., 1915), 140.

41 *Daily Mail*, 14 March 1906, 9. On Roberts' connections with the press and the public, see Heather Streets, 'Military Influence in Late Victorian and Edwardian Popular Media: The Case of Frederick Roberts', *Journal of Victorian Culture*, 8 (2003), 231–256.

42 Charles E. Gannon, in his study of the technological prognostications of future-war stories, theorises that Le Queux may have changed his

narrative as he wrote it, after being confronted by experts who read it and offered corrections. This is an interesting way of explaining inconsistencies in Le Queux's text – the sudden appearance, for example, of wireless transmitters and air-burst shells after they have been left unmentioned in the first part of the text – but the idea remains unproven. Le Queux may simply have been an inconsistent writer; and either way, the fact that Le Queux exhibited 'indifferent abilities as a military writer and prognosticator' indicates that the text, from its inception, was largely unsubstantiated by military expert knowledge, despite Le Queux's own claims to the contrary. See Charles E. Gannon, *Rumors of War and Infernal Machines: Technomilitary Agenda-Setting in American and British Speculative Fiction* (Lanham: Rowman & Littlefield Publishers, Inc., 2003), 39–42.

43 Grant Richards, *Author Hunting: By an Old Literary Sportsman. Memories of Years Spent Mainly in Publishing, 1897–1925* (London: Hamish Hamilton, 1934), 156. In what way Bernard Shaw considered himself qualified to make a judgement on this was left unanswered. Clarke cites the letter, but does not comment on it (*Voices*, 221).

44 Richards, *Author Hunting*, 156; [F.N. Maude], *The New Battle of Dorking* (London: Grant Richards, 1900).

45 James Harding, *Gerald du Maurier: The Last Actor-Manager* (London: Hodder & Stoughton, 1989), 710–771; Hynes, *Edwardian Turn of Mind*, 46.

46 Harding, *Gerald du Maurier*, 71. In an interview with the *Daily Mail*, Gerald claimed that the ending was changed during the play's rehearsals, when 'the company and everyone else said we must bring a little hope into the end, and that we have done'. (30 January 1909, 5).

47 Harding, *Gerald du Maurier*, 73.

48 *Daily Mail*, 30 January 1909, 5.

49 Harding, *Gerald du Maurier*, 72. The play was also issued as a book, in the same anonymous form that it had on its theatrical release: 'A Patriot', *An Englishman's Home* (London: Edward Arnold, 1909). For a re-evaluation of *An Englishman's Home*'s place in British pre-war culture, see Christian K. Melby, 'Rethinking British Militarism before the First World War: The Case of *An Englishman's Home* (1909), *English Historical Review*, 137 (2022), 1377–1401.

50 Clarke, *Voices*, 123. John Ramsden agrees, seeing the two works as having made 'a special impact', and arguing that Childers' work 'almost single-handedly made a German "bolt from the blue" seem a real possibility': John Ramsden, *Don't Mention the War: The British and the Germans since 1890* (London: Abacus, 2007), 71–72.

Expert opinion and public pressure 143

51 Childers took on the identity of 'editor', writing an epilogue to the book that presents the German invasion plans as real. Erskine Childers, *The Riddle of the Sands: A Record of Secret Service* (London: Thomas Nelson and Sons, Ltd., [1910, first edition published in 1903]), 371–382.

52 Erskine Childers, *In the Ranks of the C.I.V. A Narrative and a Diary of Personal Experiences with the C.I.V. Battery (Honourable Artillery Company) in South Africa* (London: Smith, Elder & Co., 1900). He also wrote two critical studies of the modern British army: *War and the Arme Blanche* (London: Edward Arnold, 1910), and *German Influence on British Cavalry* (London: Edward Arnold, 1911). *War and the Arme Blanche* contained a foreword by Lord Roberts, where he asked his 'brother officers' to 'read the book with an unbiased mind', and not be troubled by Childers' role as a civilian: 'Remember that most of our finest military histories have been written by civilians' (xvi). In fact, Childers had himself edited parts of one military history, volume V of L.S. Amery (ed.), The Times *History of the War in South Africa*, 7 vols. (London: Sampson, Low, Marsten & Co., 1900–1909), V.

53 Preferably the sea: 'My own idea is that we ought to go much farther, and train every able-bodied man for a couple of years as a sailor. Army? Oh, I suppose you'd have to give them the choice'. (Childers, *Riddle of the Sands*, 127).

54 Childers, *Riddle of the Sands*, 238.

55 Childers, *Riddle of the Sands*, v.

56 James Blyth, *The Swoop of the Vulture* (London: Digby, Long & Co., 1909), 83, 260. The book is otherwise noteworthy for its vitriolic Germanophobia – the reader is introduced to 'jeering Prussian sausage munchers' (248) – and for its description of armoured fighting vehicles, called 'motor moveable forts, or armoured fortresses' (237), and drone warfare in the form of an 'automatic kite' with a radio-controlled bomb (256).

57 Le Queux, *The Invasion of 1910*, 13–19.

58 The 'Defenders' are described as a 'strange and incongruous body. Grey-bearded Army pensioners ranged side by side with keen, enthusiastic youths'. The Legion of Frontiersmen, 'those brave fellows who had seen service in every corner of the world' (Le Queux, *The Invasion of 1910*, 360, 489), was a patriotic volunteer organisation in existence at the time Le Queux wrote his story. See Michael Humphries, ' "The Eyes of an Empire": The Legion of Frontiersmen, 1904–1914', *Historical Research*, 85 (2012), 133–158. A similar defence group is enlisted in *The Message*, published a year later. Several names are

144   *Expertise, opinion and invasion-scare fiction*

suggested for this group – 'A patriotic league, a league of defenders, a nation in arms'; 'the Liberators'; 'the Patriots' – before they finally decide on 'the Citizens': A.J. Dawson, *The Message* (London: E. Grant Richards, 1907), 249.

59 W. Douglas Newton, *War* (London: Methuen & Co., Ltd., 1914), 4.

60 Le Queux, *The Invasion of 1910*, 17.

61 *Mail*, 19 June 1895.

62 Alan H. Burgoyne, *The War Inevitable* (London: Francis Griffiths, 1908), 99, 241. That Burgoyne, an officer and later MP, would utter such blatantly anti-constitutional remarks should not necessarily come as a surprise. As discussed in previous chapters, the decades prior to the First World War saw many officers expressing their frustrations with the political system they operated in. Not everyone were as direct as Burgoyne, or as Captain Ch. Ross, author of *Representative Government and War* (London: Hutchinson & Co., 1903), who argued for the constitution to be sidelined in times of national crisis. On this trend in British military thinking, see Christian K. Melby, 'War, Public Opinion and the British Constitution, c. 1867–1914', *Journal of Modern European History*, 21 (2023), 441–457.

63 Burgoyne, *War Inevitable*, 115–121.

64 Gannon, *Rumors of War*, 55.

65 Walter Wood, *The Enemy in Our Midst: The Story of a Raid on England* (London: John Long, 1906), 49, 63, 105.

66 On the soldier as hero and masculine ideal, see Graham Dawson, *Soldier Heroes: British Adventure, Empire and the Imagining of Masculinities* (London and New York: Routledge, 1994).

67 Walter E. Houghton, *The Victorian Frame of Mind: 1830–1870* (New Haven and London: Yale University Press, 1957), 306.

68 As he noted on Ibsen's *An Enemy of the People*, 'it is easy to be in a minority and yet be wrong, [but] it is absolutely impossible to be in the majority and yet be right as to the newest social prospects' (George Bernard Shaw, *The Quintessence of Ibsenism*, 3rd edition (London: Constable and Company, Ltd., 1926), 92). The Fabian search for efficiency led them to cross-party alliances, a focus on social imperialism, and to Sidney and Beatrice Webb's creation of a 'coefficient' group, where the idea of the expert was taken very seriously. See Bernard Semmel, *Imperialism and Social Reform: English Social-Imperial Thought, 1895–1914* (Cambridge, MA: Harvard University Press, 1960). The nominally Socialist Fabians even bought into the idea of the 'businessman in politics – a 'variant on the cult of the "scientific expert"' (G.R. Searle, *The Quest for National Efficiency: A Study of British Politics and Political Thought, 1899–1914* (London: Ashfield

Expert opinion and public pressure 145

Press, 1990), 86). Spenser Wilkinson, someone who himself awkwardly straddled the divide between professional soldier and civilian theorist, claimed that he was once invited to give a talk to the Fabian Society, and ended up in a discussion with Shaw: 'A debate followed, which was wound up by Mr. Bernard Shaw. "There is one point," he [Shaw] said, "on which I cannot follow Mr. Wilkinson: he suggests that the military instructors of the nations should be its professional officers. Against professional officers I have the complaint to make that they never know their business. In spite of their many other excellent qualities, they have invariably shown themselves incompetent in the matter of war."' See Wilkinson, 'Note', in Major Stewart L. Murray, *The Reality of War: An Introduction to "Clausewitz"* (London: Hugh Rees, 1909), v.

69 Roy MacLeod, 'Introduction', in Roy MacLeod (ed.), *Government and Expertise: Specialists, Administrators and Professionals, 1860–1919* (Cambridge: Cambridge University Press, 2003), 16.

70 Searle, *National Efficiency*, 224–225.

71 Cd. 1932, 1968, 2002, *Report of the War Office (Reconstitution) Committee*, 3 vols. (London, 1904); Searle, *National Efficiency*, 222. On the background to and development of the CID and its form and function, see Franklyn Arthur Johnson, *Defence by Committee: The British Committee of Imperial Defence, 1885–1959* (London: Oxford University Press, 1960); and Rhodri Williams, *Defending the Empire: The Conservative Party and British Defence Policy, 1899–1915* (New Haven and London: Yale University Press, 1991).

72 Viscount Esher, *National Strategy* (London: A.L. Humphreys, 1904), 12–13.

73 Despite his respect for its powers, Esher was highly critical of the press influencing public opinion, and public opinion in turn forcing government policy. In early 1903, Balfour's government stood poised to jointly finance the Berlin-Baghdad railway with Deutsche Bank, but ended up having to perform a humiliating climb-down after a harrowing press campaign. Commenting on this, Esher concluded that '[t]he English people, led by a foolish, half-informed press, are children in foreign politics' (quoted in Morris, *Scaremongers*, 55–56). Though, naturally, he saw things differently when he was the one submitting writings or information to the press, as in 1884. Judging 20 years later that 'thanks to a few far-sighted writers in the Press, the Fleet … was placed upon an adequate footing': Esher, *National Strategy*, 6. However, he declined to have any direct, as opposed to indirect, involvement with newspapers, turning down an offer from Henry Labouchère in 1886 to work with the *Daily News*. See *Journals*

146   *Expertise, opinion and invasion-scare fiction*

and Letters of Reginald Viscount Esher, ed. Maurice V. Brett, 4 vols. (London: Nicholson and Watson, 1934–1938), I, 125.

74 Esher, *National Strategy,* 14. Esher was here referring to the CID.

75 Esher, *National Strategy,* 19.

76 Viscount Esher, *The Committee of Imperial Defence: Its Functions and Potentialities* (London: John Murray, 1912), 7–9, 20.

77 Cd. 1932, 4–5.

78 The articles were printed on the *Pall Mall Gazette* front page, on 18, 19, 24, 28, 29 September and 3 and 11 October 1894.

79 See Coetzee, *Party or Country,* 16; *Pall Mall Gazette,* 16 October 1894, 1. The suggestion to form a league was published in the paper on 21 November 1894, 1–2, in a letter to the editor dated 17 November. A printed copy of the letter is in NAM Spenser Wilkinson papers, 1990–11–42, 13/22–1.

80 *Pall Mall Gazette,* 11 October 1894, 2.

81 *Pall Mall Gazette,* 23 November 1894, 2. The reference to the German Field Marshall was not picked out of thin air. Wilkinson had earlier argued that Britain should adopt a centralised general staff akin to that which had won Prussia its victories in the mid-Victorian period: *The Brain of an Army: A Popular Account of the German General Staff* (London: Macmillan & Co., 1890). Wilkinson later described his plan as providing the 'Brain of a Navy', a 'forethought department' to be the directing power in naval planning and warfare: see Wilkinson, *The Brain of the Navy* (London: Archibald Constable and Company, 1895), 13.

82 NAM Spenser Wilkinson papers, 1990–11–42, 13/21 [Wilkinson to Charles Beresford], 9 October 1894.

83 F.N.M., 'Notices of Books: *The Great Alternative: A plea for a National Policy.* By Spencer [sic] Wilkinson', *Journal of the Royal United Service Institution,* 38 (June 1894), 683.

84 A.J.A. Morris, 'Wilkinson, (Henry) Spenser (1853–1937)' ODNB.

85 Coetzee, *Party or Country,* 17, 21.

86 The four 'objectives' for the new organisation listed in the letter to the *Pall Mall Gazette* were: '1. To call the attention of the public to the fact that the Navy is unequal to the demands which a war might at any moment impose upon it'; '2. To instruct the public on naval matters and on naval history, and to bring home to all British subjects the vital value to them of the Command of the Sea'; '3. To bring public opinion to bear on candidates for Parliament, so that Members may be returned who (without regard to party politics) are pledged to a naval policy which will ensure Great Britain's Command of the Sea'; '4. To secure the administration of the British Navy on lines which are

Expert opinion and public pressure 147

above party politics'. Underneath these were written, in italics: *N.B. – The League to be absolutely distinct from all party politics*'. See *Pall Mall Gazette*, 21 November 1894, 1.

87 'Constitution of the Navy League', *Navy League Pamphlet A2*, and 'Programme of Action', *Navy League Pamphlet A3* ([London: The Navy League], 1896).

88 See Coetzee, *Party or Country*, 17.

89 Coetzee, *Party or Country*, 83–84. N.C. Fleming, 'The Imperial Maritime League: British Navalism, Conflict, and the Radical Right, c.1907–1920', *War in History*, 23 (2016), 296–322.

90 NAM, Spenser Wilkinson papers, 1990–11–42, 13/22–8 [Peirson to Wilkinson], 11 February 1908.

91 NAM, Spenser Wilkinson papers, 1990–11–42, 13/22–7 [Wilkinson to Peirson], 8 March 1908.

92 NAM, Spenser Wilkinson papers, 1990–11–42, 13/22–6 Imperial Maritime League Pamphlet, 27 January 1908.

93 NAM, Spenser Wilkinson papers, 1990–11–42, 13/22–7 [Wilkinson to Peirson], 8 March 1908.

94 Wilkinson, *Brain of the Navy*, 12.

95 Mary Arnold-Forster, *The Right Honourable Hugh Oakeley Arnold-Forster: A Memoir by His Wife* (London: Edward Arnold, 1910), 362–363.

96 His letter to Balfour upon taking office as Secretary of State for War noted that he was laid up in bed, and that his acceptance was conditional on him getting better: BL Add. MS 50335 Ff. 8–9, Arnold-Forster to Balfour, 5 October 1903.

97 Coetzee, *Party or Country*, 109.

98 *Morning Leader*, 30 March 1909, 1. G.J. Marcus, 'The Naval Crisis of 1909 and the Croydon By-Election', *Journal of the Royal United Service Institution*, 103 (1958), 507, reaches a similar conclusion.

99 Coetzee, *Party or Country*, 110–111.

100 *Morning Leader*, 30 March 1909, 1.

101 See Coetzee, *Party or Country*, 109–111; Jan Rüger, *The Great Naval Game: Britain and Germany in the Age of Empire* (Cambridge: Cambridge University Press, 2009), 220–221.

102 Coetzee, *Party or Country*, 111. W. Mark Hamilton notes of the League's social composition that it had few working-class members, being mainly a bourgeois organisation – its limited political influence can be linked to this: *The Nation and the Navy: Methods and Organization of British Navalist Propaganda, 1889–1914* (New York: Garland Publishing, 1986), 360.

148   *Expertise, opinion and invasion-scare fiction*

103 Coetzee, *Party or Country*, 122. Matthew Johnson argues that this view should be somewhat tempered – British navalists could be found both in the Liberal party and on the left. In addition, Johnson has shown that Liberal membership with the Navy League was higher than previously thought, though he also notes that many of the Liberal Navy League MPs belonged to the right of their party, and later joined the Unionists: 'The Liberal Party and the Navy League in Britain before the Great War', *Twentieth Century British History*, 22 (2011), 137–163.

104 A conclusion reached by Jan Rüger as well: see *Naval Game*, 97.

105 BL Add. MS 50335 F.59, 27 October 1903.

106 Ian F.W. Beckett, *Riflemen Form: A Study of the Rifle Volunteer Movement, 1859–1908* (Barnsley: Pen & Sword, 2007), 249. A similar enquiry into the possibility of invasion had been undertaken by the CID a few years previously: in May 1905 Balfour announced to the Commons that the Committee had concluded that large-scale invasion of Britain was not seriously to be considered. The 1907–1908 inquiry reaffirmed this, though it also argued that an invader might land up to 70,000 men on British shores. See Rhodri Williams, *Defending the Empire: The Conservative Party and British Defence Policy, 1899–1915* (New Haven and London: Yale University Press, 1991), 25, 145. On the background to, and early years of the National Service League, see R.J.Q. Adams and Philip P. Poirier, *The Conscription Controversy in Great Britain, 1900–18* (Basingstoke: The Macmillan Press, 1987), 2–15; on the invasion question, see 33–48 and *passim*. See also Roger T. Stearn, '"The Last Glorious Campaign": Lord Roberts, the National Service League and Compulsory Military Training, 1902–1914', *Journal of the Society for Army Historical Research*, 87 (2009), 312–330.

107 Coetzee, *Party or Country*, 115, 117.

108 *The Times*, 12 June 1905, 6. The letter argued that 'It would not be possible under any system of organization – short of conscription – for a large reserve to be formed by the Regular Army; its numbers are too few, and the demands of foreign service prevent men from being passed with sufficient rapidity through the ranks; we must, therefore, look upon the Militia, the Yeomanry, and the Volunteers as the main reserve for the Army. When the scheme which I advocate has been fully developed it will be infinitely easier than it is at present to obtain desirable recruits for these branches of the service, and we shall have besides a potential reserve, much stronger numerically than any we could hope to create without having recourse to conscription, a measure which is so distasteful to the majority of the people of this country

Expert opinion and public pressure 149

that its adoption is greatly to be deprecated except under the pressure of an overwhelming national emergency'.

109 *The Times*, 17 February 1906, 12. Note that aside from wanting to make training legally binding, there is little difference here from the claims made in Roberts' earlier letter.

110 Archibald Hurd, 'England's Peril – Invasion or Starvation', *Fortnightly Review* (April 1910), 679.

111 Anne Summers, 'Militarism in Britain before the Great War', *History Workshop Journal*, 2 (1976), 113. See also Summers, 'The Character of Edwardian Nationalism: Three Popular Leagues', in Paul Kennedy and Anthony Nicholls (eds), *Nationalist and Racialist Movements in Britain and Germany before 1914* (London and Basingstoke: Palgrave Macmillan, 1981), 68–87; and Frans Coetzee and Marilyn Shevin Coetzee, 'Rethinking the Radical Right in Germany and Britain before 1914', *Journal of Contemporary History*, 21 (1986), 515–537.

112 Henry Spenser Wilkinson, *Thirty-Five Years: 1874–1909* (London: Constable and Company Ltd., 1933), 271. See also Summers, 'Militarism in Britain', 115. On the political sensitivity of conscription, see Adams and Poirier, *Conscription Controversy*.

113 Summers notes that the Regular Army kept away from the League: Summers, 'Three Popular Leagues', 70.

114 Quoted in Howard Roy Moon, 'The Invasion of the United Kingdom: Public Controversy and Official Planning 1888–1918' (University of London, Ph.D. thesis, 1968), 31, underlines in the original.

115 Neal Blewett, *The Peers, the Parties and the People: The General Elections of 1910* (London: Macmillan, 1972), 125–128.

Part III

Authors and readers

5

Fiction and society: the British public in invasion-scare fiction, 1871–1914

In *England's Downfall: or, the Last Great Revolution* (1893), written by 'An Ex-Revolutionist', the British government is overthrown in a violent uprising that sees the empire crumble and London mobs running amok.[1] Some critical voices were inclined to agree that Britain was indeed heading in this direction. 'It can hardly be denied, I think, by the most sanguine of Conservative optimists', an article in the April 1893 issue of the Tory *National Review* observed, 'that with the year 1893 Radical principles have cleared at one bound the space which divides practical from merely speculative politics'.[2] The author, Thomas Kebbel, directed his ire at the 'Radicalism' of Gladstone's Liberal government, but 1893 was also the founding year of the Independent Labour Party, which in time would transform the British political landscape.[3] The anarchist movement in Britain reached a high point in the early 1890s, with confrontations between labour and authorities as fertile background. In February 1894, the Greenwich Park explosion seemed to bring continental outrages home to Britain itself.[4]

The descriptions by 'An Ex-Revolutionist' were not the only examples of what might be termed 'revolution fiction' in the 1890s. *The Doom of the County Council of London* (1892), for example, describes the attempted overthrow of parliament by the eponymous council; however, a showdown with the House of Lords leads to the county council's own downfall and the restoration of normality.[5] Such 'revolution fiction' continued to appear well into the immediate pre-First World War years, and included novels like J. Twells Brex's *The Civil War of 1915* (1912), where the class war of 1915 has its antecedents (in Brex's opinion) in the bad policies of the 1906 Liberal administration.[6]

154   *Authors and readers*

As Matthew Beaumont has argued, the years after the 1871 Paris Commune – an event which coincided with the shock of the Franco-Prussian War, and taking place shortly after the 1867 Reform Act – was a period of British bourgeois fear of insurrection, paired with the fear of invasion. Beaumont has termed a certain category of fiction which followed in the wake of the Commune 'cacotopian'. Starting with *The Battle of Dorking* in 1871, he describes this as a form of anti-utopian, anti-communist literature which 'depicts the working class, *in corpore*, as dystopian', portraying its descent into revolt and insurrection.[7] In stories like *The Commune in London* (1871) and *The Siege of London* (1885), invasion serves as a catalyst for insurrection in the capital.[8] The point is made by Darko Suvin as well, who has noted that *Dorking* hints at the links between foreign aggression and revolutionary uprising.[9] British visions of a metropolitan uprising, as expressed in these and other stories, were in fact quite close to the late nineteenth century strategic outlook of the French *Jeune École*. Heavily influenced by the experience of the Paris Commune, this naval strategy, in its two-fold aim, sought to limit the risk of revolutions at home in France, and simultaneously promote it abroad through attacks on civilian targets – or, more accurately, by attacking the entire society of the enemy – a prelude to the strategic aerial bombing doctrines of the world wars. The theories of strategic bombing assumed that public opinion could be influenced from the air, forcing the government of an enemy combatant to capitulate after being subjected to pressure from its own populace. As Thomas Hippler phrases it, 'the strategy of air bombing was necessarily based on a concept of the "people" as the primordial political category'.[10] This idea was firmly established before the dawn of the aeroplane. The British public was not a uniform category, however. Some parts were more vulnerable than others: there were weak spots in the British armour. An inner as well as an outer menace loomed not only over many fictional texts, but also over military and political thinking in the years before the war.

From the discussions around *The Battle of Dorking* onwards, invasion-scare fiction throughout the period covered in this study was always more about British society itself, rather than specific external threats. Invasion-scare fiction envisioned a British populace that was not only a victim, but also an audience – and as the stories became increasingly commodified, the ways in which the

Fiction and society 155

public were expected to react to the stories changed. This chapter discusses the way the British themselves featured in invasion-scare fiction. It looks at class, gender and nation in turn, and shows how the stories developed to portray the British public and the British nation over the period between 1871 and 1914. By the Edwardian era, invasion-scare fiction was a much more inclusive genre than it had been in the 1870s. This development was reflected in a changed readership, which is discussed in more detail in the next chapter.

External and internal threats: Britain's food supply

The idea of an external attack leading to, and ultimately combining with, internal upheaval, was prevalent in a lot of British pre-war literature. It was a staple not only of invasion-scare fiction, but also as a trope in the numerous stories about civil war in Ireland, where outside influences are often paired with internal divisions on that island.[11] The potentially damaging external influences of a continental connection weighed heavily on the minds of opponents of the channel tunnel scheme. As Daniel Pick observes, 'the Channel was a crucial barrier against agitators, armies and anarchists'; in 1882 *The Sunday Times* claimed that it kept out 'Nihilists, Internationalists and Bradlaughites'.[12] The idea that there was, or should be, a separation between the 'outside' and the 'inside' of society has been perceptively linked by Laura Otis to the rise of germ theory in the nineteenth century: 'If one believes that invisible germs, spread by human contact, can make one sick, one becomes more and more anxious about penetration and about any connection with other people – the same anxieties inspired by imperialism'.[13]

Edwardian political advertisements often featured insidious foreign influences that needed to be kept out.[14] The Conservatives were particularly eager to portray the Liberals and Free Trade as opening Britain up for foreign exploitation. The German 'Herr Dumper', selling cheap German goods to the detriment of the British worker, was a threatening presence in many Tariff Reform advertisements – at times presented as a burglar.[15] The British body politic, like a physical body, could be portrayed as being threatened with dangerous infections, either through invasion, imports or foreign ideas spreading in society. This was a powerful political idea, and eagerly

156   *Authors and readers*

used in the ultimately failed Tariff Reform campaign. After all, as a lecture printed and distributed by The Women's Unionist and Tariff Reform Association (WUTRA) in 1909 proclaimed, 'Free Trade' itself was 'of foreign origin, while Protection is British'.[16] Bestsellers like Ernest Edwin Williams' *'Made in Germany'* (1896),[17] showing how products of German manufacture were supplanting British-made goods, were joined by invasion-scare fiction's depictions of a Britain where foreign labourers had taken jobs away from British-born workers. 'Here am I, a free-born Englishman', says John Steel, in Walter Wood's *The Enemy in Our Midst* (1906), 'and yet in the capital of my own country I can't get a job! I'm living in an alien colony, in an alien house, and I've got an alien landlord!'[18] In this story, the 'aliens' also constitute, as the title indicates, a fifth column, preparing the ground for a German invasion and the rising of a hidden 'Alien Army'. This trope was quite common in Edwardian invasion-scare narratives.[19]

The problem with the fear of an external threat or 'other', as expressed, for example, by *The Sunday Times* above, was that there were already enough internal divisions in society to worry about; 'Bradlaughites' need not be imported from the continent – Charles Bradlaugh, the controversial Liberal republican and atheist – was very much present in Britain already.[20] There is no foreign invasion to blame for the country's demise in *England's Downfall*, and the council is not controlled by sinister foreign influences in *The Doom of the County Council*. In stories where Britain's food supply is threatened – 'Blue Water' narratives, as discussed in chapter 2 – the effect of starvation is the complete collapse of order at home, with no need for an enemy army to set its foot on British soil. 'Our danger is starvation, not invasion', as the agricultural reformer and Unionist MP Charles Bathurst argued in a 1912 pamphlet.[21] This is the result in Charles Gleig's *When All Men Starve* (1898), subtitled *Showing how England Hazarded her Naval Supremacy, and the Horrors Which Followed the Interruption of Her Food Supply*.[22] The book's last chapter, titled 'Anarchy', sees the drunken mob dance in the light of the burning Buckingham Palace. Charles Allen Clarke had a more optimistic view of the future in *Starved into Surrender* (1904), but here too the result of a naval blockade is a violent uprising by hungry mobs. The difference from Gleig is that Clarke, a Socialist, writes approvingly of how society develops in the aftermath of the

Fiction and society 157

starvation and defeat, as a prosperous country wisely governed in the interest of its people, and free from its imperial burden.[23]

Arthur Conan Doyle, who also weighed in on the topic, penned a story where eight enemy submarines bring Britain to its knees by cutting off its food supply. The result is 'serious rioting in the Lanarkshire coalfields, and in the Midlands, together with a Socialistic upheaval in the East of London, which ... assumed the proportions of a civil war'.[24] Conan Doyle's solution to the question of how to supply Britain with food in time of war included the building of channel tunnels, encouragement of agriculture in Britain, and, in a slightly more left-field vein, 'the provision of submarine merchantmen'.[25]

With the repeal of the Corn Laws in 1846, British food imports needed to be secured by a strong navy, with a 'trade-off' between the cost of naval supremacy set against the benefits of free trade. Avner Offer notes that this trade-off worked largely to Britain's advantage until the mid-1890s. After that, 'the attractions of securing cheap grain at the cost of a fleet contracted almost every year'.[26] This was the background for the speculations over the potential consequences if Britain lost its access to imported food. 'We may figure these Islands of ours as hulks moored in a meeting place of strong tides, by the two stout hawsers of import and export'; wrote the journalist L. Cope Cornford in 1906, 'and war as the knife in the hand of an enemy, hacking at the strands'.[27]

According to Arthur Marder the 'starvation theory' – the idea that a future naval war would lead to starvation – was a 'universal belief' in Britain by the end of the century.[28] However, not everyone was convinced by the theory – or, at any rate, that it had anything to do with the strength of the navy. The 'starvation-leading-to-revolution' trope expressed in works like those of Gleig and Clarke was common enough by the mid-1890s, both in fiction and elsewhere, that a commentator in the *United Service Magazine* decried it as the 'starvation bogey', one which might in time become a self-fulfilling prophecy. Britain did not risk running out of food in case of war, the author argued, 'but the contrary impression has got such a hold of the public mind that panic about food, and a panic rise in the price of bread is a real danger'.[29]

Fears over the effects a war might have on the food supply did not come completely out of the blue – the 1905 Royal Commission on Supply of Food and Raw Material in Time of War concluded that

158 *Authors and readers*

Britain imported as much as four-fifths of its annual wheat and flour supply, the country's most important foodstuff.[30] In *The Angel of the Revolution* (1893), an enormously popular story by George Griffith where Britain is invaded by a Franco-Slavonian League, Britain's dependence on imported food is compared to that of imperial Rome.[31] This was a common refrain in these years: Matthew White Ridley, for example, a Conservative MP and Tariff Reform campaigner, thought a comparison with Rome was apt, but dismissed its implications of a future decline and fall. Speaking in the Commons in 1902, he observed that 'we have the advantage of Rome in the gradual and quickly increasing reliance that can be placed on our colonies for the food supplied that can be obtained from them'.[32] The price of imported foodstuffs was a highly politicised issue in Edwardian Britain, as illustrated by the debates over Tariff Reform, and, as Paul Readman has shown, the 'politics of land' and agrarian issues formed part of electoral contests throughout the pre-Great War period.[33] Land and national identity is explored later in this chapter.

Beyond the practicalities of a blockade, the members of the 1905 Royal Commission also discussed the possibility of what was termed a 'psychological' rise in prices: this was a reference to the fear that, even if the food supply itself was not threatened, a panicked reaction to the war might lead to an increase in prices – a similar argument to that put forward earlier in the *United Service Magazine*. A panic might give the starvation fear its own logic. Although the report was sanguine when it came to the effects of a 'psychological' rise in prices, it did acknowledge that 'it would not be safe to leave out of account that over and above the economic rise, there will be an increase due to panic, which may be very serious, but the extent of which it is impossible to foretell'.[34] Some feared that a war's impact on prices, even a psychological one, could lead to violence. 'The starving millions will not starve quietly', as Colonel Charles Yate, a Conservative MP, put it when food supply was discussed in the Commons on the eve of the First World War.[35] The danger was not necessarily the results of physical acts of warfare, but the way the British public – or its working class, at any rate – would react to the outbreak of hostilities, and respond emotionally to the war. Offer summarises this view as a combination of 'the traditional violence of the bread riot with the modern one of political revolution'.[36]

Fiction and society 159

The majority of the Royal Commission decided to dismiss the fear of a working-class uprising. But a dissenting minority argued that, with the price of bread – the most important foodstuff among the poorer classes – certain to rise if a war broke out with one or more of the great powers, the country ran the risk of being effectively ruled by the empty bellies of the poorest members of society, rather than the heads of the government ministers and defence professionals: 'the suffering in consequence among the poor, and especially if the [price] rise was much prolonged, would lead to the danger of pressure being placed upon the Government, and add to their embarrassment at moments of great crisis'.[37] This was a vision of mob rule taken to the extreme.

If the commission found it difficult to envision precisely how the country might react to an imagined future war, they could turn to the pages of fiction, where the topic, as noted, had been discussed at length. Invasion-scare literature envisioned a public that could be divided into rational versus irrational elements – and the dividing line ran through class, gender and nation.

A certain class of people?

There were indeed a large group of invasion texts which portrayed the lower classes as unfit for the role envisioned for them by the Second Reform Act. Ever since George Chesney's 1871 lamentation over how power 'was passing away from the class which had been used to rule ... into the hands of the lower classes',[38] class was a staple of invasion-scare fiction, as well as related works. The further expansion of the franchise in 1884 forms part of the litany of poor decisions that the author of the abovementioned *The Siege of London* lays at the feet of the Liberals in general, and the Radicals and William Gladstone in particular.[39] '[W]ould you give sheep the right to vote,' asks a character in *England's Downfall*, in an argument over the lack of patriotism among the Radicals, and the negative effects of the 1884 Act; 'and what are the majority but sheep as far as politics are concerned?'[40]

Studies often argue that the audience for pre-First World War invasion scares – whether in fictional or non-fictional form – was essentially middle class. Paul Kennedy, for example, has claimed

160   *Authors and readers*

that 'the middle classes were arguably the most natural audience for popular adventure stories, "invasion scare" novels and other pieces of literary ephemera'.[41] This, in turn, points forward to Modris Eksteins' argument that the First World War was shaped by middle class values, so as to become the 'first great war of the bourgeoisie'.[42] However, one should be careful with such categorisations; Jay Winter has noted of pre-Great War art that there exists an 'outmoded distinction between elite and masses, between avant-garde and rear-guard, between highbrow and middlebrow, which still bifurcates scholarship in cultural history'.[43] Although Winter was referring to the visual arts, the point still stands with reference to the written word.

This is not to say that there are no merits to a class analysis of invasion-scare narratives. There was a clear establishment mentality to some stories, characterised by an unease about popular forms of government, and the influence of the masses on politics. By cataloguing the social background of science fiction authors, Darko Suvin has argued that class ideology played an important part in the messages conveyed in Victorian science fiction in general. In the category of 'upper class', Suvin included George Chesney and Vice-Admiral Philip Colomb, due to their officer backgrounds, and he noted that '[a] glance at the names will reveal that the sons of the uppermost class wrote some of the most heavily and openly ideological narratives'.[44] This, along with Beaumont's analysis, are in turn variations of Samuel Hynes' argument that Edwardian invasion stories were Tory in nature; their anxieties were those of the ruling class.[45]

However, the depiction of a certain socio-economic subset of the population as a form of fifth column, or at the very least untrustworthy, was not uniform in invasion-scare fiction, and it changed as time went on. Numerous stories of future wars and invasions included the working class in fraternal unity with the rest of society as Britain defeats the invaders, as discussed in chapter 4, and some stories portrayed other classes as more of a threat to Britain than the workers. *The Siege of London* (1871) – not to be confused with the similarly titled 1885 pamphlet – written by 'J.W.M.', ostensibly portrays a similar situation to the one outlined in *Dorking*. But, unlike Chesney, the author pinned the blame on the ruling classes instead. A brigade of police officers, guardians of the establishment,

Fiction and society 161

contributes to the defence of London, but ends up telling the invaders to 'move on' rather than trying to stop them. Meanwhile, Queen Victoria, from comfort and safety, writes that she will record the defenders 'valour and devotion in my diary', and instructs them to look after her valuable furniture at Buckingham Palace.[46] The author notes that this description of events is probably as reliable as *The Battle of Dorking* that inspired it. As this, along with Charles Allen Clarke's *Starved into Surrender*, illustrates, there was a radical tradition among authors of invasion-scare fiction.[47] And here the working classes are often readier to defend their country than are the rich and noble. Prior to the invasion in *The Enemy in Our Midst*, the character John Steel joins a demonstration in Hyde Park along with many former soldiers, marching under banners proclaiming the foreigners and the moneyed classes as the enemies of British freedom. 'Down with the Toffs and up with the People!' flies alongside banners proclaiming 'England for the English!' in slogans replete with equal amounts of xenophobia and anti-establishment bias; real England lies neither with the aliens, nor with the 'fat, smug City man'.[48] It is the leaders who have betrayed the nation in such narratives. In this, as in other similar stories, the invasion leads to the rediscovery of a lost national unity.

When Britain is threatened with war against a European coalition in *The Swoop of the Eagles* (1889), the hero of the hour, while not working class, is an overworked and underpaid bureaucrat, not the lords of the Admiralty.[49] The story also portrays the London mob as a different animal than its continental cousins: when a crowd gathers there is shouting and protest directed at the government, but it is 'all done mildly, in that half-humorous, good natured way peculiar to the London mob, a mob that knows itself to be composed of freemen, and to have the power, in theory at least, of setting up and pulling down what governments it pleases'.[50] This crowd, with its English qualities, is the real power in the land but it is inspired by moderation, rather than revolutionary zeal.

Alongside the radical and the 'cacotopian' fiction – to borrow Beaumont's phrase – was also the more traditional image of national unity, where the various social classes know their place and respect the natural order of society. In Charles Stone's *What Happened After the Battle of Dorking* (1871), the invaders are met by a truly United Kingdom, both socially and geographically:

162   *Authors and readers*

The stalwart miners of Northumberland and Durham, of Cornwall and the Welsh coal-districts; the great muscular navvies, and healthy agricultural labourers, the sharp mechanics of the manufacturing towns, and the yeomen, gentlemen, clerks – in fact everybody rushed to arms.[51]

The working classes in invasion-scare fiction were portrayed both as threats to, and as important parts of, British society. Both tendencies were present already in 1871, although stories with a predominantly negative or paternalistic view of the workers predominated in the 1870s and 1880s. But by the time of Harmsworth's bid for a parliament seat in 1895, and in William Le Queux's forecasts from the mid-1890s onwards, there was a pronounced tendency to portray the working classes as loyal – that is, as long as they were British. In Le Queux's *The Invasion of 1910* (1906) war is described as 'a great leveller. The wealthy classes were, in proportion, losing as much as the workers'. The story also describes riots in London but these are blamed on '[t]he riff-raff from Whitechapel, those aliens whom we had so long welcomed and pampered in our midst'.[52] This was not unusual: when the narrator-journalist in H.W. Wilson and Arnold White's *When War Breaks Out* (1898) witnesses 'desperate street fighting', he notes that '[t]he crowd was largely composed of foreigners'. This mob proceeds to attack and mutilate policemen 'in true Continental style'.[53]

Le Queux includes natives in his revolutionary mob as well – 'the London unemployed and lower classes' – but Victorian commentators had long tended to describe the poorest urban dwellers, the 'residuum', as somehow foreign in themselves.[54] And when the mob runs amok in invasion-scare and related fiction, it takes on a foreign, or alien guise – the crowds in *England's Downfall*, for example, are at one point likened to the mutineers in India.[55] An Anarchist mob, on destructive rampage through London on the pages of Le Queux's *The Great War in England in 1897* (1894) sings the *Marseillaise* as they, with Le Queux's trademark heavy-handed symbolism, set the National Gallery on fire.[56] As the crowd riots in London in *The Enemy in Our Midst*, under the pressure of invasion and famine, a character is gripped by the fear that 'Great Britain was no longer a nation'. The rioting leads to the author's observation that 'it was strange that some of the worst enemies in England's midst should be Englishmen themselves; that the most

Fiction and society 163

cruel people should be Englishwomen, who had thrown aside all gentleness of sex and crushed all humanity within them'.[57] Nation as well as gender roles are here put into question – the ultimate triumph of 'alien' or 'foreign' influence.

By contrast, in *The Invasion of 1910*, a later, patriotic uprising against the German occupants in London is undertaken mostly by working-class resisters, in the working-class parts of the town.[58] A British crowd stays loyal and defends the country against invaders – whereas a crowd or mob that revolts has lost its inherent Britishness, classed in itself as somehow foreign.[59] This tendency was all the more pronounced when it came to the Celtic countries, as I return to below.

The gendered isles

As shown by the quote from *The Enemy in Our Midst* above, aside from being in a sense 'foreign', rioting crowds in invasion-scare fiction are also often female. Generally speaking, women from all classes feature in invasion-scare fiction in one of two ways: they are victims, or they form an important component part of the rioting mobs. When anarchy descends in invasion-scare and related forms of fiction, the female characteristics of the crowds are often emphasised. In Conan Doyle's blockade narrative *Danger!*, there are 'frantic mobs, composed largely of desperate women who had seen their infants perish before their eyes'.[60] Women have historically had a leading role in food-related uprisings. The price of bread played an important role in the women's march to Versailles during the French Revolution, for example,[61] but the way they form part of the crowds in invasion-scare fiction has more to do with an idea of women – and crowds in general – as somehow irrational. Gustave Le Bon, in his study of *The Crowd* – first published in English in 1896 – argued that crowds, like women, tended to extremes: they exhibited exaggerated sentiments.[62] 'Crowd theory' at the end of the century, as Joanna Bourke observes, frequently turned to gender to explain how panics broke out, seeing the 'mass' as 'feminine and thus liable to hysteria and panic'.[63] It should be noted that, although the identities of many anonymous authors of invasion-scare and related forms of fiction remain unknown, there are few indications that any of them were female.[64] While some stories have more active

164 *Authors and readers*

female characters than others,[65] it is therefore hardly surprising that women are not portrayed in more complex or flattering ways.

The 'feminine' or female nature of crowds in invasion-scare fiction also tended to make them somehow more 'foreign'. The scenes of mayhem described in Posteritas' *Siege of London* (1885) after news of an enemy landing reaches London, are described as 'resembling similar outbursts of popular fury that had so frequently disgraced Paris'. In the city, the author continues, '[w]omen went mad, and absolutely in their excitement threw themselves into the fierce flames', while 'children of tender years were tossed about like balls, and then trampled to death in the gutters'.[66] There are echoes here of the archetypal female image of the Paris Commune: the *pétroleuse*, destroying property and turning her back on her role as woman and mother. The *pétroleuse*, as Gay Gullickson has shown, was a powerful image 'not just because she embodied men's fears but because women were just as much outsiders in 1871 as they had been eighty years earlier, during the French Revolution'.[67] The *pétroleuse* was outside of society, a form of foreign or alien element, which made her even more threatening. The readers of *The Siege of London* would have been familiar with the image of an insane woman through this existing imagery. Indeed, revolution itself, Gullickson argues, could be presented as 'an unruly woman'.[68] This female, irrational and foreign quality to the crowds when they appear in invasion-scare fiction forms an important part of the symbolism of the narratives, yet it remains largely under-studied.[69]

There are also examples of women taking up arms against invaders. In *The Invasion of 1910*, for example, the working-class uprising in the area of Shoreditch and Islington is not solely male: 'Women, among them many young girls, joined in the fray, armed with pistols and knives'.[70] When the French invaders enter Edinburgh in Posteritas' *The Siege of London*, they are met by a terrifying opponent: 'Raving women, who had seen husbands, sons, sweethearts, and fathers shot down, rushed out armed with knives, pokers, and other weapons'.[71] Both Le Queux and the anonymous 'Posteritas' are eager to describe shocking scenes, however, and the women's resistance in these stories is not portrayed as exemplary – in contrast to successful British male resistance, female resistance is a sign of desperation rather than of an awakened national spirit. Women were not supposed to fight: while comments around *An Englishman's Home* (1909) often pointed out

Fiction and society 165

that the play was a wake-up call for both sexes, and that both men and women would be in the firing line if an enemy invaded,[72] they were not expected to react to the play in the same way. Men would hopefully turn to the rifle, while women should learn nursing. The Great War, as Jessica Meyer has observed, would alter traditional Edwardian ideas of masculinity and man's role in society, but there were mutterings over the challenge to gender norms in the pre-war years as well, evidenced, for example, in the reactions to the demand for women's suffrage – or 'the women's rebellion', as George Dangerfield labelled it.[73] One character in *The Enemy in Our Midst* complains that men 'have become effeminate, and women manly'. The war will hopefully lead to them finding their correct place in society again: 'in that case the young men will hurry up for voluntary service and the young women will throw aside their cigarettes and latchkeys and other idiocies and try to do some nursing and other useful work'.[74] 'I hope that not only young men will see this play, but also young women', Lord Esher observed of *An Englishman's Home*. 'They have presented to them a picture of their helplessness in face of the commonest wounds in war, which must make them realise how important a position they may occupy in the Territorial scheme'.[75] And women responded to the call: the *Penny Illustrated Paper* quoted a letter from 'Six Kensington Girls' which stated that the play had inspired them to learn nursing. '[S]hould war arise again', it stated, 'there will be, at any rate, at least half-a-dozen volunteers to the "Nursing" staff from Kensington who have made a thorough study of nursing'.[76]

More common than these variations of an active woman – either as an uncontrolled and irrational member of a crowd; as a fury taking up arms; or as a nurse, in accordance with traditional gender roles – is arguably the image of the defenceless woman, a passive victim of the aggressor. It is quite natural that there would be a skewed gender dynamic in stories where Britain is invaded by a foreign army, which would presumably be composed mainly of young men. While the foreign aggressors in invasion-scare narratives are therefore by definition masculine when they enter British civilian society, they meet a population of both men and women, young and old. The author of one invasion-scare tale in which a German army invades, observed that the army was composed of 'men who were the product of a universal military system which had brutalised them all'.[77] In *The Battle of Dorking* women and children in their

166   *Authors and readers*

villas become victims as the British lines falter under the German onslaught. There is much symbolism, both in *Dorking* and in *An Englishman's Home*, in having the invaders enter not only the country, but also forcibly occupy the private sphere of house and hearth, the traditional domain of women – and the male characters' inability to perform their traditional gender role and protect the home.[78] Even more heavy-handed symbolism can be found in references to invasion as a national rape, imagery that is perhaps unsurprising considering the gendered language of war itself. In describing the 'curious intercourse' between war and love, Paul Fussell observed that '[t]he language of military attack – *assault, impact, thrust, penetration* – has always overlapped with that of sexual importunity'.[79] As Daniel Pick has shown, the channel tunnel in particular could be presented as a form of penetration: 'The Tunnel evoked the dread not only of war and conquest, but also more subtly of miscegenation, degeneration, sexual violation and the loss of cultural identity'.[80] Such a reading is supported by Lord Randolph Churchill's oft-cited opposition to the channel tunnel in a speech he made in 1888, where he compared Britain to a 'virgo intacta' – though this was essentially a rhetorical flourish: Churchill's opposition was, after all, mostly based on economic arguments.[81]

Finally, the perceived irrationality of women meant that those who feared a 'Battle of Dorking' or invasion through a channel tunnel could in turn be presented as feminine, as with Arthur Sketchley's character 'Mrs. Brown' and her reaction to *Dorking*, discussed in chapter 1, or George Potter's comment that opposition to the channel tunnel was due to 'feminine timidity', as mentioned in chapter 3.[82] The first pages of George Meredith's *Beauchamp's Career*, a novel published in the mid-1870s, contains an entertaining description of an invasion panic earlier in the century: French soldiers' 'spectral advance on quaking London through Kentish hop-gardens, Sussex corn-fields, or by the pleasant hills of Surrey, after a gymnastic leap over the riband of salt water, haunted many pillows'. Meredith made sure to mock this panic by gendering it, thereby, as noted above, presenting it as irrational: 'Panic we will, for the sake of convenience,' he writes, 'assume to be of the feminine gender and a spinster, though properly she should be classed with the large mixed race of mental and moral neuters which are the bulk of comfortable nations'.[83] Meredith's disdain of invasion fears could hardly have been expressed more clearly than this.

Fiction and society 167

Nation and nationalities

Southern England provides the majority of the battlefields in stories where Britain is invaded, and armies trampling through Kent, Sussex and 'the pleasant hills of Surrey' formed part of the established imagery of invasion narratives from an early stage, as illustrated by Meredith's joking vision.[84] As Patrick Parrinder has pointed out, the Thames Valley became a popular destination for invading armies in a series of stories in the later nineteenth century – from Chesney to Wells' *The War of the Worlds*, via Le Queux's *The Great War in England in 1897* and *The Invasion of 1910*.[85] This should not be surprising – London, the imperial capital, is located in the south, and the channel and waters off the south coast offer the shortest distance for a continental invader to travel.[86] Robert Colls has noted that this area of Britain was open, unprotected by mountains and other natural barriers after the channel, and therefore vulnerable to invasion – but, more important than this, 'the essential England lay in the south'.[87] A similar point is made by Krishan Kumar, who describes the 'elevation of the southern English countryside to literally utopian status' in works like William Morris' *News from Nowhere* (1890).[88] There is therefore a symbolism involved in fighting in Southern England: by the end of the century, the 'south country', as Alun Howkins notes, was seen as 'the source of English culture';[89] an invader trampling through it attacked the very heart of England and Englishness. After all, as the historian R.C.K. Ensor noted in 1904, the English countryside had developed differently from its European counterparts, and was now a superior form of landscape, precisely due to its 'uninterrupted rural civilization' having been allowed to develop in peace: 'The gentry built manor-houses instead of castles; the farms, the barns, the cottages, the churches, even the hedges, were the handiwork of men who could look for comfort, and had not to look for fire and sword'.[90]

Some authors, like Le Queux, were almost gleeful in their descriptions of the consequences of the invasion on the cities. This was a regular enough trope that a German officer in P.G. Wodehouse's story *The Swoop!* (1909), which effectively satirised the entire invasion-scare genre, argues that the invaders should bombard London because 'it is always done'.[91] Yet there is a sense in many of the narratives that the real England is to be found in the countryside, in the hills around Dorking rather than the city of London, and stories therefore often

168   *Authors and readers*

focused on the image of English soil being desecrated by invaders.[92] The defenders in Louis Tracy's *The Final War* (1896), are roused by the command to 'let no d----d foreigner set foot on English soil until he steps over our dead bodies',[93] while the narrator in *Dorking* laments that he will soon be put to rest 'in the soil I have loved so well, and whose happiness and honour I have so long survived'.[94] The rural battlefield offers advantages as well as vulnerabilities, however: the invaders in Stone's *What Happened After the Battle of Dorking* are defeated – as Richard Scully points out – with the assistance of this southern English landscape, which is 'peculiarly suited to the English way of fighting'.[95] English riflemen in this story can take cover behind hedges, while the German army is denied room to manoeuvre.[96]

Landscape and locality matter in the stories: it gives an indication of what constitutes the 'nation'. The result is that smaller parts of the nation can be used symbolically, a synecdoche representing the wider community. Consequently, when French and Russian troops attack in 'The Siege of Portsmouth', discussed in the previous chapter, the city becomes a microcosm of the wider invasion and war: it is Portsmouth 'that was to witness the desecration of British soil by the foot of the foe'.[97] In Stone's pamphlet, the men of Kent take pride in their local and historical traditions of resisting invaders, and thus their role as defenders of the wider country: ' "The men of Kent have never been beaten,' as the narrator exclaims, 'and never will be" '.[98]

As fiction moved seamlessly from the local to the national level, the 'nation' could be a very inclusive category. The English focus of much invasion-scare fiction could encompass a wider 'Britishness' as well. Stone, as mentioned earlier, included Welsh miners along with the men of Kent and other defenders standing up to the invaders. Erskine Childers, author of *The Riddle of the Sands* (1903), went from British imperialist to supporter of Irish independence – illustrating, albeit with a stark example, the complexities of some authors' national loyalties. H.H. Munro, who wrote *When William Came* (1913/14) under his *nom de guerre* Saki, 'was a Highlander' as Lord Charnwood noted in the foreword of a later edition; 'and that light-footed fancy, gay or sad, in which men of Gaelic race are apt to excel, is seldom (to tell the truth) quite pleasant to mere Anglo-Saxons – the dull compatriots of Shakespeare'.[99] Even *Dorking*, with its southern English narrative, was originally published in *Blackwood's Magazine* – an Edinburgh journal. Scotland itself was

Fiction and society

169

invaded by Germans in stories like *The Invasion of 1883* and *The Channel Tunnel* (both 1876),[100] whereas it was the Russians' turn in Le Queux's *The Great War in England in 1897* – a story which also describes scenes of 'intense enthusiasm witnessed in England, Wales, and Scotland, for this was the first occasion on which the public felt the presence of invaders at their very door'.[101] The invasion in these readings unites the British nation in opposition to the invaders. This theme is brought home clearly in Posteritas' *The Siege of London*. As the French forces landing in Scotland discover,

> the Highlanders were not to be tempted from their allegiance to the British Crown. The *Bas Breton* interpreters employed by the French appealed to them as kindred Celts, but their appeals were in vain; and the country people displayed the most uncompromising hostility to the invaders.[102]

However, there are also hints at potential disunity and tension between different parts of the country. In *The Enemy in Our Midst*, the north is described as having a 'population whose lives were unknown to the Londoner, whose very language was a mystery to him, and whose concerns never aroused his interest'.[103] The most common exemption, naturally, was Ireland, which broadly features in one of two ways in invasion-scare or future-war fiction: either 'loyal', or in revolt – or, alternatively, actively supporting the invaders. The Irish are rarely equal partners with the rest of Britain in these stories. In *The Final War*, the Irish party is portrayed as an ungovernable group of schoolchildren – or perhaps something more primal:[104] 'Finding no Cabinet Minister to assail,' the story informs us, 'the Irish members consoled themselves by assailing each other'. As news of war with France and Germany reaches the floor, a Council of National Safety is set up by the Unionists and the Liberal opposition – though without the participation of the Irish nationalists. The Irish leader is instead baited into supporting the government after Joseph Chamberlain delivers a speech where he observes that the French believe Ireland is ungovernable, and rather than grant Ireland independence might instead send the Irish leaders to New Caledonia if they win the war.[105]

In the gendered language of an earlier story, *After the Battle of Dorking* (1871), Ireland and Britain are described as an unhappy couple: 'like a bickering wife, Hibernia quarrels with her husband

170 *Authors and readers*

John Bull simply because he never allows her to have another enemy'. The invasion brings the two together again: 'but now, having the opportunity, she has shown both her love and her fighting powers'.[106] When Ireland chooses to fight alongside the British, it therefore plays a subordinate role – that of a wife to a husband. The rest of Britain, on the other hand, is generally included alongside the localities of southern England in a form of expanded Englishness. The stories portray a form of 'Little Englandism' writ large, in the sense that despite their local battlefields, they encompass a wider idea of what it meant to belong to England and Britain. This inclusive Englishness could comprise the settler empire as well.

Race and empire

A common theme in stories where Britain triumphs in the face of invasion or adversity is the wielding together of a united society. In Tracy's *The Final War*, the British unite together as 'one race, one empire, one people, one party'.[107] However, as noted above, the Irish featured awkwardly in this national, or racial unity. According to Linda Colley, a British national identity was 'forged' through a process where Britons defined themselves against what they were not, primarily Catholic France, with which Britain fought a series of wars in the eighteenth century. This meant that a Catholic Ireland was difficult to reconcile within the national identity.[108] As Colley also observed, this 'Otherness' extended to the inhabitants of the British overseas empire, too – something that was increasingly apparent into the nineteenth century.[109]

That said, the empire and imperial subjects featured in invasion-scare fiction, in its various forms, in more complex ways. British fantastic fiction was partially shaped by ideas of the imperial periphery intruding on the centre. For Patrick Brantlinger, invasion-scare stories are linked with the imperial-gothic and decadence fiction of the late nineteenth century. Invasion-scare fiction as well as works like Bram Stoker's *Dracula* (1897) and H.G. Wells' *The War of the Worlds* (first serialised in 1897) are examples of British imperialism imagined in reverse.[110] This imperial connection means that invasion-scare fiction, which by definition includes an enemy attack or threat of such, also has a lot in common with 'decline narratives' of the same period, which

Fiction and society 171

do not necessarily feature external antagonists. There were numerous stories purporting to tell of *The Decline and Fall of the British Empire* throughout the pre-Great War years; narratives bearing this title were published in Britain in 1881,[111] 1890[112] and 1905.[113]

Beyond illustrating decline, 'imperialism in reverse' or imperial overstretch,[114] stories often presented the empire as a source of strength, as when contingents from settler colonies as well as 'dark-faced Indians in turbans' fight against the invaders on the streets of London in *The Invasion of 1910*.[115] Le Queux's invasion stories also specifically include descriptions of Anglo-Saxon unity across spatial distances. Canada and Australia, settler colonies within the British world, are often joined by the United States in supporting Britain, in an imagined alliance between the Anglo-Saxon peoples. In *The Cruise of the Anti-Torpedo* (1871) – a satirical story ostensibly taking place in the aftermath of the events in Chesney's *Dorking* – a lone British warship engages the combined navies of Europe in battle. As the US navy enters the scene, the crew of the eponymous Anti-Torpedo at first assume the Americans – 'our own [cousins]' – have joined their enemies. However, it turns out that the 'Yankee navy' is there to join with, not fight against, Britain in a union of *'America and old England against the World'*.[116] Satire works by emphasising existing prejudices and ideas, and while this story was tongue-in-cheek, the theme was common enough throughout the period. Imperial possessions – primarily settler colonies – were presented as favoured destinations for expatriate Britons after a successful invasion,[117] but alongside them the United States could also be a possible escape. *The Invasion of England* (1882), written by William Francis Butler, tells the reader that '[t]his story is supposed to be told in America'.[118] The US is also the chosen destination for the House of Lords in *The Battle of Newry*, a tract describing chaos in Ireland as a result of Liberal legislation. In this story, after the Lords emigrate, a group of British landowners also set up a semi-autonomous colony in Manitoba, naming it 'Lesser Britain'.[119]

Other authors dreamed of including the United States in a future federated empire, with one portraying the Republic as a 'larger, happier and freer England across the seas'.[120] A racial unity with the United States makes the former colonies preferable to an escape to non-white-majority colonies. In Saki's *When William Came*, the British monarch has fled to Delhi, where 'the king across the water'

172 *Authors and readers*

presides over a 'half-Asiatic court'.[121] There is not much left of the *British* empire in this story; its identity has been supplanted by a degenerate foreignness, like so many perfumed soldiers and effeminate governors occupying wealthy outposts in the eastern part of the Roman empire, two millennia earlier.

The racial connections between the old and new Britains indicate that the 'soil' is not necessarily the most important part of 'Englishness' in these narratives. The aforementioned 'Anti-Torpedo', for example, is described as the last true vestige of England; in another story the inhabitants of Heligoland affirm their identity as British subjects by travelling to Australia.[122] Central to such ideas was the link between the people and the sea: Britain's old wooden walls, its Royal Navy, were also wooden bridges, tying the British world together, though 'wood' was of course an anachronism by the turn of the century. It should be noted that the preoccupation with an idealised rural identity did not necessarily involve a regressive, anti-modernist mentality, despite an affinity for undisturbed rural landscapes in both fiction and other writings of the period.[123] Fantasies of a rural England were compatible with the industry that had supplanted it: it takes an industrialised society to produce thinking where industry, or certain aspects of industrialisation, can be seen as something negative.

Technological knowledge could in fact be presented as an inherent trait of racial identity, as evident in the racialised narratives of a clash between 'white' and 'yellow' civilisation, popular from the 1890s onwards. In future-war stories describing racial or civilisational threats, such as the 'Yellow Peril' stories penned by authors like Patrick Vaux and M.P. Shiel, where 'Asiatic' fleets and armies square off with European and North American counterparts, the 'us' versus 'them' trope is taken to its logical extreme.[124] In Vaux's 'The Man Who Stopped a War' (1909), a British fleet defeats a Japanese opponent aiming to conquer the Antipodes: 'Not this time was the "Nightmare of the Pacific" to inflict the horrors of invasion on Australia – that Island Continent, irreconcilably "white," and repelling the Yellow Peril in her civil life and governance'.[125] In stories like Shiel's 1898 novel *The Yellow Danger*, European nations set aside their differences in defence of civilisation itself – a common European racial identity is discovered in the face of the threat from Asia. Whether intentional or not, this pan-Europeanness was echoed in writings by academics like Sir Halford Mackinder, the

Fiction and society

father of modern geopolitics. Whereas individual nations were shaped by external threats – what Mackinder termed 'the pressure of common tribulation' – European civilisation was itself shaped by, in Mackinder's phrase, 'the secular struggle against Asiatic invasion'.[126] With the sea becoming an asset rather than a barrier to communication in the era after Columbus' discoveries, Britain, according to Mackinder, had moved from the periphery to the centre of the world.[127] Mackinder also speculated that European sea power could be challenged by the rise of an Asian land power. This is exactly what Shiel had described in *The Yellow Danger*, where 'white Europe' – led by Britain – fields a 'new Armada' against 'yellow Asia', after the Europeans have initially fought among themselves.[128] David Glover observes that this is 'a tale of multiple outsiders; or, rather, of the realignment of outsider statuses through the intervention of racial categories'.[129] A European identity is thereby, along the lines of Mackinder's theory, reshaped through a struggle against Asian invasion – and the British idea of 'us' is expanded to include all the nations of white Europe.

Throughout the period between 1871 and 1914, the British public, therefore, featured in more complex ways in invasion-scare fiction than a simple analysis of class, or even nation can explain. The public, 'us', from gender and class divisions, through local, national, imperial and racial identities, is presented as a complex and shifting entity. The stories included their readers by portraying them as part of a threatened group in a variety of ways, meaning that the texts also excluded other groups, seen as threatening 'others', depending on the narrative. How the British public were portrayed in these stories is one thing; how they read and engaged with them is a different issue. This will be explored in the next chapter.

Notes

1 'An Ex-Revolutionist' [pseud.], *England's Downfall: or, the Last Great Revolution* (London: Digby, Long & Co., [1893]).

2 T.E. Kebbel, 'The Radical Rush', *National Review* (April 1893), 162.

3 The ILP was formed in Bradford in January of that year: G.R. Searle, *A New England? Peace and War, 1886–1918* (Oxford: Clarendon Press, 2004), 232.

174 *Authors and readers*

4 See John Quail, *The Slow Burning Fuse: The Lost History of the British Anarchists* (London: Paladin Books, 1978), 162–163, 190–191; and Bernard Porter, *The Origins of the Vigilant State: The London Metropolitan Police Special Branch before the First World War* (London: Weidenfeld and Nicolson, 1987), 98–113. For a more recent study of anarchism in Britain, see Constance Bantman, *The French Anarchists in London, 1880–1914: Exile and Transnationalism in the First Globalisation* (Liverpool: Liverpool University Press, 2013), who observes that '[t]he terrorist scandals of the early 1890s reinforced the widespread belief that London was the ideological and organisational headquarters of the anarchist International' (109).

5 Anon., *The Doom of the County Council of London* (London: W.H. Allen and Co., Limited, 1892). The prospect of a revolutionary London County Council (LCC) was, of course, rather far-fetched; but debates in the aftermath of the 1888 Local Government Act often focused on the radical tendencies inherent in the LCC. Such accusations were hardly laid to rest when the Socialist John Burns, who was elected to the council when it was set up in 1889, penned a provocatively titled essay on 'The London County Council: Towards a Commune' in March 1892 – evoking the ghost of Paris in 1871: *Nineteenth Century* (March 1892), 496–514. When the essay title was criticised (R.E. Prothero, 'The London County Council: Towards Common Sense', *Nineteenth Century* (March 1892), 515–524), Burns doubled down with a passionate defence of the Paris Commune. 'A commune means to me', he wrote, 'as it meant to the workers of Paris, a free city in a free country – a community possessing all the powers of a free people for its civic, social, physical and artistic development, uncontrolled by any power other than that to which it voluntary consents': 'Let London Live', *Nineteenth Century* (April 1892), 674. I am grateful to Laura Forster for informing me of this exchange.

6 J. Twells Brex, *The Civil War of 1915* (London: C. Arthur Pearson, Ltd., 1912), 17 and *passim*. The story had originally been serialised, under the pseudonym 'St. Giles', in the *Sporting Times*, between 6 January and 16 March 1912.

7 Matthew Beaumont, 'Cacotopianism, the Paris Commune, and England's Anti-Communist Imaginary, 1870–1900', *English Literary History*, 73 (2006), 465–468.

8 Bracebridge Hemyng, *The Commune in London; or, Thirty Years Hence: A Chapter of Anticipated History* (London: C.H. Clarke, [1871]); 'Posteritas' [pseud.], *The Siege of London* (London: Wyman & Sons, 1885).

9 Darko Suvin, *Victorian Science Fiction in the UK: The Discourses of Knowledge and of Power* (Boston: G.K. Hall & Co., 1983), 342.

Fiction and society

10 Thomas Hippler, *Governing from the Skies: A Global History of Aerial Bombing*, transl. David Fernbach (London and New York: Verso, 2017), 14–15, 88–89. On the *Jeune Ecole*, see Arthur J. Marder, *British Naval Policy, 1880–1905: The Anatomy of British Sea Power* (London: Putnam & Co., [1940]), 86–91.

11 See chapter 3.

12 Daniel Pick, *War Machine: The Rationalisation of Slaughter in the Modern Age* (New Haven and London: Yale University Press, 1993), 123.

13 Laura Otis, *Membranes: Metaphors of Invasion in Nineteenth-Century Literature, Science, and Politics* (Baltimore: Johns Hopkins University Press, 1999), 5.

14 On visual political advertisements in the late Victorian and Edwardian period, see James Thompson, ' "Pictorial Lies"? – Posters and Politics in Britain c. 1880–1914', *Past & Present,* 197 (2007), 177–210.

15 See sketches in *Tariff Reform Illustrated*, a one-penny pamphlet extolling the virtues of Tariff Reform (London: Tariff Reform League, 1904), 4–6, 29–32. On 'Dumper' and 'Herr Schmit' [sic] as advertising characters, see Frank Trentmann, *Free Trade Nation: Commerce, Consumption, and Civil Society in Modern Britain* (Oxford: Oxford University Press, 2008), 93–94.

16 J.W. Welsford, *The Reign of Terror: An Experiment in Free Trade Socialism* (London: Women's Unionist & Tariff Reform Association, [1909]), 1. The WUTRA was, despite the failures of Tariff Reform in general, a largely successful attempt at creating a grassroots Unionist organisation for women. See David Thackeray, 'Home and Politics: Women and Conservative Activism in Early Twentieth-Century Britain', *Journal of British Studies,* 49 (2010), 826–848.

17 Ernest Edwin Williams, *'Made in Germany'* (London: William Heinemann, 1896).

18 Walter Wood, *The Enemy in Our Midst: The Story of a Raid on England* (London: John Long, 1906), 8. The chapter is titled 'An Englishman in Alienland'.

19 For a discussion of this, see David French, 'Spy Fever in Britain, 1900–1915', *The Historical Journal,* 21 (1978), 355–370.

20 Bradlaugh, along with the trade unionist George Odger, makes an appearance – to take one example of this internal enemy trope – in a satirical poem from 1872, purporting to be the dream of Charles Dilke. In the poem, *The Dilkiad*, Dilke dreams of a Commune in London, and of a guillotine erected in Trafalgar Square: 'Jackdaw' [pseud.], *The Dilkiad; or the Dream of Dilke: An Anti-Republican Lay* (London: Martin, 1872).

176   *Authors and readers*

21 Charles Bathurst, *To Avoid National Starvation* (London: Hugh Rees, 1912), 7. The sentiment was endorsed by Charles Beresford in the pamphlet's preface.

22 Charles Gleig, *When All Men Starve: Showing how England Hazarded her Naval Supremacy, and the Horrors Which Followed the Interruption of Her Food Supply* (London: John Lane, 1898).

23 [Charles] Allen Clarke, *Starved into Surrender* (London: C.W. Daniel, 1904).

24 Arthur Conan Doyle, *Danger! and Other Stories* (London: John Murray, 1918), 40. The story was written around eighteen months before the outbreak of the war, as Conan Doyle noted in the preface (v). It was originally published in the *Strand Magazine* in July 1914, with several 'naval experts', including Charles Beresford, Fred T. Jane and Arnold White offering their opinions on the piece in the same issue. While some, like White, were sympathetic to the argument, most found its premise exaggerated. The story proved popular in Germany as well. At least two German-language editions were published: *England in Gefahr,* transl. Waldemar Schütze (Berlin: Curtius, 1914); and *Der Tauchbootkrieg: Wie Kapitän Sirius England Niederzwang,* transl. Konter-Admiral a.D. Sta. Schanzer, 17th edition (Stuttgart: Robert Lutz, [1915]).

25 Conan Doyle, *Danger!* vi.

26 Avner Offer, *The First World War: An Agrarian Interpretation* (Oxford: Clarendon Press, 1989), 219–220. For a discussion of the role famine played in British military planning leading up to the First World War, and its impact on the conduct of the war, see 217–317.

27 L. Cope Cornford, *The Defenceless Islands: A Study of the Social and Industrial Conditions of Great Britain and Ireland; and of the Effect upon them of the outbreak of a Maritime War* (London: E. Grant Richards, 1906), 189. The book was a detailed discussion of the findings in the Royal Commission on Supply of Food and Raw Material in Time of War, discussed below. Cornford was highly critical of the Commission's majority view.

28 Marder, *British Naval Policy,* 85. Here Marder also argues that the 'starvation theory' 'formed the core of almost every one of the booklets and pamphlets on an imaginary war of the immediate future with which England was deluged in the '90s', which is an exaggeration – though the theme was a popular one.

29 A. Hilliard Atteridge, 'National Defence: Some Neglected Conditions', *United Service Magazine,* 809 (April 1896), 4, 6.

30 Cd. 2643, *Report of the Royal Commission on Supply of Food and Raw Material in Time of War. Vol. I, The Report* (London, 1905),

Fiction and society 177

6. Offer concludes that, by 1914, close to 60 per cent of the calorific value of food in Britain was imported: *Agrarian Interpretation*, 218–219.

31 George Griffith, *The Angel of the Revolution: A Tale of the Coming Terror* (London: Tower Publishing Company Limited, 1893), 257. Sam Moskowitz notes that this book was 'possibly the best-selling future-war book of the nineteenth century', setting Griffith up as one of the decade's most popular authors: Sam Moskowitz, *Strange Horizons: The Spectrum of Science Fiction* (New York: Charles Scribner's Sons, 1976), 192.

32 HPD HC Deb 28 January 1902 vol. 101 c1131.

33 See Paul Readman, *Land and Nation in England: Patriotism, National Identity, and the Politics of Land, 1880–1914* (Woodbridge: Royal Historical Society, 2008), and Matthew Cragoe and Paul Readman, 'Introduction', in Cragoe and Readman (eds), *The Land Question in Britain, 1750–1950* (Basingstoke: Palgrave Macmillan, 2010), 1–18.

34 Cd. 2643, 38.

35 HPD HC Deb 13 May 1914 vol. 62 c1236.

36 Offer, *Agrarian Interpretation*, 222. On the Commission, see 224–225.

37 Cd. 2643, 89. In all, there were no fewer than 11 signed reservations to various parts of the report. The *Saturday Review* remarked that this meant that it 'is and must remain utterly ineffective', and that a government wishing to implement the report's conclusions 'must be influenced at least as much by the recommendations of the minority as of the majority': 12 August 1905, 203–204.

38 [George T. Chesney], *The Battle of Dorking: Reminiscences of a Volunteer* (Edinburgh and London: William Blackwood and Sons, 1871), 63–64.

39 'Posteritas', *Siege of London*, 7–8.

40 'An Ex-Revolutionist', *England's Downfall*, 38.

41 Paul M. Kennedy, *The Rise of the Anglo-German Antagonism 1860–1914* (Boston: George Allen & Unwin, 1980), 382.

42 Modris Eksteins, *Rites of Spring: The Great War and the Birth of the Modern Age* (London: Bantam Press, 1989), 177.

43 Jay Winter, *Sites of Memory, Sites of Mourning: The Great War in European Cultural History* (Cambridge: Cambridge University Press, 1996), 145.

44 Darko Suvin, *Victorian Science Fiction in the UK: the Discourses of Knowledge and of Power* (Boston: G.K. Hall & Co.,1983), 232.

45 Samuel Hynes, *The Edwardian Turn of Mind* (Princeton: Princeton University Press, 1968), 34. Harry Wood has argued that the anxiety presented in Edwardian invasion narratives was more a product

178 *Authors and readers*

of the 'Radical Right' rather than what might be understood as traditional Tory Conservatism. Harry Joseph Wood, 'External Threats Mask Internal Fears: Edwardian Invasion Literature 1899–1914' (University of Liverpool, Ph.D. thesis, 2014). I am grateful to Harry for letting me read his thesis. Also Wood, 'Radical Reactionary: The Politics of William Le Queux', *Critical Survey*, 32 (2020), 139–158.

46 J.W.M., *The Siege of London* (London: Robert Hardwicke, 1871), 41, 30.

47 The signature J.W.M. was also behind another 1871 pamphlet, *The Coming Cromwell*, where a future civil war between parliament and crown leads to the victory of a radical republican faction under the eponymous leader, taking his inspiration from his historical namesake. The new British Commonwealth, having survived a 'Teuton' invasion in support of the royal forces, proceeds to invade the continent to spread republican ideals. The pamphlet, written in the form of a future history, ends with British commonwealth rule across much of the world. This was no nightmare scenario, with 'J.W.M.' praising the original Cromwell and dreaming of both Irish Home Rule and of republican government relegating monarchy to the dustbin of history: J.W.M., *The Coming Cromwell* (London: British & Colonial Publishing Company, 1871).

48 Wood, *The Enemy in Our Midst*, 15–16.

49 As Nicola Bishop points out, '[t]he clerkly type became a crucial literary "everyman" during the early twentieth century': 'Ruralism, Masculinity and National Identity: The Rambling Clerk in Fiction, 1900–1940', *Journal of British Studies,* 54 (2015), 655. While *The Swoop of the Eagles* is from an earlier period, the choice of protagonist in the story hints at a development towards 'everyman' heroes that the readers could identify with – as well as illustrating how Britain was in the process of becoming a 'professional society', as Harold Perkin termed this period: *The Rise of Professional Society: England since 1880* (London and New York: Routledge, 2001). And the clerk, this 'everyman' creation, was of course also a newspaper reader – preferring the *Daily Mail*, as Lord Salisbury once remarked. Adrian Gregory notes that, by 1914, the 'very identity of the "clerk," culturally and politically, had in important respects been formed by this newspaper': 'A Clash of Cultures: The British Press and the Opening of the Great War', in Troy R.E. Paddock (ed.), *A Call to Arms: Propaganda, Public Opinion, and Newspapers in the Great War* (Westport: Praeger, 2004), 16. The volunteer army that marched into battle in the Great War, as Gregory notes, was composed of 'more clerks than miners and railwaymen combined', whereas the rural population largely declined

Fiction and society 179

the call to volunteer. See *The Last Great War: British Society and the First World War* (Cambridge: Cambridge University Press, 2008), 81.

50 'V.', *The Swoop of the Eagles: An Episode from the Secret History of Europe* (London: Ward and Downey, 1889), 87.

51 [Charles Stone], *What Happened after the Battle of Dorking; or, the Victory at Tunbridge Wells* (London: George Routledge and Sons, [1871]), 5. The more pessimistic Saki (H.H. Munro), writing forty years later, imagines a similar, yet more exclusive group, as his protagonist Murrey Yeovil tries to convince himself that among the participants in the East Wessex hunting season – 'small squires and yeoman farmers, doctors, country tradesmen, auctioneers and so forth' – there could be found 'the local nucleus of revolt against the enslavement of the land': *When William Came: A Story of London under the Hohenzollerns* (London: John Lane 1914 [1913]), 117–118.

52 William Le Queux, *The Invasion of 1910. With a Full Account of the Siege of London* (London: Eveleigh Nash, 1906), 280–283. Elsewhere, Le Queux is eager to portray the difference between the courageous Londoners who resist the German occupation, and the 'alien rabble of the East End' (475). For another story describing war as a leveller of class differences, see Donal Hamilton Haines, 'The Leveller', *Pall Mall Magazine* (January 1913), 13–24. See also Wood, *The Enemy in Our Midst*, where the War Secretary observes that 'we have the riff-raff of creation on our hands, to say nothing of our own dregs' (148), and where men of different classes find common cause.

53 H.W. Wilson and Arnold White, *When War Breaks Out* (London and New York: Harper Brothers, 1898), 30–31. 'The riot', as the narrator later observes, 'was not provoked or sustained by native-born English' (42).

54 Dorothy Porter, '"Enemies of the Race": Biologism, Environmentalism, and Public Health in Edwardian England', *Victorian Studies*, 34 (1991), 159–160.

55 'Ex-Revolutionist', *England's Downfall*, 101.

56 William Le Queux, *The Great War in England in 1897* (London: Tower Publishing Company Limited, 1894), 47.

57 Wood, *The Enemy in Our Midst*, 140.

58 Le Queux, *The Invasion of 1910*, 477–484.

59 The tendency to describe rioters as foreign continued into the inter-war years, and Adrian Gregory has mused that it was their own use of violence that destroyed the British Fascist movement, as its violent excesses meant that opponents could present it as un-British and alien. See Adrian Gregory, 'Peculiarities of the English? War, Violence and Politics: 1900–1939', *Journal of Modern European History*, 1 (2003), 55–56.

180 *Authors and readers*

60 Conan Doyle, *Danger!*, 41.

61 See George Rudé, *The Crowd in the French Revolution* (Oxford: Clarendon Press, 1959), 61–79.

62 Gustave Le Bon, *The Crowd: A Study of the Popular Mind* (London: T. Fisher Unwin, 1903), 56. The crowd was also, Le Bon claimed, akin to barbarians, or bacteria: 'In consequence of the purely destructive nature of their power, crowds act like those microbes which hasten the dissolution of enfeebled or dead bodies' (19).

63 Joanna Bourke, *Fear: A Cultural History* (London: Virago, 2005), 62. See also 65–66.

64 The narrator in the short pamphlet *Gortschakoff and Bismarck, or Europe in 1940: A Dream* (Oxford: James Parker and Co., 1878), is a woman, which is unusual, and could possibly indicate that the author was also a woman. The pamphlet describes a war between Britain on the one hand, and Germany, Austria and Russia on the other, but without an invasion of Britain. It all ends up being, as the title suggests, 'a dream'. Anonymity influenced the way Victorian audiences approached writings, as James A. Secord notes of a different type of work published earlier in the century: 'controversy about the authorship demonstrates the power of readers as makers of meaning. Any conjecture expressed a reading of the work's politics, gender, religion, and expertise'. *Victorian Sensation: The Extraordinary Publication, Reception, and Secret Authorship of* Vestiges of the Natural History of Creation (Chicago and London: University of Chicago Press, 2003) 23. See also Rachel Sagner Buurma, 'Anonymity, Corporate Authority, and the Archive: The Production of Authorship in Late-Victorian England', *Victorian Studies*, 50 (2007), 15–42.

65 See, for example, George Griffith's Natasha in *The Angel of the Revolution*; and the eponymous character in its sequel, *Olga Romanoff: Or, the Syren of the Skies* (London: Tower Publishing Company Limited, 1894). Among more traditional invasion-scare narratives, a woman plays an important role in Robert Cromie's *For England's Sake* (London and New York: Frederick Warne and Co., 1889), where India is invaded by Russia; however, the woman in question serves more as an object of desire than a protagonist. Similar female characters can be found in, among other stories, Anon., *England's Danger; or, Rifts within the Lute. A Russian Plot* (Portsmouth: Griffin & Co., 1889); and 'An Ex-Revolutionist', *England's Downfall*.

66 'Posteritas', *Siege of London*, 33. In Bracebridge Hemyng, *The Commune in London; or, Thirty Years Hence: A Chapter of Anticipated History* (London: C.H. Clarke, [1871]), working-class

Fiction and society 181

women also take up arms against the rightful government: 'The more violent [women] among the lower orders formed themselves into a body called the Amazons of the East, and were regularly armed and instructed. The partial defence of the barricades ... was entrusted to those desperate viragos, who were the first to begin to talk openly of "death" for all enemies of the Commune' (17).

67 Gay L. Gullickson, *Unruly Women of Paris: Images of the Commune* (Ithaca: Cornell University Press, 1996), 223.

68 Gullickson, *Unruly Women*, 225. See also 218–228.

69 Though the links between *pétroleuses* and the women in Le Queux's descriptions of warfare in London has been pointed out by Antony Taylor, '"At the Mercy of the German Eagle": Images of London in Dissolution in the Novels of William Le Queux', *Critical Survey*, 32 (2020), 64–65.

70 Le Queux, *The Invasion of 1910*, 482.

71 'Posteritas', *Siege of London*, 49.

72 See, for example, *Daily Mail*, 2 February 1909, 4.

73 Jessica Meyer, *Men of War: Masculinity and the First World War in Britain* (Basingstoke: Palgrave Macmillan, 2009); George Dangerfield, *The Strange Death of Liberal England* (New York: Perigee Books, 1980), 139.

74 Wood, *The Enemy in Our Midst*, 115.

75 *Daily Mail*, 29 January 1909.

76 *Penny Illustrated Paper*, 13 February 1909, 3.

77 Wood, *The Enemy in Our Midst*, 100. However, the story did not object to voluntary service (115), and the book ends with the 'lesson' that 'universal military service in Great Britain is essential' (320).

78 On this aspect of masculinity, see Meyer, *Men of War*, 6; and John Tosh, *A Man's Place: Masculinity and the Middle-Class Home in Victorian England* (New Haven and London: Yale University Press, 1999), 3, 6–7. See also John Tosh, *Manliness and Masculinities in Nineteenth-Century Britain: Essays on Gender, Family and Empire* (Harlow: Pearson Longman, 2005), esp. 192–209. As Eloise Moss has shown, late Victorian and Edwardian insurance sellers made use of a 'culture of fear', exacerbating existing fears about burglars, to sell insurance: 'Burglary Insurance and the Culture of Fear in Britain, c. 1889–1939', *The Historical Journal*, 54 (2011), 1039–1064. The image of 'Herr Dumper' as a burglar, mentioned earlier, is an example of how the images of foreign intrusion and burglary coexisted and played on each other. The similarities between burglaries, or home invasions, and foreign or military invasion are many, as A. Michael Matin has also noted: '"We Aren't German Slaves Here, Thank

God": Conrad's Transposed Nationalism and British Literature of Espionage and Invasion', *Journal of Modern Literature*, 21 (1997–1998), 270–271, notes 67 and 69.

79 Paul Fussell, *The Great War and Modern Memory* (Oxford, 2000), 270. Italics in the original.

80 Pick, *War Machine*, 121.

81 HPD HC Deb 27 June 1888 vol. 327 c1500. The Randolph Churchill quote is mentioned in Pick, *War Machine*, 131, but the assertion that it was 'reciprocal penetration which so horrified the [channel tunnel] scheme's opponents' is somewhat exaggerated.

82 Arthur Sketchley [George Rose], *Mrs. Brown on The Battle of Dorking* (London, [1871]); George Potter, *The Channel Tunnel and International Progress* (London: 14 Fetter Lane, [1882]), 14.

83 George Meredith, *Beauchamp's Career*, 3 vols. (London: Chapman & Hall, 1876), I, 2–4.

84 Meredith lived at Flint Cottage on Box Hill, near the battlefields in *Dorking*, for over forty years until his death in 1909. The ashes of the 'Sage of Box Hill' are buried in Dorking cemetery: Margaret Harris, 'Meredith, George (1828–1909)', ODNB.

85 As well as being the scene of natural disasters and catastrophes. Patrick Parrinder, 'From Mary Shelley to *The War of the Worlds*: The Thames Valley Catastrophe', in David Seed (ed.), *Anticipations: Essays on Early Science Fiction and Its Precursors* (Syracuse: Syracuse University Press, 1995), 58.

86 Thanet, in Kent, has historically been a favoured landing spot for invaders – so much so that it is a running joke in W.C. Sellar and R.J. Yeatman, *1066 and All That* (London: Penguin Books, 1962), first published in 1930. However, as Alan H. Burgoyne points out in his invasion story, *The War Inevitable* (London: Francis Griffiths, 1908): 'It is a strange fact that in all works of fiction dealing with future wars, and in which an invasion of these Isles is attempted, the rising town of Worthing is almost invariably chosen for the hostile landing' (115). However, as a map of invasion routes in a selection of invasion literature shows, invaders tended to land and ramble across much of southern England: See map in Franco Moretti, *Atlas of the European Novel, 1800–1900* (London and New York: Verso, 2009), 139. Burgoyne's comment is an indication of how self-referential and, in a sense, mature the genre had become by the Edwardian era. Many stories made a point out of playing up their own artificiality and their own fictitious nature: on this, see Christian K. Melby, 'Rethinking British Militarism before the First World War: The Case of *An*

Fiction and society 183

Englishman's Home (1909)', *English Historical* Review, 137 (2022), 1398–1399.

87 Robert Colls, 'Englishness and the Political Culture', in Robert Colls and Philip Dodd (eds), *Englishness: Politics and Culture 1880–1920* 2nd edition (London: Bloomsbury Academic, 2014), 69.

88 Krishan Kumar, *The Making of English National Identity* (Cambridge: Cambridge University Press, 2003), 211.

89 Alun Howkins, 'The Discovery of Rural England', in Colls and Dodd, *Englishness*, 95.

90 R.C.K. Ensor, 'The English Countryside', in Lucian Oldershaw (ed.), *England: A Nation. Being the Papers of the Patriots' Club* (London and Edinburgh: R. Brimley Johnson, 1904), 96–97. Though this reading required Ensor to classify the English Civil War somewhat awkwardly as a 'singularly humane war', characterised by 'wonderful moderation' – at least in comparison with the fighting in the Thirty Years' War on the continent.

91 P.G. Wodehouse, *The Swoop! Or, How Clarence Saved England* (London: Alston Rivers, 1909), 36. Scarborough, which was bombarded by the German navy in December 1914, was a favourite target for naval bombardment in pre-Great War stories as well: See 'Untruthful Thomas' [pseud.], *The Bombardment of Scarbro' by the Russian Fleet in 1891* (London: The Crown Printing Company, [1889]); 'A. Nelson Seaforth' [George Sydenham Clarke], *The Last Great Naval War: An Historical Retrospect* (London: Cassell & Company, Limited, 1891); The Earl of Mayo [Dermot Bourke], *The War Cruise of the 'Aries'* (Dublin: Edward Ponsonby, 1894). Visions of a London in ruins has a long pedigree in British culture: see Antony Taylor, *London's Burning: Pulp Fiction, the Politics of Terrorism and the Destruction of the Capital in British Popular Culture, 1840–2005* (London: Bloomsbury, 2013); and Taylor, 'Images of London'.

92 A negative outlook on metropolitan life was common across the political spectrum by the turn of the century. Arnold White decried the unsanitary and crowded conditions of modern cities in *The Problems of a Great City* (London: Remington & Co. Publishers, 1886) and *Efficiency and Empire* (London: Methuen & Co., 1901), 95–121 and *passim*. J.A. Hobson believed the routine of city life had weakened its inhabitants' minds, and made them more amenable to Jingoism as a consequence: *The Psychology of Jingoism* (London: Grant Richards, 1901), 8.

93 Louis Tracy, *The Final War: A Story of the Great Betrayal* (London: C. Arthur Pearson Limited, 1896), 25.

184 *Authors and readers*

94 [Chesney], *Dorking*, 64. Chesney's narrator also encounters occupying troops using looted silverware to eat beef – food long associated with old ideas of Englishness and liberty – adding a symbolic defeat to the military disaster (57). On the symbolism of beef, see Ben Rogers, *Beef and Liberty: Roast Beef, John Bull and the English Nation* (London: Vintage, 2004).

95 Richard Scully, *British Images of Germany: Admiration, Antagonism & Ambivalence, 1860–1914* (Basingstoke: Palgrave Macmillan, 2012), 97.

96 [Stone], *After Dorking*, 56. 35 years later, another author reached a different conclusion, in a story where British arms are again defending (and losing) against a German invader in the area between Dorking and Guildford. The English countryside, the anonymous author notes, is 'more suitable to attack than to defence', though it may be utilised for delaying actions: 'General Staff' [pseud.], *The Writing on the Wall* (London: William Heinemann, 1906), 97.

97 *Mail,* Monday 18 June 1895, 1.

98 [Stone], *After Dorking*, 50.

99 Lord Charnwood [Godfrey Benson], 'Introduction', in 'Saki' (H.H. Munro), *When William Came: A Story of London under the Hohenzollerns* (London: John Lane/The Bodley Head, Ltd., 1926), viii. Although this seems condescending, Charnwood was full of praise for Saki's literary prognostication.

100 Anon., *The Invasion of 1883: A Chapter from the Book of Fate* (Glasgow: James Maclehose, 1876), 18; 'Cassandra', *The Channel Tunnel; or, England's Ruin* (London: Wm. Clowes and Sons, 1876), 27.

101 Le Queux, *The Great War,* 22.

102 'Posteritas', *Siege of London*, 42. A satirical inversion of this is a story written by the pseudonymous 'Jingo Jones, M.P.', titled *The Sack of London by the Highland Host: A Romance of the Period* (London: Simpkin, Marshall, Hamilton, Kent, & Co., Ltd., 1900).

103 Wood, *The Enemy in Our Midst*, 94.

104 As L. Perry Curtis, Jr. has shown, the English stereotype of the Irish in the Victorian era was frequently that of a simian, or ape-man: *Apes and Angels: The Irishman in Victorian Caricature* (Newton Abbot: David and Charles, 1971). However, R.F. Foster has argued that the Irish were presented in more complex ways in British culture than Curtis acknowledges: *Paddy and Mr. Punch: Connections in Irish and English History* (London: Allen Lane, 1993), in particular 171–194. The Irish are, however, generally speaking portrayed as caricatures in invasion-scare and related forms of fiction. The narrator's

Irish valet – called 'Pat', of course – in Edward Lester's *The Siege of Bodike* (1886) is described as a 'faithful native', in what is perhaps an unintentional nod to how the Irish could be seen as foreign, like the natives of imperial possessions elsewhere. See *The Siege of Bodike: A Prophecy of Ireland's Future* (London: John Heywood, 1886), 15. This is a story of an Irish rebellion, not an invasion text, though there are foreign influences involved. W. Douglas Newton, himself Irish, wrote with more understanding and sympathy of the Irish plight in a story published right before the outbreak of the First World War that portrayed a revolt in Ulster: *The North Afire: A Picture of What May Be* (London: Methuen & Co., Ltd., 1914). Here, a colonel complains, '[g]ood men on each side are at each other's throats, and ourselves [the army] in the middle' (63).

105 Tracy, *The Final War*, 15, 18–19. A similar argument – that the foreign yoke will be far worse than rule from London – is outlined in a story published in 1917: 'Baron von Kartoffel' [pseud.], *The Germans in Cork: Being the letters of His Excellency the Baron von Kartoffel (Military Governor of Cork in the year 1918) and Others* (Dublin: The Talbot Press Ltd., 1917).

106 Anon., *After the Battle of Dorking; or What Became of the Invaders!* (London: George Maddick, 1871), 14–15.

107 Tracy, *The Final War*, 18. See also, for example, Wood, *The Enemy in Our Midst*, 290.

108 Linda Colley, *Britons: Forging the Nation 1707–1837* (London: Pimlico, 1994).

109 Linda Colley, 'Britishness and Otherness: An Argument', *Journal of British Studies*, 31 (1992), 311, 316. Catholicism as a foreign 'invader' was the theme of some stories on the fringes of the wider invasion-scare genre. Thomas Godfrey Jack, *Anti-Papa: or, the Invasion of England by the Priests of Satan* (London: C.T. Lipshytz, [1895]), while not a work of fiction, portrayed the Catholic church as no less than a satanic-influenced threat to England, while Allen Upward was more tongue in cheek in his description of a Catholic subjugation in *The Fourth Conquest of England* (London: The Tyndale Press, [1904]), where a German invasion is also included for good measure. Of note is also the fact that at least some invasion-scare texts had clear antisemitic undertones. Interestingly, however, in the story *The Swoop of the Eagles*, the 'Bosschild' family – an obvious allusion to the Jewish Rothschilds – use their international financial network to ensure that Britain's enemies are prevented from descending upon the country (V. *Swoop of the Eagles*, 77–86). Along with gender, religious imagery – in particular eschatology and apocalyptic elements – and

186　　　*Authors and readers*

the portrayal of religious 'others' remain a largely understudied part of invasion-scare literature. On 'the apocalyptic imagination in art' before 1914, see Winter, *Sites of Memory*, 145–177. For an interesting discussion of religion in early science fiction in general, see Moskowitz, *Strange Horizons*, 3–49.

110 Patrick Brantlinger, *The Rule of Darkness: British Literature and Imperialism, 1830–1914* (Ithaca: Cornell University Press, 1988), 233. Matin, referring to Brantlinger and Joseph S. Meisel ('The Germans are Coming! British Fiction of a German Invasion, 1871–1913' in *War, Literature and the Arts*, 2 (1990), 41–79) argues that invasion-scare fiction 'illustrates the imperial imagination turned in upon itself' (' "We Aren't German Slaves Here, Thank God": Conrad's Transposed Nationalism and British Literature of Espionage and Invasion', *Journal of Modern Literature*, 21 (1997–1998), 254). See also Ailise Bulfin, ' "To Arms!": Invasion Narratives and Late-Victorian Literature', *Literature Compass*, 12 (2015), 482–496; and Tom Reiss, 'Imagining the Worst: How a Literary Genre Anticipated the Modern World', *The New Yorker*, 28 Nov 2005, 106–114. On Wells, see Ingo Cornils, 'The Martians are Coming! War, Peace, Love and Reflection in H.G. Wells's *The War of the Worlds* and Kurd Laßwitz's *Auf Zwei Planeten*', in Fred Bridgham (ed.), *The First World War as a Clash of Cultures* (Rochester, NY: Camden House, 2006), 129–143. Cornils sees *The War of the Worlds*, as 'a satirical mirror that turns all the colonial powers into well-organized Martian colonies' (133).

111 'Lang-Tung' [pseud.], *The Decline and Fall of the British Empire. Being a History of England between the Years 1840–1981* (London: F.V. White and Co., 1881).

112 [H.C.M. Watson], *The Decline and Fall of the British Empire; or, the Witch's Cavern* (London: Trischler & Company, 1890).

113 [E.E. Mills], *The Decline and Fall of the British Empire* (Oxford: Alden & Co., Ltd., Bocardo Press, 1905). In the same vein, a short story in the September 1911 issue of *Strand Magazine* described a New Zealand expedition to the former metropole, a reference to Thomas Macaulay's vision of a future New Zealander visiting the ruins of London in the future; Macaulay was quoted on the first page of the story, in case anyone missed the point: 'Prof. Blyde Muddersnook' [pseud.], 'When the New Zealander Comes', *Strand Magazine* (September 1911), 284–291. See also Grant Allen, *The British Barbarians: A Hill-top Novel* (London: John Lane, 1895); and H.D. Traill, *The Barbarous Britishers: A Tip-top Novel* (London: John Lane, [1896]), a parody of Allen's story. On 'degeneration' in British

Fiction and society 187

fiction, see Daniel Pick, *Faces of Degeneration: A European Disorder, c.1848-c.1918* (Cambridge: Cambridge University Press, 1989), 155–175.

114 On overstretch, see, for example, [Chesney], *Dorking*, 7.

115 Le Queux, *The Invasion of 1910*, 531. The various ways in which the empire, racial identities and national identity could overlap and contradict each other in invasion-scare and future-war fiction is discussed in more detail in Christian K. Melby, 'Empire and Nation in British Future-War and Invasion-Scare Fiction, 1871–1914', *Historical Journal*, 63 (2020), 389–410. Some of the remarks made in the final paragraphs of this chapter have previously been made or expanded on in this article.

116 Anon., *The Cruise of the Anti-Torpedo* (London: Tinsley Brothers, 1871), 43–44. Italics in the original.

117 See, for example, Anon., *Europa's Fate: or the Coming Struggle. A History Lesson in New Zealand, A.D. 2076* (London: Griffith and Farran, 1875); and William Delisle Hay, *The Doom of the Great City; being the Narrative of a Survivor, written A.D. 1942* (London: Newman & Co., [1880]), two stories were natural disaster plays a role. See also 'An Ex-Revolutionist', *England's Downfall*, and Upward, *The Fourth Conquest;* as well as the 'Decline and Fall' narratives above.

118 'An Old Soldier' [William F. Butler], *The Invasion of England: Told Twenty Years After* (London: Sampson Low, Marston, Searle, & Rivington, 1882), 4.

119 'Ulidia' [pseud.], *The Battle of Newry: Or the Result of Thirty Years' Liberal Legislation,* 2nd edition (Dublin: Hodges, Figgis, and Co., 1883), 10, 15.

120 'A. Nelson Seaforth' [George Sydenham Clarke], *The Last Great Naval War: An Historical Retrospect* (London: Cassell & Company, Limited, [1891]), 4. See also Geoffrey Danyers, *Blood is Thicker than Water: A Political Dream* (London: Tower Publishing Company Limited, 1894), which was dedicated to 'All true Britons and to all true Americans', as well as to George Clarke.

121 'Saki', *When William Came* (1914), 53.

122 'Motly Ranke McCauley' [pseud.], *The Battle of Berlin (Die Slacht von Königsberg)* 5th edition (London: Tinsley Brothers, 1890 [1871]), 53. Anon., *Anti-Torpedo*, 14–15.

123 I am referring here to the theory of 'declinism' postulated, for example, in Martin J. Wiener, *English Culture and the Decline of the Industrial Spirit, 1850–1980* (Cambridge: Cambridge University Press, 1981). For two different critiques of Wiener, see Peter Mandler, 'Against "Englishness": English Culture and the Limits to Rural

188 *Authors and readers*

Nostalgia, 1850–1940', *Transactions of the Royal Historical Society* (1997), 155–175; and Paul Readman, 'The Place of the Past in English Culture, c. 1890–1914', *Past & Present*, 186 (2005), 147–199.

124 On the 'yellow peril', see John Kuo Wei Tchen and Dylan Yeats (eds), *Yellow Peril! An Archive of Anti-Asian Fear* (London and New York: Verso, 2014). David Glover notes that the 'Yellow Peril' was pan-European, originating in Germany in the 1890s. David Glover, *'Die Gelbe Gefahr, le Péril Jaune,* the Yellow Peril: the Geopolitics of a Fear', in Kate Hebblethwaite and Elizabeth McCarthy (eds), *Fear: Essays on the Meaning and Experience of Fear* (Dublin: Four Courts Press, 2007), 47–59. Japan, a British *ally* by the Edwardian era, could also feature as a stalwart supporter of Britain, alongside its colonial contingents, in such stories as Alan H. Burgoyne, *The War Inevitable* (London: Francis Griffiths, 1908).

125 Patrick Vaux, 'The Man Who Stopped a War', *Pall Mall Magazine* (June 1909), 727. Visions of Asian invasion, and of miscegenation and loss of cultural identity were prevalent in the US as well around the turn of the century. In Vaux's 'War and a Woman' (*The Idler* (June 1909), 269–275), an American fleet squares off with a Japanese navy attempting to wrest control of the Philippines and Hawaii from the United States. The American author Jack London wrote extensively on the 'yellow peril': see John N. Swift, 'Jack London's "The Unparalleled Invasion": Germ Warfare, Eugenics, and Cultural Hygiene', *American Literary Realism*, 35 (2002), 59–71.

126 H.J. Mackinder, 'The Geographical Pivot of History', *Geographical Journal*, 23 (1904), 421–437. In discussing future developments, Mackinder referred to the potential might of a Russian empire in control of the 'Pivot Area' in Eurasia. But, as the final lines of the paper observed: 'Were the Chinese, for instance, organized by the Japanese, to overthrow the Russian Empire and conquer its territory, they might constitute the yellow peril to the world's freedom just because they would add an oceanic frontage to the resources of the great continent, an advantage as yet denied to the Russian tenant of the pivot region' (437). Japan could be envisioned as either opponent or ally in theories outlining the dangers of Asia.

127 See H.J. Mackinder, *Britain and the British Seas* (London: William Heinemann, 1902), 4.

128 M.P. Shiel, *The Yellow Danger* (London: Grant Richards, 1898), 320. On sea power against land power, see comments by Spenser Wilkinson and Mackinder in 'The Geographical Pivot of History – Discussion', *Geographical Journal*, 23 (1904), 437–444.

129 Glover, 'Geopolitics of a Fear', 51–52.

6

Readers and receptions: the British public as audience and consumers, from the 1870s to the Edwardian high point

On 24 January 1902, H.G. Wells took the stage at the Royal Institution and delivered a paper on 'The Discovery of the Future'.[1] There existed, he postulated, two types of mind: the dominant one, the mind of the majority of people, was oriented towards the past, towards precedent – he described this as the mind of the lawyer. This was in contrast to a more modern type – and Wells presumably placed himself in this category – which was oriented towards the future. This was the creative, the legislative and the masterful mind.[2] Wells was arguing that, just as science had expanded our knowledge of the past, humans should now turn towards investigating what the future might look like.

Wells' fiction had, of course, already done this, for instance in his description of a journey to a dystopian future in *The Time Machine* (1895).[3] However, in a series of 'Anticipations', published in the *Fortnightly Review* between April and December 1901, he argued against using fiction to predict the developments of the next century. Even though there existed an abundance of fictional forecasts – '*Stories of the Year* 2000, and *Battles of Dorking*, and the like' – Wells thought these suffered from being 'concrete and definite', therefore permitting no 'open alternatives':

> The very form of fiction carries with it something of disavowal; indeed, very much of the Fiction of the Future pretty frankly abandons the prophetic altogether and becomes polemical, cautionary or idealistic, and a mere footnote and commentary to our present discontents.[4]

At this stage in life, Wells turned more towards non-fictional analyses of the future. He would, however, continue to write fictional

190 *Authors and readers*

forecasts, such as *The War in the Air* (1908). It might therefore seem curious that one of the most famous authors of fantastic fiction would deprecate the use of his own medium. Wells was obviously not opposed to all fictional speculation. In his lecture he praised M.P. Shiel's *The Purple Cloud* (1901), a story about the last man left alive on Earth.[5] But he mocks Bert Smallways, his own protagonist in *The War in the Air*, who gets interested in flight after reading a 'sixpenny edition of that aeronautic classic, Mr. George Griffith's "The Outlaws of the Air"'.[6] Despite the tongue-in-cheek description of Bert as 'a progressive Smallways', the hero of his future-war story was hardly the kind of man Wells imagined as a discoverer of the future, and his choice of reading material is not meant to reflect well on Griffith, or on the readers of this kind of fiction.[7]

Wells was not alone in his assessment: the July 1901 issue of the *Fortnightly Review* – where the fourth instalment in Wells' 'Anticipations' also appeared – contained an article by William Laird Clowes titled 'The Cheapening of Useful Books'. 'With comparatively few exceptions', Clowes argued, 'the only very cheap books to be had in England are novels – books, that is, which are primarily amusing rather than instructive and useful'.[8] Clowes had himself produced 'instructive and useful' works; under the pseudonym 'Nauticus' he had written extensively about naval issues, and was in 1901 in the process of compiling a history of the Royal Navy.[9] He had also dabbled in fiction, however: aside from his contribution to 'The Siege of Portsmouth' in 1895, he had written several tales of future wars, invasion threats and battles.[10] But he was relaxed about the way some of his fiction was approached, as he noted in an 'advertisement' at the beginning of *The Great Peril* (1893):

> This story is not intended to found a school of philosophic doubt, to advocate a fad, to preach a sermon, to illustrate a theory, to point a moral, to teach a lesson, to throw contempt upon a cause, to deride a set of religious convictions, to attack an individual or a party, or to advertise a patent medicine. Excellent stories to do all these and many other things have been written, and have had their effect. It now occurs to me humbly to endeavour to strike out a novel course, and to tell a story the object of which shall be merely to entertain the benevolent reader.[11]

The Great Peril certainly is an entertaining romp, a satire on the invasion theme, where an American syndicate – The Old Country Development Trust – attempts to take over Britain through brainwashing its population. This was simple entertainment, and it was presumably understood as such by its readers.

Even some more serious works were, however, of questionable instructive quality. Fred T. Jane, who illustrated stories by Clowes and Griffith among others, and who gave his name to a series of reference books that are still published in new editions today, wrote a future naval war story of his own in 1895.[12] Jane was vitriolic in his criticism of British naval policy and of the Liberals; he also condemned the non-partisan attitude of the Navy League, of which he was a member. Indeed, he jumped ship and joined the rival Imperial Maritime League when this was founded in 1908.[13] *Blake of the 'Rattlesnake'*, his fictional take on what a future naval war might look like, contained strong criticism of 'Little Englanders' and the '"six hundred talking asses" at Westminster', but this was mentioned as an 'apology for not having prated on the need of Admiralty reform': 'the chiefest glory of a democracy', he wrote, 'is the privilege of every fool to teach other men their business'. The point of his story was not to change policy, nor was it to 'settle any vexed questions of theories or tactics'. His aim was rather more prosaic: 'I have tried instead to work into story-form some of the romance that clings thick around the torpedo service, to set forth some of the poetry latent in torpedo craft'.[14]

Another of William Laird Clowes' stories, *The Captain of the 'Mary Rose'* (1892), was written with the intention of presenting his readers with a description of modern naval warfare, as well as to argue for a strong naval presence in the Mediterranean. However, Clowes also noted that his aim was to provide a readable narrative, one whose aspects 'will especially recommend themselves to British boys'.[15] A stirring story with 'romance' and 'poetry' was important – and there was clearly a market for this kind of literature, either in humorous form or written in more sombre tones.[16] Grant Richards, who contemplated the unsatisfactory reception of *The New Battle of Dorking* in chapter 4, still had enough faith in the marketability of the invasion-scare genre to publish A.J. Dawson's invasion tract *The Message* seven years later – illustrated by the watercolourist Henry Matthew Brock – not to mention that he

192   *Authors and readers*

republished the original *Battle of Dorking* after the outbreak of war in 1914, with an introduction by G.H. Powell – a 'book man' and antiquarian rather than an authority on either war or the future.[17]

Authors like Wells and Clowes were concerned with making prognostications and suggestions about what a future war might entail, but fiction was not necessarily their preferred way of communicating their message. Clowes did note that he hoped *The Captain of the 'Mary Rose'* might awaken an interest in the navy among the boys reading it – but presumably as an introduction to more serious literature: 'If they will take an intelligent interest in modern naval developments, we shall not, twenty or thirty years hence, have to lament that upon naval questions the tax-paying public is ignorant or apathetic'; he noted, 'for not only the boy is the father of the man, but also the study of matters naval is so seductive that, I believe, no Englishman who has once taken it up has ever willingly relinquished it'.[18]

Clowes' argument – that there was a distinction between 'useful' factual literature and stirring fiction – illustrates an under-explored aspect of invasion-scare literature and its reception. This chapter investigates the link between how the stories were published and marketed, and how the idea of invasion was seen from the perspective of their readers. The chapter examines the changes in publishing over the decades between the publication of *Dorking* and the Edwardian era, and the effects these changes had on the way invasion-scare fiction was marketed and read. The chapter also discusses how readers and commenters understood and reinterpreted fiction in the decades before the First World War. Rather than uncritically accepting the premises of fantastic literature, British readers took away their own ideas from the fictional worlds presented to them, and these ideas could at times be quite contradictory.

Fiction and the reading public

Up until the late 1880s and early 1890s, most 'Dorking'-like stories were published in pamphlet form and as individual short stories, but the genre was always deeply intertwined with the developments in publishing taking place at the same time, and with the rise of popular periodicals and newspapers. In their separate studies of

Readers and receptions 193

British Victorian science fiction, Brian Stableford and Darko Suvin both stress the 1890s as a dividing line for the way such fiction was written and disseminated. Before 1894 and the demise of the three-decker novel, Victorians were often served their novels in multivolume form; this influenced the way stories were written.[19] Science fiction – or 'Scientific romance' – was arguably well suited to shorter forms of writing, meaning that authors were now given more room to experiment.[20] For Richard Altick, 'the 1890's saw the ultimate victory of the cheap-book movement',[21] though publication of invasion-scare fiction in book format was making headway in the 1880s. The 1890s also witnessed the rise of the popular periodical, with George Newnes, Alfred Harmsworth and Arthur Pearson radically upsetting the magazine publishing industry in Britain. These developments effectively created a whole new market for authors of science fiction. Stableford sees the 1890s as the decade when the wider genre of 'speculative fiction' not only became commercially viable in a way that it had not been before; it also inaugurated a period of literary experimentation.[22] This analysis is broadly true for invasion-scare fiction as well.

Periodicals and newspapers 'are best adapted to the needs of a mass audience' – they are topical, short and cheaper to acquire than books.[23] No wonder then that the Victorian era saw such a proliferation and wide dissemination of them – in 1897 the Liberal *Speaker* even exclaimed that 'if this century is to have any special character, it is doubtful whether any name could describe it so well as the Century of Periodicals'.[24] It could have added newspapers to the description as well – though it would be fairer to say that it was the last half of the century that deserved the moniker. Newspapers were not a novelty in the nineteenth century, but they had initially been curtailed by a political establishment fearful of the radical influences papers might have on readers. After the Napoleonic Wars, the Stamp Act of 1819 set out to restrict the industry; yet even under the Act there was room for cheap papers specialising in fantastic tales aimed at a wide audience – a sign of things to come later in the century.[25] Still, cheap newspapers, properly understood, were a product of the mid-Victorian era after the paper duties – the last 'tax on knowledge' – were finally abolished in 1861.[26]

Even so, it would take another 35 years before newspapers started circulating widely among the working classes, marked, for

194   *Authors and readers*

example, by Harmsworth's *Daily Mail* in 1896.[27] By the 1880s and 1890s, proprietors like W.T. Stead, Harmsworth, Newnes and Pearson had created a mass circulation press in Britain.[28] The same development could be seen in periodical publishing, and with many of the same actors. While the first part of the century was dominated by relatively small-circulation literary reviews of the *Blackwood's Magazine* type,[29] the last quarter of the century witnessed a profound change in the market. Magazines like Newnes' *Tit-Bits* (1881) had a circulation of over 300,000 by the mid-1880s, while its imitators *Pearson's Magazine* (1896) and *Harmsworth's Magazine* (1898) achieved circulation figures of around the quarter-million mark by 1900.[30] The first issue of Newnes' *Strand Magazine* initiated what Sam Moskowitz has termed the 'golden age of magazines', between 1891 and 1914: 'Never before had the middle class and even the working class had such an incredible selection of superb magazines of well-balanced general interest at a reasonable price'.[31] Older, established middle-class periodicals, as well as satirical magazines like *Punch*, continued to publish as well, meaning that British readers, from working class through to the middle classes, had a larger selection of reading material to choose from than ever before.

Changes in the medium necessarily also affected the ways in which texts were presented to readers. Newspapers and journals probably had a larger and more influential circulation than books in the Victorian era,[32] but the distinction between them was not always clear. After the three-decker was effectively abolished in the 1890s, authors began to 'market the text rather than the book', as Alexis Weedon observes: 'collecting their journal and newspaper articles into volumes for republication, and rewriting novels serialized in the periodical press for the different formats available'.[33]

Graham Law and Robert L. Patton point out that there was a considerable overlap between serial publication and book publication in the Victorian era.[34] Indeed, there was never an obvious barrier between serialising a story in one form or another, or publishing it in book form – this was after all still the era of Charles Dickens. The new century continued the trend: William Le Queux's *The Invasion of 1910* went from its first inception in Alfred Harmsworth's *Daily Mail* to being issued as a book.[35] This was the norm rather than exception, and hints at the interlinked nature of the British publishing industry. H.O. Arnold-Forster, to take another example, worked

Readers and receptions 195

for the publisher Cassell before commencing his career in parliament, and whereas his naval warfare story *In a Conning Tower* had originally been published by *Murray's Magazine*, the 1891 pamphlet was released under the Cassell imprint.[36] Max Pemberton, a prolific author of fantastic literature, also made a name for himself as an imaginative author at Cassell when he, as editor of the publisher's boys' magazine *Chums* contributed the story 'The Iron Pirate' as a serial; it was published in book form in 1893.[37] At the time, Pemberton claimed that he had gained extensive knowledge about 'the reading tastes of the masses' – a credible assertion, as his friendship with Harmsworth must have given him at least some insights.[38] Although he left the magazine in 1894, he returned to the publisher again a few years later to edit *Cassell's Magazine*, and attracted popular authors to the publication over the course of his editorship, among them William Le Queux.[39]

The rise of a truly popular press changed the way stories were written. As Philip Waller observes, Victorian authors were often themselves journalists.[40] The two trades were therefore linked – this was one of the defining features of invasion-scare fiction in the later years of the century. In an attempt to present realistic scenarios or add colour to the narratives, stories often adopted and adapted the recognisable traits of newspaper publishing. Perhaps most famous, and certainly pioneering in this respect, was 'The Great War of 1892', published in *Black and White* in 1892. Here, a fictional European Great War was presented through reports and sketches, as if it had been a real event.[41] Brian Stableford notes that William Le Queux's 1894 invasion-scare story 'The Poisoned Bullet', serialised in Harmsworth's *Answers*, and later republished as *The Great War in England in 1897*, was 'not so much a novel as an exercise in "speculative non-fiction"', using the tools of journalism to drive the narrative forward.[42] Le Queux's strength as an author was the way he dramatically presented his narrative, rather than his somewhat limited writing abilities. Le Queux wrote for shock effect, and he used the journalist's tools to enhance this.[43]

Aside from the portrayal of women – which remained largely static and rather one-dimensional throughout the decades discussed in this book – invasion-scare fiction became more 'inclusive' as time went on. The cacotopian trend identified by Matthew Beaumont,

196 *Authors and readers*

discussed in the previous chapter and evident in literature like *England's Downfall*, was becoming anachronistic by the 1890s, at least in descriptions of future wars. Indeed, the portrayal of the 'residuum' in alliance with 'the respectable working classes' as a societal threat was largely a product of the 1880s, and was no longer seen as pressing by the middle classes in the 1890s, as Gareth Stedman Jones has observed.[44] The reactionary attitude of most literature of the 1870s and 1880s, then, can be contrasted with the all-encompassing nation-in-arms portrayed in Le Queux's *The Invasion of 1910*.

As the stories changed, so did the readership. An expanded audience meant that the stories were aimed at readers with more varied political interests. John Ramsden perceptively remarked on Le Queux's writing that he 'shamelessly flattered' his readers by hinting that they shared the cosmopolitan habits he claimed for himself and his characters.[45] But spreading a wide net to encompass a large group of readers also meant that the political arguments of invasion-scare fiction, like that of Le Queux, became watered down. As invasion-scare fiction moved into the 1890s and 1900s – the Harmsworth era – its political and technical arguments were atomised as the idea of a future war was explored in more fantastical narratives, like those of George Griffith, along with more traditional politico-military focused stories. Sam Moskowitz's argument that the popularity of Griffith meant that he 'reflected the attitudes of his time', and 'obviously helped shape them', is tempered by H.G. Wells' criticism of him as 'a purveyor of wild "*pseudo*" scientific extravaganza'.[46] From the 1890s onwards, invasion-scare fiction became an element of consumer culture, and even though narratives extolled policies like national service and decried a variety of perceived societal ills, their readership approached them with more varied interests.

By the turn of the century the visual aspect became more important than before – an indication that invasion-fiction had become a spectacle of consumerism. Stories now existed as part of visual culture, as part of advertising and in forms other than purely textual – both as theatre plays, of which *An Englishman's Home* (1909) was hardly the first,[47] and as board games. An early example of the latter was *The Battle of Dorking*, directly inspired by Chesney's story;[48] another was the 1889 game *Invasion*, which dealt with the question of a channel tunnel;[49] and one, *War Tactics: or Can Great Britain be Invaded?*, may have been published in 1911, though could also be from after the outbreak of the war.[50] Soon invasion stories also made an appearance as films in the era of cinematography.[51]

Drawings and caricatures of invasions and future wars were arguably more widespread than feature films and board games. As print culture in the 1890s produced cheap journals, newspapers and books, illustrations became an important component of fiction, including invasion-scare literature. The Tower Publishing Company, for example, specialised in books with high quality printing and illustrations, and beautiful illustrated covers, sold at low prices. The firm published highly popular stories by Le Queux, W. Laird Clowes, George Griffith and Fred T. Jane, among others, before ultimately going bankrupt in the mid-1890s.[52] When the journal *Black and White* advertised for its serialised narrative 'The Great War of 1892', it was eager to not only underline that the narrative was supported by naval and military experts, but that it would also be illustrated by numerous artists.[53]

The visual culture of invasion-scare fiction coincided with the rise of a Victorian advertising culture. As Philip Waller in his comprehensive work on Victorian authors and readers notes, '[t]he style of Victorian advertising owed much to the theatre, with its fashion for spectacle and sensation'.[54] The popularity of invasion-scare fiction was fuelled by successful marketing, and by a tendency among authors and, importantly, publishers, to see their readers as consumers, and their fictional invasions as commodities in a marketplace.

Advertising constitutes part of a society's culture – this was no less true for Victorian Britain. 'Advertising is, next to the bookseller, the most important factor in the sale of books', an article in the December 1896 issue of the *Nineteenth Century* noted: 'In England publishers spend larger sums in advertising than in any other country in the world, some indeed spending thousands of pounds annually in trying to make their books sell'.[55] Advertisements in general, not just for books, were ubiquitous in turn-of-the-century Britain, in particular in the newspaper columns of the mass circulation press. 'It might be said, indeed,' one commentator in the *Monthly Review* in 1905 observed, 'that newspapers are nowadays but purveyors of news in order that they may be mediums for advertisements'. That said, he also argued that this was not necessarily a bad thing; it also meant more news was made available to the readers.[56]

198 *Authors and readers*

Authorial intent versus popular reaction: insecurity, militarism and the paradoxes of fear

In early February 1882, as the debate over the proposed channel tunnel was intensifying in the press,[57] a short interview with Sir Garnet Wolseley was published in the *Standard*. 'Any tunnel is objectionable', Wolseley argued – a common refrain from the outspoken opponent of such a scheme – 'on the account of the extreme danger it would entail upon England'.[58] After reading the interview, Thomas Berney, Rector and Officiating Minister of Bracon Ash in the diocese of Norwich, penned a letter to William Gladstone. In the letter, which the clergyman also had printed and presented not only to every member of the legislature, but also to the Queen herself, Berney ramblingly described the possibility of a French seizure of Dover Castle, and of the prospective tunnel itself. He naturally chose to illustrate his warning by including a fictional account. The French invasion force, he imagined, would first take the castle by tricking the garrison into peeking over the parapets, then dispatch them with a volley. 'But what might follow?' he asked, 'Let us picture the scene; happily not yet a fact!'[59] If Gladstone was ever persuaded by any of the letter's confused arguments, he was probably dissuaded by the time he reached the last page, where Berney offered his services to the Scientific and Expediency Committees looking into the tunnel project, adding that he could also present them with 'certain sacred prophecies concerning the future'.[60] Thomas Berney was presumably not among the people Sir Garnet Wolseley wanted, or needed, in his campaign against the tunnel.

Berney's pamphlet is illustrative of how debates sparked by various national security questions were never easy to control or to limit. As discussed in chapter 3, Wolseley's channel tunnel campaign itself took on the form of an invasion-scare narrative, inspiring others to do the same. Berney's invective was published alongside both subtle satirical digs and more serious invasion-scare fiction. These, in turn, were all presented to a varied reading public, who reacted to their messages in different ways. This had been true ever since *The Battle of Dorking* – the majority of fictional responses to Chesney were either critical of his conclusions, or satirised his premise. By the end of the century, the increased literacy and political influence of the voting public meant that invasion scares were read and commented on by a large group of people, many of whom may have taken entirely different lessons from the texts. In 1914, on the cusp of the First World War, Colonel Louis Jackson surmised that the 'wild imaginings' in fictional depictions of aerial attack could lead to the public missing out on the real danger, 'because the common sense of the public rejects them, and is prejudiced to the extent of thinking the whole danger illusory'.[61] If the popular reactions to invasion-scare and similar types of literature were difficult to control or manage, the question still remains: how were the stories read and understood by their audience?

The idea that invasion-scare fiction shaped, influenced, or in some way changed ideas in society has traditionally been analysed on three levels. First is the military level, or the impact of fiction on military planning. A. Michael Matin has investigated the debates at the Royal United Service Institution in 1872 over the feasibility of a *Dorking*-style invasion; but these debates were essentially between a civilian – the Liberal politician William Harcourt – and soldiers, not between soldiers planning the details of a future war.[62] Chesney had placed his fictive invaders in a natural position to take London, not invented a new invasion plan, nor changed British military thinking regarding how to defend London. Dorking and Guildford had, after all, been invasion targets for the French at least since the 1760s.[63] The extent to which fiction directly influenced military thinking – as opposed to the other way around – is difficult to assess, but was probably rather limited. That said, future-war fiction was written and discussed by service personnel, and stories showed a willingness among professionals to engage with technological developments, as touched upon in chapter 2. It is something of a truism that generals always fight the last war, but planning naturally requires forethought as well. The *Recent Publications of Military Interest*, a quarterly pamphlet issued by the General Staff and the War Office, was in April 1907 full of praise for a German vision of *The Battle of the Future*, which it said, 'while being a scientific tactical text book, is yet eminently readable'.[64] Others were more ambivalent about predicting the future: a review of Captain Sydney Eardley-Wilmot's 1894 story *The Next Naval War* in the *Journal of the Royal United Service Institution*, while recommending the narrative to the journal's readers, opened by stating that '[w]e are rather inclined to doubt the wisdom of attempts to forecast the results of the next great war'.[65] More research is needed

200   *Authors and readers*

about the links between planning for war and the writing of fiction, but inter-service debate is anyway beyond the scope of this book.[66]

Second, the popularity of invasion-scare and other, related forms of fiction, has been read as a sign of societal insecurity – in particular after the South African War at the turn of the century. According to Matin, the ebb and flow in the production of invasion-scare fiction was a measure of British anxieties throughout the decades before the war.[67] Samuel Hynes saw an Edwardian feeling of unease, the 'Decline and Fall of Tory England', as symbolised on the one hand by Victoria's death, and illustrated on the other by works of fiction like *The Riddle of the Sands* (1903) and plays like *An Englishman's Home*.[68] Edwardian Britain, in Hynes' analysis, saw itself as sinking into relative decline, opposed by rising rivals like Germany. An alternative version of this is the idea of pre-Great War Britain, as well as Europe, as a place of optimism, as an 'Edwardian garden party'.[69] But this idea does not exclude pessimism. As Heather Jones and Arndt Weinrich note: a European-wide 'geography of unease', and a similar optimism were 'corollaries of each other' in the years before the war; the idea of 'progress' in some form or other coexisted with an idea that it might suddenly come to an abrupt end.[70] Nowhere has this idea of a paradox – coexisting optimism and pessimism – been better formulated than in the words of George Dangerfield. In *The Strange Death of Liberal England* he described the immediate pre-war years as a form of illogical drama, with violent undercurrents tearing the familiar world apart. In this setting, as Dangerfield saw it, 'public fears of Germany were a kind of self-indulgence':

> The Public was only aware of an inner tension, a need for stimulants; and what could be more exciting than to gather all the political rages, all the class hatreds, all the fevers for spending and excitement and speed, which then seemed to hang like a haunted fog over England – to gather them and condense them into one huge shape and call it *Germany*?[71]

Finally, and linked with the idea that Edwardian Britain was a fearful or decline-obsessed society, is the view of the country as militarised and jingoistic. In G.R. Searle's estimate, it was the setbacks in South Africa that finally meant that latent insecurities and fears within British society could be expressed, and led to a 'Quest for National Efficiency', as British political theorists sought to put the

Readers and receptions 201

country on the right track.[72] Anne Summers has claimed that '[i]t might be more appropriate to label it a quest for military efficiency', and argues that this Edwardian quest inverted the earlier Victorian efforts to domesticate Tommy Atkins: 'now, society was to be militarized'.[73] Recent studies have focused on the dynamic and multifaceted nature of this pre-war British militarism, though the term itself remains contested.[74]

As far as the sociologist Herbert Spencer was concerned, a move towards, or rather 'recrudescence' of, militarism, or 'militancy' in British society was well underway before the Edwardian period. Writing in the closing decades of Victoria's reign, Spencer was one of the more influential social theorists of the period, though his ideas are much less discussed today. Spencer divided societies into the 'industrial' and the 'militant', with the former being the ideal – the focus in an 'industrial' society being on rational organisation and liberal individualism. By contrast, in a 'militant' society, individual rights are subjected to the needs of the state. Spencer included German militarism as well as socialism in this definition of militancy: 'For the socialistic *régime* is simply another form of the bureaucratic *régime*. Military regimentation, civil regimentation, and industrial regimentation, are in their natures essentially the same'.[75] In Britain, Spencer argued, a move towards a militant society had in the nineteenth century been fuelled by war scares and alarmist reports of Britain's defencelessness – in which invasion-scare tracts can naturally be seen to belong. The result was increased expenditure on army and navy, and a society geared towards militant pursuits:

> For a generation the volunteer movement has been accustoming multitudes of civilians to military rule, while re-awakening their fighting instincts. On groups of upper-class boys in public schools, who have their drills and even their sham fights, and on groups of lower-class boys in London, such as the Church Lads Brigade, regimental discipline is similarly brought to bear ...[76]

For Spencer, a tangible result of the 'growth of armaments' was a 'growth of aggressiveness'. Specifically, as he saw it, the increase of militancy within a society led to outward expansion through imperialism. In this, Britain, Spencer argued, was as guilty as France.[77] The increased 'aggressiveness' of Britain was therefore a direct result of its feeling of insecurity at home. There are echoes of

202 *Authors and readers*

Richard Cobden in this reading: writing in 1862, Cobden decried what he saw as the unnecessary defence 'panics', and their impact on defence expenditure and international cooperation, beginning with the French invasion-scare of 1847–1848.[78]

Spencer's analysis has its flaws. His terms are wide and unwieldy – 'industry', for example, seems like an arbitrary and confusing label, and was used to describe a form of classic Liberal idea of individual freedom and innovation, rather than what may be more commonly understood as industrial organisation. But his understanding of the ability of state or social structures to quite literally regiment people's lives remains one of the more perceptive and original analyses of late Victorian and Edwardian Britain.

Where Spencer saw ideas of vulnerability as a catalyst for militancy in Britain, others have seen support for the military as at least in part the result of genuine enthusiasm. Michael Paris uses the phrase 'pleasure culture of war' to describe what he sees as British preoccupation with things military and imperial by the final decades of the nineteenth century.[79] The focus in this and similar studies has been cultural rather than social. Writing in the mid-1980s, John MacKenzie saw a link between imperialism and militarism in British society, and discussed both tendencies in *Propaganda and Empire*.[80] As with MacKenzie, W.J. Reader also saw culture as part of the militarisation process, with the publishing revolution of the 1880s onwards leading to a wide dissemination of such ideas in society. Juvenile fiction for boys, and war correspondents writing in British newspapers had an extensive readership, but even literature reaching a smaller part of society had an impact, in Reader's estimate, as their message of patriotism filtered through society and were picked up even outside the immediate readership.[81] Cecil D. Eby reached a similar conclusion regarding what he terms the 'Martial Spirit' of British readers, but he argued that militaristic writing was a symptom of existing tastes among the readers, rather than an influence on them: 'In most cases', he notes in his study, 'we suspect that the writer, like a sensitive radar apparatus, responds to frequencies already pulsating in the ether'.[82] Paris concurs: for him, from the 1850s onwards Britain was – and indeed continues to be – a 'Warrior Nation', as evidenced in the contents of the reading material presented to the British public, and its youth in particular.[83] For Reader, Eby and Paris, British ideas of war and militarism in the pre-Great War period are closely linked with Britain's identity as an imperial power. Invasion-scare and future-war fiction constituted part of this wider culture of war, patriotism, militarism and imperialism.

MacKenzie specifically mentions Antonio Gramsci's theory of hegemony, though his own study of imperialism did not engage directly with Gramscian thinking.[84] However, most of the above-mentioned cultural studies in one way or another analysed British pre-War society as being influenced by, or finding its expression through, a cultural elite – a very Gramscian idea, even if Gramsci is not explicitly referred to.[85] A Gramscian reading of invasion-scare fiction specifically would conclude that it constituted a form of mobilisation of consent regarding British militarism and imperialism. This is the argument made by C.J. Keep: beginning with *Dorking*, Keep claims, stories were being used to organise consent for imperialism among a wide social stratum in the British settler empire. Using a Gramscian analysis, Keep assumed that readers ('the office clerk in Manchester or the printer's apprentice in Toronto') who picked up the pamphlet would 'recognize Chesney's upper-class English Imperialist concerns as their own'; the story 'aroused emotions that cut across class-lines and oceans, instilling a fervent new patriotism'.[86]

Keep's reading seems to argue that the empire was tied together by a bourgeois mentality; in this analysis, the print culture of future-war and invasion-scare fiction was forming identities across time and space. This, of course, is conjecture, and implies that the stories functioned as a form of 'social control' – a somewhat nebulous term, as F.M.L. Thompson noted in 1981, used by social historians to describe top-down efforts to control the lower classes. Thompson argued that theories of the efficacy of social control are based on a view which 'plac[es] the working classes perpetually on the receiving end of outside forces and influences, and portraying them as so much putty in the hands of a masterful and scheming bourgeoisie'.[87] As Hobsbawm noted of 'invented traditions', official attempts at 'mass-producing' traditions could easily fail if popular engagement was lacking.[88] It would be a mistake to automatically read the mass-production of invasion literature as evidence of popular acceptance of its message. Le Queux later worked more overtly to mobilise consent after the real Great War broke out, as

204 *Authors and readers*

discussed in the next chapter, producing anti-German propaganda and publishing it under George Newnes' imprint.[89] But his work's impact on morale is of course less certain. Both before and after 1914, stories were not read and accepted uncritically, and they did not and could not on their own cement any consensus on empire either in Britain or elsewhere – *Dorking* was, for example, met with much criticism from the Liberals, even as they eagerly read the narrative, as discussed in chapter 1. The stories should instead be read as dynamic parts of wider social and political debates.

For the remainder of this chapter I want to return to the idea of invasion-scares as a paradox: as examples of an optimistic vision of British military prowess, and simultaneously as part of a 'geography of unease'. As Adrian Gregory has pointed out, the reaction to the Great War, when it finally broke out, was one of ambiguity: 'awful as it is', one diarist noted of the declaration of war on 4 August, '– it is very thrilling'.[90] This lived duality was, in many ways, replicated in the pre-war invasion fiction itself, with its extreme swing from either eschatological scenes of defeat and humiliation, or a successful – almost utopian – reinvention of an imagined and lost national unity. The answer to what the stories meant and how they were interpreted lies in the little-explored and much less understood grey area between these two extremes.

'The more ignorant public': reactions to *The Invasion of 1910*

The reaction to Le Queux's most famous novel, the 1906 story *The Invasion of 1910*, offers a case study of how invasion-scare fiction was discussed, and of how such stories could be read and interpreted in the Edwardian years. The contents and background to Le Queux's story were outlined in chapter 5; the focus here is on the reception of, and public engagement with, its publication.

Speaking in the House of Commons on 13 March 1906, the MP Rudolph Lehmann brought Le Queux's *The Invasion of 1910* to the attention of the Liberal Prime Minister, Henry Campbell-Bannerman. Lehmann referred to adverts for the story in the morning papers, and asked Campbell-Bannerman whether the government could 'take any steps or express any opinion which will discourage the publication of matter of this sort, calculated to prejudice our relations with other Powers'.[91] In Darko Suvin's reading, it was Lehmann's class snobbery more than his affiliation with the Liberal party that determined his reaction to Le Queux, the 'hack writer for Harmsworth'.[92] This, Suvin argues, was the 'Establishment man' speaking out against the *'arriviste'*. Whatever his motivation was, the response from Campbell-Bannerman was in the negative: 'I do not know what step the Government can take in the matter; I am afraid they can do nothing. We can safely leave it, I think, to be judged by the good sense and good taste of the British people'.[93] Hynes, who also comments on the exchange, argues that the Prime Minister's words were spoken 'with evident regret'.[94] There was a sense of defeat in the statement, but the Liberal leader may also have been perceptive in his *laissez-faire* attitude: Harmsworth's effort to capitalise politically on the invasion-scare genre was not particularly successful, as chapter 4 illustrated, and *The Invasion of 1910* was later described by its own author as ineffective (of which more later).

The affair did not end here, however. Showing his knack for self-promotion, Le Queux immediately went on the offensive: he forwarded a letter to *The Times* that he had sent to Campbell-Bannerman, in which he protested at the way his novel had been described.[95] In the answer, also printed in the newspaper, Arthur Ponsonby, on behalf of the Prime Minister, argued that it was not the book itself that was the problem, but its promotional material, a 'full-page map giving the position of the German fleet and army corps'. This, Ponsonby opined, was 'an objectionable form of advertisement which Sir Henry considered was likely to produce irritation abroad and might conceivably alarm the more ignorant public at home'.[96] Le Queux was not impressed by the last sentence: 'On the contrary', he wrote,

> I believe the English public to be at least as well educated and intelligent as that of any Continental nation, and I am somewhat surprised that you, Sir, as Prime Minister, should cast that reflection upon us as a people.[97]

The debate ended with Ponsonby's response in the next day's paper: 'The phrase "the more ignorant public at home" ', he tersely replied, 'was obviously intended to refer to "the more ignorant section of the public at home" '.[98]

206   *Authors and readers*

The exchanges, both in parliament and in *The Times,* show that Lehmann and Campbell-Bannerman did not object to invasion-scare fiction as such, but to the way it was commodified and presented to its potential readership through aggressive marketing. In addition to the invasion maps, the serialisation was also promoted through the use of sandwich-board men, wearing German uniforms and parading through the streets of London – a visual reminder of what an invading army could look like, but this one more focused on selling newspapers than fighting.[99] In May, H.O. Arnold-Forster, the former Unionist Secretary of State for War, was one of those who asked the Liberal Home Secretary in parliament if he was 'aware that this abuse of the national uniform is likely to be resented by the officers and men of the German army, as a similar use of the British uniform would be resented by our own Army'; the Home Secretary, Herbert Gladstone, answered that this form of advertisement 'appears to me both foolish and offensive', and informed the Commons that 'the Commissioner of Police is taking steps to deal with the matter'.[100]

Tories and Liberals were in perfect agreement over the poor taste of the display, but the idea that it could potentially stoke the fear of invasion in the British populace does not seem to have been their main concern. The advertisements, both the printed maps and the sandwich-board men, were not dangerous; they were vulgar. The other thing to note is Ponsonby's argument that the public could be divided into an 'ignorant section' and the rest. It is not immediately obvious that Suvin's class analysis can be used here; one 'section' of the public were not trusted to understand that the adverts should be judged as inappropriate, rather than taken seriously, but there is no clear indication that either Campbell-Bannerman or Ponsonby intended this to mean the working classes.

With questions raised in parliament, and letters exchanged between the author and the Prime Minister, *The Invasion* got more free publicity than its author and Harmsworth could have dreamed of. Clement King Shorter, writing his weekly literary letter in the *Sphere,* noted that Lehmann's question gave Le Queux 'an advertisement that his brother novelists of similar calibre will envy'.[101] The *Daily News* surmised that it was 'accident' that had given Le Queux's story 'a fame, or perhaps notoriety, which it might not otherwise have acquired'.[102] The newspaper was highly critical

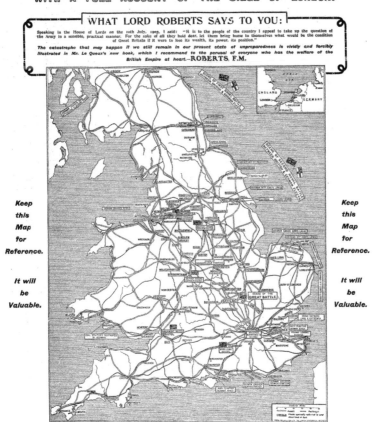

Figure 6.1 Advertisement for William Le Queux, *The Invasion of 1910* (1906), in *The Times*, 13 March 1906, 11.
Source: DMG Media, reproduced with permission

208 *Authors and readers*

of *The Invasion of 1910*; hardly a surprising stance for a Liberal paper where Rudolph Lehmann had been editor only a few years previously.[103] The story was the literary talk over the summer of 1906, even if the author's claims that the book sold a million copies in its various editions should be taken with a pinch of salt.[104] Reginald Glossop, later a rather obscure author of fantastic fiction, wrote a short imagined-invasion tract in response to Le Queux, and had it published in the *Daily Mail* – this one a Hull paper, not the Harmsworth one.[105] A notice in *The Citizen*, a Gloucester paper, on 26 May was more esoteric: it advertised a lecture in the Christadelphian Lecture Hall on the theme of 'The Invasion of 1910 – Will it be possible? England's Destiny in the latter day. Scripture prophecies on War'.[106]

Aside from eschatological pronouncements like this, the story was largely read with good humour, or ridiculed. Will Evans, a music hall performer who, *The Era* claimed, 'always catches the whim of the passing hour, and knowing generally how exercised in its mind is the British public over the story by Mr. William Le Queux', created a short parody of it which was evidently well received by its audiences.[107] The *Pall Mall Gazette* lumped Le Queux's tale together with even less probable fiction in a review of Francis Hernaman-Johnson's novel *The Polyphemes*, also published in 1906: 'What with threatening a German invasion in 1910, and a number of raids by gigantic ants (capable of using poisonous airships), the sensational novelists of the day are doing their best to finish off the British Empire'.[108] While Le Queux's story was popular, its message was drowned out; there were simply too many sensational stories around to take them all seriously. 'Mr. Le Queux's clever war story which has been advertised with such amusing ingenuity', observed the *New London Journal*, 'is but the new statement of a very old theme'. Noting the existence of similar literature in Germany as well, the *Journal* continued by pointing out that ' "The Battle of Dorking" is perhaps the most celebrated book dealing with the subject: but fiction writers by the score have attempted to picture the great war of the future':

> Happily, the prophetic horrors of the sensational novelist are rarely fulfilled. Did not Mr. Le Queux himself, some years ago, write about a terrible European war which was to happen in 1897?[109]

Readers and receptions   209

The paper was here referring to *The Great War in England in 1897* (1894). Readers interested in perusing stories of British defeats and military setbacks were spoiled for choice, even if they limited themselves to Le Queux's corpus alone. As such comments indicate, the saturated invasion-scare market was widely mocked and satirised. In large parts this trend goes back to the reactions to *The Battle of Dorking* and is a tendency that has largely been overlooked by historians.[110]

The Yellow Peril? Newspapers as vehicles for scares

In May 1906 the society journal *Tatler* countered Le Queux's vision of the future with a story of its own, and imagined a British invasion of Germany in 1908, led by authors and journalists instead of professional soldiers and sailors: 'all the ships and regiments were officered by eminent literary men, who alone understood modern warfare'. The invading British army was, naturally, commanded by General Le Queux.[111] While the *Daily News* had a clear disagreement with Le Queux, *Tatler*'s satire was a more left-field affair, from a journal that one might expect would have stayed out of any discussion of such literature.

What this and similar parodies of Le Queux took aim at was the form his and similar invasion scares took in the Edwardian era, with the fourth estate for all intents and purposes having declared war on Germany on its own; the pen, it seemed, had finally been sharpened to the extent that it supplanted the sword entirely. *Punch*, in a satirical story about irresponsible journalism, imagined the great powers being brought to the brink of war by the writings of 'yellow patriots' – the journalists of the yellow press. In this story, the situation is defused when the political leadership announces that it will send the journalists to fight if war breaks out; the result is that the tense language in the newspaper reports is quickly toned down.[112] As with *Tatler*, *Punch* also pointed out the link between authors like Le Queux and the newspapers that printed and supported their stories. In 1909, it printed the short skit 'The Invaders', where William Le Queux and Leo Maxse, editor of the *National Review*, successfully invade Germany on their own.[113] The political

210 *Authors and readers*

leadership and Britain's professional soldiers and sailors, these publications joked, had finally been brushed aside by the authors and publishers who used to cooperate with them. There was perhaps a sense of unease in these satires: as with the questions raised over *The Invasion* in parliament in 1906, there was an undertone of uncertainty in what the result of Harmsworth's aggressive marketing of anti-German propaganda could have to say for the relationship between the two countries. What would the 'more ignorant section of the public' think?

Perhaps surprisingly, Le Queux himself was bitterly disappointed in the effect of his novel. In his autobiography, he claimed that the result of *The Invasion of 1910* was the opposite of what he had hoped: after initial indications that it might have had an impact – '[a]t last England seemed about to wake up!' – Le Queux became despondent. 'I saw that we had advanced no further in arousing the public', he wrote, and, claiming that his warnings of German perfidiousness were going unheeded, he described the 'situation' between 1910 and 1913 as 'hopeless': 'How pitiable, how absolutely criminal was our apathy!' The author claimed that while people 'read my book eagerly', they then 'simply set it aside, and, admitting that it was quite an exciting work of imagination, set me down as a second-class Jules Verne!'[114]

The story had a longer shelf-life than Le Queux here hints at: *The Invasion* was published in numerous editions all the way up to, and indeed after, the outbreak of the Great War in 1914. But the rest of his analysis was closer to the mark. It has been theorised that the popularity of the story, and the engagement with it in parliament, meant that it had 'a profound political impact at the very highest level of the Empire's government'.[115] This theory echoes claims that Le Queux himself made in 1915, in a book discussing German spies, where he darkly hinted at a conspiracy to keep the public uninformed: 'the British public have so long been officially deluded, reassured and lulled to sleep'.[116] But Campbell-Bannerman's reply in the commons indicates annoyance rather than 'impact' in any meaningful political sense. What he objected to was the way the story was 'staged'; the theatricals of its advertisement campaign, not the story itself. Another way of looking at *The Invasion*'s reception would be to see it as simply not very convincing in the first place. If the newspaper reactions cited above are anything to go by, *The Invasion* was indeed mostly met with sighs and ridicule – though the wider publishing industry behind it was certainly not so disparaged.

The rise of the 'yellow press', and of mass-market publishing in Britain, encompassed a wide range of publications. In 1906, the wider newspaper industry included not only the mass-readership Harmsworth press, but papers with a narrower focus, like the Unionist *National Review*, edited by Leo Maxse – the other 'invader' in *Punch*'s satire. Reading a story like J.N. Hampson's 1898 'Great Britain v. France and Russia' gives us a detailed narrative of a near-future war between the three countries, amply supplied with details and quotations from the writings of Alfred Mahan, the American proponent of naval power. The simple fact that the story was a Navy League prize essay, published in the *National Review* is perhaps more instructive than the story itself, however.[117] Maxse, a proponent of a large navy – he would abandon the Navy League for the more aggressive Imperial Maritime League in 1908 – was an obvious choice to publish such an essay.[118] The *National Review* was firmly in the corner of the Royal Navy, the empire and the Unionists. It published extensively on political and military issues – the June 1898 issue included, beside Hampson's imaginary war, some thoughts on the ongoing struggle between the United States and Spain, written by Admiral Philip Colomb.[119] Hampson's story was clearly meant to be read and discussed in all seriousness.[120]

Whether the press was able to substantially change public perceptions in one way or another is a complex question. Politicians before 1914 tended to pussyfoot around press magnates like Harmsworth, eager not to offend those who were understood to influence the public.[121] But, as Stephen Koss has observed, the political press generally belonged to a specific social and geographical location: the metropolitan elite in London.[122] The readership increased throughout the period covered in this book, but even in 1913 F.W. Hirst, updating Cobden's 1862 treatise on panics for a new era, argued that the impact of a mass press was limited: 'You cannot imagine all the towns and villages of England, Ireland, Scotland and Wales reduced to a state of terror by a stage whisper, even though it ran through the whole of the newspaper press'.[123] Newspapers were read for different reasons – and there were a myriad of opinions, including anti-war messages, presented on the pages of a diverse

212 *Authors and readers*

British press before the war – though an effective and influential mass-circulation socialist paper was conspicuously absent.[124] Glenn R. Wilkinson has claimed that the Edwardian press is illustrative of societal attitudes towards war, and that the positive presentation of warfare in newspapers helps us understand attitudes towards war in the years before 1914.[125] This is a somewhat unsatisfactory analysis, however. As Dominik Geppert has shown, press barons like Harmsworth were hardly consistent in their anti-German campaigns, and did not present war as an unquestionable good. 'The popular press', as Geppert notes, 'represented a more ambivalent force in British-German relations than either the accusation of warmongering or the emphasis on international business cooperation indicate'.[126] People read newspapers, that much is clear, but what they took away from them is less certain. The same is true for invasion-scare fiction and similar forms of literature published on the pages of the newspapers, journals and magazines in increasing numbers throughout this period.

The sheer volume of invasion-scare stories published in the new magazines from the late-1880s onwards often makes it a little more difficult to assess whether there was a political agenda behind publishing them. Juvenile publications like *Chums* and *Boy's Own Paper* fit awkwardly in a discussion of how invasion-literature attempted to discuss and influence defence thinking, though they have been included in some existing studies of militarism.[127] Leaving such publications aside, magazines and periodicals were not always as outspoken in their policies as Maxse's *National Review*. Another journal, the *Pall Mall Magazine* – an upmarket publication which served as the literary companion to the *Pall Mall Gazette* – also discussed the prospect of invasion in its pages throughout the early years of the twentieth century, and found ample space for invasion fiction alongside it.[128] The magazine was particularly interested in aerial warfare, serialising H.G. Wells' *The War in the Air* throughout 1908. The following year it published 'The War Hawks', a short story by Ernest Bramah about an attempted German aerial invasion. Bramah, a novelist, imagined that British airmen wearing wings on their persons, in self-propelled flight, would do battle with German airships.[129]

Four years later, the magazine published a story written with at least a more professionally informed description of future aerial

Readers and receptions 213

war: In 'The Great Day in 1920' Captain S.W. Beeman described a dream where a well-prepared Britain, with a massive air armada, defeats an unnamed would-be invader in the near-future year of 1920. 'The following narrative, though cast in the form of fiction – as all such attempts to see into the future must necessarily be – carries all the weight of a carefully balanced article,' the *Pall Mall Magazine*'s introduction to the story began, 'since it is written by a military expert who has given much study to the problem of human flight'.[130] Rudyard Kipling published a spy story, involving a silenced aeroplane invented by an American friend of the unnamed narrator, in the December 1913 issue of the magazine.[131] This story, 'The Edge of the Evening', can be read as a warning about British complacency, faced with the aggression of an unnamed foreign power, but it is also a slightly tongue-in-cheek description of a somewhat different intrusion: 'I represent the business end of the American Invasion', jokes Laughton O. Zigler, the US inventor in the story, who proceeds, along with a motley group of British notables, to accidentally kill two enemy spies. 'Next to marrying one of its women, killing one of its men makes for pretty close intimacy with any country', the narrator observes earlier in the story, but the readers are none the wiser as to what extent the unfit and trigger-happy spies of unknown nationality could really pose a threat to British security.

In contrast to the heavy-handed arguments of the *National Review*, stories about invasion in the more moderate *Pall Mall Gazette* provide a multifaceted version of how the invasion threat was presented to a British audience. 'The Edge of the Evening' was certainly more realistic than two stories Kipling had written about aircraft earlier: 'With the Nightmail' and 'As Easy as A.B.C.' described the benign, if somewhat ominous, worldwide dictatorship of a fictional Aerial Board of Control – 'a small group of international technocrats and experts' as Michael Paris describes it – at the turn of the twenty-first century.[132] However, Kipling's readers may have read his 1913 *Pall Mall Magazine* story for sheer enjoyment, rather than as an instructive warning. The periodical did certainly publish other stories that hinted at the dangers of invasion, alongside articles about the need for military preparation. A story about different social classes of civilians coming together as brothers-in-arms and defeating an enemy invasion was published in the January 1913 issue; its author, Donal Hamilton Haines, was

214   *Authors and readers*

American, but his message of national unity was generic enough that a British audience may not have noticed any difference.[133] Yet, alongside such tales of national service, there was also ample space to joke about invasion fears. A humorous short story by Inglis Allen in the January 1912 issue introduced a narrator who defends his habit of going to a barber: 'I still maintain that my threepences have purchased for me a knowledge of the German character and language which may stand me in good stead when the invasion comes' – a not-so-subtle dig at the spy fever fuelled by authors such as William Le Queux.[134] In other words, *Pall Mall Magazine* found space for professionally written invasion-scares, serious stories by amateur authors, and stories making fun of any invasion threat. Its readers were asked to keep an intellectual distance from the idea that a future war would play out as the fiction authors described it.

There are indications – as hinted at in the above discussion – that there was considerable political establishment bias against fictions and advertising campaigns that could be misconstrued by sections of the public. There are also indications that a wider readership was welcomed. But this does not mean that the popular engagement with the narratives indicate an increased interest in issues of national defence. 'As a rule, strangely enough', the *Penny Illustrated Paper* noted in the wake of *An Englishman's Home*'s success, '"plays with a purpose" are seldom popular with the majority of the general public'.[135] Rather than active attempts at mobilising consent, invasion-scare fiction – and theatre plays – were quite often seen as entertaining parts of a wider genre of speculative fiction. To work as recruitment tools or political statements, plays like *An Englishman's Home* needed to be aggressively promoted and connected with existing campaigns.[136] Only rarely did this happen, and the results were often mixed.

As had been their Victorian predecessors, Edwardians were treated to a cornucopia of invasions in books, newspapers and magazines, on stage, and through marketing campaigns. Studies of this period often ignore, however, that just as the Victorians had done, the Edwardians reacted to these spectacles in different ways – as audiences encountered fictitious invaders they did not silently nod along to the stories and their often-confused messages. Stories were taken seriously, but they were also satirised, their advertisement campaigns were criticised and their authors mocked – the

Readers and receptions

invasion trope, in short, was used and reinterpreted by different audiences. This does not mean that Edwardians were unconcerned with invasion or with questions of war, but it does show how optimism and pessimism coexisted when the 'Great War' was still only an imagined spectacle and a fictional concept. When Le Queux felt dismissed as a second-class Jules Verne, he might therefore have shown more insight into the mentality of his readers than subsequent historians have done.

Notes

1 H.G. Wells, *The Discovery of the Future: A Discourse Delivered to the Royal Institution on January 24, 1902* (London: T. Fisher Unwin, 1902).
2 Wells, *Discovery*, 7–10.
3 See the 'Atlantic Edition' of *The Works of H.G. Wells*, 28 vols. (London: T. Fisher Unwin, 1924–1927). Other works worth mentioning are *When the Sleeper Awakes*, or *The Sleeper Awakes*, first published in book form in 1899, and *A Dream of Armageddon* – described by Wells as 'obviously a by-product of the manufacture of "The Sleeper Awakes" (III, x), in addition, of course, to Wells' other fantastic fiction – all dealing in some way with the possibilities of the near future.
4 H.G. Wells, 'Anticipations: An Experiment in Prophecy. I – Locomotion in the Twentieth Century', *Fortnightly Review*, 69 (April 1901), 747, note 2.
5 Wells, *Discovery*, 86; M.P. Shiel, *The Purple Cloud* (London: Chatto & Windus, 1901).
6 H.G. Wells, *The War in the Air: And Particularly How Mr. Bert Smallways Fared while It Lasted* (London: George Bell and Sons, 1908), 9. The book in question – George Griffith, *The Outlaws of the Air* (London: Tower Publishing Company Limited, 1895) – imagined a future air war and was published in book form the same year as H.G. Wells' *The Time Machine*.
7 Wells, *The War in the Air*, 4. Indeed, Smallways is later described as 'a vulgar little creature, the sort of pert, limited soul that the old civilization of the early twentieth century produced by the million in every country of the world' (67).
8 Wm. Laird Clowes, 'The Cheapening of Useful Books', *Fortnightly Review*, 70 (July 1901), 89.

216   *Authors and readers*

9 S.E. Fryer, 'Clowes, Sir William Laird (1856–1905)', rev. Roger Morriss, ODNB.

10 Anon., [W. Laird Clowes and possibly Alan H. Burgoyne or Commander Charles Napier Robinson], *The Great Naval War of 1887* (London: Hatchards, 1887); W. Laird Clowes, *The Captain of the 'Mary Rose': A Tale of To-morrow* (London: Tower Publishing Co., Ltd., 1892); W. Laird Clowes, *The Great Peril, and How it was Averted* (London: Black and White, 1893) – this had originally been printed in *Black and White*; and W. Laird Clowes and Alan H. Burgoyne, *Trafalgar Re-Fought* (London: Thomas Nelson and Sons, [1905]).

11 Clowes, *The Great Peril,* iv.

12 A list of the works Jane wrote, edited and/or illustrated can be found in Richard Brooks, *Fred T. Jane: An Eccentric Visionary* (Coulsdon: Jane's Information Group, 1997), 239–242. The work in question here is *Blake of the 'Rattlesnake', or; The Man Who Saved England: A Story of Torpedo Warfare in 189-* (London: Tower Publishing Company Limited, 1895). The story was illustrated by Jane.

13 Frans Coetzee, *For Party or Country: Nationalism and the Dilemmas of Popular Conservatism in Edwardian England* (New York and Oxford: Oxford University Press, 1990), 79, 84. Jane also tried to run for parliament as an independent naval candidate in the 1906 General Election for – where else? – Portsmouth. 1906 was a bad year to challenge the Liberals at the polls, and Jane came in last. See Brooks, *Fred T. Jane*, 133–135.

14 Jane, *Blake of the 'Rattlesnake'*, 7, 9. Jane wrote other fictional stories as well, some of which were even more focused on telling a good story rather than present accurate forecasts. *The Violet Flame,* for instance, described the end of the world (*The Violet Flame: A Story of Armageddon and After* (London: Ward, Lock & Co., 1899)); while *To Venus in Five Seconds* was a more light-hearted adventure (*To Venus in Five Seconds: An Account of the Strange Disappearance of Thomas Plummer, Pill-maker* (London: Innes & Co., 1897)). Jane illustrated both stories himself.

15 Clowes, *'Mary Rose'*, xiv–xv.

16 This market included naval personnel as well as 'British boys': F.T. Hamilton, newly appointed to the rank of commander in the navy, noted in a letter to Clowes in August 1892 that he was 'reading your "Mary Rose" with great interest'. Caird Library, National Maritime Museum Greenwich, MS/93/001 letter from F.T. Hamilton to William Laird Clowes, 5 August [1892].

17 A.J. Dawson, *The Message* (London: E. Grant Richards, 1907); [George Tomkyns Chesney], *The Battle of Dorking, with an Introduction by*

Readers and receptions 217

G.H. *Powell* (London: Grant Richards Ltd.,1914). See [G.H. Powell], 'A Discourse of Rare Books', *Macmillan's Magazine*, 68 (June 1893), 115–126. The reissue of *Dorking* is discussed in more detail in the next chapter.

18 Clowes, *'Mary Rose'*, xiv.

19 John Sutherland, 'Nineteenth-Century SF and the Book Trade', in Darko Suvin, *Victorian Science Fiction in the UK: The Discourses of Knowledge and of Power* (Boston: G.K. Hall & Co., 1983), 124–125. (Sutherland, though technically the author of this chapter, stresses that the arguments therein are those of Suvin.); Brian Stableford, *Scientific Romance in Britain: 1890–1950* (London: Fourth Estate, 1985), 14–15. For a discussion of the three-decker format, see Troy J. Bassett, 'The Production of Three-volume Novels in Britain, 1863–97', *The Papers of the Bibliographical Society of America*, 102 (2008), 61–75.

20 Stableford, *Scientific Romance*, 14.

21 Richard D. Altick, *The English Common Reader: A Social History of the Mass Reading Public 1800–1900* (Chicago: Phoenix Books, 1967), 316.

22 Stableford, *Scientific Romance*, 15.

23 Altick, *Common Reader*, 318.

24 *Speaker*, 23 January 1897, 92–94.

25 Altick, *Common Reader*, 321–322, 328.

26 Alan J. Lee, *The Origins of the Popular Press in England: 1855–1914* (London: Croom Helm, 1976), 48.

27 Altick, *Common Reader,* 355.

28 Joel H. Wiener, 'The Nineteenth Century and the Emergence of a Mass Circulation Press', in Martin Conboy and John Steel (eds), *The Routledge Companion to British Media History* (London: Routledge, 2015), 209.

29 In the 1860s and 1870s *Blackwood's* circulation averaged around 6,500. See David Finkelstein, 'The Role of the Literary and Cultural Periodical', in Conboy and Steel (eds), *Routledge Companion to British Media History*, 265.

30 Finkelstein, 'Literary and Cultural Periodical', 265–266.

31 Sam Moskowitz, 'Preface', in Moskowitz (ed.), *Science Fiction by Gaslight: A History and Anthology of Science Fiction in the Popular Magazines, 1891–1911* (Cleveland: World Publishing Co., 1968), 11. What role, if any, the education acts had in this development is difficult to say. Writing in 1876, a 'Journeyman Engineer' wrote in *Good Words* that most of the working classes were 'badly educated' but also that 'the great bulk of them can read'. The problem, he argued, was

218 *Authors and readers*

that they often read literature of poor instructive quality: 'Readers and Reading', *Good Words* (December 1876), 315–320.

32 This is the opinion of John S. North: see J. Don Vann and Rosemary T. VanArsdel, 'Introduction', in Vann and VanArsdel (eds), *Victorian Periodicals and Victorian Society* (Toronto: University of Toronto Press, 1995), 3.

33 Alexis Weedon, *Victorian Publishing: The Economics of Book Production for a Mass Market, 1836–1916* (Aldershot: Ashgate, 2003), 143.

34 Graham Law and Robert L. Patten, 'The Serial Revolution', in David McKitterick (ed.), *The Cambridge History of the Book in Britain, vol. VI: 1830–1914* (Cambridge: Cambridge University Press, 2009), 144.

35 After the serialisation in the *Daily Mail* between 14 March and 4 July 1906, Eveleigh Nash brought out the first book edition: *The Invasion of 1910. With a Full Account of the Siege of London* (London: Eveleigh Nash, 1906). A colonial edition, part of 'Macmillan's Colonial Library', was published the same year (London: Macmillan & Co., 1906). Everett & Co. brought out its own edition, *The Invasion* (London: Everett & Co., [1913]), and George Newnes brought out an abridged version before the war – *The Invasion: Abridged from the Original Edition* (London: George Newnes, Ltd., [1910]) – and one after, part of the 'Newnes Trench Library': *The Invasion* (London: George Newnes, Ltd., 1917). These are just examples of editions published in London. It was claimed that the book was translated into 27 languages (see N. St. Barbe Sladen, *The Real Le Queux: The Official Biography of William Le Queux* (London: Nicholson & Watson, 1938), 195), though this number might have been an invention.

36 See chapter 3.

37 The first instalment appeared in *Chums* no. 25, 1 March 1893, and ran until no. 47, 2 August 1893. The book was published by Cassell: Max Pemberton, *The Iron Pirate: A Plain Tale of Strange Happenings on the Sea* (London: Cassell & Company, 1893). See Simon Nowell-Smith, *The House of Cassell 1848–1958* (London: Cassell and Company, Ltd., 1958), 186; Max Pemberton, *Sixty Years Ago and After* (London: Hutchinson & Co., 1936), 115.

38 Pemberton, *Sixty Years*, 112; Pemberton, *Lord Northcliffe: A Memoir* (London: Hodder and Stoughton Limited, [1922]).

39 Nowell-Smith, *Cassell*, 187.

40 Philip Waller, *Writers, Readers and Reputations: Literary Life in Britain 1870–1918* (Oxford: Oxford University Press, 2006), 399. As Stableford notes, several 'scientific romancers were essayists as well as novelists': *Scientific Romance*, 6.

Readers and receptions 219

41 This story was discussed in more detail in chapter 4. Another example is *When War Breaks Out* (London and New York: Harper Brothers, 1898), authored by H.W. Wilson and Arnold White. The story was written as a series of letters from a correspondent in London to a US weekly, during a near-future war between Britain and France and Russia.

42 Stableford, *Scientific Romance*, 109. The story was printed in *Answers* between 23 December 1893 and 2 June 1894. By 17 February it was referred to as 'The Great War in 1897', presumably so that the theme would be more recognisable. The book edition, referred to earlier, was published later that same year: *The Great War in England in 1897* (London: Tower Publishing Company Limited, 1894). Le Queux had indeed worked as a journalist before he turned to fiction: see Roger T. Stearn, 'The Mysterious Mr Le Queux: War Novelist, Defence Publicist and Counterspy', *Soldiers of the Queen*, 70 (1992), 7.

43 Aside from journalists, the profession that was most imitated by authors of future-war narratives was probably that of the historians. The idea of writing a 'history' from the future was particularly common in the 1870s. See Christian K. Melby, 'Empire and Nation in British Future-War and Invasion-Scare Fiction, 1871–1914', *Historical Journal*, 63 (2020), 399–400.

44 Gareth Stedman Jones, *Outcast London: A Study in the Relationship Between Classes in Victorian Society* (Oxford: Clarendon Press, 1971), 327–328.

45 John Ramsden, *Don't Mention the War: The British and the Germans since 1890* (London: Abacus, 2007), 57.

46 Both quotes are from Moskowitz, *Strange Horizons*, 182–183.

47 A theatrical invasion-scare tradition goes back at least to *The Battle of Dorking*, as discussed in chapter 1. A play titled *The Invasion of Britain, or the Siege of Glasgow* premiered in that city in April 1900, at a time when the sending of an expeditionary force to South Africa led to discussions of British vulnerability at home: in the play, the enemy takes advantage of the 'denudation of this country of its regular troops' (*The Era*, 21 April 1900, 9). The play was reportedly positively received by 'an audience which seemed to enjoy the invasion' (*Glasgow Herald*, 17 April 1900, 3). I am grateful to Brian Wallace for informing me of this play. There might have been numerous similar stage dramas which dealt with the topic of invasion, in particular in local settings, through the period covered in this study. Anne Summers observes that the National Service League was particularly eager to have invasion plays written: Anne Summers, 'The Character of Edwardian Nationalism: Three Popular Leagues', in Paul Kennedy and Anthony Nicholls (eds), *Nationalist and Racialist Movements in*

220   *Authors and readers*

Britain and Germany before 1914 (London and Basingstoke: Palgrave Macmillan, 1981), 75. More research is needed on the way such plays were disseminated, staged and received. A more detailed analysis of the staging of and reaction to *An Englishman's Home* can be found in Christian K. Melby, 'Rethinking British Militarism before the First World War: The Case of *An Englishman's Home* (1909)', *English Historical Review*, 137 (2022), 1377–1401.

48 *Westminster Papers: A Monthly Journal of Chess, Whist, Games of Skill, and the Drama,* 1 February 1872, 175. The journal noted that the game was 'an excellent recreation for the long evenings'.

49 See Christopher George Lewin, *War Games and their History* (Stroud: Fonthill Media, 2012), 83–85 for details on this game. I am grateful to Peter Keeling for informing me of the existence of this and *The Battle of Dorking* board games.

50 Lewin lists the game as being from 1915 (*War Games*, 140–141); Brett Holman, in an informative description and analysis of this and other board games, surmises a pre-1914 date might be more accurate: https://airminded.org/2007/08/05/war-games/. The Imperial War Museum lists the game as being made in 1911: www.iwm.org.uk/collections/item/object/30082434.

51 A 1909 film promised its viewers a vision of *Invasion: Its Possibilities*, and showed the repulse of an enemy army by British troops (*Kinematograph and Lantern Weekly*, 4 March 1909, 1180). Michael Paris lists some films, portraying aerial warfare, from the immediate pre-war years, beginning with *The Airship Destroyer*, also from 1909: Michael Paris, *Winged Warfare: The Literature and Theory of Aerial Warfare in Britain, 1859–1917* (Manchester and New York: Manchester University Press, 1992), 56–57. More films of imaginary warfare would follow after the outbreak of war in 1914, as discussed in more detail in the next chapter.

52 See Moskowitz, *Strange Horizons*, 191–200.

53 *Black and White*, 2 January 1892, 2.

54 Waller, *Writers, Readers and Reputations,* 332.

55 J. Shaylor, 'On the Selling of Books', *The Nineteenth Century* (December 1896), 939.

56 Michael MacDonagh, 'The Craft of Newspaper Advertising', *Monthly Review* (August 1905), 102.

57 See chapter 3.

58 *Standard*, 6 February 1882, 3.

59 Rev. Thomas Berney, *The Battle of the Channel Tunnel and Dover Castle and Forts. A Letter to the Right Honourable Wm. Ewart Gladstone, M.P.* (Bracon Ash: Thomas Berney, 1882), 4.

60 Berney, *Channel Tunnel*, 12.
61 Colonel Louis Jackson, 'The Defence of Localities against Aerial Attack', *Journal of the Royal United Service Institution*, 58 (June 1914), 701–702. On ideas of aerial warfare, fictional and otherwise, see Brett Holman, *The Next War in the Air: Britain's Fear of the Bomber, 1908–1941* (Farnham: Ashgate, 2014).
62 A. Michael Matin, 'Scrutinizing *The Battle of Dorking*: The Royal United Service Institution and the Mid-Victorian Invasion Controversy', *Victorian Literature and Culture*, 39 (2011), 385–407.
63 Frank McLynn, *Invasion: From the Armada to Hitler, 1588–1945* (London: Routledge & Kegan Paul, 1987), 61.
64 General Staff, War Office, *Recent Publications of Military Interest*, No. 1 (April 1907), 20.
65 'Notices of Books: *The Next Naval War*. By S. Eardley-Wilmot', *Journal of the Royal United Service Institution*, 38 (August 1894), 895.
66 For a more in-depth look at the links between future-war fiction/science fiction and war, see David Seed (ed.), *Future Wars: The Anticipations and the Fears* (Liverpool: Liverpool University Press, 2012); Antulio J. Echevarria II, *Imagining Future War: The West's Technological Revolution and Visions of Wars to Come, 1880–1914* (Westport and London: Praeger Security International, 2007); Charles E. Gannon, *Rumors of War and Infernal Machines: Technomilitary* Agenda-Setting in American and British Speculative Fiction (Lanham: Rowman & Littlefield Publishers, Inc., 2005); also Matin, 'The Creativity of War Planners: Armed Forces Professionals and the Pre-1914 British Invasion Scare Genre', *English Literary History*, 78 (2011), 801–831. For a concrete example of how military thinking could be presented as fiction, outside the format of a traditional future-war narrative, see 'Backsight Forethought' [pseud.], *The Defence of Duffer's Drift: A Few Experiences in Field Defence for Detached Posts Which May Prove Useful in Our Next War* (London: William Clowes & Sons, Limited, 1904).
67 A. Michael Matin, ' "The Hun is at the Gate!": Historicizing Kipling's Militaristic Rhetoric, from the Imperial Periphery to the National Center: Part One: The Russian Threat to British India', *Studies in the Novel*, 31 (1999), 318.
68 Samuel Hynes, *The Edwardian Turn of Mind* (Princeton: Princeton University Press, 1968), 15–53.
69 The title of Hynes' first chapter: *Edwardian Turn of Mind*, 3–14. In a similar vein, I.F. Clarke, focusing on the way future-war fiction presented technology, saw pre-1914 stories as part of a 'gospel of progress', compared to what came after. See I.F. Clarke,

222 *Authors and readers*

Voices Prophesying War: Future Wars 1763–3749 (Oxford: Oxford University Press, 1992), 46. 'The world knows only too well', he concluded, 'what the effects of another total war could be' (*Voices*, 4). Following Clarke, in studies where the technological aspects of future-war fiction is the main focus, pre-war optimism is contrasted with the pessimism of the world that emerged after 1914. According to Antulio J. Echevarria II, '[d]ark futures and bright ones competed with one another. The era generally put its faith in the latter, a faith that remained intact until the full extent of the Great War's ruinous effects became known' (*Imagining Future War*, 96). See also chapter 3 in Chris Morgan, *The Shape of Futures Past: The Story of Prediction* (Exeter: Webb & Bower, 1980), 36–73. Lawrence Freedman follows a similar logic, contrasting 'what can now seem the naïve optimism from before the First World War' with 'the fearful realism that preceded the Second World War, or the attempts to come to terms with the utterly terrifying prospect of a nuclear conflict': *The Future of War: A History* (London: Allen Lane, 2017), xvii.

70 Heather Jones and Arndt Weinrich, 'The Pre-1914 Period: Imagined Wars, Future Wars. Introduction', *Francia*, 40 (2013), 309. Holger Afflerbach argues that the two contrasting beliefs of the future Great War as both improbable and inevitable existed side by side in pre-war Europe: 'The Topos of Improbable War in Europe before 1914', in Holger Afflerbach and David Stevenson (eds), *An Improbable War? The Outbreak of World War I and European Political Culture before 1914* (New York and Oxford: Berghahn, 2007), 174–175.

71 George Dangerfield, *The Strange Death of Liberal England* (New York: Perigee Books, 1980), 119.

72 G.R. Searle, *The Quest for National Efficiency: A Study in British Politics and Political Thought, 1899–1914* (London: Ashfield Press, 1990), 34.

73 Anne Summers, 'Militarism in Britain before the Great War', *History Workshop Journal*, 2 (1976), 112.

74 On militarism and the left, see Matthew Johnson, *Militarism and the British Left, 1902–1914* (Basingstoke: Palgrave Macmillan, 2013) – a study that, despite its title, focuses mostly on the Liberal party. On 'Patriotism' and the left more generally, see Paul Ward, *Red Flag and Union Jack: Englishness, Patriotism and the British Left, 1881–1924* (Woodbridge: The Royal Historical Society/Boydell Press, 1998). On the concept of a technologically focused British 'Liberal Militarism', see David Edgerton, 'Liberal Militarism and the British State', *New Left Review*, 185 (1991), 138–169; and Edgerton, *England and the Aeroplane: Militarism, Modernity and Machines* (London: Penguin

Books, 2013). For a good discussion on the complexities of the term 'militarism', see Johnson, *Militarism and the Left*, 1–19. See also Melby, 'Empire and Nation'; and Melby, 'Rethinking British Militarism', where some of the arguments in this chapter regarding militarism and imperialism in invasion-scare and future-war fiction have previously been outlined and discussed.

75 Herbert Spencer, *The Principles of Sociology*, 3 vols. (London: Williams and Norgate, 1876–1896), II, 658–730; III, 585–586. See also Spencer, 'The New Toryism', *Contemporary Review* (February 1884), 153–167. On Spencer's thought, see J.W. Burrow, *Evolution and Society: A Study in Victorian Social Theory* (Cambridge: Cambridge University Press, 1970), 179–227.

76 Spencer, *Principles*, III, 590.

77 It should be noted that Spencer did not use the word 'imperialism': he described British expansion as the process where '[m]ore and more lands belonging to weak peoples are being seized on one or other pretext'. Spencer, *Principles*, III, 590; on French imperialism, see 586–587.

78 Richard Cobden, *The Three Panics: An Historical Episode*, 6th edition (London: Ward & Co., 1862).

79 Michael Paris, *Warrior Nation: Images of War in British Popular Culture, 1850–2000* (London: Reaktion, 2000), 8. See also Graham Dawson, *Soldier Heroes: British Adventure, Empire and the Imagining of Masculinities* (London and New York: Routledge, 1994), in particular 233–258.

80 John M. MacKenzie, *Propaganda and Empire: The Manipulation of British Public Opinion, 1880–1960* (Manchester: Manchester University Press 1984). See also 'Introduction: Popular imperialism and the military', in MacKenzie (ed.), *Popular Imperialism and the Military: 1850–1950* (Manchester: Manchester University Press, 1992), as well as the other essays in this volume.

81 W.J. Reader: *At Duty's Call: A Study in Obsolete Patriotism* (Manchester: Manchester University Press, 1988), 19, 27.

82 Cecil D. Eby, *The Road to Armageddon: The Martial Spirit in English Popular Literature, 1870–1914* (Durham and London: Duke University Press, 1987), 7–8. Note that Eby nominally looked at 'England', not 'Britain'.

83 Paris, *Warrior Nation*.

84 MacKenzie, *Propaganda and Empire*, 8.

85 On Gramsci, see James Joll, *Gramsci* (Glasgow: Fontana, 1977); and Peter Ives, *Language and Hegemony in Gramsci* (London: Pluto Press, 2004). Gramsci, of course, was partly echoing ideas Karl Marx and Friedrich Engels had originally had in the 1840s, where they argued

224 *Authors and readers*

that the class which controls the material means of production 'consequently also controls the means of mental production': Karl Marx and Friedrich Engels, *The German Ideology* (Amherst: Prometheus Books, 1998), 67.

86 C.J. Keep, 'Fearful Domestication: Future-War Stories and the Organization of Consent, 1871–1914', *Mosaic*, 23 (1990), 3, 6.

87 F.M.L. Thompson, 'Social Control in Victorian Britain', *Economic History Review*, 34 (1989), 189, 207.

88 Eric Hobsbawm, 'Mass-Producing Traditions: Europe 1870–1914', in Hobsbawm and Terence Ranger (eds), *The Invention of Tradition* (Cambridge: Cambridge University Press, 1983), 263–264.

89 For example, William Le Queux, *German Atrocities: A Record of Shameless Deeds* (London: George Newnes, [1914]). This naturally included an advert for Newnes' abridged edition of Le Queux's *The Invasion of 1910*.

90 Adrian Gregory, 'British "War Enthusiasm" in 1914: A Reassessment', in Gail Braybon (ed.), *Evidence, History and the Great War: Historians and the Impact of 1914–18* (New York and Oxford: Berghahn, 2003), 81.

91 HPD HC Deb 13 March 1906 vol. 153 c1120.

92 Suvin, *Victorian Science Fiction*, 234. This is, of course, only one possible reading: Lehmann, as a Radical Liberal, was certainly also opposed to Harmsworth's militarism, had opposed the Boer War, and was offered the editorship of the *Daily News* when the paper 'reverted to its former radical and anti-jingo course', as his son observed. To say that it was social, rather than political differences that primarily made him view Le Queux with distaste, is probably an overstatement: see John Lehmann, *The Whispering Gallery: Autobiography I* (London: Longmans, Green, 1955), 35–37. See also Eric Halladay, 'Lehmann, Rudolph Chambers (1856–1929)', ODNB. Interestingly, when the exchange between Lehmann and the Prime Minister was reported in *The Times*, the newspaper wrote that it was the Liberal member for Coventry, A.E.W. Mason, another novelist and author of adventure fiction, who had asked the question, instead of Lehmann (14 March 1906, 6). Mason had an *erratum* posted in the next day's paper: 'The question was not asked by me', he wrote, 'and since it would not have been in the best of taste for me to put a question of the kind, I shall be greatly obliged if you would publish this correction' (*The Times*, 15 March 1906, 8).

93 HPD HC Deb 13 March 1906 vol. 153 c1120.

94 Hynes, *Edwardian Turn of Mind*, 42. Suvin refers to Hynes in his above analysis.

95 *The Times*, 14 March 1906, 11.

96 *The Times*, 16 March 1906, 11.

97 *The Times*, 16 March 1906, 11.

98 *The Times*, 17 March 1906, 8.

99 Clarke, *Voices*, 122.

100 HPD HC Deb 14 May 1906 vol. 157 cc187–188. In addition to Arnold-Forster, the Conservative Sir Howard Vincent also disapproved of the advertising, and inquired whether anything could be done about it.

101 *Sphere*, 24 March 1906, 288.

102 *Daily News*, 4 April 1906, 4.

103 See *Daily News*, 14 March 1906, 6; and 7 April 1906, 6.

104 William Le Queux, *German Spies in England: An Exposure* (London: Stanley Paul & Co., 1915), 17. The claim is repeated in N. St. Barbe Sladen, *The Real Le Queux: The Official Biography of William Le Queux* (London: Nicholson & Watson, 1938), 195. Eveleigh Nash, the publisher behind the book edition, claimed that *The Invasion of 1910* gained 'a million readers' (see advertisement in *Pall Mall Gazette*, 30 July 1906, 3), which might be where the number is from. But a million readers is of course not the same thing as a million copies sold, in particular for a story that had been serialised in a mass circulation newspaper. In an attempt to calculate the number of copies sold, Ailise Bulfin concludes that the book must have sold several thousand copies, and can conceivably be characterised as a bestseller, reaching a large audience. Ailise Bulfin, 'The International Circulation and Impact of Invasion Fiction: Case Study of William Le Queux's *The Invasion of 1910* – "Not an ordinary 'pot-boiler' " ', *Critical Survey*, 32 (2020), 171.

105 *[Hull] Daily Mail*, 14 November 1906, 4.

106 *The Citizen*, 26 May 1906, 2.

107 See *The Era*, 14 April 1906, 20. At the Granville, the paper reported, Evans caused 'uproarious laughter': see *The Era* 28 April 1906, 21. Evans was not the only satirist: a less traditional parody was a 'laughable water sketch' performed at the East Ham Swimming Club's annual swimming club gala in August, reported in the *Essex County Chronicle*, 17 August 1906, 3.

108 *Pall Mall Gazette*, 16 June 1906, 10. Francis Hernaman-Johnson, *The Polyphemes: A Story of Strange Adventures among Strange Beings* (London: Ward, Lock & Co., 1906), does indeed describe an intelligent species of ants who, having mastered air travel, go to war with mankind.

226   *Authors and readers*

109 *New London Journal*, 5 May 1906, 10.
110 For a reading of satire in invasion-scare stories, see Melby, 'Rethinking British Militarism', 1394–1399.
111 *Tatler*, 16 May 1906, 183–184, 'The Invasion of 1908. With a Full Account of the Siege of Berlin'. The story was supposedly written by Frank Richardsheimer, with naval chapters by Lieutenant-Colonel Newnham Davis.
112 *Punch*, 14 March 1906, 188–189, 'The Yellow Patriots'.
113 *Punch*, 7 March 1909, 187–188, 'The Invaders'. *Punch* also made fun of Le Queux later that year, in the short 'The Secret of the Army Aeroplane': *Punch*, 26 May 1909, 366.
114 William Le Queux, *Things I know about King's, Celebrities, and Crooks* (London: Eveleigh Nash and Grayson Limited, 1923), 249–253. A later biography of Le Queux argues that '[t]he claims which Le Queux made in novels such as *The Invasion* and *Spies of the Kaiser* were in general treated as good, clean fun ...' – this is a reasonable assumption: Chris Patrick and Stephen Baister, *William Le Queux: Master of Mystery* (Purley: Chris Patrick & Stephen Baister, [2007]), 66.
115 Gannon, *Rumors of War*, 37.
116 Le Queux, *German Spies*, 8.
117 J.N. Hampson, 'Great Britain v. France and Russia', *National Review* (June 1898), 502–522.
118 See Andrew S. Thompson, 'Maxse, Leopold James (1864–1932)', ODNB.
119 Vice-Admiral P.H. Colomb, 'First Impressions of the War', *National Review* (June 1898), 523–535.
120 Although the *National Review* apparently inspired more sensationalist stories as well: Walter Wood claimed that he wrote *The Enemy in Our Midst: The Story of a Raid on England* (London: John Long, 1906) after having read 'a sensational article by a "German Staff Officer"' in the periodical (5).
121 A.J.A. Morris, *The Scaremongers: The Advocacy of War and Rearmament, 1896–1914* (London: Routledge & Kegan Paul, 1984), 368.
122 Stephen Koss, *The Rise and Fall of the Political Press in Britain* (Chatham: Fontana Press, 1990), 21.
123 F.W. Hirst, *The Six Panics and Other Essays* (London: Methuen & Co., 1913), 2.
124 Adrian Gregory, 'A Clash of Cultures: The British Press and the Opening of the Great War', in Troy R.E. Paddock (ed.), *A Call to Arms: Propaganda, Public Opinion, and Newspapers in the Great War* (Westport: Praeger, 2004), 18.
125 See Glenn R. Wilkinson, ' "The Blessings of War": The Depiction of Military Force in Edwardian Newspapers', *Journal of Contemporary*

History, 33 (1998), 97–115; Wilkinson, 'Literary Images of Vicarious Warfare: British Newspapers and the Origin of the First World War, 1899–1914', in Patrick J. Quinn and Steven Trout (eds), *The Literature of the Great War Reconsidered: Beyond Modern Memory* (Basingstoke: Palgrave, 2001), 24–34; Wilkinson, *Depictions and Images of War in Edwardian Newspapers, 1899–1914* (Basingstoke: Palgrave Macmillan, 2003).

126 Dominik Geppert, ' "The foul-visaged anti-Christ of journalism"? The Popular Press between Warmongering and international Cooperation', in Dominik Geppert and Robert Gerwarth (eds), *Wilhelmine Germany and Edwardian Britain: Essays on Cultural Affinity* (Oxford: Oxford University Press, 2008), 388.

127 See, for example, Paris, *Warrior Nation*; and Eby, *Armageddon*.

128 *Pall Mall Magazine* was owned by William Waldorf Astor, who had bought the *Gazette* in 1892 and turned it into a Conservative paper. Under the editorship of George Halkett in particular, from the turn of the century to 1905 the magazine published extensively on the issue of invasion and national defence: see Mike Ashley, *The Age of the Storytellers: British Popular Fiction Magazines 1880–1950* (London: British Library, 2006), 147, 150–151. Examples include two essays by foreign officers on the prospect of invading Britain, by Lieutenant-Colonel Delauney of France in the November 1901 issue, 395–398; and by Major Hoenig of the German Army in the February 1902 issue, 230–234.

129 Ernest Bramah, 'The War Hawks', *Pall Mall Magazine* (September 1909), 384–393. On the fear of aerial invasion in 1908–1909, see Alfred M. Gollin, 'England Is No Longer an Island: The Phantom Airship Scare of 1909', *Albion*, 13 (1981), 43–57. Gollin notes that while there were reports of 'phantom airships' over Britain in May 1909, many newspapers were dismissive of these – Northcliffe and the *Daily Mail* were particularly scathing. The *Pall Mall Gazette*, in a bemused commentary, observed that: 'We are not sure that the "scare" is so widespread as all that. The suggestion of foreign airships over these islands has inspired a spirit of curiosity rather than alarm, since it is so obvious that there could be nothing to be alarmed about, even though certain of our contemporaries have been ill-advised enough to ascribe a sinister origin to the harmless phenomena of the past few days' (21 May 1909, 7).

130 Captain S.W. Beeman, 'The Great Day in 1920', *Pall Mall Magazine* (April 1913), 441.

131 Rudyard Kipling, 'The Edge of the Evening', *Pall Mall Magazine* (December 1913), 714–726.

228   *Authors and readers*

132 Michael Paris, *Winged Warfare: The Literature and Theory of Winged Warfare in Britain, 1859–1917* (Manchester and New York: Manchester University Press, 1992), 39. Paris lists the stories as written in c.1904 and 1907, respectively. 'With the Nightmail' can be found in Rudyard Kipling, *Actions and Reactions* (London: Macmillan & Co., 1909), 109–167; 'As Easy as A.B.C.' is printed in Kipling, *A Diversity of Creatures* (London: Macmillan & Co., 1917), 1–44.
133 Donal Hamilton Haines, 'The Leveller', *Pall Mall Magazine* (January 1913), 13–24.
134 Inglis Allen, 'Woman Disposes: The Story of a Night's Adventures', *Pall Mall Magazine* (January 1912), 39.
135 *Penny Illustrated Paper*, 13 February 1909, 3.
136 See Melby, 'Rethinking British Militarism'.

Part IV

Fiction goes to war

7

Invasion-scare literature and the First World War

'I'd got so used to the war with Germany that I never imagined it would happen'.

> - Mr. Lawrence Carmine, in H.G. Wells'
> *Mr Britling Sees It Through*, 1916.[1]

Britain went to war with Germany on 4 August 1914. It would take more than four years, the creation and mobilisation of a mass army, and the almost complete commitment of most of the British economy and society before victory could be declared. In scope, magnitude and impact on British society, the First World War was, in most respects, unlike anything seen on the pages of fictional war stories in the decades leading up to 1914. No wonder, then, that as early as November 1914 the satirical magazine *Punch* could quip that:

> Amongst the (more or less) skilled industries that have been gravely affected by the outbreak of hostilities must now be placed the making of prophetic fiction. It is calculated that the number of novels dealing with "*The Next Great War*" that have had to be scrapped must run well into four figures.[2]

Punch, however, was wide off the mark in this respect. Far from killing off the industry, the First World War would continue a pre-war trend, wherein stories could be presented and utilised as arguments in new debates and discussions. Both old and new stories would appear, more often than not in the same format and guise as the pre-war literature, and offer their audience the opportunity to make sense of the ongoing conflict.

232 *Fiction goes to war*

This chapter shows what happened when invasion- and future-war fiction went to war in 1914–1918. While the war has at times been presented – notably by I.F. Clarke[3] – as more or less a black hole when it came to the writing and reading of future-war stories, it was actually an active period where the idea of invasion played out much as it had done before the conflict. A main contention of this book has been that the stories of imaginary wars were more flexible and constituted a more multilayered genre than a first glance at the stories might indicate. The ultimate proof of this thesis is the way the stories were repurposed and reimagined when the real 'Great War' came along.

Contested prophets, or Chesney goes to war

It was perhaps to be expected that one of the first British pre-war invasion-scare texts to be reissued during the First World War was the tale that started the genre back in the summer of 1871, *The Battle of Dorking*. Already in September 1914, shortly after the outbreak of war, the publisher Grant Richards brought out a new sixpence pamphlet edition of Chesney's story, capitalising, it would seem, on the very real contest between Britain and Germany. In a foreword to the pamphlet G.H. Powell noted that, while there were obvious differences, 'few readers will not recognize parallel features to those of our own situation in September 1914'. While most of the foreword was taken up with a more or less dreamy discourse on the just cause of the war against Germany, this point – that Chesney had somehow foretold and warned against coming catastrophes, from the 1870s until 1914 – was also central to Powell's introduction: '*Mutatis mutandis*', he observed, 'doubtless, much of General Chesney's advice and warning might have been repeated on the occasion of the Boer War'.[4] This was echoed elsewhere: 'the moral of the book – a pregnant warning against national unreadiness – is still valid', noted the *Sheffield Daily Telegraph* of the reissued story.[5]

Chesney was rediscovered by other commentators as well. On 18 August, while complaining of the lack of good poetic descriptions of the current war, the author Arthur Machen in the London *Evening News* had called for poets to render descriptions of the

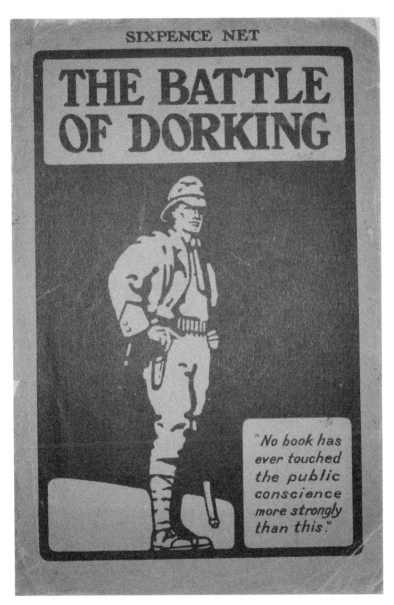

Figure 7.1 George Tomkyns Chesney, *The Battle of Dorking, with an Introduction by G.H. Powell* (London: Grant Richards Ltd., 1914). Source: Author's own collection

234   *Fiction goes to war*

'nightmare' of war, now reality: 'I can well remember when we first began to dream this ill-dream', he wrote.

> It was soon after the Franco-Prussian War that the "Battle of Dorking," a dismal augury of German invasion and English defeat, was written; and again and again in varying forms the terror has recurred, and we have shuddered a little and paled for a moment, and then laughed our fears away.[6]

During the early months of the war, warnings abounded of the possibility of a real 'battle of Dorking' taking place,[7] and the story, along with its later cousins, were picked up and re-read as Britain mobilised for a war on the continent. While not all of these new readers were convinced by the idea that Chesney's story, or others like it, had much to say about the present war, *Dorking* was still praised as having given at least an indication of developments leading up to 1914. 'Its republication at this moment by Mr. Grant Richards is opportune', wrote the *Yorkshire Post*,

> for though the picture Sir George Chesney draws has more contrasts than similarities to the existing situation, the general impression made on the mind of the reader will be wholesome and stimulating. Invasion of these shores is still a possibility should there be any slackening in the national spirit, and it is well that one should realise what it means.[8]

Stories both old and new could all be instructive, in their different ways. In the *Bystander* magazine on 19 August, two weeks after the British declaration of war, Ralph Straus dug up a set of old future-war stories, mostly from the previous two decades or so, but going back all the way to *Dorking* and an even earlier story, *The Reign of George VI* (from 1763), to see how war had been imagined before. Straus observed that some of these authors' work 'reads rather ludicrous today, but that is only to be expected. International relations can and do change very rapidly'. He found many of the developments described in such books as Alan H. Burgoyne's *The War Inevitable* rather incredible by modern eyes, but the ongoing war was still in its early days and its future development as yet unclear.[9] Pre-war literature was seen as both predictive and fantastic, with the war seeming stranger than fiction even for those who had written predictions of it. T.W. Offin, author of the 1900 pamphlet *How the Germans took London*, told his local paper in August 1914 that 'recent events have shown how accurately I had summed up the situation at the time'. While this is debatable – the pamphlet describes a fairly fantastic and bloodless surprise attack on London, where German planning and forethought overwhelm the hapless defenders – Offin still found the present situation surreal: 'I little thought, however,' he stated, 'that I should ever see any of my own land taken possession of by our Military Authorities, and pretty hedgerows levelled with the ground as necessary preparations to protect us from a real German invasion'.[10]

Not everyone found in the fiction of old something to be admired or to be instructed by. The Fabian *New Statesman* published a 'Special War Supplement' in November 1914, consisting of a long, critical essay – titled 'Common Sense about the War' – by George Bernard Shaw. Early in his essay, Shaw remarked on the British equivalent of German militarist literature:

> We soon produced the first page of the Bernhardian literature: an anonymous booklet entitled *The Battle of Dorking*. ... And its moral was "To Arms; or the Germans will besiege London as they besieged Paris." From that time until the present the British propaganda of war with Germany has never ceased. The lead given by *The Battle of Dorking* was taken up by articles in the daily press and the magazines.[11]

The link between Bernhardi and Chesney was echoed by a young Harold Laski in the pages of the *Herald* in January 1915, as he analysed the US's view on the war: 'Militarism of any kind', he wrote, 'whether of Potsdam or of Whitehall, whether in Bernhardi or in the resuscitated author of the Battle of Dorking, whether expressed in Von Moltke or expressed in Kitchener, she [America] shrinks from as from an evil thing'.[12] Britain, the argument went, had been as guilty of promoting militarist fantasies as Germany; Chesney's place in British culture was proof of this.

The 'resuscitation' of Chesney and his narrative, and the debate over what the story meant or could say about Britain's relationship with Germany, did not necessarily indicate that *Dorking* had a deep-seated place in the British national psyche, however. An angry rebuttal of Shaw's 'Common Sense' essay in the Northcliffe-owned *Weekly Dispatch*, penned by the bellicose journalist Robert Blatchford, seems to have got most of the narrative wrong: 'The

236 *Fiction goes to war*

author of the pamphlet (a British general)', he wrote of *The Battle of Dorking*, 'chose Germany as the invader because he thought Germany the least likely of European nations to make an attempt [at invasion], and therefore judged that the Germans would not take offence. But the invader the pamphlet was aimed at was France'. This is a slightly dubious reading of Chesney's intentions behind the pamphlet, to say the least. Blatchford even got the publication year wrong: '"The Battle of Dorking," if I remember rightly, was published somewhere about 1873 or 1874'.[13]

Blatchford was certainly not alone in having mostly forgotten about *Dorking*, before it was exhumed in time for a new European war. William Archer, a friend and acquaintance of Shaw, wrote in the *Daily News and Leader* that '[t]he younger readers of Mr. Shaw's sixpenny startler on the war have probably been asking themselves "What on earth was or is "The Battle of Dorking"?"' Archer wrote that he had found and re-read the pamphlet, for these younger readers' benefit, but that he thought the statement that the pamphlet was anti-German was a step too far: true, an unnamed Germany was the enemy in the story, '[b]ut the design was obviously not to indicate any special danger from the side of Germany, but to show up British unpreparedness and inefficiency'.[14] This was a more perceptive reading than Blatchford's or even Shaw's, but it is also an indication that even at this point, four decades after its publication and with a real war raging against Germany, the meaning and interpretation of Chesney's story was still contested. As Britain entered its first war winter, how this first invasion-scare story should be read and understood remained a battleground, with readers able to infer their own ideas on *Dorking*'s pages.

As the example of *Dorking* shows, older stories were interpreted and re-read with new eyes, even as pre-war imagery found its way into the British view of Germany in the early months of the war. German treatment of civilians in an occupied Britain had been portrayed in much of the pre-war fictional invasion stories, from *The Battle of Dorking* to *An Englishman's Home*. Whether this provided an impetus to descriptions of German behaviour in Belgium – and of potential behaviour in Britain, should the country be invaded – is less clear, though at least some used *An Englishman's Home* as an illustration of what the horrors of war entailed. As Mr. Brown had taken up a rifle against the invaders in du Maurier's play, men and

Invasion-scare literature and the war

women were also taking up weapons against the German invaders in Belgium, with the same result. A 'legal correspondent' in the *Globe*, referring to a story of 'Belgian women who repulsed the Uhlans from the National Arms Factory at Herstal', found such behaviour problematic: 'If people who are not actually in the army take it upon themselves to defend their own houses or workshops, they not only run the risk of being captured and shot, like the man in "An Englishman's Home," but the chances are that they will induce the enemy to take severe reprisals on the rest of the population'.[15] A letter to *The Times* in October 1914 agreed: if civilians were to take up arms against invaders, they would be in breach of international law: 'the sad, but inevitable consequence of which was … truthfully represented on the stage in *An Englishman's Home*'.[16] 'We do not want to see repeated in England the famous scene from *An Englishman's Home*', wrote the military correspondent for *The Times*, Charles à Court Repington, in late August 1914, 'which has recently been enacted in many a Belgian village'.[17] For these, as well as other commentators, du Maurier's pre-war story could be used to describe the present war. However, the meaning of the story was filtered through the experiences of the real war, and interpreted in light of the new developments in Belgium.

It is possible to read such comments as an indication of a long-lasting fear of invasion, expressed through invasion-scare fiction, ever lurking under the surface and ready to emerge when the German army neared the channel. Stephen Badsey has argued that the British public prior to the war had been 'sensitised through imaginative fiction to the idea of foreign invaders wreaking havoc upon their own peaceful communities'.[18] Indeed, the portrayal of German behaviour towards civilians in stories ranging from *The Battle of Dorking* to *An Englishman's Home* must have taken on a new significance when read alongside reports of German treatment of Belgian civilians in the autumn of 1914. However, it is also possible to see how the earlier future-war narratives could be reused and reinterpreted for a new reality, illustrating not a lasting influence and continuous fear but a reimagining or rediscovering of earlier narratives where present-day ideas were attached to older stories.

Fears of invasion were prevalent in Britain during the summer and autumn months of 1914. Catriona Pennell has shown, looking at the popular responses to the war in the south-east of England, that '[t]he primary reaction of the Essex population between August

238   *Fiction goes to war*

and December 1914 was a fear of invasion by a German army'.[19] However, while some of these fears might have been inspired by pre-war invasion stories, it is not at all clear that such pre-war sentiments were what shaped the immediate fears in the autumn of 1914. While Pennell notes that such stories were indicative of at least some continued form of Edwardian invasion fears, it is also clear that the more immediate reason for the nervousness was the very real effects of the war currently ongoing on the continent, not least in Belgium, in the later months of 1914.[20] Recruitment numbers for the Army shot up noticeably as British newspapers reported of British setbacks at Amiens on 29 August, for example.[21]

In short, part of the problem in trying to assess the influence of pre-war invasion and future-war stories on the UK's reaction to the war in the late summer and autumn of 1914, is that the stories seem to have been superseded by the war itself. When references to pre-war stories emerge in the press, they are not seen as blueprints for how the conflict will play out, and only rarely – and conflictingly – touted as 'prophecies'. As such, pre-war invasion-scare fiction followed the same development as other cultural products and ideas when the war broke out: pre-war sentiments and ideas formed part of the language and ideas regarding war and Germany, but the war soon took on a logic of its own. This does not mean that fictional depictions of war and invasion were gone and had been superseded by events, as *Punch* had argued; but it did mean that the production and consumption of invasion-scare fiction took on a new function. While pre-war invasion texts had for the most part been inward-looking – commentaries on British society itself, rather than on external threats – the war, and the emergence of a concrete enemy in the form of Germany, offered a new logic to how old and new stories were interpreted. Before exploring this, we need to understand the ways in which British society approached the war, and how the conflict changed views on Germany as well as on British vulnerabilities.

Recycled ideas

In September 1914, Arthur Machen and the *Evening News* – who in the month before had called for poets to apply their pens to describe the conflict – would publish one of the first famous fictionalisations from the war. In the story 'The Bowmen' supernatural aid is rendered the British army during the troops' retreat from Mons.[22] By 1915, as the fronts had frozen in the stalemate of trench warfare, this story ballooned into an enormously popular legend: that the British soldiers had been saved by angels.[23]

That a story ended up with an afterlife of its own – with new interpretations and ideas attached to it – means that Machen's 'The Bowmen' had a lot in common with the invasion-scare literature that preceded it. In addition, whether due to the exigencies and stresses of wartime, or due to some other reasons, it illustrates the extent to which British society seemed particularly receptive to myths and fantasies in the war years – not to mention rumours. As Paul Fussell noted, the conflict 'seems especially fertile in rumor and legend. It was as if the general human impulse to make fictions had been dramatically unleashed by the novelty, immensity, and the grotesqueness of the proceedings'.[24] Soldiers, of course, are wont to be superstitious, and the First World War was no exception in this regard.[25] But aside from individual soldiers' superstitions, more widespread beliefs were accepted or at least spread among civilian society at home in Britain – such as the myth, prevalent in the months between August and November 1914, that thousands of Russian soldiers had been seen marching through Britain, with snow on their boots, on their way to assist the hard-pressed British Expeditionary Force on the Western Front.[26]

Some of these myths, including the legend of the angels of Mons, were based on or inspired by older conceptions and ideas.[27] As Daniel Pick has commented, First World War propaganda was organic, and not readily settled on easily defined stereotypes, but it nonetheless drew on pre-war language.[28] The widely circulated idea that the German army recycled the dead bodies of their own troops in a 'Corpse Exploitation Establishment',[29] was not a fabrication of the propaganda apparatus in Britain – as with the myth of the Russian soldiers, it was a *popular* invention, circulated long before any official notice was taken of it.[30]

Understanding this background helps explain how and in which ways British invasion-scare fiction – both from before and after the outbreak of war – was received in Britain after August 1914. The war created a new situation, one with real material consequences as well as new fears and worries for communities across Britain. To

240   *Fiction goes to war*

an extent, however, these fears and worries were based on earlier ideas both of war in general and of Germany in particular. These ideas circulated on a popular, ground level – below official government messaging and the nascent propaganda of state and newspapers. It is perhaps understandable, then, that the invasion-scare and future-war fiction that was published, re-released or reimagined during the war years was to a large extent, in form as well as function, the same literature that had been read and consumed before the war.

The afterlife of *Dorking*, and the references to earlier invasion-scare and future-war fiction in 1914 have already been mentioned, but more would follow as the war dragged on. As with the rediscovery of Chesney's novel, this literature often consisted of older stories, geared for a new market and a new reality. William Le Queux reinvented himself as a spy catcher and propagandist (albeit an unofficial one) after the war broke out (of which more below) but his earlier *The Invasion of 1910* led a profitable existence as a war novel, including as part of George Newnes' 'Newnes Trench Library', where the novel was marketed as 'the book that foretold the war'.[31] A film version of the story, to be made by Gaumont Cinematograph Company, had been in the works since 1912: Le Queux had written to Lord Roberts about this and asked for his assistance with the film, which Le Queux claimed would give a 'graphic idea of the state of England under invasion'.[32] The film seems to have run into troubles with the censors, which explains why it was not released until October 1914, after the outbreak of war. However, the film had never seriously been intended as a propaganda feature, as such. Le Queux had claimed, in his 1912 letter to Roberts, that the film would hopefully 'bring home to the thousands who go to "picture palaces" what war really means', but the plans reportedly included preparation for making two versions of the film: one where British arms triumphed and an alternative one with the Germans victorious at the end, the latter aimed, naturally, at the German market.[33] However, when the film was finally released at the end of October 1914, in markedly different circumstances and under the new title *If England Were Invaded*, it was promoted as a 'great patriotic film'.[34] The trade magazine *Bioscope* thought it was 'one of the best of many films which have been prepared to meet the great demand for patriotic fare'.[35]

Another old story made its screen debut in the opening months of the war, as film makers looked around for stirring narratives to turn into patriotic films. *An Englishman's Home* was filmed and released in picture theatres in September 1914.[36] In a commentary that might just as well have been taken from the 1909 reactions to du Maurier's stage version of the play, the film industry magazine *Kinematograph and Lantern Weekly* described it as a ' "recruiting" film'.[37] *Pictures and the Picturegoer* dedicated a large spread over three pages to the film, arguing that it threw a gauntlet down to the slackers. 'For years many patriots have been trying to bring home to Britons the great need of being prepared for war in times of peace. The result of these warnings were not gratifying'.[38] Little seemed to have changed in the five years since 1909: the story as well as the comments it received were the same, even as a real war was raging on the continent.[39]

A third pre-war invasion narrative that was turned into a film in 1914 was *Wake Up! A Dream of To-Morrow*, a film based on an earlier stage play by Laurence Cowen. Reportedly written a couple of years prior to the war, for a production at the London Opera House, the story was picked up by the Eclair Company 'with the cordial approval and co-operation of the authorities'.[40] The 'patriotic photo-play', of about an hour running time, received the enthusiastic backing of the Boy Scouts' Association, as well as the War Office. *Kinematograph and Lantern Weekly* reported that, 'so far as the military and spectacular part of the production is concerned, the whole thing may be said to have been filmed under the auspices of the War Office', and that, at the 15 October premiere, 'about 20,000 boy scouts from various parts of the London area are to march to Cambridge Circus and parade'.[41] The story was later serialised in the *Daily Express* between 5 January and 26 February 1915, and the paper joined forces with the Boy Scouts' Association in promoting the film version.[42] Throughout the serialisation, the *Daily Express* linked the two versions of the story – serialisation and film adaptation – in its promotion of the tale, including by listing places where the film version was screened. The newspaper was overt in stating that its reasoning was to increase recruitment. 'After reading the above', notices underneath the serialisation proclaimed, 'no man worthy the name must remain untrained'.[43] The success of the film in this respect was also trumpeted: a notice on 24 February proclaimed that a screening at the Coliseum in Harringay had resulted

242   *Fiction goes to war*

in 42 new recruits signing up.[44] A slightly amended book version of the serialised story was published the same year,[45] making "*Wake Up!*" one of the few invasion-scare tracts that appeared as a theatre production, film production, newspaper serialisation and finally in book format. Despite this, the story is largely forgotten today.

"*Wake Up!*" is a strange story, and despite its active use as a recruitment tool, its content was to a large extent out of touch with the political situation in 1915. In the novel we are introduced to Field-Marshal Sir Robert Mars – a character clearly inspired by Lord Roberts – who is a proponent of national service. Opposed to Mars' plan is the Secretary of State for War, named Lord Pax. As Britain is treacherously attacked and invaded by the country of Vaevictia, Lord Pax gets ample opportunity to regret his opposition to national service. The untrained British soldiery put up a brave resistance, but the Vaevictian soldiers prove too much, and civilians are subjected to the brutal behaviour of the invaders. London, naturally, is bombed. By the end of the story, Pax wakes up in his office – the invasion, the British defeat and the humiliation at the hands of the enemy troops, has all been a dream. Swiftly converted to the cause of national service, the story ends with Mars and Pax meeting and shaking hands in the former's office. Said Pax:

> Yes, Mars. I am convinced that you are right; that only in universal military service can Britain find safety, because the very knowledge of her strength will keep her from attack, as the knowledge of her weakness will invite it.[46]

'And when The Day came', a final paragraph informs the reader, 'and Britannia drew the sword, she was ready'.[47]

The country of Vaevictia is clearly meant to represent Wilhelmine Germany, but why Cowen decided to follow *An Englishman's Home* in blurring the true identity of the invaders is less clear; presumably no one was much worried about offending Germany in 1915, so naming them as the invaders would not have made much difference. Other parts of the narrative also seem to belong to the pre-war years, rather than to 1915, including Mars/Roberts' promotion of national service. Early in the story this turns into a heated discussion between Mars and Pax, wherein many of the pre-war arguments for conscription, including the risk of a 'bolt from the blue' – an attack without prior declaration of war – are presented.[48]

Invasion-scare literature and the war 243

That a story promoting conscription was chosen as a recruitment tool for voluntary enlistment was also curious, and echoes some of the issues that arose in debates between the proponents of conscription and those in favour of recruitment for the Territorials that followed *An Englishman's Home* in 1909. Other elements of the story that are clearly in line with other pre-war invasion-scare and spy fiction include the presence of a Vaevictian spy, the aptly named Hostis, and the assertion that Vaevictians 'of various social ranks', from waiters and hairdressers to Count Hostis himself, have been preparing the ground for an invasion of Britain.[49] This part of the plot would not have been out of place in a story by William Le Queux, as would the bloody descriptions of the war's effect on civilians.

Despite its promotion in the *Daily Express*, its rapid – and at least in part officially sanctioned – film adaptation, and the support it received at a time when British recruitment was in full swing, *"Wake Up!"* belongs as much to the Edwardian and pre-war years as it does to the First World War. This was a reworked, reimagined version of an earlier idea – showing yet again how pre-war invasion-scare fiction could take on new roles in the new reality that the war provided, at least in the earlier part of the conflict.

Invasion-scare narratives in visual culture: from films to postcards

The early burst of film adaptations of invasion-scare stories was not sustained throughout the conflict. Part of this can presumably be explained by the changed circumstances in the fighting, as the Western Front settled in for stalemate by late 1914.[50] Another reason was the lack of official support for fictional depictions of war. Private productions like *Wake Up!* may have received some tacit War Office support: at the beginning of the war, there was a sense that film could be an effective tool for raising patriotism in Britain, and cinema soon became part of the official British propaganda effort. The official propaganda, however, was geared towards the production of factual films, and these only appeared from 1915 onwards. Official British film propaganda during the war years was therefore dominated by such 'factual' productions as *Britain*

244   *Fiction goes to war*

Prepared (1915), *Battle of the Somme* (1916) and *The Battle of the Ancre and the Advance of the Tanks* (1917).[51]

The success of the 'factual' approach to propaganda filmmaking was mixed: on the one hand, *Battle of the Somme* was extremely popular, but as Nicholas Reeves has shown, the popularity of such films declined from 1917. Nor was cinema a fool-proof tool of propaganda, and audiences reacted differently to the same or similar films.[52] *Kinematograph and Lantern Weekly* was certainly not happy with the situation, commenting in September 1917 that British films compared unfavourably with those of its allies. The factual films, like *Britain Prepared* and *Battle of the Somme*, had a drawback in 'their lack of human interest and want of cohesion', noted the magazine. 'What we want to do', the writer continued, 'is to point out to the British producer that he is losing valuable ground by neglecting the opportunity of presenting story pictures, which will incite and enthuse the people to greater effort and soften their sacrifices and burdens by comparison with what they see others have borne'.[53] In short: what was needed was more melodrama. Official British propagandists seem to have agreed, with a move towards drama towards the end of the war. As part of this newfound impulse, British cinema audiences in 1918 almost got the opportunity to see what would presumably have been a rather remarkable invasion-scare narrative on the silver screen.

The short version is as follows: while Reeves lists only two feature-length British propaganda fiction films made by the official propaganda apparatus in Britain during the war, one of these, a film titled *Hearts of the World* from mid-1918, was mostly a Hollywood production, made by the director D.W. Griffith and starring Lillian Gish.[54] This leaves only one truly official British feature-length propaganda fiction film from the war. This film, provisionally titled *The National Film*, would be a massive production under the auspices of official film propagandists, with the Ministry of Information being heavily involved. However, the first print of the film was destroyed in a fire, and a re-shoot was finished too late to be distributed during the war. Indeed, the film was never released, its remaining copies destroyed. What we know of the film, however, indicates a heavy-handed invasion-scare narrative in what would probably have constituted a truly spectacular film. The screenplay was by Hall Caine, with help from numerous other authors, among them Thomas Hardy and Rudyard Kipling; a musical score had been prepared by, among others, Edward Elgar. Shot on location in Chester, the film aimed to portray the brutal behaviour of German invaders in England, and the effect an invasion would have on the civilian population.[55]

Aside from films, British propaganda efforts during the war did make occasional use of at least the idea of invasion. Ephemera such as printed posters, of which there were many during the conflict, sometimes referenced invasion, for example, to promote enlistment. A 1915 Irish poster, showing *pickelhaube*-wearing German troops bursting into a house and disturbing the breakfast of an unsuspecting family, bears the inscription 'IS YOUR HOME WORTH FIGHTING FOR?', and informs the reader that 'IT WILL BE TOO LATE TO FIGHT WHEN THE ENEMY IS AT YOUR DOOR SO JOIN TO-DAY'. Despite its Irish background and intended audience, the image, if not the text, would not have been out of place as an illustration for either *The Battle of Dorking* or *An Englishman's Home*.[56] The prospect of a German invasion of Ireland was mooted in other propaganda material as well: 'GERMANY WANTS IRELAND!' warned one poster (possibly) from 1916.[57] Irish recruitment posters often made use of women as recruiting agents, and appealed to Irish men to defend their home and family.[58] Other Irish recruitment posters drew direct links between Ireland on the one hand, and Belgium's experience of German occupation on the other.[59]

Visual propaganda, in the form of caricatures or posters, were central to all the belligerents' propaganda, as mobilisation got underway.[60] Recruitment posters, such as those discussed above, can be included here, but postcards too enjoined its recipients to support the war effort, or mocked the opposing forces – including, in Britain's case, the prospect of Germany ever invading Britain.[61] As such examples indicate, propaganda was – and is – a multifaceted concept, not easily defined or separated from other forms of communication and marketing. While much propaganda is, by modern definition at least, composed of lies or at least exaggerations, this was not necessarily how it was understood or seen during the war. Jay Winter has described propaganda as 'a state-dominated lawyers' brief, pleading the cause of the nation before its population and that of the world'.[62] Propaganda is rarely accepted when it is a top-down imposition, but it can function rather well – as it did during the First World War – when it is combined with popular ideas and sentiments;

Figure 7.2 'Is your home worth fighting for?', 1915 Irish poster.
Source: Imperial War Museum, reproduced with permission

Figure 7.3 Postcard, postmarked August 1918.
Source: Author's own collection

248 *Fiction goes to war*

the 'state-dominated' in Winter's quote does therefore not mean 'state-directed', as he writes.[63] The links between private enterprise, popular sentiment and government guidance was central to British propaganda efforts, as evidenced by attempts both at supporting private film enterprises, and to steer such productions from above.

Invasion-scare literature in official propaganda: a missing element?

Visual imagery, from film to recruitment posters was different from written invasion literature, however, and the latter seems to have held a more awkward position in official British propaganda.

Britain's propaganda apparatus took time to organise, and changed over the course of the conflict.[64] The August 1914 Defence of the Realm Act – or DORA – went beyond the voluntary pre-war censorship by adding coercive powers to government control of the press. However, the legislation was mostly aimed at preventing the press from printing information that could be valuable to the enemy, not as a means of controlling public opinion in Britain.[65] Intention is one thing, of course, and control of newspaper reporting – or lack thereof – did of course influence the public back home in Britain. In the first month of the war, as censorship was still rather disorganised, *The Times*' printed a dispatch from the front – the 'Amiens Dispatch' – with the blessing of F.E. Smith, the head of the newly established Official Press Bureau. The consternation both among the political apparatus and the public was substantial, and led to Smith resigning his post. 'The entire sequence of events leading both to and from the Amiens Dispatch', writes Stephen Badsey, 'arose from confusion within the government over propaganda, and from the lack of a system that had been agreed and understood by the press itself of accreditation for reporters, and of press handling and censorship'.[66]

Censorship, as in the control of information and separate from overt propaganda, was only one aspect of British attempts to control information during the war. Beyond recruitment, which remained 'the dominant theme of domestic propaganda until the introduction of conscription in January 1916',[67] the system of propaganda that was built up over the following years was likewise mainly aimed at foreigners – either intended to sap the morale of the enemy, or to

Invasion-scare literature and the war 249

convince neutrals, most importantly the United States, to support Britain's cause. To this end, Charles Masterman, Chancellor of the Duchy of Lancaster and a friend of the Prime Minister, was tasked with setting up a propaganda organisation in Britain. Organised out of the building that would give it its nickname, Wellington House, the War Propaganda Bureau tapped numerous literary figures – including J.M. Barrie, G.K. Chesterton, Arthur Conan Doyle and H.G. Wells. Newspapermen were also mobilised.[68] William Le Queux, the most prolific pre-war, anti-German author was conspicuously absent from the Wellington House list, presumably, as A. Michael Matin theorises, due to a combination of his low-brow literary standing and his eclectic personality.[69] Neither did Le Queux's novels appear among the *Schedule of Wellington House Literature*, where commissioned or reissued books that were part of Wellington House's propaganda were listed.[70]

What Masterman's Wellington House did during the war remains shrouded in some mystery,[71] but it seems clear that Le Queux would not have been a good fit with the War Propaganda Bureau's overall strategy. 'From the beginning, the guiding principle of Wellington House was that propaganda should be based on accurate information and measured argument', as M.L. Sanders and Philip M. Taylor write in their study of British First World War propaganda. 'The facts and arguments presented in Wellington House literature had to be reliable and sensible. Mass distribution was avoided'.[72] This was hardly an approach suited to Le Queux or indeed to much of invasion-scare literature, where shock effect and reaching a mass readership was often the goal. In addition, of course, stories portraying an invasion of Britain would presumably not be of much use in trying to persuade other countries, such as the United States, of the need to support Britain.[73] By the end of the war, literature, as initially promoted by Wellington House, had been superseded by an emphasis on visual culture, such as film.[74]

War literature

In summary, the war started with a reuse and reimagining of earlier invasion-scare fiction, adapted to the new reality of war. Beyond the ad hoc efforts to support 'patriotic' films in 1914 and the abortive

250 *Fiction goes to war*

attempt to make *The National Film* later in the war, there seems to have been minimal effort on the part of the official propaganda apparatus to promote invasion-scare narratives. This did not mean that authors, at least those outside the halls of Wellington House, did not write about and discuss the prospect of invasion, or muse about the development of the ongoing war, though here as well most authors seem to have strayed little from the pre-war tropes of the genre. Even as a real world war was raging, few writers thought about reinventing the wheel in their descriptions of invasion and foreign conquest; the genre in 1914–1918 would therefore have largely been recognisable to a pre-war readership.

For William Le Queux, to take one prolific example, the war meant new opportunities, and the writer published extensively throughout the war years. Much of this output was geared towards factual – broadly defined – publications, such as his contributions to the publisher George Newnes' series *The War of the Nations*.[75] Other 'factual' output included books on the German spy peril – a topic Le Queux claimed to be thoroughly *au fait* with, and which he had written extensively about before the war.[76] In *German Spies in England* and its 'sequel', *Britain's Deadly Peril*, Le Queux continued his campaign against the supposed threat from the German spy system which, he claimed, was allowed to operate more or less unhindered in Britain.[77] He also hinted at the continued possibility of a German invasion of Britain – albeit not on the same scale as described in *The Invasion of 1910*. 'Few people would be daring enough to say', he wrote in *Britain's Deadly Peril*,

> that it would be impossible for the Germans, aided undoubtedly by spies on shore, to land suddenly in the neighbourhood of one of the big East Coast towns a force strong enough to overpower, for the moment, the local defences, and establish itself – if only for a few days – in a position where it could lay waste with fire and sword a very considerable section of country.[78]

As this quotation illustrates, along with his continued crusade against an elusive spy threat, Le Queux was able to reorient his pre-war *oeuvre* into a wartime body of work that continued his Germanophobic rants in a different setting. Le Queux did not need to make substantial changes to his writing, since he had already spent years outlining and denigrating the supposed perfidy of

Wilhelmine Germany. But his wartime writings also show that Le Queux was, to a large extent, trapped in the pre-war genre and tropes he had created; there was little new in his writings after August 1914, and his readers might as well have picked up one of his Edwardian novels as investing in any of the newer literature he created as Britain found itself engaged in the war Le Queux had spent so much ink trying to foretell and describe. His fiction writing from the war years – books such as *The Zeppelin Destroyer* and *Number 70, Berlin*, to name but two[79] – can be said to fall into the same category as his pre-war stories: Le Queux did not change his writing style or choice of topic just because a war had broken out. Nor did he need to, as the stories dealt with the familiar tropes – dastardly foreign agents, oblivious British officials, and the ever-looming threat of Germany, on which his earlier writings had also focused.

In fact, much of the wartime invasion and future-war fiction literature – and related forms of fiction – were quite similar, both in terms of style and theme, as the pre-war literature. It is perhaps no coincidence that the most memorable spy novel from the war, John Buchan's *The Thirty-Nine Steps*, takes place before the outbreak of war, despite being published in 1915.[80] The short story, *The Germans in Cork* by 'Baron von Kartoffel', published in 1917 after the Easter Rising of the previous year, echoed pre-war arguments that the Irish were ungovernable on their own, and would be far worse off under a German yoke than they were when ruled from London.[81] There would have been little new for Irish readers in this pamphlet.

It was perhaps to be expected that authors would stick to a tried and tested formula, rather than attempt to reinvent the genre during the war. It is also understandable that it would be difficult to write about potential developments in future wars, when a war was already raging on the continent; sticking to pre-war settings, or using Victorian and Edwardian plot points to muse on developments in the world war, makes sense in this respect. As such, *Punch* had a point when the magazine joked that ideas on 'The Next Great War' would have to be scrapped; the past and the present took precedent over future developments in many of the novelisations of war, invasion, occupation and spying that were printed between 1914 and 1918.

252   *Fiction goes to war*

Some future-war stories did look towards a time after the First World War, however – though one of these, F. Herbert Stead's novel *No More War!* can hardly be termed a 'future-war' narrative, as the title hints. Published in 1917, the story envisages an end to the ongoing war, and a German defeat after the assassination (by a German woman, no less) of the German Crown Prince. As allied armies push the German troops back, revolution threatens in Germany, and the Social Democratic party mobilises to take power and oust the Hohenzollerns.[82] This was not too far, one could argue, from how the war actually ended in 1918, but it was still an airy, dreamy narrative to put forward in 1917, and the author's long-term hopes for the future would also not live up to expectations. 'The author still clings to the crushed and shattered Hague movement', complained *The Globe* in a review of the book, 'as if it were an unbroken thread upon which the future of Europe could be woven'.[83] 'All that matters just now is that we should get on with the war', another reviewer wrote, criticising the book's 'curious medley of fantasy and realism, historical fact and religious thought'.[84] *No More War!* was, in short, a strange and, if nothing else, different example of the future-war fiction published during the First World War.

More in line, perhaps, with the reviewers' views on *No More War!* was a 1915 narrative by the popular novelist Edgar Wallace. In *"1925"*, subtitled *The Story of a Fatal Peace* and dedicated to 'the creator of armies, "K."', Wallace warned of the danger inherent in coming to a premature peace with Germany. In the story, Britain and the allies signed a peace with Germany in 1915, ending the world war through the 'Peace of Copenhagen'. Ten years later, in 1925, Germany is planning its revenge, while Britain languidly believes herself safe behind the protection of her fleet. By the end of the short novel, the British fleet has been destroyed – 'submarined', to be precise – and a quarter of a million German soldiers have landed at 'Kemby Cove', presumably somewhere in the south of England, with more men to follow. Prior to this, Germany has tricked over half a million UK veterans from the First World War to visit Germany, under the guise of a peace rally, where they have all been interned. The efforts of an intrepid newspaper editor to warn the country of the coming danger has all been in vain. Apart from this, the novel contains a few familiar tropes, such as the machinations of a suave German spy, and a secret invention by a British

Invasion-scare literature and the war 253

inventor that would presumably have turned the tables against the German submarines had it been utilised in time.[85] Wallace's point was hammered home to his 1915 readers: peace with a still undefeated Germany would mean a new war in the future.

Wallace's novel is a rarity in that it was a story from the First World War that imagined what a future war would look like *after* the war had ended. Despite this, it was, as most novels published during the war, anchored in the present conflict – preoccupied with the ongoing war rather than with future developments. The war, it would seem, made new arguments from old fiction, and new fiction spoke to the present. Here, as well, the invasion narratives that were circulated during the years between 1914 and 1918 had much in common with the pre-war iterations of the genre.

If British invasion-scare and future-war fiction underwent few developments during the 1914–1918 war, there are many plausible explanations for this. In a war imbued with its own logic, pre-war literature could only go so far in explaining the conflict and mobilising consent. And while much of pre-war literature and theatre plays were utilised and discussed in the early phase of the conflict, the changing nature of the war – including, one would assume, the reality of industrialised slaughter, the frozen stalemate on the Western Front and, from 1916, the imposition of conscription in Britain (though not in Ireland) – made the genre less relevant for the purposes of recruitment propaganda and to warn of the danger of imminent invasion. In addition, as the official propaganda apparatus concentrated its efforts in other directions, there were few attempts to create official invasion-scare narratives; symptomatic of this trend is the belated support for *The National Film*, which stands out as a lone attempt and an exceptional effort at portraying a fictitious invasion, with public funding and under the supervision of Britain's established propaganda machinery. That the film was not finished on time, and remained unreleased, shows that British official attempts in this respect were too little, too late.

This left much of the wartime publication of invasion-scare and future-war fiction to private enterprise, and here, too, pre-war publication trends were in evidence. William Le Queux continued his career as alarmist and self-proclaimed spy catcher, and large commercial publishers like George Newnes published and distributed his work, much like in the years prior to the outbreak of war.

254 *Fiction goes to war*

The First World War – the real 'Great War' that authors like William Le Queux and H.G. Wells had imagined, warned about and tried to describe for decades – ended, therefore, with the invasion-scare genre more or less unchanged from how it had looked in the Edwardian era. Far from indicating that this meant that the genre was 'dead', its arguments outdated and its constituting tropes no longer relevant to its readers, this chapter has shown how invasion-scare fiction and the exercise of imagining future war retained its ability to be reimagined, reused, reinterpreted and re-presented, even in the face of a world war. As such, the war years illustrated a trend that had been evident in one form or another since the unnamed invaders marched across Surrey in Chesney's 1871 story *The Battle of Dorking*: the history of imagined war in Britain is one of adaptability, of a genre that changed meaning depending on its context and readership.

The First World War did not kill off the 'Next World War' industry, as *Punch* had joked in 1914. It was natural, instead, that such ideas – old as well as new – would be published long after the guns had fallen silent in November 1918. It should come as no surprise that in August 1939, as another, even more devastating world war neared its beginning, a writer in the *Birmingham Post* would invoke Chesney's story again. Leith Hill, a correspondent to the paper had noted, offered 'at least temporary escape from the present troubles' with its beautiful scenery and nature. 'But', as the *Birmingham Post*'s writer countered, 'for a much older generation Leith Hill and its environment are haunted by a tradition associated with a most grim prophecy of dread things to come'.

> It was hereabouts that a highly imaginative soldier in the 'seventies placed the story of an imaginary battle that hurried to its close an imaginary struggle for armed supremacy in Europe. ... Leith Hill may be a fine vantage point for counting the blessings of peace, but also, because of its contiguity to the scene of the imaginary Battle of Dorking, it must ever be a constant reminder that preparedness to defend those blessings is part of the price that must be paid by the true patriot.[86]

If *Dorking* was a warning and a call to be prepared for some readers, others took a different view. The following year, Chesney's story appeared in German translation, as a threat and a promise, under the title *Was England Erwartet*.[87] Yet again, Chesney's story proved its usefulness and its flexibility. Invasion-scare and future-war

Invasion-scare literature and the war 255

fiction was, and remains today, a flexible form of literature, able to be read and interpreted and presented in myriad different ways. Rather than change this fact, the First World War cemented it.

Notes

1 H.G. Wells, *Mr Britling Sees It Through* (New York: The Macmillan Company, 1916), 200.
2 *Punch,* 4 November 1914, 376.
3 Clarke's treatment of the First World War is rather cursory. His book, *Voices Prophesying War,* moves from pre-1914 literature to a chapter covering the entire period 'from the Somme and Verdun to Hiroshima and Nagasaki'; and most of this chapter is concerned with literature published after 1918, not from the war itself. See I.F. Clarke, *Voices Prophesying War: Future Wars 1763–3749* (Oxford: Oxford University Press, 1992), 131–163.
4 G.H. Powell, 'Preface', in [George Tomkyns Chesney], *The Battle of Dorking, with an Introduction by G.H. Powell* (London: Grant Richards Ltd., 1914), v, vi.
5 *Sheffield Daily Telegraph*, 24 September 1914.
6 *Evening News* [London], 18 August 1914, 2.
7 For example, by Sir Lancelot Gubbins at a Red Cross Society meeting in Wimbledon: *Wimbledon Boro' News*, 22 August 1914, 5. Gubbins had stated that 'the moral of that story had been forgotten', and that there could be 'a real "battle of Dorking," or of Epsom, or even of Wimbledon Common'. Others were less concerned, at least with the naval aspect of the story: David Hannay in the *Manchester Guardian* (12 January 1915, 8) doubted that the Germans could make effective use of mines in a naval battle with the Royal Navy, a 'supposition as old as the "Battle of Dorking"'.
8 *Yorkshire Post*, 28 September 1914, 6.
9 Ralph Straus, 'Armageddon in Prophecy: How Near Scare-Fictionists Have Come to The Truth', *Bystander*, 19 August 1914, 429–430. The anonymous short book *The Reign of George VI* was known to early twentieth-century British readers after having been reissued by the historian Charles Oman in 1899: Anon., *The Reign of George VI, 1900–1925: A Forecast Written in the Year 1763*, ed. Charles Oman (London: Rivingtons, 1899). It would probably have been forgotten otherwise. Alan H Burgoyne's story *The War Inevitable* (London: Francis Griffiths, 1908) was closer to memory.

256   *Fiction goes to war*

10 *Essex County Chronicle*, 21 August 1914, 3; T.G. Offin, *How the Germans took London. Forewarned, Forearmed* (Chelmsford: Edmund Durrant & Co., 1900).

11 G. Bernard Shaw, 'Common Sense about the War', *The New Statesman Special War Supplement*, 14 November 1914, 4. Friedrich von Bernhardi, a German general, had written a book with the descriptive title *Germany and the Next War*, that had been published in English in 1912: Friedrich von Bernhardi, *Germany and the Next War*, transl. Allen H. Powles (London: Edward Arnold, 1912). The bellicose title and Bernhardi's discourse on war created quite a stir in Britain and the book was frequently pointed to both before and after August 1914 as proof of German militarism.

12 *Herald*, 9 January 1915, 4.

13 *Weekly Dispatch*, 22 November 1914, 3.

14 *Daily News and Leader*, 20 November 1914, 4. Archer noted that Chesney's pamphlet 'might well be re-issued', which led to a terse letter to the editor from Grant Richards in the next day's issue of *Daily News*: 'It was reissued, by me, on Sept. 16, at sixpence' (*Daily News and Leader*, 21 November 1914, 4).

15 *Globe*, 12 August 1914, 7.

16 *The Times*, 27 October 1914, 9.

17 *The Times*, 20 August 1914, 4.

18 Stephen Badsey, *The German Corpse Factory: A Study in First World War Propaganda* (Warwick: Helion & Company, 2019), 24.

19 Catriona Pennell, '"The Germans have Landed!" Invasion Fears in the South-East of England, August to December 1914', in Heather Jones, Jennifer O'Brien and Cristoph Schmidt-Supprian (eds), *Untold War: New Perspectives in First World War Studies* (Leiden and Boston: Brill, 2008), 96.

20 Pennell, '"The Germans have Landed!"', 98, 102.

21 See Stephen Badsey, 'Strategy and Propaganda: Lord Kitchener, the Retreat from Mons and the Amiens Dispatch, August-September 1914', in Mark Connelly, Jo Fox, Stefan Goebel and Ulf Schmidt (eds), *Propaganda and Conflict: War, Media and Shaping the Twentieth Century* (London: Bloomsbury Academic, 2019), 31–32.

22 *Evening News*, 29 September 1914, 3.

23 On the 'angels of Mons' myth, see David Clarke, 'Rumours of Angels: A Legend of the First World War', *Folklore*, 113 (2002), 151–173. 'In my view', writes Clarke, 'both stories [Machen's 'The Bowmen' and the later myth of the angels] had their origins partly in fiction and partly from the background of popular belief and tradition upon which "The Bowmen" was itself based' (Clarke, 'Rumours of Angels', 170–171). Machen himself did not doubt that his story of the bowmen had led to

Invasion-scare literature and the war   257

the myth of the angels, and he underlined this when 'The Bowmen' was republished in 1915: see Arthur Machen, *The Angels of Mons: The Bowmen and Other Legends of the War* (London: Simpkin, Marshall, Hamilton, Kent & Co., Ltd., 1915), 5–27.

24 Paul Fussell, *The Great War and Modern Memory* (Oxford: Oxford University Press, 2000), 115.

25 Robert Graves, for example, recounted in his memoirs how, after some unlucky words had been uttered and with Graves the only officer present able to 'touch wood' in time (a pencil he had kept in his pocket), he was the only survivor among the officers a few days later: Robert Graves, *Goodbye to All That* (Harmondsworth: Penguin Books, 1985), 161–164. Then, of course, there is also Graves' conviction that the preservation of his virginity kept him safe during his stints at the front: see Fussell, *Great War,* 124.

26 Catriona Pennell, 'Believing the Unbelievable: The myth of the Russians with "snow on their boots" in the United Kingdom, 1914', *Cultural and Social History*, 11 (2014), 69–87.

27 Clarke, 'Rumours of Angels'.

28 Daniel Pick, *War Machine: The Rationalisation of Slaughter in the Modern Age* (New Haven & London: Yale University Press, 1993), 140.

29 The term is from *The Times*, 16 April 1917, 7. A story in *The Times*, 21 August 1917, 6, wrote of the 'German callousness to their dead', as they were transported to the rear: 'There is, of course, no evidence that the bodies are actually being taken to corpse utilization factories; but they are certainly being taken somewhere by train, with officers and men superintending the operation, and the way the bodies are tied together is callous and inhuman almost beyond belief'.

30 Adrian Gregory, *The Last Great War: British Society and the Great War* (Cambridge: Cambridge University Press, 2008), 41–42; Pennell, 'Believing the Unbelievable'; Badsey, *The German Corpse Factory*, 18–19.

31 William Le Queux, *The Invasion* (London, George Newnes, Ltd., 1917).

32 NAM, Roberts papers, 7101/23/47, William Le Queux to Lord Roberts, 27 October 1912.

33 See Nicholas Hiley, 'The Play, the Parody, the Censor and the Film', *Intelligence and National Security*, 6 (1991), 225–226; Roger T. Stearn, 'The Mysterious Mr Le Queux: War Novelist, Defence Publicist and Counterspy', *Soldiers of the Queen*, 70 (1992), 21. This change of ending had already happened with the book version of *The Invasion of 1910*, where the heavily edited German version ended with a German victory: see Clarke, *Voices*, 123. The German translation was published as William Le Queux, *Die Invasion von 1910: Einfall*

258 *Fiction goes to war*

der Deutschen in England, transl. Traugott Tamm (Berlin: Concordia Deutsche Verlags-Anstalt, [n.d., probably 1906/1907]).

34 For example, in advert in *Bioscope*, 1 October 1914, 32–33. Though this accolade was also added to other films, such as the 'great patriotic film' *"England Expects"*: *Bioscope*, 1 October 1914, 36; or *On His Majesty's Service*, touted as '[u]ndoubtedly the finest patriotic film of the moment': *Bioscope*, 1 October 1914, 38.

35 *Bioscope*, 8 October 1914, 174. The film was not Le Queux's only venture into cinema: in April, *Bioscope* reported on the success of the film serial *The White Lie*, and the production of *The Staircase of Death*; a French film company had reportedly been contracted to 'cinematise seven more of Mr Le Queux's books during the present year': *Bioscope*, 23 April 1914, 34.

36 Hiley, 'The Play', 226.

37 *Kinematograph and Lantern Weekly*, 17 September 1914, 71.

38 *Pictures and the Picturegoer*, 3 October 1914, 114.

39 On the 1909 debates on the meaning of *An Englishman's Home*, see Christian K. Melby, 'Rethinking British Militarism before the First World War: The Case of *An Englishman's Home* (1909)', *English Historical Review*, 137(2022), 1377–1401.

40 For example, notice in *Bioscope*, 3 September 1914, 862.

41 *Kinematograph and Lantern Weekly*, 8 October 1914, 13.

42 See, for example, advert in *Bioscope*, 7 January 1915, 22. The Boy Scouts are praised in the book version of the story, as a 'remarkable organisation [that] had proved of great service in many ways' during the fighting that followed the invasion: Laurence Cowen, *"Wake Up!" A Dream of To-Morrow* (London: Everett & Co., [1915]), 164.

43 For example, *Daily Express*, 7 January 1915, 2.

44 *Daily Express*, 24 February 1915, 7.

45 Cowen, *"Wake Up!"*. A notice in the book informs that the story was serialised between 3 January and 26 February (2), but this is incorrect: the first instalment appeared on 5 January, as noted above. Among other changes, the chapter structure had been changed in the book version. The same notice also states that the book was 'conceived and written long before the outbreak of the present war' (2).

46 Cowen, *"Wake Up!"*, 255–256. This summary is from the book version.

47 Cowen, *"Wake Up!"*, 256.

48 Cowen, *"Wake Up!"*, 43–38. Perhaps wisely, this lengthy discussion is abridged in the serialised version of the story, shortened, in most respects, to the brief statement that the two discussants 'went at it hammer and tongs': *Daily Express,* 7 January 1915, 2.

49 Cowen, *"Wake Up!"*, 68–69, 79.

Invasion-scare literature and the war 259

50 1914 was the high point of invasion fears during the war: Pennell, ' "The Germans have Landed!" ', 98–101. Another reason may have been a shift from patriotic fervour in the early part of the war, to escapism. According to Eberhard Demm, cinema in the belligerent countries 'reverted to escapist entertainment as early as 1915 because people wanted to forget the terrible war for a few hours': Eberhard Demm, *Censorship and Propaganda in World War I: A Comprehensive History* (London: Bloomsbury Academic, 2019), 74.

51 Nicholas Reeves, 'Official British Film Propaganda', in Michael Paris (ed.), *The First World War and Popular Cinema: 1914 to the Present* (New Brunswick: Rutgers University Press, 2000), 31.

52 Reeves, 'Film Propaganda', 31, 45. See also Reeves, *The Power of Film Propaganda: Myth or Reality?* (London: Continuum, 2003), 31–38.

53 *Kinematograph and Lantern Weekly*, 27 September 1917, 107. The article was titled 'Where is the British patriotic film?'

54 Nicholas Reeves, *Official British Film Propaganda During the First World War* (London: Croom Helm, 1986), 212.

55 The background to and making of *The National Film*, is discussed in detail in Reeves, *Official British Film*, 125–130 and *passim*. Caine claimed that it was the prime minister himself, David Lloyd George, who had tasked him with making the film: *Kinematograph and Lantern Weekly*, 15 November 1917, 11.

56 Imperial War Museum poster collection, Art.IWM PST 13623 www.iwm.org.uk/collections/item/object/31622.

57 Trinity College Dublin Library, digital collections, OLS Papyrus Case 16 no. 4 https://digitalcollections.tcd.ie/concern/works/s1784k724?locale=en.

58 Mark Tierney, Paul Bowen and David Fitzpatrick, 'Recruiting Posters', in David Fitzpatrick (ed.), *Ireland and the First World War* (Dublin: Trinity History Workshop, 1986), 48.

59 See Catriona Pennell, 'Presenting the War in Ireland, 1914–1918', in Troy R.E. Paddock (ed.), *World War I and Propaganda* (Leiden and Boston: Brill, 2014), 42–64. On the politics and propaganda of Irish recruitment, see also Tim Bowman, 'The Irish Recruiting and Anti-Recruiting Campaigns, 1914–1918', in Bertrand Taithe and Tim Thornton (eds), *Propaganda: Political Rhetoric and Identity 1300–2000* (Stroud: Sutton Publishing, 1999), 223–238.

60 J.M. Winter, 'Propaganda and the Mobilization of Consent', in Hew Strachan (ed.), *The Oxford Illustrated History of the First World War* (Oxford: Oxford University Press, 2000), 220.

61 In the author's own collection is a British postcard, a part of the 'Patriotic Series', with a caricature of Kaiser Wilhelm holding a map

260 *Fiction goes to war*

of Britain, with the headline: 'THIS YEAR! NEXT YEAR! SOMETIME! NEVER!' The postcard is postmarked 18 August 1918: see figure 7.3. Similar mockery can be seen in the illustrations that went with *The Kaiser's Kalendar for 1915* (London, Daily Express, [1914]), published as a one-penny pamphlet by the *Daily Express*. In this calendar, Emperor William is portrayed as dreaming of conquering Britain, before waking up and discovering that his conquest was all a dream.

62 Winter, 'Propaganda and Mobilization of Consent', 216.

63 Winter, 'Propaganda and Mobilization of Consent', 217.

64 M.L. Sanders and Philip M. Taylor, *British Propaganda during the First World War, 1914–18* (London and Basingstoke: The Macmillan Press Ltd., 1982), remains the most authoritative study on British propaganda in the war. See also the other works cited in this chapter.

65 Sanders and Taylor, *British Propaganda*, 9. On the pre-1914 background to press control in war, see Badsey, 'Strategy and Propaganda', 22–23.

66 Badsey, 'Strategy and Propaganda', 33. On the Press Bureau, see Sanders and Taylor, *British Propaganda*, 18–32.

67 Sanders and Taylor, *British Propaganda*, 16.

68 On the background to, and establishment and organisation of Wellington House, see Sanders and Taylor, *British Propaganda*, 38–40.

69 Michael Matin, 'Gauging the Propagandist's Talents: William Le Queux's Dubious Place in Literary History, Part One', *Critical Survey*, 32 (2020), 79–98. There is a throwaway remark criticising the low-brow quality of Le Queux's writing in Wells' *Mr Britling Sees It Through*, where a letter from the front states: 'We can do with all sorts of books, but I don't think the ordinary sensational novel is quite the catch it was for them in peace time. ... He [Old Park] used to regard Florence Warden and William Le Queux as the supreme delights of print'. Wells, *Mr Britling*, 334.

70 Matin, 'Propagandist's Talents, Part One', 80–81.

71 Matin, 'Gauging the Propagandist's Talents: William Le Queux's Dubious Place in Literary History, Part Two', *Critical Survey*, 32 (2020), 203.

72 Sanders and Taylor, *British Propaganda*, 41–42.

73 Perhaps it is unsurprising, then, that the only invasion-scare story Matin mentions from the *Schedule of Wellington House Literature* is a text aimed at a US audience: the 1918 story *Der Tag for Us*. See Matin, 'Propagandist's Talents, Part One', 94 n.4.

74 Matin, 'Propagandist's Talents, Part Two', 203. Pictures and paintings were also emphasised: 'In April 1916', writes Eberhard Demm, 'Masterman created a picture section in Wellington House, employed

Invasion-scare literature and the war 261

90 official painters and founded the magazine *War Pictorial* with a circulation of 50,000 copies and art series such as *The Western Front* (Demm, *Censorship and Propaganda*, 75).

75 William Le Queux was the author of the first volume, published as early as late August, 1914: William Le Queux, *The War of the Nations: A History of the Great European Conflict*, vol. I (London: George Newnes, [1914]). On Le Queux's output during the war, see Brett Holman, 'William Le Queux, the Zeppelin Menace and the Invisible Hand', *Critical Survey*, 32 (2020), 99–118.

76 For example, in the fictional *Spies of the Kaiser: Plotting the Downfall of England* (London: Hurst & Blackett, Ltd., 1909).

77 William Le Queux, *German Spies in England: An Exposure* (London: Stanley Paul & Co., 1915); idem, *Britain's Deadly Peril: Are We Told the Truth?* (London: Stanley Paul & Co., 1915). The latter was written, as its introduction opened, 'partly as a sequel' to *German Spies in England* (7). In addition to these, Le Queux also wrote the introduction to a third book on German spies, also from 1915: 'Ex-Intelligence Officer', *The German Spy System from Within* (London: Hodder and Stoughton, 1915). The cover illustration of this exposé depicts a waiter – clearly a German spy, as per the pre-war trope – observing two British officers who in turn are busy inspecting some papers by a table.

78 Le Queux, *Britain's Deadly Peril*, 143.

79 William Le Queux, *The Zeppelin Destroyer: Being Some Chapters of Secret History* (London: Hodder and Stoughton, 1916); Le Queux, *Number 70, Berlin: A Story of Britain's Peril* (London: Hodder and Stoughton, 1916).

80 John Buchan, *The Complete Richard Hannay* (London: Penguin Books Ltd., 1992). Buchan's narrative has been adapted numerous times, not least as a film by Alfred Hitchcock, and the book's storyline has changed considerably in some of these adaptations: *The Thirty-Nine Steps* falls into that category of literature that is adaptable, able to be reworked and reimagined as one sees fit.

81 'Baron von Kartoffel' [pseud.], *The Germans in Cork: Being the letters of His Excellency the Baron von Kartoffel (Military Governor of Cork in the year 1918) and Others* (Dublin: The Talbot Press Ltd., 1917). The pamphlet purported to be a translation from the German, and described the effects of a future German occupation of Ireland. Real translations – as opposed to spurious ones, like the pamphlet by 'Baron von Kartoffel' – also made their way to British readers. Einem Deutschen Dichter [Paul Georg Münch], *Hindenburgs Einmarsch in London* (Leipzig: Grethlein & Co., 1915), describes a German

262   *Fiction goes to war*

invasion and occupation of Britain. It was translated and published in Britain as *Hindenburg's March into London: Being a Translation from the German Original*, ed. L.G. Redmond-Howard (London: John Long, Limited, 1916). 'Had the present bombastic adventure been by way of warning, or even by way of threat', wrote L.G. Redmond-Howard in the introduction to the English edition, 'and had it come from the pen of an Englishman, like, say, "The Battle of Dorking," or Wells' "War in the Air," or even William Le Queux's "Invasion," we might have questioned its good taste'. Since it is a German work, however, Redmond-Howard contends that the story 'simply indicates a blindness and an unconscious sense of irony, which will some day place "Hindenburg's March into London" among their masterpieces of satirical self-criticism': L.G. Redmond-Howard, 'Introduction', in [Münch], *Hindenburg's March*, 13–14. Münch is identified as the author by Everett F. Bleiler and Richard J. Bleiler, *Science Fiction: The Early Years* (Kent, OH, & London: Kent State University Press, 1990), 529; also https://sf-encyclopedia.com/entry/munch_paul_georg.

82 F. Herbert Stead, *No More War! "Truth Embodied in a Tale"* (London: Simpkin, Marshall, Hamilton, Kent & Co., Ltd., 1917).

83 *The Globe*, 22 December 1917, 6. The paper judged the book 'pacifist poison', and its contents nearly treasonous.

84 *Yorkshire Post*, 20 February 1918, 3.

85 Edgar Wallace, *"1925": The Story of a Fatal Peace* (London: George Newnes, Limited, 1915). In line with British hopes of convincing the United States to join the war, the story also portrays the US as a potential target for Germany's aggrandisement (e.g., 115).

86 *Birmingham Post*, 25 August 1939, 6. The writer did, however, get the publication date wrong, and claimed that Chesney's story had appeared in 1875, rather than 1871. This was closer to the mark than some other inter-war commentators who invoked *The Battle of Dorking*: a notice in *Dover Express and East Kent News*, 5 August 1938, 2, claimed that the story had been written 'somewhere between the years 1860 to 1870', and that it described 'an imaginary invasion by the Emperor Louis Napoleon, who had not then met his Sedan'. In the 1920s a claim circulated that *The Battle of Dorking* had been authored by 'General Hamley' – presumably Edward Bruce Hamley: for example, *The Northern Whig and Belfast Post*, 8 May 1926, 10.

87 Will-Erich Peuckert/Chesney, *Was England Erwartet: Ein Zukunftsroman von 1871* (Berlin: August Groß Verlag, 1940).

Conclusion

'They have no imagination. They are blinded by an idiotic vanity.
What they want just now is a jolly good scare'.
                    - Mr. Vladimir, in Joseph Conrad's *The Secret Agent*, 1907.[1]

There is something inherently modern about the invasion-scare genre. As Marshall Berman described the term, modernity entails living in a world of 'unity of disunity', 'of perpetual disintegration and renewal'.[2] The numerous 'Battles of Dorking' published after 1871 imagined the tearing apart and destruction of old worlds, the creation of new realities and of new social relationships and political alignments. The genre flourished partly due to modern means of mass communication, and by reaching an audience on a scale that would have been unimaginable in earlier centuries. The genre has also proven to be remarkably resilient, and in some senses immune to change. Britain and Europe have continued to be invaded by paper armies in the decades since 1918, much in a similar vein to earlier stories. Though they may not have realised it, authors of more modern stories wrote in a genre that belonged as much to the nineteenth century as it did to the later centuries in which they were published.[3]

There is a spatial fluidity as well as timelessness to the genre. Pre-1914 invasion-scare literature did not respect borders. Stories were produced in large numbers in Germany and France, for example, and translations of British stories made their way across the channel and became part of the European cultural scene, and *vice versa* – albeit to a lesser extent. This was true of smaller countries as well. Scandinavian invasion-scare fiction, which can be traced back at least to 1840, saw an upswing in the number of stories

264   *Invasions*

published from 1889 onwards.[4] If the genre had a life outside of the period discussed in these chapters, and outside of Britain, what makes British invasion-scare fiction special, and what does it tell us about the country in the decades between 1871 and 1918?

'Our concern with history', a teacher tells W.G. Sebald's young Austerlitz in the eponymous novel, 'is a concern with pre-formed images already imprinted on our brains, images at which we keep staring while the truth lies elsewhere'.[5] Part of the problem with how scholars have approached invasion-scare literature is a similar tendency to see it through the images we have of 1914–1918. But, as H.G. Wells noted, the many 'Battles of Dorking' were anchored in the immediate, focused on the present more than on the future. While they tell us something about the British view of their own time, they form an imperfect guide to the future and need to be read with this in mind, rather than as sibylline prognostications on warfare. This book has outlined how invasion-scare stories, especially from the 1890s onwards, were commodified as spectacles in a marketplace, linked with developments taking place in the publishing industry. As Troy Paddock notes of newspapers at the turn of the century, their focus on striking headlines had the effect of creating spectacles out of news, and with a concomitant focus on the immediate.[6] Stories of future warfare had a similar trajectory.

While the use of 'expert' knowledge in various forms continued to be used to market and sell stories after 1871, the genre's continued success from the later nineteenth century into the Edwardian and war years owed little to the various defence debates of the time. More or less heavily politicised texts were published, of course – and the dividing lines between argument and fiction were not always clear[7] – but the trend pointed towards invasion-scare fiction being read for other reasons than a desire to be informed about how the navy or the army should be organised.

The genre matured and developed in a specific political context, with politics moving towards a recognisably democratic system – though just what this new socio-political order should look like was not at all clear. Edwardian Liberal commentators tended to invoke the United States when they, clearly dismayed by the system's perceived shortcomings, criticised the power of the masses. In the first decade of the twentieth century the social psychologist, Graham

Conclusion 265

Wallas, observed of the United States, where representative democracy had existed for longer than in Britain, that 'politicians and political students seem puzzled and disappointed by their experience of it'.[8] While the jab was directed at America, Wallas clearly had his home country in mind when he wrote these words. He also claimed to have overheard, on two separate occasions, his own canvassers in a municipal election use the phrase 'it's a queer business' to describe the ongoing British experiment in representative democracy.[9] In his opinion, the illogical and immediate dominated the electorate's minds, rather than any calculated long-term ideas of good governance; this, in Wallas' analysis, was the element of 'human nature' intruding upon the world of politics. A similar point was made by Wallas' fellow Liberal James Bryce in 1909, by then ambassador to Washington D.C. While his lecture on *The Hindrances to Good Citizenship* was delivered to an American audience at Yale, it was, by his own admittance, mostly based on his experience with British politics.[10] 'Freedom has done much for the European and American continents', Bryce observed, 'yet far less than expected':

> The citizens have failed to respond to the demand for active virtue and intelligent public spirit which free government makes and must make. Everywhere there is the same contrast between that which the theory of democracy requires and that which the practice of democracy reveals.[11]

In a modern democracy, as Bryce later argued, newspapers were a double-edged sword: making democratic discourse possible in a large country, while also constituting a threat to the same democracy. Newspapers, driven by a search for profits, appealed to a readership that, while it may have increased in size, had not become more critical or intelligent in their engagement with the press and, by extension, politics.[12]

Liberal critique like this was common in the aftermath of the South African War, and was clearly shaped by a general disappointment with the voting public.[13] Arguments over the compatibility of good government with the will of easily swayed masses and the power of the press went back further than this, however, having been an integral part of the society in which invasion-scare fiction was written and read – from the 1867 and 1884 Reform Acts to the rise of the Labour movement and beyond. But explaining the popularity of invasion-scare literature as driven solely by readers' increased access to newspapers and reading material would be unsatisfactory – as would, of course, the idea that the British public uncritically accepted everything these newspapers told them. Other factors clearly played a role in the genre's popularity; and these were inextricably linked with the form and content of the stories.

For a genre built on the premise that Britain could be threatened by outside forces, the stories tended to be flexible about the threat itself. *Dorking*, while clearly describing German invaders, never actually mentioned the invading troops' nationality. The stories seldom offered an unambiguous enemy akin to France during the earlier rivalry between the two countries in the long eighteenth century, where, as Linda Colley has argued, British identity was defined in opposition to the enemy across the channel.[14] Invasion-scare fiction between 1871 and 1914, and even during the war, by contrast, was always more inward-looking: the stories presented various ideas about 'Britishness' through descriptions of the result of the enemy invasion and Britons' reaction to it, rather than of the enemy itself.

That said, the genre was certainly not immune to shifts in the international power balance, and the Great Powers alternated as antagonists according to developments on the world stage. France and Russia were popular enemies until Germany replaced them in the early years of Edward VII's reign, as the fronts between what would become the Great War belligerents were crystallising. Between 1914 and 1918, of course, Germany's role as antagonist continued. But the stories were rarely indicators of such world-stage developments. The enemy itself was interchangeable, and throughout the period between 1871 and the early Edwardian era, stories often portrayed coalitions of enemies joining forces against Britain. This presentation of the 'outside' as a threat partly explains the genre's readability. Invasion-scare fiction brought great power conflicts home, quite literally, to the reading masses. It created a society of readers – by the end of the century, literacy, as well as access to reading material, was high among all classes – and tied it together through invoking an idealised British nation. This trend was first evident in some of the many responses to *Dorking* in 1871, and it was firmly established by the mass-readership stories of the 1890s onwards.

Conclusion 267

Behind the magazines, pamphlets, books, newspapers and marketing machinery was also a culture in which the prospect of invasion could flourish. The country's physical separation from external threats – its island status – meant that invasion was in and of itself a spectacular vision to imagine for Britons. Invasion-scare stories represented the clash between two competing ideas of British society: as forcibly projecting strength outwards, and as more introspective, or fearful of foreign impulses. Both could be indulged by opening books like Le Queux's *The Invasion of 1910*, and either agreeing with or scoffing at their premise.

The idea that Britain was threatened by foreign enemies was of course not conjured completely out of thin air; nor was it created or sustained by invasion-scare fiction alone. 'In every era', as Jonathan Parry has observed, 'a small insular nation can be made to feel vulnerable about its physical and moral security'.[15] In an earlier study, Paul Kennedy detected a feeling of '*Angst,* an excessive suspicion of perceived foreign rivals' among pre-war politicians and journalists, 'in other words, among a high proportion of the "upper ten thousand"'.[16] Such feelings could also be found elsewhere in British society. It was hardly a coincidence that the programme for the 'Grand Empire Pageant' in Lincolnshire in 1909 contained a stirring 'Appeal to the Young Men of Lincoln', asking if the reader 'wish your country to be adequately protected against any possibility of foreign invasion?'[17]

The aim of this book has not been to disprove the existence of such feelings of apprehension, but rather to show how invasion fears were not one-sided arguments in Victorian and Edwardian society. In short, while the genre illustrates a public awareness of the foreign threats to British interests – to claim otherwise would be absurd – and often referred to, or organically mirrored, foreign policy and national defence debates, the stories' popularity does not automatically indicate a widespread fear of invasion. There has been a marked tendency to overstate the influence of invasion-scare and related forms of fiction in shaping the pre-war mind in Britain, and a concomitant tendency to underestimate the ability of the reading public to engage critically with the literature of future wars.

Even in a parliamentary system like that of Britain, the feeling of the man or woman in the street had an unclear influence on foreign and defence questions. When it comes to Great Power politics,

268 *Invasions*

public opinion could, from politicians' points of view, be seen as little more than 'an external force pressing on government ... like a fog pressing on the window panes of ministerial offices', and that could be ignored, or excluded from their own domain without much difficulty.[18] Consequently, according to Gordon Martel, the late nineteenth century Britain of the Earl of Rosebery was one where foreign policy was 'relatively free of domestic concerns'.[19] Of course, in a question of whether it was the *Primat der Innen-* or *Aussenpolitik* which set the stage for the First World War, the former cannot easily be written off altogether. For Keith Wilson, despite his outline of the policy of the Entente largely as a product of contradictory ideas expressed within the halls of the Foreign Office, 'the primacy of the *Innenpolitik,* even in the case of Great Britain, cannot lightly be set aside'.[20] The external pressures of public opinion could also be invoked as an imagined constraint. As shown in chapters 2–4, appeals to the public on defence questions often took the form of invoking an abstract or invented idea of public opinion – this was true in particular with the 1884 naval scare, discussed in chapter 3. Both chapters 3 and 4 also described attempts to insulate defence policy from the vagaries of popular interference. There were natural domestic constraints – real or imagined – to the foreign policy the government could pursue, both prior to and after August 1914. In addition, the separation between the two spheres – the domestic and the foreign – can, and has been, overstated.[21] Within this context, fictional invasions were dismissed or supported by the political establishment according to whether they were considered useful or not – though there was never much chance for a government, and much less an interest group, to control the public reaction to invasion-scare narratives.

Invasion-scare fiction reflected the social and cultural developments of British society, while also being detached from, and in many cases running against the political current. Some conclusions, then, can be drawn about the genre's role in British society. First, the genre became more inclusive as the stories changed over time and appealed to a wider public of consumers. The popularity of such fiction was linked with the increased access to it, but also by the way it invited readers – and theatre audiences and, later, cinematograph audiences – to be a part of the unfolding narrative. Linked

Conclusion 269

with this development was the way stories were entertaining and colourful. Hugh Cunningham has argued that the 'audience knew and responded to the essentially theatrical conventions of the portrayal of war in popular entertainment'.[22] This can broadly be said to be the case for many invasion texts and plays too.

Second, although Victorian and Edwardian politics and culture were interlinked, the invasion-scare genre had an incongruous relationship with popular politics. Invasion-scare fiction was political in so far as it spoke to and referenced political questions of the period, from the Cardwell reforms to conscription, and it frequently invoked an audience of rational consumers – as such, the genre was separate from juvenile fiction, even though the lines between the two are blurry. However, there are no indications that the genre functioned as a successful vehicle for specific policies, or that its readers primarily understood it as such. 'With the *Battle of Dorking*,' I.F. Clarke remarked, 'Chesney had invented an ideal mode for continuing politics by means of fiction'.[23] In reality, the opposite was the case: insofar as stories promoted specific political arguments, these were often ignored. Victorian and Edwardian invasion-scare literature should therefore not be read as an indication of the popular acceptance of Conservative/Tory or 'radical right' ideas in British society – even if the anti-Liberal, pro-national service arguments in some stories overlapped with or were directly linked to the political outlook of the British right. Invasion-scare fiction was malleable, and readers and audiences took away different things from the stories. This also meant that there was no ready-made image of Germany to reach for in August 1914, created and sustained through the writings of Chesney, Clowes, Childers and Le Queux. Nor did the stories lose all meaning as the reality of modern warfare became clear on continental battlefields; *The Battle of Dorking* and *The Invasion of 1910* continued to enjoy a healthy existence as war literature.

The preceding chapters have outlined a genre that, in the decades before 1918, was both more and less than the sum of its parts. Judgements of it as inconsequential and unimportant are as misguided as the argument that it shaped Britons' world views. Rather than an indicator of popular feeling, or a genre giving vent to popular anxieties, invasion-scare stories were limited in their impact on politics, and the various messages of the genre do not seem to have

270   *Invasions*

seriously moved public opinion on specific issues. That said, the genre was undeniably popular; at times it sold extremely well, and for Edwardians in particular it would have been difficult to ignore the avalanche of stories and their promotion in newspapers and magazines. Invasion-scare literature shaped the way Britons talked about themselves and the outside world, it reflected and appealed to a shared British identity, and it changed the way they wrote about the present as well as the future.

It is difficult to imagine invasion-scare fiction reaching the heights of popularity it did in a society that was not as mindful of its position of relative decline, confronted by the rise of external powers and with a powerful and established political press as Britain had. Stories like *The Battle of Dorking* entered the vocabulary of generations of writers and politicians. Fiction helps to illustrate the ways in which authors negotiated the changing nature of British identity and what it meant to belong to the body politic in a period of increasingly 'democratic' government. Pre-war invasion-scare literature was a modern genre, both in the way it was written and how it was distributed, promoted and read. It was by its very nature immediate and headline-grabbing. It appealed to an audience who wanted to read about the spectacle of conflict brought home. 'All these books shared a common assumption that war was a splendid thing', note Zara Steiner and Keith Neilson, in discussing the many pre-war stories of future conflict.[24] This is too simplistic. The literature did not prepare Britain for a Great War, and its popularity does not indicate that the British wanted a conflict or that Germany had always been the enemy when one came along. 'Scares', either in fiction or as part of campaigns like the 1884 naval scare, were not one-sided arguments. The 'psychology of crowds' meant that it was relatively easy to cause a panic among a group of people, as F.W. Hirst observed in 1913. 'But a nation is not a crowd'.[25] Pre-war Britain was, as any other society, a country of individuals, and of readers, commentators and theatre-goers with agency and their own ideas, worries and dreams. For all the arguments that war would be beneficial, and for all the fears that the country was vulnerable, there were also voices who proclaimed, as Frank W. Green and Carl Bernstein did in 1871, in response to the story that started the modern invasion-scare genre: 'England invaded, What a strange idea!'[26]

Conclusion

271

Notes

1 Joseph Conrad, *The Secret Agent: A Simple Tale* (Oxford: Oxford University Press, 2008), 22, first published in 1907.

2 Marshall Berman, *All That Is Solid Melts into Air: The Experience of Modernity* (London and New York: Verso, 2010), 15.

3 For a discussion of the genre's development until the twenty-first century, see Lawrence freedman, *The Future of War: A History* (London: Allen Lane, 2017). On the prognosticative problems with newer attempts to describe future wars, see Christian K. Melby, 'Litteraturen om krigen som aldri kommer', *Nytt norsk tidsskrift*, 40 (2023), 191–203.

4 See Claes Ahlund, 'Den svenska invasionsberättelsen – en bortglömd litteratur', *Tidskrift för litteraturvetenskap*, 3 (2003), 82–103; and Christian K. Melby, 'Norsk fremtidskrigs- og invasjonslitteratur før 1914 i et skandinavisk og europeisk perspektiv', *Historisk tidsskrift*, 102 (2023), 202–216. On stories published after 1914, see Ahlund, 'Rats and Anthills: The First World War in the Scandinavian Spy Novel', in Claes Ahlund (ed.), *Scandinavia in the First World War: Studies in the War Experience of the Northern Neutrals* (Lund: Nordic Academic Press, 2012), 109–127.

5 W.G. Sebald, *Austerlitz*, transl. Anthea Bell (London: Penguin Books, 2011), 101.

6 [Troy R.E. Paddock], 'Introduction: Newspapers, Public Opinion, and Propaganda', in Troy R.E. Paddock (ed.), *A Call to Arms: Propaganda, Public Opinion, and Newspapers in the Great War* (Westport: Praeger, 2004), 6.

7 See, for example, H.W. Wilson's evocative description of the consequences of a future naval defeat in *Navy League Pamphlet C2*, 'The Meaning of Defeat' ([London: The Navy League], 1896): 'we will raise the curtain of the future', Wilson wrote, in a text that was clearly inspired by, and shared much in common with, existing future-war fiction of the same period.

8 Graham Wallas, *Human Nature in Politics* (London: Archibald Constable & Co., 1908), 2.

9 Wallas, *Human Nature*, 3.

10 James Bryce, *The Hindrances to Good Citizenship* (New Haven: Yale University Press, 1909), 4. Bryce's knowledge of the American political system and society was extensive: see Edmund Ions, *James Bryce and American Democracy 1870–1922* (London: Macmillan, 1968).

11 Bryce, *Hindrances*, 15–16.

272 *Invasions*

12 James Bryce, *Modern Democracies*, 2 vols. (London: Macmillan and Co., 1921), I, 123. The Great War made Bryce wary of how militarism might influence British society, arguing that '[o]nly constitutional habit stood between Britain and Prussian autocracy – but even habit was no match for passions in time of war, as he remembered well from the Boer War': John T. Seaman, Jr., *A Citizen of the World: The Life of James Bryce* (London and New York: I.B. Tauris, 2006), 214.

13 This is particularly prevalent in the writings of J.A. Hobson. See *The Psychology of Jingoism* (London: Grant Richards, 1901) and *The Crisis of Liberalism: New Issues of Democracy* (London: P.S. King & Son., 1909). In 1904, L.T. Hobhouse doubted if foreign policy could ever be controlled by the popular will, and questioned whether democracy could be said to exist at all alongside imperialism: *Democracy and Reaction* (London: T. Fisher Unwin, 1904), 144–145, 169.

14 Linda Colley, *Britons: Forging the Nation 1707–1837* (London: Pimlico, 1994).

15 Jonathan Parry, 'What's the big idea?', *London Review of Books*, 39, no. 23 (30 November 2017), 31–32.

16 Paul Kennedy, *The Realities Behind Diplomacy: Background Influences on British External Policy, 1865–1980* (London: George Allen & Unwin, 1981), 59.

17 Angela Bartie, Linda Fleming, Mark Freeman, Tom Hulme, Alex Hutton, Paul Readman, 'The Grand Empire Pageant 1909', The Redress of the Past, www.historicalpageants.ac.uk/pageants/1075/.

18 Christopher Clark, *The Sleepwalkers: How Europe Went to War in 1914* (London: Penguin Books, 2013), 236–237.

19 Gordon Martel, *Imperial Diplomacy: Rosebery and the Failure of Foreign Policy* (Montreal: McGill-Queen's University Press, 1986), ix. A similar point is made in James Joll and Gordon Martel, *The Origins of the First World War*, 3rd edition (Harlow: Pearson Longman, 2007), 170–174.

20 Keith M. Wilson, *The Policy of the Entente: Essays on the Determinants of British Foreign Policy 1904–1914* (Cambridge: Cambridge University Press, 1985), 3. For a presentation of the *Primat der Innenpolitik* thesis, see Arno J. Mayer, 'Domestic Causes of the First World War', in Leonard Krieger and Fritz Stern (eds), *The Responsibility of Power: Historical Essays in Honor of Hajo Holborn* (London and Melbourne: Macmillan, 1968), 286–300, and Mayer, 'Internal Crisis and War Since 1870', in Charles L. Bertrand (ed.), *Revolutionary Situations in Europe, 1917–1922: Germany, Italy, Austria-Hungary* (Montreal: Interuniversity Centre for European Studies, 1977), 201–233.

Conclusion 273

21 Paul Readman, 'Patriotism and the Politics of Foreign Policy, c. 1870-c. 1914', in William Mulligan and Brendan Simms (eds), *The Primacy of Foreign Policy in British History, 1660–2000: How Strategic Concerns Shaped Modern Britain* (Basingstoke: Palgrave Macmillan, 2010), 260–276. On the interconnection between the two spheres in the naval context, see Jan Rüger, *The Great Naval Game: Britain and Germany in the Age of Empire* (Cambridge: Cambridge University Press, 2009), 219–221 and *passim*.

22 Hugh Cunningham, 'The Language of Patriotism', *History Workshop Journal*, 12 (1981), 26.

23 I.F. Clarke, 'The Battle of Dorking: Second Thoughts', *Extrapolation*, 40 (1999), 289.

24 Zara S. Steiner and Keith Neilson, *Britain and the Origins of the First World War*, 2nd edition (Basingstoke and New York: Palgrave Macmillan, 2003), 167.

25 F.W. Hirst, *The Six Panics and Other Essays* (London: Methuen & Co., 1913), 1.

26 Frank W. Green and Carl Bernstein, *The Battle of Dorking: A Dream of John Bull's* (London: C. Sheard, [1871]).

Bibliography

Primary sources

Archival Sources

British Library, London:
The Lord Chamberlain's plays and day-books
Arnold-Forster papers
Dilke papers
Northcliffe Papers
Caird Library, National Maritime Museum Greenwich
National Army Museum, London:
Spenser Wilkinson papers
Roberts papers
National Library of Scotland, Edinburgh:
Blackwood's papers

Official publications

Cd. 1932, 1968, 2002, *Report of the War Office (Reconstitution) Committee*, 3 vols. (London, 1904).
Cd. 2643, 2644, 2645, *Report of the Royal Commission on Supply of Food and Raw Material in Time of War*, 3 vols. (London, 1905).
General Staff, War Office, *Recent Publications of Military Interest*, No. 1 (April 1907).
Hansard Parliamentary Debates
House of Commons papers, 1884–1885, vol. 48, no. 46, 'Navy. Explanations of differences. Statement showing the explanations of the differences between the amounts proposed in the navy estimates for 1885–86, and the amounts voted for 1884–85'.

Bibliography

Newspapers and periodicals

Academy
Answers
Army and Navy Gazette
Athenæum
Bioscope
Birmingham Post
Black and White
Blackwood's Magazine
Broad Arrow
Bystander
Chums
The Citizen
City Press [London]
Civil and Military Gazette [Lahore, India]
Contemporary Review
Daily Express
Daily Mail
Daily Mail [Hull]
Daily News (also published as *Daily News and Leader*)
Dover Express and East Kent News
Engineering
The Era
Essex County Chronicle
Evening Gazette [Middlesbrough, Stockton, and District]
Evening News
Fortnightly Review
Fun
Geographical Journal
Glasgow Herald
Globe
Good Words
Hampshire Advertiser
Herald
The Idler
John Bull
Journal of the Royal United Service Institution
Kinematograph and Lantern Weekly
Liverpool Mercury
London Society
Macmillan's Magazine
Mail [Portsmouth]
Manchester Guardian
Merry England
Monthly Review

276   Bibliography

Morning Leader
Morning Post
Murray's Magazine
National Review
New London Journal
Nineteenth Century
North American Review
The Northern Whig and Belfast Post
Pall Mall Gazette
Pall Mall Magazine
Penny Illustrated Paper
Pictures and the Picturegoer
Punch
Review of Reviews
Reynold's Newspaper
Saturday Review
The Scotsman
Sheffield Daily Telegraph
Speaker
Spectator
Sphere
Sporting Times
St James's Gazette
Standard
Strand Magazine
Tatler
Time
The Times
United Service Magazine (also printed as *Colburn's United Service Magazine*)
Westminster Papers
Weekly Dispatch
Wimbledon Boro' News
Yorkshire Post

Edited primary sources

The Diary of Gathorne Hardy, Later Lord Cranbrook, 1866–1892: Political Selections, ed. Nancy E. Johnson (Oxford: Clarendon Press, 1981).

Fear God and Dread Nought: The Correspondence of Admiral of the Fleet Lord Fisher of Kilverstone, ed. Arthur J. Marder, 3 vols. (London: Jonathan Cape, 1952–1959).

The Gladstone Diaries, ed. M.R.D. Foot and H.C.G. Matthew, 14 vols. (Oxford: Clarendon Press, 1968–1994).

History of Herodotus, ed. George Rawlinson, 4 vols. (London: John Murray, 1875).

Bibliography

Journals and Letters of Reginald Viscount Esher, ed. Maurice V. Brett, 4 vols. (London: Nicholson and Watson, 1934–1938).

Books, pamphlets and articles

Note: For serialisations, only the first and final instalments are listed.

A., F., 'The Seizure of the Channel Tunnel: A Tale of the Twentieth Century', *Time* (April 1882), 91–121.

A., F., 'The Yellow Patriots', *Punch,* 14 March 1906, 188–189.

'Adjourned Discussion of Mr. Vernon Harcourt's Paper', *Journal of the Royal United Service Institution*, 16 (1872), 607–632.

Allen, Grant, *The British Barbarians: A Hill-top Novel* (London: John Lane, 1895).

Allen, Inglis, 'Woman Disposes: The Story of a Night's Adventures', *Pall Mall Magazine* (January 1912), 39–45.

Amery L.S. (ed.), The Times *History of the War in South Africa*, 7 vols. (London: Sampson, Low, Marsten & Co., 1900–1909).

Anon., 'What We May Learn', *Blackwood's Magazine* (February 1871), 131–144.

_____ 'Position of the Government', *Blackwood's Magazine* (February 1871), 258–276.

_____ 'Der Ruhm, or the Wreck of German Unity: The Narrative of a Brandenburger Hauptmann', *Macmillan's Magazine* (July 1871), 230–240.

_____ 'Fifty Years Ago', *Colburn's United Service Magazine* (August 1871), 475–493, and (September 1871), 75–89.

_____ 'The Defeat of the Navy in the "Battle of Dorking"', *Colburn's United Service Magazine* (August 1871), 551–562.

_____ *After the Battle of Dorking; or What Became of the Invaders!* (London: George Maddick, 1871).

_____ *The Cruise of the Anti-Torpedo* (London: Tinsley Brothers, 1871).

_____ 'The Fall of England! The Battle of Dorking: Reminiscences of a Volunteer by a Contributor to "Blackwood"', *North American Review*, 113 (1871), 473–476.

_____ *The Hens Who Tried to Crow* (London: Robert Hardwicke, 1871).

_____ 'The Battle of Berlin in 1875', *Colburn's United Service Magazine* (August 1872), 533–537.

_____ 'The Wiltshire Campaign', *Colburn's United Service Magazine* (October 1872), 226–239 and (November 1872), 367–387.

_____ *Europa's Fate: or the Coming Struggle. A History Lesson in New Zealand, A.D. 2076* (London: Griffith and Farran, 1875).

_____ *The Invasion of 1883: A Chapter from the Book of Fate* (Glasgow: James Maclehose, 1876).

_____ *A Parallel Case; or, the Straits of Dover Question A.D. 2345* (Darlington: Bell, 1876).

278 *Bibliography*

_____ *Fifty Years Hence: An Old Soldier's Tale of England's Downfall* (London: G.W. Bacon & Co., 1877).

_____ 'Lord Hartington's Resolutions, and the Position of the Opposition', *Blackwood's Magazine* (September 1878), 357–363.

_____ *Gortschakoff and Bismarck, or Europe in 1940. A Dream* (Oxford: James Parker and Co., 1878).

_____ 'The Battle of Wilton. By A Survivor', *Colburn's United Service Magazine* (September 1880), 93–97.

_____ 'The War of 1886 between the United States and Great Britain' [review], *Colburn's United Service Magazine* (October 1882), 216–218.

_____ 'The Battle of Port Said: A Chapter in the History of the Future', *Engineering*, 6 July 1883 to 10 August 1883.

_____ *The Battle of Port Said: A Chapter in the History of the Future* (London: Offices of 'Engineering', 1883).

_____ *The Battle of the Moy, or How Ireland gained Her Independence: 1892–1894* (Boston, MA: Lee and Shepard Publishers, 1883).

_____ *The Battle of To-Morrow* (London: Chappell and Company, Limited, 1885).

_____ 'Newry Bridge; a story of Ireland in 1887', *St James's Gazette*, 3 May 1886 to 11 May 1886.

_____ *Newry Bridge, or Ireland in 1887* (Edinburgh and London: William Blackwood and Sons, 1886).

_____ *In the Year One (A.D. 1888) of Home Rule* de Jure (London: W.H. Allen & Co., 1886).

_____ *'Down with England!' A French Prophesy* (London: Chapman and Hall, 1888).

_____ *The 'Russia's Hope', or, Britannia no Longer Rules the Waves*, transl. Charles James Cooke (London: Chapman and Hall, Limited, 1888).

_____ *England's Danger; or, Rifts within the Lute. A Russian Plot* (Portsmouth: Griffin & Co., 1889).

_____ 'Mr. Punch's Naval Novel', *Punch*, 3 October 1891, 160–161.

_____ *The Doom of the County Council of London* (London: W.H. Allen and Co., Limited, 1892).

_____ 'Notices of Books: *The Next Naval War.* By S. Eardley-Wilmot', *Journal of the Royal United Service Institution*, 38 (August 1894), 895.

_____ *The Reign of George VI, 1900–1925: A Forecast Written in the Year 1763*, ed. Charles Oman (London: Rivingtons, 1899).

_____ 'The Invaders', *Punch*, 7 March 1909, 187–188.

[Arnold-Forster, H.O.], *The Truth About the Land League, Its Leaders and Its Teaching, by 'One Who Knows'* (Dublin: The National Press Agency, Limited, 1882).

_____ 'Our Position as a Naval Power', *Nineteenth Century* (January 1883), 1–13.

_____ 'The People of England versus Their Naval Officials', *Nineteenth Century* (November 1884), 702–714.

_____ 'In a Conning Tower: How I Took H.M.S. "Majestic" into Action', *Murray's Magazine* (July 1888), 59–78.

Bibliography

_____ *In a Conning Tower; or, How I took H.M.S. 'Majestic' Into Action: A Story of Modern Ironclad Warfare* (London: Cassell & Company, Limited, 1891).

Arnold-Forster, Mary, *The Right Honourable Hugh Oakeley Arnold-Forster: A Memoir by His Wife* (London: Edward Arnold, 1910).

Atteridge, A. Hilliard, 'National Defence: Some Neglected Conditions', *United Service Magazine*, 809 (April 1896), 1–13.

B., A.G.F., *Plus Encore d'Angleterre; or, Repulse of the French* (Bristol and London: J.W. Arrowsmith, [1888]).

Baedeker, K. [J.F. Muirhead], *Great Britain, England, Wales and Scotland as far as Loch Maree and the Cromarty Firth: Handbook for Travellers* (London: Karl Baedeker, 1887).

Bathurst, Charles, *To Avoid National Starvation* (London: Hugh Rees, 1912).

Beckett, Arthur A., 'How the Prussians Invaded Brighton: A Story of the Review', *London Society* (May 1871), 453–460.

Beeman, Captain S.W., 'The Great Day in 1920', *Pall Mall Magazine* (April 1913), 440–452.

Berney, Rev. Thomas, *The Battle of the Channel Tunnel and Dover Castle and Forts. A Letter to the Right Honourable Wm. Ewart Gladstone, M.P.* (Bracon Ash: Thomas Berney, 1882).

Bernhardi, Friedrich von, *Germany and the Next War*, transl. Allen H. Powles (London: Edward Arnold, 1912).

'Blower, Sergt.' and 'Cheeks the Marine' [pseud.], *Our Hero!! Or; Who Wrote 'The Battle of Dorking?' A Military and Naval Review of the Now Celebrated Pamphlet* (London: Bradbury, Evans & Co., 1871).

Blyth, James, *The Swoop of the Vulture* (London: Digby, Long & Co., 1909).

Bradlaugh, Charles, *The Channel Tunnel: Ought the Democracy to Oppose or Support It?* (London: A. Bonner, 1887).

Bramah, Ernest, 'The War Hawks', *Pall Mall Magazine* (September 1909), 384–393.

Brex, J. Twells, *The Civil War of 1915* (London: C. Arthur Pearson, Ltd., 1912).

_____ [under the pseudonym 'St. Giles'], 'The Civil War of 1915', *Sporting Times*, 6 January to 16 March 1912.

Bryce, James, *The Hindrances to Good Citizenship* (New Haven: Yale University Press, 1909).

_____ *Modern Democracies*, 2 vols. (London: Macmillan and Co., Limited, 1921).

Buchan, John, *The Complete Richard Hannay* (London: Penguin Books Ltd., 1992).

Burgoyne, Alan H., *The War Inevitable* (London: Francis Griffiths, 1908).

Burns, John, 'The London County Council: Towards a Commune', *Nineteenth Century* (March 1892), 496–514.

_____ 'Let London Live', *Nineteenth Century* (April 1892), 673–685.

280 Bibliography

[Butler, William F.], 'An Old Soldier', *The Invasion of England, Told Twenty Years After* (London: Sampson Low, Marston, Searle, & Rivington, 1882).

_____ 'The Invasion of England', *Merry England* (November 1888) to (April 1889).

'A Captain of the Royal Navy' [pseud.], *The Battle off Worthing: Why the Invaders Never Got to Dorking* (London: The London Literary Society, 1887).

'Cassandra' [pseud.], *The Channel Tunnel; or, England's Ruin* (London: Wm. Clowes and Sons, 1876).

Charnwood, Lord [Godfrey Benson], 'Introduction', in 'Saki' (H.H. Munro), *When William Came: A Story of London under the Hohenzollerns* (London: John Lane/The Bodley Head, Ltd., 1926), vii–xiii.

Chesney, Lieut.-Col. C.C., R.E., 'Our Panics and Their Remedy', *Macmillan's Magazine* (April 1871), 449–457.

[Chesney, George Tomkyns], 'The Battle of Dorking: Reminiscences of a Volunteer', *Blackwood's Magazine* (May 1871), 539–572.

_____ *The Battle of Dorking: Reminiscences of a Volunteer* (Edinburgh and London: William Blackwood and Sons, 1871).

_____ *Slaget vid Dorking: En Skarpskytts Minnen* (Fahlun: Carl Nordins Förlag, 1872).

_____ *A True Reformer,* 3 vols. (Edinburgh and London: William Blackwood and Sons, 1873).

_____ 'The New Ordeal', *Blackwood's Magazine* (October 1878), 385–405 to (November 1878), 511–535.

_____ *The New Ordeal* (Edinburgh and London: Blackwood and Sons, 1879).

_____ 'The English Genius and Army Organization', *Journal of the Royal United Service Institution,* 44 (1900), 53–64.

_____ *The Battle of Dorking, with an Introduction by G.H. Powell* (London: Grant Richards Ltd., 1914).

Childers, Erskine, *In the Ranks of the C.I.V. A Narrative and a Diary of Personal Experiences with the C.I.V. Battery (Honourable Artillery Company) in South Africa* (London: Smith, Elder & Co., 1900).

_____ *The Riddle of the Sands: A Record of Secret Service* (London: Thomas Nelson and Sons, Ltd., [1910]).

_____ *War and the Arme Blanche* (London: Edward Arnold, 1910).

_____ *German Influence on British Cavalry* (London: Edward Arnold, 1911).

Clarke, [Charles] Allen, *Starved into Surrender* (London: C.W. Daniel, 1904).

Clowes, W. Laird, *The Captain of the 'Mary Rose': A Tale of To-morrow* (London: Tower Publishing Co., Ltd., 1892).

_____ *The Great Peril, and How it was Averted* (London: Black and White, 1893).

Bibliography 281

_____ 'The Cheapening of Useful Books', *Fortnightly Review*, 70 (July 1901), 88–98.

Clowes, W. Laird and Alan H. Burgoyne, *Trafalgar Re-Fought* (London: Thomas Nelson and Sons, [1905]).

[Clowes, W. Laird and possibly Alan H. Burgoyne or Commander Charles Napier Robinson], 'The Great Naval War of 1887', *St James's Gazette*, 5 November 1886 to 10 November 1886.

_____ *The Great Naval War of 1887* (London: Hatchards, 1887).

Cobden, Richard, *The Three Panics: An Historical Episode*, 6th edition (London: Ward & Co., 1862).

Coleridge, Samuel Taylor, *Fears in Solitude* (London: J. Johnson, 1798).

Colomb, Vice-Admiral P.H., 'First Impressions of the War', *National Review* (June 1898), 523–535.

Colomb, Rear Admiral P., Colonel J.F. Maurice, R.A., Captain F.N. Maude, Archibald Forbes, Charles Lowe, D. Christie Murray, and F. Scudamore, 'The Great War of 1892: A Forecast', *Black and White*, 2 January 1892 to 21 May 1892.

_____ *The Great War of 189-: A Forecast* (London: William Heinemann, 1893).

Conan Doyle, Arthur, 'Danger! Being the Log of Captain John Sirius' *Strand Magazine* (July 1914), 3–22.

_____ *England in Gefahr*, transl. Waldemar Schütze (Berlin: Curtius, 1914).

_____ *Der Tauchbootkrieg: Wie Kapitän Sirius England Niederzwang*, transl. Konter-Admiral a.D. Sta. Schanzer, 17th edition (Stuttgart: Robert Lutz, [1915]).

_____ *Danger! and Other Stories* (London: John Murray, 1918).

Conrad, Joseph, *The Secret Agent: A Simple Tale* (Oxford: Oxford University Press, 2008).

Cornford, L. Cope, *The Defenceless Islands: A Study of the Social and Industrial Conditions of Great Britain and Ireland; and of the Effect upon them of the outbreak of a Maritime War* (London: E. Grant Richards, 1906).

Cowen, Laurence, *'Wake Up!' A Dream of To-Morrow* (London: Everett & Co., [1915]).

_____ ' "Wake Up!" A Dream of To-Morrow', *Daily Express* 5 January to 26 February 1915.

Cromie, Robert, *For England's Sake* (London and New York: Frederick Warne and Co., 1889).

_____ *The Next Crusade* (London: Hutchinson & Co., 1896).

Danyers, Geoffrey, *Blood is Thicker than Water: A Political Dream* (London, Tower Publishing Company Limited, 1894).

Dawson, A.J., *The Message* (London: E. Grant Richards, 1907).

'The Demure One' [pseud.], *The Battle of Boulogne; Or, How Calais became English Again: Another Version of the Channel Tunnel Affair* (London: C.F. Roworth, 1882).

282 Bibliography

Dilke, Charles Wentworth, *Greater Britain: A Record of Travel in English-Speaking Countries during 1866 and 1867*, 2 vols. (London: MacMillan and Co., 1868).

Dilke, Sir Charles Wentworth and Spenser Wilkinson, *Imperial Defence* (London: MacMillan and Co., 1892).

DO, CD., *The Channel Tunnel. A True View of it! Regarded as a Great Whole* (London: Hamilton, Adams, & Co., 1882).

Donovan, Rev. Alexander, *The Irish Rebellion of 1898: A Chapter in Future History* (Dublin: Hodges, Figgis, and Co., Ltd., 1893).

Dunsany, Lord, 'The Silver Streak', *Nineteenth Century*, 51 (May 1881), 737–755.

_____ 'The Proposed Channel Tunnel', *Nineteenth Century*, 60 (February 1882), 288–304.

Ensor, R.C.K., 'The English Countryside', in Lucian Oldershaw (ed.), *England: A Nation. Being the Papers of the Patriots' Club* (London and Edinburgh: R. Brimley Johnson, 1904), 95–129.

Esher, Viscount [Reginald Brett], *National Strategy* (London: A. L. Humphreys, 1904).

_____ *The Committee of Imperial Defence: Its Functions and Potentialities* (London: John Murray, 1912).

Evans, Arthur J., *Through Bosnia and the Herzegóvina on Foot during the Insurrection, August and September 1875. With an Historical Review of Bosnia and a Glimpse at the Croats, Slavonians, and the Ancient Republic of Ragusa* (London: Longmans, Green, and Co., 1876).

'Ex-Intelligence Officer' [pseud.], *The German Spy System from Within* (London: Hodder and Stoughton, 1915).

'An Ex-Revolutionist' [pseud.], *England's Downfall: or, the Last Great Revolution* (London: Digby, Long & Co., [1893]).

'Forethought, Backsight' [pseud.], *The Defence of Duffer's Drift: A Few Experiences in Field Defence for Detached Posts Which May Prove Useful in Our Next War* (London: William Clowes & Sons, Limited, 1904).

Freeman, Edward A., 'The Panic and its Lessons', *Macmillan's Magazine* (May 1871), 1–12.

'General Staff' [pseud.], *The Writing on the Wall* (London: William Heinemann, 1906).

Gissing, George, *New Grub Street* (Hertfordshire: Wordsworth Editions Limited, 1996).

Gleig, Charles, *When All Men Starve: Showing How England Hazarded her Naval Supremacy, and the Horrors Which Followed the Interruption of Her Food Supply* (London: John Lane, 1898).

Glossop, Reginald, 'Invasion of Britain', [Hull] *Daily Mail*, 14 November 1906, 4.

Gopčevik, Spiridion, *The Conquest of Britain in 1888, and the Fights and Battles that Led to It*, transl. Commander F.H.E. Crowe (Portsmouth: Griffin and Co., 1887).

Bibliography

283

Green, Frank W. and Carl Bernstein, *The Battle of Berlin* (London: C. Sheard, [1871]).

_____ *The Battle of Dorking: A Dream of John Bull's* (London: C. Sheard, [1871]).

Greer, Tom, *A Modern Dædalus* (London: Griffith, Farran, Okeden & Welsh, 1885).

Greg, W.R., 'Popular Versus Professional Armies', *Contemporary Review* (December 1870), 351–373.

Griffith, George, *The Angel of the Revolution: A Tale of the Coming Terror* (London: Tower Publishing Company Limited, 1893).

_____ *Olga Romanoff: Or, the Syren of the Skies* (London: Tower Publishing Company Limited, 1894).

_____ *The Outlaws of the Air* (London: Tower Publishing Company Limited, 1895).

Griffiths, Robert J., *Under the Deep Deep Sea: The Story of the Channel Tunnel* (London: Moffatt & Paige, [1887]).

'Grip' [pseud.], *How John Bull lost London; or, the Capture of the Channel Tunnel*, 4th edition (London: Sampson Low, Marston, Searle, & Rivington, 1882).

Gwynn, Stephen and Gertrude M. Tuckwell, *The Life of the Rt. Hon. Sir Charles W. Dilke*, 2 vols. (London: John Murray, 1917).

Haines, Donal Hamilton, 'The Leveller', *Pall Mall Magazine* (January 1913), 13–24.

[Hamley, Edward Bruce], 'Lessons from the War', *Blackwood's Magazine* (February 1856), 232–242.

Hampson, J.N., 'Great Britain v. France and Russia', *National Review* (June 1898), 502–522.

Harcourt, W. Vernon, 'Our naval and military establishments regarded with reference to the dangers of invasion', *Journal of the Royal United Service Institution*, 16 (1872), 575–607.

Hay, William Delisle, *The Doom of the Great City; being the Narrative of a Survivor, written A.D. 1942* (London: Newman & Co., [1880]).

[Hayward, Abraham], 'The Second Armada', *The Times*, 22 June 1871, 5.

Hemyng, Bracebridge, *The Commune in London; or, Thirty Years Hence: A Chapter of Anticipated History* (London: C.H. Clarke, [1871].

Hernaman-Johnson, Francis, *The Polyphemes: A Story of Strange Adventures among Strange Beings* (London: Ward, Lock & Co., 1906).

'Hibernicus' [pseud.], 'The Services and Civilians', *United Service Magazine*, 807 (February 1896), 537–546.

Hirst, F.W., *The Six Panics and Other Essays* (London: Methuen & Co., 1913).

Hobhouse, L.T., *Democracy and Reaction* (London: T. Fisher Unwin, 1904).

Hobson, J.A., *The Psychology of Jingoism* (London: Grant Richards, 1901).

_____ *The Crisis of Liberalism: New Issues of Democracy* (London: P.S. King & Son, 1909).

284 *Bibliography*

Hozier, Captain H.M., *The Invasions of England: A History of the Past, with Lessons for the Future*, 2 vols. (London: Macmillan and Co., 1876).

Hunter, Lieut.-Col. William, *Army Speech Dedicated to Those Who Have been Frightened by the Battle of Dorking* (London: Simpkin Marshall, 1871).

Hurd, Archibald, 'England's Peril – Invasion or Starvation', *Fortnightly Review* (April 1910), 679–692.

Ibsen, Henrik, 'An Enemy of the People', in *The Collected Works of Henrik Ibsen*, with introductions by William Archer, 11 vols. (London: W. Heinemann, 1906–1912), VIII.

Jack, Thomas Godfrey, *Anti-Papa: or, the Invasion of England by the Priests of Satan* (London: C.T. Lipshytz, [1895]).

'Jackdaw' [pseud.], *The Dilkiad; or the Dream of Dilke: An Anti-Republican Lay* (London: Martin, 1872).

Jackson, Colonel Louis, 'The Defence of Localities against Aerial Attack', *Journal of the Royal United Service Institution*, 58 (June 1914), 701–724.

Jane, Fred T., *Blake of the 'Rattlesnake', or; The Man Who Saved England: A Story of Torpedo Warfare in 189-* (London: Tower Publishing Company Limited, 1895).

_____ *To Venus in Five Seconds: An Account of the Strange Disappearance of Thomas Plummer, Pill-maker* (London: Innes & Co., 1897).

_____ *The Violet Flame: A Story of Armageddon and After* (London: Ward, Lock & Co., 1899).

'Jones, Jingo, M.P.' [pseud.], *The Sack of London by the Highland Host: A Romance of the Period* (London: Simpkin, Marshall, Hamilton, Kent, & Co., Ltd., 1900).

Jones, Major W. P., 'The Invasion of England', *Colburn's United Service Magazine*, July 1872, 363–367.

The 'Journeyman Engineer' [pseud.], 'Readers and Reading', *Good Words* (December 1876), 315–320.

The Kaiser's Kalendar for 1915 (London: Daily Express, 1914]).

'Kartoffel, Baron von' [pseud.], *The Germans in Cork: Being the letters of His Excellency the Baron von Kartoffel (Military Governor of Cork in the year 1918) and Others* (Dublin: The Talbot Press Ltd., 1917).

Kebbel, T.E., 'The Radical Rush', *National Review* (April 1893), 162–173.

Kipling, Rudyard, *Actions and Reactions* (London: Macmillan & Co., 1909).

_____ *A Diversity of Creatures* (London: Macmillan & Co., 1917).

_____ 'The Edge of the Evening', *Pall Mall Magazine* (December 1913), 714–726.

'A Landlord' [pseud.], *The Great Irish Rebellion of 1886* (London: Harrison & Sons, 1886).

'Lang-Tung' [pseud.], *The Decline and Fall of the British Empire. Being a History of England between the Years 1840–1981* (London: F.V. White and Co., 1881).

Bibliography

Le Bon, Gustave, *The Crowd: A Study of the Popular Mind* (London: T. Fisher Unwin, 1903).

Le Queux, William, 'The Poisoned Bullet' ['The Great War (in England) in 1897'], *Answers*, 23 December 1893 to 2 June 1894.

_____ *The Great War in England in 1897* (London: Tower Publishing Company Limited, 1894).

_____ 'The Invasion of 1910', *Daily Mail*, 14 March 1906 to 4 July 1906.

_____ *The Invasion of 1910. With a Full Account of the Siege of London* (London: Eveleigh Nash, 1906).

_____ *The Invasion of 1910. With a Full Account of the Siege of London* (London: Macmillan & Co., 1906).

_____ *Spies of the Kaiser: Plotting the Downfall of England* (London: Hurst & Blackett, Ltd., 1909).

_____ *The Invasion: Abridged from the Original Edition* (London: George Newnes, Ltd., [1910]).

_____ *The Invasion* (London: Everett & Co., [1913]).

_____ *German Atrocities: A Record of Shameless Deeds* (London: George Newnes, [1914]).

_____ *The War of the Nations: A History of the Great European Conflict*, vol. I (London: George Newnes, [1914]).

_____ *Britain's Deadly Peril: Are We Told the Truth?* (London: Stanley Paul & Co., 1915).

_____ *German Spies in England: An Exposure* (London: Stanley Paul & Co., 1915).

_____ *Number 70, Berlin: A Story of Britain's Peril* (London: Hodder and Stoughton, 1916).

_____ *The Zeppelin Destroyer: Being Some Chapters of Secret History* (London: Hodder and Stoughton, 1916).

_____ *The Invasion* (London: George Newnes, Ltd., 1917).

_____ *Things I Know about Kings, Celebrities, and Crooks* (London: Eveleigh Nash and Grayson Limited, 1923).

_____ *Die Invasion von 1910: Einfall der Deutschen in England*, transl. Traugott Tamm (Berlin: Concordia Deutsche Verlags-Anstalt, [n.d.]).

Leighton, Sir Baldwyn, *The Lull before Dorking* (London: Richard Bentley and Son, 1871).

Lester, Edward, *The Siege of Bodike: A Prophecy of Ireland's Future* (London: John Heywood, 1886).

Lester, H.F., *The Taking of Dover* (Bristol: J.W. Arrowsmith, 1888).

M., A.A., 'The Secret of the Army Aeroplane': *Punch*, 26 May 1909, 366.

M., F.N., 'Notices of Books: *The Great Alternative: A plea for a National Policy*. By Spencer [sic] Wilkinson', *Journal of the Royal United Service Institution*, 38 (June 1894), 683.

M., H.C., 'Wake, England Wake!', *Blackwood's Magazine* (February 1871), 257–258.

M., J.W., *The Coming Cromwell* (London: British & Colonial Publishing Company, 1871).

286   *Bibliography*

_____ *The Siege of London* (London: Robert Hardwicke, 1871).

'Macaulay, Clarendon' [pseud.], *The Carving of Turkey: A Chapter of European History, from Sources hitherto unpublished* (London: Mead and Co., 1894 [1874]).

'McCauley, Motly Ranke' [pseud.], *The Battle of Berlin (Die Slacht von Königsberg)* 5th edition (London: Tinsley Brothers, 1890 [1871]).

MacDonagh, Michael, 'The Craft of Newspaper Advertising', *Monthly Review* (August 1905), 102–117.

Machen, Arthur, *The Angels of Mons: The Bowmen and Other Legends of the War* (London: Simpkin, Marshall, Hamilton, Kent & Co., Ltd., 1915).

MacKay, Charles, *Memoirs of Extraordinary Popular Delusions and the Madness of Crowds*, 3rd edition, 2 vols. (London: G. Routledge & Co., 1856).

MacKay, Donald, *The Dynamite Ship* (London: Page, Pratt, & Turner, 1888).

Mackinder, H.J., *Britain and the British Seas* (London: William Heinemann, 1902).

_____ 'The Geographical Pivot of History', *Geographical Journal*, 23 (1904), 421–437.

_____ 'The Geographical Pivot of History – Discussion', *Geographical Journal*, 23 (1904), 437–444.

Marx, Karl and Friedrich Engels, *The German Ideology* (Amherst: Prometheus Books, 1998).

[Maude, F.N.], *The New Battle of Dorking* (London: Grant Richards, 1900).

Maurice, Brevet-Lieutenant Colonel J.F., *Hostilities without the Declaration of War: An Historical Abstract of the Cases in Which Hostilities Have Occurred Between Civilized Powers Prior to Declaration or Warning. From 1700 to 1870* (London: Clowes and Sons, 1883).

Mayo, The Earl of [Dermot Bourke], *The War Cruise of the 'Aries'* (Dublin: Edward Ponsonby, 1894).

Meredith, George, *Beauchamp's Career*, 3 vols. (London: Chapman & Hall, 1876).

[Mills, E.E.], *The Decline and Fall of the British Empire* (Oxford: Alden & Co., Ltd., Bocardo Press, 1905).

Moore, G.H., *Openings and Proceedings of the Irish Parliament* (London: Reeves & Turner, 1886).

'Muddersnook, Prof. Blyde' [pseud.], 'When the New Zealander Comes', *Strand Magazine* (September 1911), 284–291.

[Münch, Paul Georg], 'Einem Deutschen Dichter' [pseud.], *Hindenburgs Einmarsch in London* (Leipzig: Grethlein & Co., 1915).

_____ *Hindenburg's March into London: Being a Translation from the German Original*, ed. L.G. Redmond-Howard (London: John Long, Limited, 1916).

Murray, Major Stewart L., *The Reality of War: An Introduction to "Clausewitz"* (London: Hugh Rees, 1909).

Bibliography 287

Navy League Pamphlet A2, 'Constitution of the Navy League' ([London: The Navy League], 1896).

Navy League Pamphlet A3, 'Programme of Action' ([London: The Navy League], 1896).

Navy League Pamphlet C2, 'The Meaning of Defeat' ([London: The Navy League], 1896).

Newton, W. Douglas, *War* (London: Methuen & Co., Ltd., 1914).

_____ *The North Afire: A Picture of What May Be* (London: Methuen & Co., Ltd., 1914).

'An Octogenarian' [pseud.], *The British Federal Empire in the Twentieth Century* (London: Charles H. Clarke, [1872]).

Offin, T.G., *How the Germans took London. Forewarned, Forearmed* (Chelmsford: Edmund Durrant & Co., 1900).

Oldershaw, Lucian (ed.), *England: A Nation. Being the Papers of the Patriots' Club* (London and Edinburgh: R. Brimley Johnson, 1904).

'A Patriot' [Guy du Maurier], *An Englishman's Home* (London: Edward Arnold, 1909).

Peddie, James, *The Capture of London* (London: General Publishing Company, [1887]).

Pemberton, Max, 'The Iron Pirate', *Chums*, 1 March 1893 to 2 August 1893.

_____ *The Iron Pirate: A Plain Tale of Strange Happenings on the Sea* (London: Cassell & Company, 1893).

_____ *Lord Northcliffe: A Memoir* (London: Hodder and Stoughton Limited, [1922]).

_____ *Sixty Years Ago and After* (London: Hutchinson & Co., 1936).

Peuckert, Will-Erich/Chesney, *Was England Erwartet: Ein Zukunftsroman von 1871* (Berlin: August Groß Verlag, 1940).

Porter, Mrs. Gerald, *Annals of a Publishing House: John Blackwood. The Third Volume of William Blackwood and his Sons: Their Magazine and Friends* (Edinburgh and London: William Blackwood and Sons, 1898).

'Posteritas' [pseud.], *The Siege of London* (London: Wyman & Sons, 1885).

Potter, George, *The Channel Tunnel and International Progress* (London: 14 Fetter Lane, [1882]).

[Powell, G.H.], 'A Discourse of Rare Books', *Macmillan's Magazine*, 68 (June 1893), 115–126.

Prothero, R.E., 'The London County Council: Towards Common Sense', *Nineteenth Century* (March 1892), 515–524.

[Pullen, Henry William], *The Fight at Dame Europa's School: Shewing how the German Boy Thrashed the French Boy; and how the English Boy Looked On* (London: Simpkin, Marshall and Co., [1870]).

Redmond-Howard, L.G., 'Introduction', in [Paul Georg Münch], *Hindenburg's March into London: Being a Translation from the German Original*, ed. L.G. Redmond-Howard (London: John Long, Limited, 1916), 11–19.

Reed, Sam Rockwell, *The War of 1886 between the United States and Great Britain* (Cincinnati: Robert Clarke & Co., 1882).

288 *Bibliography*

Richardsheimer, Frank [pseud.], 'The Invasion of 1908: With a Full account of the Siege of Berlin', *Tatler*, 16 May 1906, 183–184.

Robinson, Admiral Sir R. Spencer, 'Causes Which Have Hindered the Development of the Fleet', *Journal of the Royal United Service Institution*, 32 (1888), 505–523.

Ross, Ch., *Representative Government and War* (London: Hutchinson & Co., 1903).

Saki [H.H. Munro], *When William Came: A Story of London under the Hohenzollerns* (London: John Lane, 1914 [1913]).

_____ *When William Came: A Story of London under the Hohenzollerns* (London: John Lane/The Bodley Head, Ltd., 1926).

'Seaforth, A. Nelson' [George Sydenham Clarke], *The Last Great Naval War: An Historical Retrospect* (London: Cassell & Company, Limited, 1891).

Shaw, George Bernard, 'Common Sense about the War', *The New Statesman Special War Supplement*, 14 November 1914.

_____ *The Quintessence of Ibsenism*, 3rd edition (London: Constable and Company, Ltd., 1926).

Shaylor, J., 'On the Selling of Books', *Nineteenth Century* (December 1896), 937–943.

Shiel, M.P., *The Yellow Danger* (London: Grant Richards, 1898).

_____ *The Purple Cloud* (London: Chatto & Windus, 1901).

Sketchley, Arthur [George Rose], *Mrs. Brown on The Battle of Dorking* (London: George Routledge and Sons, [1871]).

Spencer, Herbert, *The Principles of Sociology*, 3 vols. (London: Williams and Norgate, 1876–1896).

_____ 'The New Toryism', *Contemporary Review* (February 1884), 153–167.

Stead, F. Herbert, *No More War! "Truth Embodied in a Tale"* (London: Simpkin, Marshall, Hamilton, Kent & Co., Ltd., 1917).

Stead, W.T, 'Government by Journalism', *Contemporary Review* (May 1886), 653–674.

_____ 'The Rebuilding of the British Navy: How a Great Imperial Work was Begun', *Review of Reviews* (July 1897), 77–81.

_____ 'Character Sketches: The Three Most Notable Men in the Empire', Review of Reviews (January 1904), 21–29.

[Stone, Charles], *What Happened after the Battle of Dorking; or, the Victory at Tunbridge Wells* (London: George Routledge and Sons, [1871]).

Straus, Ralph, 'Armageddon in Prophecy: How Near Scare-Fictionists Have Come to The Truth', *Bystander*, 19 August 1914, 429–430.

Tariff Reform Illustrated (London: Tariff Reform League, 1904).

Tracy, Louis, *The Final War: A Story of the Great Betrayal* (London: C. Arthur Pearson Limited, 1896).

Traill, H.D., *The Barbarous Britishers: A Tip-top Novel* (London: John Lane, [1896]).

Bibliography 289

'Ulidia' [pseud.], *The Battle of Newry; or, the Result of Thirty Years' Liberal Legislation*, 2nd edition (Dublin: Hodges, Figgis, and Co., 1883).

'Untruthful Thomas' [pseud.], *The Bombardment of Scarbro' by the Russian Fleet in 1891* (London: The Crown Printing Company, [1889]).

Upward, Allen, *The Fourth Conquest of England* (London: The Tyndale Press, [1904]).

V., *The Swoop of the Eagles: An Episode from the Secret History of Europe* (London: Ward and Downey, 1889).

'Vates' [pseud.], 'The Revenge for Fashoda', *Fortnightly Review*, 73 (May 1903), 773–808.

Vaux, Patrick, 'The Man Who Stopped a War', *Pall Mall Magazine* (June 1909), 722–727.

_____ 'War and a Woman', *The Idler* (June 1909), 269–275.

'Vindex' [pseud.], *England Crushed; the Secret of the Channel Tunnel Revealed* (London: P.S. King, 1882).

Wallace, Edgar, *"1925": The Story of a Fatal Peace* (London: George Newnes, Limited, 1915).

Wallas, Graham, *Human Nature in Politics* (London: Archibald Constable & Co., 1908).

[Watson, H.C.M.], *The Decline and Fall of the British Empire; or, the Witch's Cavern* (London: Trischler & Company,1890).

'A Wayside Observer' [pseud.], *The Years before the Battle* (London: Elliot Stock, [1871]).

Wells, H.G., 'Anticipations: An Experiment in Prophecy', *Fortnightly Review*, 69 (April 1901) to 70 (December 1901).

_____ *The Discovery of the Future: A Discourse Delivered to the Royal Institution on January 24, 1902* (London: T. Fisher Unwin, 1902).

_____ *The War in the Air: And Particularly How Mr. Bert Smallways Fared While It Lasted* (London: George Bell and Sons, 1908).

_____ *Mr Britling Sees It Through* (New York: The Macmillan Company, 1916).

_____ *The Works of H.G. Wells*, 28 vols. (London: T. Fisher Unwin, 1924–1927).

_____ *The War in the Air: And Particularly How Mr. Bert Smallways Fared While It Lasted* (Harmondsworth: Penguin Books, 1941).

Welsford, J.W., *The Reign of Terror: An Experiment in Free Trade Socialism* (London: Women's Unionist & Tariff Reform Association, [1909]).

White, Arnold, *The Problems of a Great City* (London: Remington & Co. Publishers, 1886).

_____ *Efficiency and Empire* (London: Methuen & Co., 1901).

[White, William], *The Illustrated Handbook of the Royal Alhambra Palace, Leicester Square* (London: Nicholls Brothers, [1869]).

Wilkinson (Henry) Spenser, *The Brain of an Army: A Popular Account of the German General Staff* (London: Macmillan & Co., 1890).

_____ *The Brain of the Navy* (London: Archibald Constable and Company, 1895).

290   *Bibliography*

_____ 'Note', in Major Stewart L. Murray, *The Reality of War: An Introduction to "Clausewitz"* (London: Hugh Rees, 1909), v–xiv.

_____ *Thirty-Five Years: 1874–1909* (London: Constable and Company Ltd., 1933).

Williams, Ernest Edwin, *'Made in Germany'* (London: William Heinemann, 1896).

[Wilson. Beccles, and W. Laird Clowes], 'The Siege of Portsmouth', *Mail*, 17 June 1895 to 16 July 1895.

Wilson, H.W., and Arnold White, *When War Breaks Out* (London and New York: Harper Brothers, 1898).

Wodehouse, P.G., *The Swoop! Or, How Clarence Saved England* (London: Alston Rivers, Limited, 1909).

Wood, Walter, *The Enemy in Our Midst: The Story of a Raid on England* (London: John Long, 1906).

Secondary Sources

Adams, R.J.Q. and Philip P. Poirier, *The Conscription Controversy in Great Britain, 1900–18* (Basingstoke: The Macmillan Press, 1987).

Afflerbach, Holger, 'The Topos of Improbable War in Europe before 1914', in Holger Afflerbach and David Stevenson (eds), *An Improbable War? The Outbreak of World War I and European Political Culture before 1914* (New York and Oxford: Berghahn, 2007), 161–182.

Afflerbach, Holger and David Stevenson (eds), *An Improbable War? The Outbreak of World War I and European Political Culture before 1914* (New York and Oxford: Berghahn, 2007).

Ahlund, Claes, 'Den svenska invasionsberättelsen – en bortglömd litteratur', *Tidsskrift för litteraturvetenskap*, 3 (2003), 82–103.

_____ (ed.), *Scandinavia in the First World War: Studies in the War Experience of the Northern Neutrals* (Lund: Nordic Academic Press, 2012).

_____ 'Rats and Anthills: The First World War in the Scandinavian Spy Novel', in Claes Ahlund (ed.), *Scandinavia in the First World War: Studies in the War Experience of the Northern Neutrals* (Lund: Nordic Academic Press, 2012), 109–127.

Altick, Richard D., *The English Common Reader: A Social History of the Mass Reading Public, 1800–1900* (Chicago: Phoenix Books, 1967).

Amis, Kingsley, *New Maps of Hell: A Survey of Science Fiction* (London: Penguin Books, 2012).

Ashley, Mike, *The Age of the Storytellers: British Popular Fiction Magazines 1880–1950* (London: British Library, 2006).

Badsey, Stephen, *The German Corpse Factory: A Study in First World War Propaganda* (Warwick: Helion & Company, 2019).

_____ 'Strategy and Propaganda: Lord Kitchener, the Retreat from Mons and the Amiens Dispatch, August-September 1914', in Mark

Bibliography

Connelly, Jo Fox, Stefan Goebel and Ulf Schmidt (eds), *Propaganda and Conflict: War, Media and Shaping the Twentieth Century* (London: Bloomsbury Academic, 2019), 21–37.

Bantman, Constance, *The French Anarchists in London, 1880–1914: Exile and Transnationalism in the First Globalisation* (Liverpool: Liverpool University Press, 2013).

Bassett, Troy J., 'The Production of Three-volume Novels in Britain, 1863–97', *The Papers of the Bibliographical Society of America*, 102 (2008), 61–75.

Baylen, J.O., 'Politics and the "New Journalism": Lord Esher's Use of the "Pall Mall Gazette"', *Victorian Periodicals Review*, 20 (1987), 126–141.

Beaumont, Matthew, 'Cacotopianism, the Paris Commune, and England's Anti-Communist Imaginary, 1870–1900', *English Literary History*, 73 (2006), 465–487.

Beckett, Ian F.W., *Riflemen Form: A Study of the Rifle Volunteer Movement 1859–1908* (Barnsley: Pen & Sword, 2007).

_____ *A British Profession of Arms: The Politics of Command in the Late Victorian Army* (Norman, OK: University of Oklahoma Press, 2018).

Beeler, John, 'In the Shadow of Briggs: A New Perspective on British Naval Administration and W.T. Stead's 1884 "Truth about the Navy" Campaign', *International Journal of Naval History*, 1 (2002), [1–10].

Bell, Duncan, *The Idea of Greater Britain: Empire and the Future of World Order, 1860–1900* (Princeton and Oxford: Princeton University Press, 2007).

Benjamin, Walter, *The Arcades Project*, ed. Rolf Tiedemann, transl. Howard Eiland and Kevin McLaughlin (Cambridge, MA: The Belknap Press, 2002).

Berman, Marshall, *All That Is Solid Melts into Air: The Experience of Modernity* (London and New York: Verso, 2010).

Bertrand, Charles L. (ed.), *Revolutionary Situations in Europe, 1917–1922: Germany, Italy, Austria-Hungary* (Montreal: Interuniversity Centre for European Studies, 1977).

Bishop, Nicola, 'Ruralism, Masculinity and National Identity: The Rambling Clerk in Fiction, 1900–1940', *Journal of British Studies*, 54 (2015), 654–678.

Bleiler, Everett F., *The Checklist of Science-Fiction and Supernatural Fiction* (Glen Rock: Firebell Books, 1979).

_____ *Science Fiction: The Early Years* (Kent, OH, and London: Kent State University Press, 1990).

Blewett, Neal, 'The Franchise in the United Kingdom 1885–1918', *Past & Present*, 32 (1965), 27–56.

_____ *The Peers, the Parties and the People: The General Elections of 1910* (London: Macmillan, 1972).

Bond, Brian, *The Victorian Army and the Staff College, 1854–1914* (London: Eyre Methuen, 1972).

292 *Bibliography*

Bond, Brian and Nigel Cave (eds), *Haig: A Reappraisal 70 Years On* (Barnsley: Leo Cooper, 1999).

Bösch, Frank, 'Transfers and Similarities: Journalists, Politicians and Scandals in Imperial Germany and Britain', in Frank Bösch and Dominik Geppert (eds), *Journalists as Political Actors: Transfers and Interactions between Britain and Germany since the late 19th Century* (Augsburg: Wissner Verlag, 2008), 16–34.

Bösch, Frank and Dominik Geppert (eds), *Journalists as Political Actors: Transfers and Interactions between Britain and Germany since the late 19th Century* (Augsburg: Wissner Verlag, 2008).

Bourke, Joanna, *Fear: A Cultural History* (London: Virago, 2006).

Bowman, Tim, 'The Irish Recruiting and Anti-Recruiting Campaigns, 1914–1918', in Bertrand Taithe and Tim Thornton (eds), *Propaganda: Political Rhetoric and Identity 1300–2000* (Stroud: Sutton Publishing, 1999), 223–238.

Brantlinger, Patrick, *The Rule of Darkness: British Literature and Imperialism, 1830–1914* (Ithaca: Cornell University Press, 1988).

Braybon, Gail (ed.), *Evidence, History and the Great War: Historians and the Impact of 1914–18* (New York and Oxford: Berghahn, 2003).

Bridgham, Fred (ed.), *The First World War as a Clash of Cultures* (Rochester, NY: Camden House, 2006).

Briggs, Asa, 'The Language of "Mass" and "Masses" in Nineteenth-Century England', in David E. Martin and David Rubinstein (eds), *Ideology and the Labour Movement: Essays Presented to John Saville* (London: Croom Helm, 1979), 62–83.

Brooks, Richard, *Fred T. Jane: An Eccentric Visionary* (Coulsdon: Jane's Information Group, 1997).

Brown, Lucy, *Victorian News and Newspapers* (Oxford: Clarendon Press, 1985).

Buchanan, R.A., 'Engineers and Government in Nineteenth-Century Britain', in Roy MacLeod (ed.), *Government and Expertise: Specialists, Administrators and Professionals, 1860–1919* (Cambridge: Cambridge University Press, 1988), 41–58.

Bulfin, Ailise, '"To Arms!": Invasion Narratives and Late-Victorian Literature', *Literature Compass*, 12 (2015), 482–496.

———— *Gothic Invasions: Imperialism, War and Fin-de-Siècle Popular Fiction* (Cardiff: University of Wales Press, 2018).

———— 'The International Circulation and Impact of Invasion Fiction: Case Study of William Le Queux's *The Invasion of 1910* – "Not an ordinary 'pot-boiler' " ', *Critical Survey,* 32 (2020), 159–192.

———— ' "Fast lapsing back into barbarism": Social Evolution, the Myth of Progress and the Gothic Past in Late-Victorian Invasion and Catastrophe Fiction', *Victorian Popular Fictions*, 5 (2023), 37–57.

Burrow, J.W., *Evolution and Society: A Study in Victorian Social Theory* (Cambridge: Cambridge University Press, 1970).

Bibliography

Buurma, Rachel Sagner, 'Anonymity, Corporate Authority, and the Archive: The Production of Authorship in Late-Victorian England', *Victorian Studies*, 50 (2007), 15–42.

Calhoun, Craig (ed.), *Habermas and the Public Sphere* (Cambridge, MA and London, 1992).

_____ 'Introduction: Habermas and the Public Sphere', in Craig Calhoun (ed.), *Habermas and the Public Sphere* (Cambridge, MA and London, 1992), 1–48.

Cannadine, David, *Class in Britain* (New Haven and London: Yale University Press, 1998).

Carey, John, *The Intellectuals and the Masses: Pride and Prejudice among the Literary Intelligentsia, 1880–1939* (London: Faber and Faber, 1992).

Cesario, Bradley, *New Crusade: The Royal Navy and British Navalism, 1884–1914* (Oldenburg: De Gruyter, 2021).

Chancellor, Valerie E., *History for their Masters: Opinion in the English History Textbook: 1800–1914* (Bath: Adams & Dart, 1970).

Clark, Christopher, *The Sleepwalkers: How Europe Went to War in 1914* (London: Penguin Books, 2013).

Clarke, David, 'Rumours of Angels: A Legend of the First World War', *Folklore*, 113 (2002), 151–173.

Clarke, I.F., 'The Battle of Dorking', *Victorian Studies*, 8 (1965), 309–328.

_____ *Voices Prophesying War, 1763–1984* (London: Oxford University Press, 1966).

_____ 'Forecasts of Warfare in Fiction 1803–1914', *Comparative Studies in Society and History*, 10 (1967), 1–25.

_____ *The Tale of the Future, from the Beginning to the Present Day*, 3rd edition (London: The Library Association, 1978).

_____ *The Pattern of Expectation, 1644–2001* (London: Jonathan Cape, 1979).

_____ *Voices Prophesying War: Future Wars 1763–3749*, 2nd edition (Oxford: Oxford University Press, 1992).

_____ (ed.), *The Tale of the Next Great War, 1871–1914: Fictions of Future Warfare and of Battles still-to-come* (Liverpool: Liverpool University Press, 1995).

_____ 'The Origins of Future War Fiction', *Science Fiction Studies*, 23 (1996), 546–548.

_____ 'Before and after "The Battle of Dorking"', *Science Fiction Studies*, 24 (1997), 33–46.

_____ 'Future-War Fiction: The First Main Phase 1871–1900', *Science Fiction Studies*, 24 (1997), 387–412.

_____ (ed.), *The Great War with Germany, 1890–1914: Fictions and Fantasies of the War-to-come* (Liverpool: Liverpool University Press, 1997).

_____ 'Trigger-Happy: An Evolutionary Study of the Origins and Development of Future-War Fiction, 1763–1914', *Journal of Social and Evolutionary Systems*, 20 (1997), 117–136.

294   *Bibliography*

_____ 'The Battle of Dorking: Second Thoughts', *Extrapolation*, 40 (1999), 277–283.

Coetzee, Frans, *For Party or Country: Nationalism and the Dilemmas of Popular Conservatism in Edwardian England* (New York and Oxford: Oxford University Press, 1990).

Coetzee, Frans and Marilyn Shevin Coetzee, 'Rethinking the Radical Right in Germany and Britain before 1914', *Journal of Contemporary History*, 21 (1986), 515–537.

Colley, Linda, 'Britishness and Otherness: An Argument', *Journal of British Studies*, 31 (1992), 309–329.

_____ *Britons: Forging the Nation 1707–1837* (London: Pimlico, 1994).

Collini, Stefan, *Public Moralists: Political Thought and Intellectual Life in Britain 1850–1930* (Oxford: Clarendon Press, 1991).

Colls, Robert, 'Englishness and the Political Culture', in Robert Colls and Philip Dodd (eds), *Englishness: Politics and Culture 1880–1920* 2nd edition (London: Bloomsbury Academic, 2014), 53–84.

Colls, Robert and Philip Dodd (eds), *Englishness: Politics and Culture 1880–1920,* 2nd edition (London: Bloomsbury Academic, 2014).

Conboy, Martin and John Steel (eds), *The Routledge Companion to British Media History* (London: Routledge, 2015).

Connelly, Mark, Jo Fox, Stefan Goebel and Ulf Schmidt (eds), *Propaganda and Conflict: War, Media and Shaping the Twentieth Century* (London: Bloomsbury Academic, 2019).

Connery, Brian A. and Kirk Combe (eds), *Theorizing Satire: Essays in Literary Criticism* (Basingstoke: Macmillan, 1995).

_____ 'Theorizing Satire: A Retrospective and Introduction', in Brian A. Connery and Kirk Combe (eds), *Theorizing Satire: Essays in Literary Criticism* (Basingstoke: Palgrave Macmillan, 1995), 1–15.

Cornils, Ingo, 'The Martians are Coming! War, Peace, Love and Reflection in H.G. Wells's *The War of the Worlds* and Kurd Laßwitz's *Auf Zwei Planeten*', in Fred Bridgham (ed.), *The First World War as a Clash of Cultures* (Rochester, NY: Camden House, 2006), 129–143.

Cragoe, Matthew and Paul Readman (eds), *The Land Question in Britain, 1750–1950* (Basingstoke: Palgrave Macmillan, 2010).

_____ 'Introduction', in Matthew Cragoe and Paul Readman (eds), *The Land Question in Britain, 1750–1950* (Basingstoke: Palgrave Macmillan, 2010), 1–18.

Crawshaw, Michael, 'The Impact of Technology on the BEF and its Commander', in Brian Bond and Nigel Cave (eds), *Haig: A Reappraisal 70 Years On* (Barnsley: Leo Cooper, 1999), 155–175.

Cunningham, Hugh, *The Volunteer Force: A Social and Political History 1859–1908* (London: Croom Helm, 1975).

_____ 'The Language of Patriotism', *History Workshop Journal*, 12 (1981), 8–33.

Curtis, L. Perry, Jr., *Apes and Angels: The Irishman in Victorian Caricature* (Newton Abbot: David and Charles, 1971).

Bibliography 295

Dangerfield, George, *The Strange Death of Liberal England* (New York: Perigee Books, 1980).

Dawson, Graham, *Soldier Heroes: British Adventure, Empire and the Imagining of Masculinities* (London and New York: Routledge, 1994).

Demm, Eberhard, *Censorship and Propaganda in World War I: A Comprehensive History* (London: Bloomsbury Academic, 2019).

Eby, Cecil D., *The Road to Armageddon: The Martial Spirit in English Popular Literature, 1870–1914* (Durham and London: Duke University Press, 1987).

Echevarria II, Antulio J., *Imagining Future War: The West's Technological Revolution and Visions of Wars to Come, 1880–1914* (Westport and London: Praeger Security International, 2007).

Edgerton, David, 'Liberal Militarism and the British State', *New Left Review*, 185 (1991), 138–169.

_____ 'British Scientific Intellectuals and the Relations of Science, Technology and War', in Paul Forman and José M. Sánchez-Ron (eds), *National Military Establishments and the Advancement of Science and Technology* (Dordrecht: Kluwer Academic, 1996), 1–35.

_____ *England and the Aeroplane: Militarism, Modernity and Machines* (London: Penguin Books, 2013).

Edstadler, Katharina, Sandra Folie and Gianna Zocco (eds), *New Perspectives on Imagology* (Leiden: and Boston: Brill, 2022).

Eksteins, Modris, *Rites of Spring: The Great War and the Birth of the Modern Age* (London: Bantam Press, 1989).

Falk, Bernard, *Bouquets for Fleet Street: Memories and Musings over fifty years* (London: Hutchinson & Co., 1951).

Ferguson, Niall, *The Pity of War* (London, 1998).

Finkelstein, David, *The House of Blackwood: Author-Publisher Relations in the Victorian Era* (University Park, 2002).

_____ 'From Textuality to Orality – the Reception of *The Battle of Dorking*', in John Thompson (ed.), *Books and Bibliography: Essays in Commemoration of Don McKenzie* (Wellington: Victoria University Press, 2002), 87–102.

_____ (ed.), *Print Culture and the Blackwood Tradition, 1805–1930* (Toronto: University of Toronto Press, 2006).

_____ 'The Role of the Literary and Cultural Periodical', in Martin Conboy and John Steel (eds), *The Routledge Companion to British Media History* (London: Routledge, 2015), 263–272.

Fitzpatrick, David (ed.), *Ireland and the First World War* (Dublin: Trinity History Workshop, 1986).

Forman, Paul and José M. Sánchez-Ron (eds), *National Military Establishments and the Advancement of Science and Technology* (Dordrecht: Kluwer Academic, 1996).

Foster, R.F., *Paddy and Mr. Punch: Connections in Irish and English History* (London: Allen Lane, 1993).

Franklin, Alexandra, 'John Bull in a Dream: Fear and Fantasy in the Visual Satires of 1803', in Mark Philp (ed.), *Resisting Napoleon: The British*

296 *Bibliography*

Response to the Threat of Invasion, 1797–1815 (Aldershot: Ashgate, 2006), 125–139.

Franklin, H. Bruce, *Future Perfect: American Science Fiction of the Nineteenth Century* (New York, 1966).

_____ *War Stars: The Superweapon and the American Imagination* (New York, 1988).

Freedman, Lawrence, *The Future of War: A History* (London: Allen Lane, 2017).

Freedman, Lawrence, Paul Hayes and Robert O'Neill (eds), *War, Strategy, and International Politics: Essays in Honour of Sir Michael Howard* (Oxford: Clarendon Press, 1992).

French, David, 'Spy Fever in Britain, 1900–1915', *The Historical Journal*, 21 (1978), 355–370.

Fussell, Paul, *The Great War and Modern Memory* (Oxford, 2000).

Gannon, Charles E., *Rumors of War and Infernal Machines: Technomilitary Agenda-Setting in American and British Speculative Fiction* (Lanham: Rowman & Littlefield Publishers, Inc., 2003).

Geppert, Dominik, ' "The foul-visaged anti-Christ of journalism"? The Popular Press between Warmongering and International Cooperation', in Dominik Geppert and Robert Gerwarth (eds), *Wilhelmine Germany and Edwardian Britain: Essays on Cultural Affinity* (Oxford: Oxford University Press, 2008), 369–389.

_____ *Pressekriege: Öffentlichkeit und Diplomatie in den deutsch-britischen Beziehungen (1896–1912)* (Munich, 2007).

Geppert, Dominik and Robert Gerwarth (eds), *Wilhelmine Germany and Edwardian Britain: Essays on Cultural Affinity* (Oxford: Oxford University Press, 2008).

Glover, David, '*Die Gelbe Gefahr, le Péril Jaune,* the Yellow Peril: the Geopolitics of a Fear', in Kate Hebblethwaite and Elizabeth McCarthy (eds), *Fear: Essays on the Meaning and Experience of Fear* (Dublin: Four Courts Press, 2007), 47–59.

Gollin, Alfred M., 'England Is No Longer an Island: The Phantom Airship Scare of 1909', *Albion*, 13 (1981), 43–57.

Gooch, John, *The Prospect of War: Studies in British Defence Policy 1847–1942* (London, 1981).

Gowan, Peter, 'The Origins of the Administrative Elite', *New Left Review*, 162 (March–April 1987), 4–34.

Graves, Robert, *Goodbye to All That* (Harmondsworth: Penguin Books, 1985).

Gregory, Adrian, 'British "War Enthusiasm" in 1914: A Reassessment', in Gail Braybon (ed.), *Evidence, History and the Great War: Historians and the Impact of 1914–18* (New York and Oxford: Berghahn, 2003), 67–85.

_____ 'Peculiarities of the English? War, Violence and Politics: 1900–1939', *Journal of Modern European History*, 1 (2003), 44–59.

Bibliography

_____ 'A Clash of Cultures: The British Press and the Opening of the Great War', in Troy R.E. Paddock (ed.), *A Call to Arms: Propaganda, Public Opinion, and Newspapers in the Great War* (Westport: Praeger, 2004), 15–49.

_____ *The Last Great War: British Society and the First World War* (Cambridge: Cambridge University Press, 2008).

Gullickson, Gay L., *Unruly Women of Paris: Images of the Commune* (Ithaca: Cornell University Press, 1996).

Habermas, Jürgen, *The Structural Transformation of the Public Sphere: An Inquiry into a Category of Bourgeois Society*, transl. Thomas Burger and Frederick Lawrence (Cambridge, 1992).

Hamer, W.S., *The British Army: Civil-Military Relations 1885–1905* (Oxford, 1970).

Hamilton, W. Mark, *The Nation and the Navy: Methods and Organization of British Navalist Propaganda, 1889–1914* (New York: Garland Publishing, 1986).

Harding, James, *Gerald du Maurier: The Last Actor-Manager* (London: Hodder & Stoughton, 1989).

Hattendorf, John B., 'The Conundrum of Military Education in Historical Perspective', in Gregory C. Kennedy and Keith Neilson (eds), *Military Education: Past, Present, and Future* (Westport, CT: Praeger, 2002), 1–12.

Hawkins, Angus, '"Parliamentary Government" and Victorian Political Parties, c.1830-c.1880', *The English Historical Review*, 104 (1989), 638–669.

_____ *Victorian Political Culture: 'Habits of Heart and Mind'* (Oxford, 2015).

Hebblethwaite, Kate and Elizabeth McCarthy (eds), *Fear: Essays on the Meaning and Experience of Fear* (Dublin: Four Courts Press, 2007).

Hiley, Nicholas, 'The Play, the Parody, the Censor and the Film', *Intelligence and National Security*, 6 (1991), 218–228.

Hippler, Thomas, *Governing from the Skies: A Global History of Aerial Bombing*, transl. David Fernbach (London: and New York: Verso, 2017).

Hobsbawm, Eric, 'Mass-Producing Traditions: Europe 1870–1914', in Eric Hobsbawm and Terence Ranger (eds), *The Invention of Tradition* (Cambridge: Cambridge University Press, 1983), 263–307.

Hobsbawm, Eric and Terence Ranger (eds), *The Invention of Tradition* (Cambridge: Cambridge University Press, 1983).

Holman, Brett, *The Next War in the Air: Britain's Fear of the Bomber, 1908–1941* (Farnham: Ashgate, 2014).

_____ 'William Le Queux, the Zeppelin Menace and the Invisible Hand', *Critical Survey*, 32 (2020), 99–118.

Houghton, Walter E., *The Victorian Frame of Mind: 1830–1870* (New Haven and London: Yale University Press, 1957).

Howkins, Alun, 'The Discovery of Rural England', in Robert Colls and Philip Dodd (eds), *Englishness: Politics and Culture 1880–1920*' 2nd edition (London, 2014), 85–111.

Bibliography

Hughes, Michael and Harry Wood, 'Crimson Nightmares: Tales of Invasion and Fears of Revolution in Early 20th Century Britain', *Contemporary British History*, 28 (2014), 294–317.

Humphries, Michael, '"The Eyes of an Empire": The Legion of Frontiersmen, 1904–1914', *Historical Research*, 85 (2012), 133–158.

Hynes, Samuel, *The Edwardian Turn of Mind* (Princeton: Princeton University Press, 1968).

Ions, Edmund, *James Bryce and American Democracy 1870–1922* (London: Macmillan, 1968).

Ives, Peter, *Language and Hegemony in Gramsci* (London: Pluto Press, 2004).

James, Edward, 'Science Fiction by Gaslight: An Introduction to English-Language Science Fiction in the Nineteenth Century', in David Seed (ed.), *Anticipations: Essays on Early Science Fiction and its Precursors* (Syracuse: Syracuse University Press), 26–45.

Jenkins, Roy, *Sir Charles Dilke: A Victorian Tragedy* (London and Glasgow: Fontana Books, 1968).

Johnson, Franklyn Arthur, *Defence by Committee: The British Committee of Imperial Defence, 1885–1959* (London: Oxford University Press, 1960).

Johnson, Matthew, 'The Liberal Party and the Navy League in Britain before the Great War', *Twentieth Century British History*, 22 (2011), 137–163.

_____ *Militarism and the British Left, 1902–1914* (Basingstoke: Palgrave Macmillan, 2013).

Joll, James, *Gramsci* (Glasgow: Fontana, 1977).

Joll, James and Gordon Martel, *The Origins of the First World War*, 3rd edition (Harlow: Pearson Longman, 2007).

Jones, Aled, *Powers of the Press: Newspapers, Power and the Public in Nineteenth-Century England* (Aldershot: Scolar Press: 1996).

Jones, Heather, Jennifer O'Brien and Cristoph Schmidt-Supprian (eds), *Untold War: New Perspectives in First World War Studies* (Leiden and Boston: Brill, 2008).

Jones, Heather and Arndt Weinrich, 'The Pre-1914 Period: Imagined Wars, Future Wars. Introduction', *Francia,* 40 (2013), 305–315.

Keep, C.J., 'Fearful Domestication: Future-War Stories and the Organization of Consent, 1871–1914', *Mosaic*, 23 (1990), 1–16.

Kennedy, David, *A World of Struggle: How Power, Law and Expertise Shape Global Political Economy* (Princeton, 2016).

Kennedy, Paul M., *The Rise of the Anglo-German Antagonism 1860–1914* (Boston: George Allen & Unwin, 1980).

_____ *The Rise and Fall of British Naval Mastery* (London: Penguin Books, 2017).

_____ *The Realities behind Diplomacy: Background Influences on British External Policy, 1865–1980* (London: George Allen & Unwin, 1981).

Bibliography

_____ *The Rise and Fall of the Great Powers: Economic Change and Military Conflict from 1500 to 2000* (London: Unwin Hyman, 1988).

Kennedy, Paul and Anthony Nicholls (eds), *Nationalist and Racialist Movements in Britain and Germany before 1914* (London and Basingstoke: Palgrave Macmillan, 1981).

Kirkwood, Patrick M., 'The Impact of Fiction on Public Debate in Late Victorian Britain: *The Battle of Dorking* and the "Lost Career" of Sir George Tomkyns Chesney', *Graduate History Review*, 4 (2012), 1–16.

Koss, Stephen, *The Rise and Fall of the Political Press in Britain* (Chatham: Fontana Press, 1990).

Krever, Tor, 'Spectral Expertise', *New Left Review*, 106 (July–August 2017), 148–160.

Krieger, Leonard and Fritz Stern (eds), *The Responsibility of Power: Historical Essays in Honor of Hajo Holborn* (London and Melbourne: Macmillan, 1968).

Kumar, Krishan, *The Making of English National Identity* (Cambridge: Cambridge University Press, 2003).

_____ *The Idea of Englishness: English Culture, National Identity and Social Thought* (Farnham, 2015).

Lambert, Andrew, 'Education in the Royal navy: 1854–1914', in Geoffrey Till (ed.), *The Development of British Naval Thinking: Essays in Memory of Bryan McLaren Ranft* (London: Routledge, 2006), 34–59.

Law, Graham and Robert L. Patten, 'The Serial Revolution', in David McKitterick (ed.), *The Cambridge History of the Book in Britain, vol. VI: 1830–1914* (Cambridge: Cambridge University Press, 2009), 144–171.

Lee, Alan J., *The Origins of the Popular Press in England 1855–1914* (London: Croom Helm, 1976).

Leersen, Joep, 'Enmity, Identity, Discourse: Imagology and the State', in Katharina Edstadler, Sandra Folie and Gianna Zocco (eds), *New Perspectives on Imagology* (Leiden and Boston: Brill, 2022), 49–69.

Leggett, Don, *Shaping the Royal Navy: Technology, Authority and Naval Architecture, c.1830–1906* (Manchester: Manchester University Press, 2015).

Lehmann, John, *The Whispering Gallery: Autobiography I* (London: Longmans, Green, 1955).

Lewin, Christopher George, *War Games and their History* (Stroud: Fonthill Media, 2012).

Longmate, Norman, *Island Fortress: The Defence of Great Britain, 1603–1945* (London: Grafton, 1993).

Luckhurst, Roger, 'Scientific Romance, Fantasy and the Supernatural', in Michael Saler (ed.), *The Fin-De-Siècle World* (London: Routledge, 2015), 677–690.

Luvaas, Jay, *The Education of an Army: British Military Thought, 1815–1940* (London: Cassell, 1965).

300 Bibliography

MacKenzie, John M., *Propaganda and Empire: The Manipulation of British Public Opinion, 1880–1960* (Manchester: Manchester University Press, 1985).

—— (ed.), *Popular Imperialism and the Military: 1850–1950* (Manchester: Manchester University Press, 1992).

—— 'Introduction: Popular imperialism and the military', in John M. MacKenzie (ed.), *Popular Imperialism and the Military: 1850–1950* (Manchester: Manchester University Press, 1992).

McKitterick, David (ed.), *The Cambridge History of the Book in Britain, vol. VI: 1830–1914* (Cambridge: Cambridge University Press, 2009).

MacLeod, Roy (ed.), *Government and Expertise: Specialists, Administrators and Professionals, 1860–1919* (Cambridge: Cambridge University Press, 1988).

MacLeod, Roy, 'Introduction', in Roy MacLeod (ed.), *Government and Expertise: Specialists, Administrators and Professionals, 1860–1919* (Cambridge: Cambridge University Press, 1988) 1–24.

McLynn, Frank, *Invasion: From the Armada to Hitler, 1588–1945* (London: Routledge & Kegan Paul, 1987).

Mandler, Peter, 'Against "Englishness": English Culture and the Limits to Rural Nostalgia, 1850–1940', *Transactions of the Royal Historical Society* (1997), 155–175.

—— 'The Problem with Cultural History', *Cultural and Social History*, 1 (2004), 94–117.

—— *The English National Character: The History of an Idea from Edmund Burke to Tony Blair* (New Haven and London, 2006).

Marcus, G.J., 'The Naval Crisis of 1909 and the Croydon By-Election', *Journal of the Royal United Service Institution*, 103 (1958), 500–514.

Marder, Arthur J., *British Naval Policy 1880–1905: The Anatomy of British Sea Power* (London: Putnam & Co., [1940]).

Martel, Gordon, *Imperial Diplomacy: Rosebery and the Failure of Foreign Policy* (Montreal: McGill-Queen's University Press, 1986).

Martin, David E. and David Rubinstein (eds), *Ideology and the Labour Movement: Essays Presented to John Saville* (London: Croom Helm, 1979).

Matin, A. Michael, '"We Aren't German Slaves Here, Thank God"': Conrad's Transposed Nationalism and British Literature of Espionage and Invasion', *Journal of Modern Literature*, 21 (1997–1998), 251–280.

—— '"The Hun is at the Gate!": Historicising Kipling's Militaristic Rhetoric, From the Imperial Periphery to the National Center: Part One: The Russian Threat to Imperial India', *Studies in the Novel*, 31 (1999), 317–356.

—— '"The Hun is at the Gate!": Historicising Kipling's Militaristic Rhetoric, From the Imperial Periphery to the National Center: Part Two: The French, Russian, and German Threats to Great Britain', *Studies in the Novel*, 31 (1999), 432–470.

Bibliography

_____ 'The Creativity of War Planners: Armed Forces Professionals and the Pre-1914 British Invasion Scare Genre', *English Literary History*, 78 (2011), 801–831.

_____ 'Scrutinizing *The Battle of Dorking*: The Royal United Service Institution and the Mid-Victorian Invasion Controversy', *Victorian Literature and Culture*, 39 (2011), 385–407.

_____ 'Gauging the Propagandist's Talents: William le Queux's Dubious Place in Literary History: Part One', *Critical Survey*, 32 (2020), 79–98.

_____ Gauging the Propagandist's Talents: William le Queux's Dubious Place in Literary History: Part Two', *Critical Survey*, 32 (2020), 193–218.

Matos, T. Carlo, *Ibsen's Foreign Contagion: Henrik Ibsen, Arthur Wing Pinero, and Modernism on the London Stage, 1890–1900* (Bethesda: Academica Press, 2012).

Matz, Aaron, *Satire in an Age of Realism* (Cambridge: Cambridge University Press, 2010).

Mayer, Arno J., 'Domestic Causes of the First World War', in Leonard Krieger and Fritz Stern (eds), *The Responsibility of Power: Historical Essays in Honor of Hajo Holborn* (London and Melbourne: Macmillan, 1968), 286–300.

_____ 'Internal Crisis and War Since 1870', in Charles L. Bertrand (ed.), *Revolutionary Situations in Europe, 1917–1922: Germany, Italy, Austria-Hungary* (Montreal: Interuniversity Centre for European Studies, 1977), 201–233.

Meisel, Joseph S., 'The Germans are Coming! British Fiction of a German Invasion, 1871–1913' *War, Literature and the Arts*, 2 (1990), 41–79.

Melby, Christian K., '"Of Paramount Importance to Our Race": H.O. Arnold-Forster and South African Soldier-Settlement', *History*, 102 (2017), 596–616.

_____ 'Empire and Nation in British Future-War and Invasion-Scare Fiction, 1871–1914', *Historical Journal*, 63 (2020), 389–410.

_____ 'Rethinking British Militarism before the First World War: The Case of *An Englishman's Home* (1909)', *English Historical Review*, 137 (2022), 1377–1401.

_____ 'Litteraturen om krigen som aldri kommer', *Nytt norsk tidsskrift*, 40 (2023), 191–203.

_____ 'Norsk fremtidskrigs- og invasjonslitteratur før 1914 i et skandinavisk og europeisk perspektiv', *Historisk tidsskrift*, 102 (2023), 202–216.

_____ 'War, Public Opinion and the British Constitution, c. 1867–1914', *Journal of Modern European History*, 21 (2023), 441–457.

Meyer, Jessica, *Men of War: Masculinity and the First World War in Britain* (Basingstoke: Palgrave Macmillan, 2009).

Middleton, Alex, 'William Rathbone Greg, Scientific Liberalism, and the Second Empire', *Modern Intellectual History*, 19 (2022), 681–707.

Millman, Richard, *Britain and the Eastern Question, 1875–1878* (Oxford: Clarendon Press, 1979).

302 *Bibliography*

Moretti, Franco, *Atlas of the European Novel, 1800–1900* (London and New York: Verso, 2009).

Morgan, Chris, *The Shape of Futures Past: The Story of Prediction* (Exeter: Webb & Bower, 1980).

Morgan-Owen, David G., *The Fear of Invasion: Strategy, Politics, and British War Planning, 1880–1914* (Oxford: Oxford University Press, 2017).

_____ 'Strategy, Rationality, and the Idea of Public Opinion in Britain, 1870–1914', *Historical Research*, 94 (2021), 397–418.

_____ 'Scares, Panics, and Strategy: The Politics of Security and British Invasion Scares before 1914', *Diplomacy & Statecraft*, 33 (2022), 442–473.

Morris, A.J.A., *The Scaremongers: The Advocacy of War and Rearmament, 1896–1914* (London: Routledge & Kegan Paul, 1984).

Moskowitz, Sam (ed.), *Science Fiction by Gaslight: A History and Anthology of Science Fiction in the Popular Magazines, 1891–1911* (Cleveland: World Publishing Co., 1968).

_____ 'Preface', in Sam Moskowitz (ed.), *Science Fiction by Gaslight: A History and Anthology of Science Fiction in the Popular Magazines, 1891–1911* (Cleveland: World Publishing Co., 1968), 11–14.

_____ *Strange Horizons: The Spectrum of Science Fiction* (New York: Charles Scribner's Sons, 1976).

Moss, Eloise, 'Burglary Insurance and the Culture of Fear in Britain, c. 1889–1939', *The Historical Journal*, 54 (2011), 1039–1064.

Mulligan, William and Brendan Simms (eds), *The Primacy of Foreign Policy in British History, 1660–2000: How Strategic Concerns Shaped Modern Britain* (Basingstoke: Palgrave Macmillan, 2010).

Mullins, Robert E., *The Transformation of British and American Naval Policy in the Pre-Dreadnought Era: Ideas, Culture and Strategy*, ed. John Beeler (Basingstoke: Palgrave Macmillan, 2016).

Newton, Douglas, *The Darkest Days: The Truth Behind Britain's Rush to War, 1914* (London and New York: Verso, 2014).

Nichols, David, *The Lost Prime Minister: A Life of Sir Charles Dilke* (London and Rio Grande: The Hambledon Press, 1995).

Nowell-Smith, Simon, *The House of Cassell 1848–1958* (London: Cassell and Company, Ltd., 1958).

Offer, Avner, *The First World War: An Agrarian Interpretation* (Oxford: Clarendon Press, 1989).

Ortega y Gasset, José, *The Revolt of the Masses* (London: George Allen & Unwin, Ltd., 1932).

Otis, Laura, *Membranes: Metaphors of Invasion in Nineteenth-Century Literature, Science, and Politics* (Baltimore: Johns Hopkins University Press, 1999).

Paddock, Troy R.E. (ed.), *A Call to Arms: Propaganda, Public Opinion, and Newspapers in the Great War* (Westport: Praeger, 2004).

Bibliography

_____ 'Introduction: Newspapers, Public Opinion, and Propaganda', in Troy R.E. Paddock (ed.), *A Call to Arms: Propaganda, Public Opinion, and Newspapers in the Great War* (Westport: Praeger, 2004), 1–13.

_____ (ed.), *World War I and Propaganda* (Leiden and Boston: Brill, 2014).

Paris, Michael, *Winged Warfare: The Literature and Theory of Aerial Warfare in Britain, 1859–1917* (Manchester and New York: Manchester University Press, 1992).

_____ *Warrior Nation: Images of War in British Popular Culture, 1850–2000* (London: Reaktion, 2000).

_____ (ed.), *The First World War and Popular Cinema: 1914 to the Present* (New Brunswick: Rutgers University Press, 2000).

Parrinder, Patrick, 'From Mary Shelley to *The War of the Worlds*: The Thames Valley Catastrophe', in David Seed (ed.), *Anticipations: Essays on Early Science Fiction and Its Precursors* (Syracuse: Syracuse University Press), 58–74.

Parry, Jonathan, *The Politics of Patriotism: English Liberalism, National Identity and Europe, 1830–1886* (Cambridge: Cambridge University Press, 2006).

_____ 'What's the big idea?', *London Review of Books*, 39, no. 23 (30 November 2017), 31–32.

Partridge, Michael Steven, *Military Planning for the Defence of the United Kingdom, 1814–1870* (Westport: Praeger, 1989).

Patrick, Chris and Stephen Baister, *William Le Queux: Master of Mystery* (Purley: Chris Patrick & Stephen Baister, [2007]).

Patten, Robert L. and David Finkelstein, 'Editing *Blackwood's*; or, What Do Editors Do?', in David Finkelstein (ed.), *Print Culture and the Blackwood Tradition, 1805–1930* (Toronto: University of Toronto Press, 2006), 143–183.

Pelling, Henry, *Social Geography of British Elections, 1885–1910* (Aldershot: Gregg Revivals, 1994).

Pennell, Catriona, ' "The Germans have Landed!" Invasion Fears in the South-East of England, August to December 1914', in Heather Jones, Jennifer O'Brien and Cristoph Schmidt-Supprian (eds), *Untold War: New Perspectives in First World War Studies* (Leiden and Boston: Brill, 2008), 95–116.

_____ *A Kingdom United: Popular Responses to the Outbreak of the First World War in Britain and Ireland* (Oxford: Oxford University Press, 2012).

_____ 'Believing the Unbelievable: The myth of the Russians with "snow on their boots" in the United Kingdom, 1914', *Cultural and Social History*, 11 (2014), 69–87.

_____ 'Presenting the War in Ireland, 1914–1918', in Troy R.E. Paddock (ed.), *World War I and Propaganda* (Leiden and Boston: Brill, 2014).

Perkin, Harold, *The Rise of Professional Society: England since 1880* (London and New York: Routledge, 2001).

304   *Bibliography*

Philp, Mark, 'Introduction: The British Response to the Threat of Invasion, 1797–1815', in Mark Philp (ed.), *Resisting Napoleon: The British Response to the Threat of Invasion, 1797–1815* (Aldershot: Ashgate, 2006), 1–17.

Pick, Daniel, *Faces of Degeneration: A European Disorder, c.1848-c.1918* (Cambridge: Cambridge University Press, 1989).

_____ *War Machine: The Rationalisation of Slaughter in the Modern Age* (New Haven and London: Yale University Press, 1993).

Porter, Andrew, *Victorian Shipping, Business and Imperial Policy: Donald Currie, the Castle Line and Southern Africa* (Woodbridge: Boydell, 1986).

Porter, Bernard, *The Origins of the Vigilant State: The London Metropolitan Police Special Branch before the First World War* (London: Weidenfeld and Nicolson, 1987).

Porter, Dorothy, '"Enemies of the Race": Biologism, Environmentalism, and Public Health in Edwardian England', *Victorian Studies*, 34 (1991), 159–178.

Pugh, Martin, *The Making of Modern British Politics, 1867–1945*, 3rd edition (Oxford: Blackwell Publishing, 2001).

Quail, John, *The Slow Burning Fuse: The Lost History of the British Anarchists* (London: Paladin Books, 1978).

Quinn, Patrick J. and Steven Trout (eds), *The Literature of the Great War Reconsidered: Beyond Modern Memory* (Basingstoke: Palgrave, 2001).

Ramsden, John, *Don't Mention the War: The British and the Germans since 1890* (London: Abacus, 2007).

Ranft, Bryan, 'Parliamentary Debate, Economic Vulnerability, and British Naval Expansion, 1860–1905', in Lawrence Freedman, Paul Hayes and Robert O'Neill (eds), *War, Strategy, and International Politics: Essays in Honour of Sir Michael Howard* (Oxford: Clarendon Press, 1992), 75–93.

Reader, W.J., *At Duty's Call: A Study in Obsolete Patriotism* (Manchester: Manchester University Press, 1988).

Readman, Paul, 'The 1895 General Election and Political Change in Late Victorian Britain', *The Historical Journal*, 42 (1999), 467–493.

_____ 'The Place of the Past in English Culture, c. 1890–1914', *Past & Present*, 186 (2005), 147–199.

_____ *Land and Nation in England: Patriotism, National Identity, and the Politics of Land, 1880–1914* (Woodbridge: Royal Historical Society, 2008).

_____ 'Patriotism and the Politics of Foreign Policy, c. 1870–1914', in William Mulligan and Brendan Simms (eds), *The Primacy of Foreign Policy in British History, 1660–2000: How Strategic Concerns Shaped Modern Britain* (Basingstoke: Palgrave Macmillan, 2010), 260–276.

_____ '"The Cliffs are not Cliffs": The Cliffs of Dover and National Identities in Britain, c.1750-c.1950', in *History*, 99 (2014), 241–269.

Redford, Duncan, 'Opposition to the Channel Tunnel, 1882–1975: Identity, Island Status and Security', *History*, 99 (2014), 100–120.

Reeves, Nicholas, *Official British Film Propaganda During the First World War* (London: Croom Helm, 1986).

Bibliography 305

_____ 'Official British Film Propaganda', in Michael Paris (ed.), *The First World War and Popular Cinema: 1914 to the Present* (New Brunswick: Rutgers University Press, 2000), 27–50.

_____ *The Power of Film Propaganda: Myth or Reality?* (London: Continuum, 2003).

Reiss, Tom, 'Imagining the Worst: How a Literary Genre Anticipated the Modern World', *The New Yorker*, 28 Nov 2005, 106–114.

Richards, Grant, *Author Hunting: By an Old Literary Sportsman. Memories of Years Spent Mainly in Publishing, 1897–1925* (London: Hamish Hamilton, 1934).

Richards, Thomas, *The Commodity Culture of Victorian England: Advertising and Spectacle, 1851–1914* (London: Verso, 1990).

Rogers, Ben, *Beef and Liberty: Roast Beef, John Bull and the English Nation* (London: Vintage, 2004).

Rose, Andreas, *Between Empire and Continent: British Foreign Policy before the First World War*, transl. Rona Johnston (New York & Oxford: Berghahn, 2019).

Rose, Jonathan, *The Intellectual Life of the British Working Classes*, 2nd edition (New Haven and London: Yale University Press, 2001).

Rudé, George, *The Crowd in the French Revolution* (Oxford: Clarendon Press, 1959).

Rüger, Jan, *The Great Naval Game: Britain and Germany in the Age of Empire* (Cambridge: Cambridge University Press, 2009).

_____ 'Revisiting the Anglo-German Antagonism', *Journal of Modern History*, 83 (2011), 579–617.

_____ *Heligoland: Britain, Germany, and the Struggle for the North Sea* (Oxford: Oxford University Press, 2017).

Ryan, W. Michael, 'The Invasion Controversy of 1906–1908: Lieutenant-Colonel Charles à Court Repington and British Perceptions of the German Menace', *Military Affairs*, 44 (1980), 8–12.

Saler, Michael (ed.), *The Fin-De-Siècle World* (London: Routledge, 2015).

Sanders, M.L., and Philip M. Taylor, *British Propaganda during the First World War, 1914–18* (London and Basingstoke: The Macmillan Press Ltd., 1982).

Schults, Raymond L., *Crusader in Babylon: W.T. Stead and the Pall Mall Gazette* (Lincoln, NE: University of Nebraska Press, 1972).

Schurman, D.M., *The Education of a Navy: The Development of British Naval Strategic Thought, 1867–1914* (London: Cassell, 1965).

Scully, Richard, *British Images of Germany: Admiration, Antagonism & Ambivalence, 1860–1914* (Basingstoke: Palgrave Macmillan, 2012).

Seaman, John T., Jr., *A Citizen of the World: The Life of James Bryce* (London and New York: I.B. Tauris, 2006).

Searle, G.R., *The Quest for National Efficiency: A Study in British Politics and Political Thought, 1899–1914* (London: Ashfield Press, 1990).

_____ *A New England? Peace and War 1886–1918* (Oxford: Clarendon Press, 2004).

306 *Bibliography*

Sebald, W.G., *Austerlitz*, transl. Anthea Bell (London: Penguin Books, 2011).

Secord, James A., *Victorian Sensation: The Extraordinary Publication, Reception, and Secret Authorship of* Vestiges of the Natural History of Creation (Chicago and London: University of Chicago Press, 2003).

Seed, David (ed.), *Anticipations: Essays on Early Science Fiction and Its Precursors* (Syracuse: Syracuse University Press, 1995).

—— (ed.), *Future Wars: The Anticipations and the Fears* (Liverpool: Liverpool University Press, 2012).

Sellar, W.C. and R.J. Yeatman, *1066 and All That* (London: Penguin Books, 1962).

Semmel, Bernard, *Imperialism and Social Reform: English Social-Imperial Thought, 1895–1914* (Cambridge, MA: Harvard University Press, 1960).

Smith, Steven R.B., 'Public Opinion, the Navy and the City of London: the Drive for British Naval Expansion in the Late Nineteenth Century', *War & Society*, 9 (1991), 29–50.

Spiers, Edward M., *The Late Victorian Army, 1868–1902* (Manchester: Manchester University Press, 1992).

St. Barbe Sladen, N., *The Real Le Queux: The Official Biography of William Le Queux* (London: Nicholson & Watson, 1938).

Stableford, Brian, *Scientific Romance in Britain, 1890–1950* (London: Fourth Estate, 1985).

Stafford, David A.T., 'Spies and Gentlemen: 'The Birth of the British Spy Novel, 1893–1914', *Victorian Studies,* 24 (1981), 489–509.

Stearn, Roger T., 'Victorian and Edwardian Fiction of Future War', *Soldiers of the Queen*, 69 (1992), 26–32.

—— 'The Mysterious Mr Le Queux: War Novelist, Defence Publicist and Counterspy', *Soldiers of the Queen*, 70 (1992), 6–27. (Reprinted in *Critical Survey*, 32 (2020), 17–58).

—— 'General Sir George Chesney', *Journal of the Society for Army Historical Research*, 75 (1997), 106–118.

—— '"The Last Glorious Campaign": Lord Roberts, the National Service League and Compulsory Military Training, 1902–1914', *Journal of the Society for Army Historical Research*, 87 (2009), 312–330.

Stedman Jones, Gareth, *Outcast London: A Study in the Relationship Between Classes in Victorian Society* (Oxford: Clarendon Press, 1971).

Steiner, Zara S. and Keith Neilson, *Britain and the Origins of the First World War*, 2nd edition (Basingstoke and New York: Palgrave Macmillan, 2003).

Strachan, Hew (ed.), *The Oxford Illustrated History of the First World War* (Oxford: Oxford University Press, 2000).

Summers, Anne, 'Militarism in Britain before the Great War', *History Workshop Journal,* 2 (1976), 104–123.

—— 'The Character of Edwardian Nationalism: Three Popular Leagues', in Paul Kennedy and Anthony Nicholls (eds), *Nationalist and Racialist*

Movements in Britain and Germany before 1914 (London and Basingstoke: Palgrave Macmillan, 1981), 68–87.

Sutherland, John, 'Nineteenth-Century SF and the Book Trade', in Darko Suvin, *Victorian Science Fiction in the UK: The Discourses of Knowledge and of Power* (Boston: G.K. Hall & Co., 1983), 123–126.

Suvin, Darko, *Metamorphoses of Science Fiction: On the Poetics and History of a Literary Genre* (New Haven and London: Yale University Press, 1979).

_____ *Victorian Science Fiction in the UK: The Discourses of Knowledge and of Power* (Boston: G.K. Hall & Co., 1983).

Swift, John N., 'Jack London's "The Unparalleled Invasion": Germ Warfare, Eugenics, and Cultural Hygiene', *American Literary Realism*, 35 (2002), 59–71.

Taithe, Bertrand, and Tim Thornton (eds), *Propaganda: Political Rhetoric and Identity 1300–2000* (Stroud: Sutton Publishing, 1999).

Taylor, Antony, *London's Burning: Pulp Fiction, the Politics of Terrorism and the Destruction of the Capital in British Popular Culture, 1840–2005* (London: Bloomsbury, 2013).

_____ '"At the Mercy of the German Eagle": Images of London in Dissolution in the Novels of William Le Queux', *Critical Survey*, 32 (2020), 59–78.

Tchen, John Kuo Wei and Dylan Yeats (eds), *Yellow Peril! An Archive of Anti-Asian Fear* (London and New York: Verso, 2014).

Thackeray, David, 'Home and Politics: Women and Conservative Activism in Early Twentieth-Century Britain', *Journal of British Studies*, 49 (2010), 826–848.

Thompson, Andrew S., *Imperial Britain: The Empire in British Politics, c.1880–1932* (Harlow: Pearson Education, 2000).

Thompson, F.M.L., 'Social Control in Victorian Britain', *Economic History Review*, 34 (1989), 189–208.

Thompson, J. Lee, *Politicians, the Press, & Propaganda: Lord Northcliffe & the Great War, 1914–1919* (Kent, OH, and London: The Kent State University Press 1999).

_____ *Northcliffe: Press Baron in Politics, 1865–1922* (London: John Murray, 2000).

Thompson, James, '"Pictorial Lies"? – Posters and Politics in Britain c. 1880–1914', *Past & Present,* 197 (2007), 177–210.

_____ *British Political Culture and the Idea of 'Public Opinion', 1867–1914* (Cambridge: Cambridge University Press, 2013).

Thompson, John (ed.), *Books and Bibliography: Essays in Commemoration of Don McKenzie* (Wellington: Victoria University Press, 2002).

Tierney, Mark, Paul Bowen and David Fitzpatrick, 'Recruiting Posters', in David Fitzpatrick (ed.), *Ireland and the First World War* (Dublin: Trinity History Workshop, 1986).

Tosh, John, *A Man's Place: Masculinity and the Middle-Class Home in Victorian England* (New Haven and London: Yale University Press, 1999).

308   *Bibliography*

_____ *Manliness and Masculinities in Nineteenth-Century Britain: Essays on Gender, Family and Empire* (Harlow: Pearson Longman, 2005).

Travis, Anthony S., 'Engineering and Politics: The Channel Tunnel in the 1880s', *Technology and Culture*, 32 (1991), 461–497.

Tredrey, F.D., *The House of Blackwood, 1804–1954: The History of a Publishing Firm* (Edinburgh: William Blackwood and Sons, 1954).

Trentmann, Frank, *Free Trade Nation: Commerce, Consumption, and Civil Society in Modern Britain* (Oxford: Oxford University Press, 2008).

Tucker, Albert, 'Military', in J. Don Vann and Rosemary T. VanArsdel (eds), *Victorian Periodicals and Victorian Society* (Toronto: University of Toronto Press, 1995), 62–80.

Vann, J. Don and Rosemary T. VanArsdel (eds), *Victorian Periodicals and Victorian Society* (Toronto: University of Toronto Press, 1995).

_____ 'Introduction', in J. Don Vann and Rosemary T. VanArsdel (eds), *Victorian Periodicals and Victorian Society* (Toronto: University of Toronto Press, 1995), 3–8.

Waller, Philip, *Writers, Readers and Reputations: Literary Life in Britain 1870–1918* (Oxford: Oxford University Press, 2006).

Ward, Paul, *Red Flag and Union Jack: Englishness, Patriotism and the British Left, 1881–1924* (Woodbridge: The Royal Historical Society/Boydell Press, 1998).

Watson, Alexander, *Enduring the Great War: Combat, Morale and Collapse in the German and British Armies, 1914–1918* (Cambridge: Cambridge University Press, 2008).

Weedon, Alexis, *Victorian Publishing: The Economics of Book Production for a Mass Market, 1836–1916* (Aldershot: Ashgate, 2003).

Wiener, Joel H., 'The Nineteenth Century and the Emergence of a Mass Circulation Press', in Martin Conboy and John Steel (eds), *The Routledge Companion to British Media History* (London: Routledge, 2015), 206–213.

Wiener, Martin J., *English Culture and the Decline of the Industrial Spirit, 1850–1980* (Cambridge: Cambridge University Press, 1981).

Wilkinson, Glenn R., '"The Blessings of War": The Depiction of Military Force in Edwardian Newspapers', *Journal of Contemporary History*, 33 (1998), 97–115.

_____ 'Literary Images of Vicarious Warfare: British Newspapers and the Origin of the First World War, 1899–1914', in Patrick J. Quinn and Steven Trout (eds), *The Literature of the Great War Reconsidered: Beyond Modern Memory* (Basingstoke: Palgrave, 2001), 24–34.

_____ *Depictions and Images of War in Edwardian Newspapers, 1899–1914* (Basingstoke: Palgrave Macmillan, 2003).

Williams, Rhodri, *Defending the Empire: The Conservative Party and British Defence Policy, 1899–1915* (New Haven and London: Yale University Press, 1991).

Bibliography

Wilson, Keith M., *The Policy of the Entente: Essays on the Determinants of British Foreign Policy 1904–1914* (Cambridge: Cambridge University Press, 1985).
_____ *Channel Tunnel Visions, 1850–1945: Dreams and Nightmares* (London, 1994).
Winter, Jay, *Sites of Memory, Sites of Mourning: The Great War in European Cultural History* (Cambridge: Cambridge University Press, 1996).
_____ 'Propaganda and the Mobilization of Consent', in Hew Strachan (ed.), *The Oxford Illustrated History of the First World War* (Oxford: Oxford University Press, 2000).
Wood, Harry, 'Radical Reactionary: The Politics of William Le Queux', *Critical Survey*, 32 (2020), 139–158.

Unpublished theses

Moon, Howard Roy, 'The Invasion of the United Kingdom: Public Controversy and Official Planning 1888–1918' (University of London, Ph.D. thesis, 1968).
Wood, Harry Joseph, 'External Threats Mask Internal Fears: Edwardian Invasion Literature 1899–1914' (University of Liverpool, Ph.D. thesis, 2014).

Internet resources

Airminded	www.airminded.org
British Museum, London	www.britishmuseum.org
Encyclopedia of Science Fiction	www.sf-encyclopedia.com
Imperial War Museum	www.iwm.org.uk
International Journal of Naval History	www.ijnhonline.org
The Invasion Network	invasionnetwork.wordpress.com
Island Mentalities	invasionscares.wordpress.com
Oxford Dictionary of National Biography	www.oxforddnb.com
The Redress of the Past	www.historicalpageants.ac.uk
The Riddle of the Sands	www.theriddleofthesands.com
Trinity College Dublin Library	https://digitalcollections.tcd.ie

Index

Note: 'n.' after a page reference indicates the number of a note on that page

1925 – Story of a Fatal Peace, The (Wallace) 252

'A Patriot' 125
About the Battle of Dorking (play) 35
Academy, The (periodical) 120
Admiralty 67, 89, 90, 91, 127, 129, 133, 134, 161, 191
advertising culture 199–200
Aerial Board of Control 213
aerial warfare 154, 199, 212, 213
Afflerbach, Holger 222n.70
After the Battle of Dorking (Anon.) 169
After Dorking (Stone) 184n.96
Aldershot 83
Alison, Sir Archibald 104, 114n.101
Allen, Inglis 214
Altick, Richard D. 193
amateurs 56, 58, 60, 83, 120, 121, 123, 127, 128, 130, 137, 214
'Amiens Dispatch' 248
Amis, Kingsley 7
anarchist movement 153
Angel of the Revolution, The (Griffith) 158
angels of Mons legend 239
Anglo-Saxons 168, 171

Answers (periodical) 195, 219n.42
anti-channel tunnel campaign 99
'Anticipations' (Wells) 189, 190
anti-establishment bias 161
anti-German propaganda 204, 210, 212, 236
anxieties over invasion 7–8, 103, 155, 200
Archer, William 234–235, 256n.14
armaments, growth of 35, 96, 201
Arnold-Forster, Hugh Oakeley 84, 85, 90, 92, 93, 94, 95, 96, 97, 106n.25, 106n.31, 107n.46, 110n.69, 119, 120, 134, 135, 138n.14, 147n.96, 194, 206
views on expertise 87–88
views on navy and its significance 88–89
Arnold-Forster, Mary 90
Arnold, Matthew 109n.63
'As Easy as A.B.C.' (Kipling) 213
Ashley, Evelyn 117, 123
Astor, William Waldorf 203, 227n.128
Athenæum (periodical) 139n.15
Atkins, Tommy 201
Atteridge, A. Hilliard 61
Australia 65, 171, 172
authorial intent versus popular reaction 198–199

Index

Badsey, Stephen 237, 248
Baedeker 21
Bagehot, Walter 4
Balfour, Arthur 84, 130, 131,
    147n.96
Barrie, J.M. 125, 249
Bathurst, Charles 156
Battle of Berlin, The
    ('McCauley') 37
Battle of Berlin, The (music) 37
'Battle of Berlin in 1875, The'
    (Anon.) 72, 82n.75
Battle of Bolougne, The (The
    Demure One) 114n.10
Battle of Dorking, The (Chesney)
    5, 10, 55–56, 60, 65, 68,
    83, 94, 101, 103, 104,
    114n.108, 154, 161, 165,
    196, 198, 208, 209, 232,
    235, 236, 237, 245, 254,
    262n.86, 269, 270
    audience of 41–44
    criticism 26–27
    in culture 34–38
    and invasion panics of
        1870–1871 28–32
    mocking of 35–37, 42–43
    narrative of 23–27
    politics of 38–41
    public opinion and impact
        of 31–32
    and service writers 62–64
    success of 21–22, 39–41
Battle of Dorking, The (music) 37
Battle of Newry, The (Ulidia) 171
Battle of Port Said, The (Anon.) 96
Battle of the Ancre and the
    Advance of the Tanks,
    The (film) 244
Battle of the Future, The 199
Battle of the Somme (film) 244
Battle of To-Morrow, The
    (Anon.) 113n.86
'Battle of Wilton' (Anon.) 73
Battle off Worthing, The
    ('A Captain of the Royal
    Navy') 96

Beauchamp's Career
    (Meredith) 166
Beaumont, Matthew 154, 160,
    161, 195
Beckett, Ian F.W. 3, 32
Bee-Hive 100
Beeler, John 105, 109n.51
Benjamin, Walter 42
Benson, Godfrey, Lord
    Charnwood 168
Beresford, Charles 84, 86, 90,
    121, 136, 176n24
Berman, Marshall 263
Berney, Rev. Thomas 198
Bernhardi, Friedrich von
    256n.11
Bernstein, Carl 270
Bioscope (magazine) 240, 258n.35
Birmingham Post 254
Bishop, Nicola 178n.49
Black and White (periodical) 120,
    195, 197
Blackwood, John 22, 24–25, 37,
    39, 41, 99
Blackwood, William 32, 39–41
Blackwood's Magazine 22, 23,
    27, 36, 39, 41, 44, 70, 99,
    168, 194
Blake of the 'Rattlesnake'
    (Jane) 191
Blatchford, Robert 235–236
Blewett, Neal 109n.62, 136
'Blue Water' 71, 96, 156
blue-blooded contingents 30
Blyth, James 127
Boer War 56
    see also South African War
'Bolt from the Blue' 71, 96, 242
Bond, Brian 76n.23
Bösch, Frank 110n.70
bourgeois ideology 38, 154, 203
Bourke, Joanna 4, 163
'Bowmen, The' (Machen) 239
Boxing Day invasion 125, 127
Boy Scouts 258n.42
Boy's Own Paper 212
Bracon Ash 198

Index

Bradlaugh, Charles 101, 102, 156, 175n.20
Bradlaughites 155, 156
Bramah, Ernest 212
Brantlinger, Patrick 170
Brassey, Sir Thomas 91, 92
Brett, Reginald, Lord Esher 89, 94, 130, 145n.73, 165
Brex, J. Twells 153
Briggs, Asa 5
Britain Prepared (film) 244
Britain's Deadly Peril (Le Queux) 250
British Expeditionary Force 2, 32, 239
Britons: Forging the Nation 1707–1837 (Colley) 6
Broad Arrow (newspaper) 63
Brock, Henry Matthew 191
Bryce, James 265, 272n.12
Buchan, John 251, 261n.80
Bulfin, Ailise 7, 225n.104
Burgoyne, Alan H. 71, 96, 128, 144n.62, 182n86, 234
Burnand, Francis Cowley 35–37, 39
Burns, John 174n5
Butler, Lady Elizabeth 97
Butler, William Francis 97, 112n.81, 171
Bystander (magazine) 234

cacotopian fiction 154, 161, 195
Caine, Hall 244, 259n.55
Cambridge, Duke of 41, 98, 115n.111
Campbell-Bannerman, Henry 130, 204, 205, 206, 210
Canada 171
Captain of the 'Mary Rose,' The (Clowes) 191, 192
Cardwell, Edward 23, 43
Cardwell army reforms 23, 30, 58–59, 68, 131, 269
Carey, John 62
Carving of Turkey, The ('Macaulay') 71, 72

Cassell's Magazine 195
Catholicism 170, 185n.109
censorship 248
Cesario, Bradley 105n.18
Chamberlain, Joseph 84, 87, 169
Chancellor, Valerie E. 62
channel tunnel 98–100, 119, 155, 166
    and 1884 naval scare 103–104
    opposition and debates on 100–103
Charteris, Francis, Lord Elcho 43
'Cheapening of Useful Books, The' (Clowes) 190
Checklist of Science-Fiction and Supernatural Fiction, The (Bleiler) 79n.60
Chesney, Charles 28–29, 69
Chesney, George Tomkyns 5, 10, 21, 23, 32, 55, 59–60, 83, 84, 85, 160, 269
    on lack of organisation 32
    political intentions 38
    RUSI lecture 55–56, 64
    see also Battle of Dorking, The
Chesterton, G.K. 249
Childers, Erskine 125–127, 128, 168, 269
Chums (magazine) 195, 212
Churchill, Lord Randolph 166
Citizen, The (newspaper) 208
City Imperial Volunteers 125
Civil War of 1915, The (Brex) 153
civilian writers 58, 62
civilisational threats 172
Clarke, Charles Allen 156, 157, 161
Clarke, David 256n.23
Clarke, I.F. 6–7, 22, 26, 32, 70, 79n.60, 88, 119, 122, 123, 125, 113n.86, 142n.43, 221n.69, 232, 255n.3, 269
class 9, 26, 42, 94, 135, 159–163, 173, 206
Clowes, William Laird 96, 118, 191, 192, 197, 269
Cobden, Richard 3, 202, 211

Index 313

Colburn, Henry 66
Colburn's United Service
Magazine 63, 64, 66–67, 69,
72–73, 82n.79, 136
Coleridge, Samuel Taylor 2
Colley, Linda 6, 170, 266
Colls, Robert 167
Colomb, John 86
Colomb, Philip 86, 160, 211
Coming Cromwell, The
(J.W.M.) 178n.47
'Command of the Sea, The'
(Wilkinson, *Pall Mall*
Gazette) 132
Committee of Imperial Defence
(CID) 130–131, 135
commodification 5, 13n26
Commune in London, The
(Hemyng) 154
communication 57–59
Conan Doyle, Arthur 157, 163, 249
Conrad, Joseph 263
conscription 32, 71, 123, 135, 242,
243, 248, 253, 269
Contemporary Review 31
Corn Laws (1846) 157
Cornford, L. Cope 157
Corpse Exploitation
Establishment 239
Council of National Safety 169
Cowen, Laurence 241, 242
Crawshaw, Michael 59
Crimean War 59, 67, 122
Crowd, The (Le Bon) 163
crowds 93, 95, 96, 129, 161, 162
angry 129
era of 4
female, irrational and foreign
quality 164, 165
psychology of 270
riots 162, 163
theory 163
women 163
see also public
Croydon by-election 134
Cruise of the Anti-Torpedo, The
(Anon.) 171

cultural hegemony 203
cultural navalism 105n.18
Cunningham, Hugh 14n.30, 269
Currie, Sir Donald 91
Curtis, L. Perry, Jr. 184n.104

Daily Express 241, 243, 259n.61
Daily Mail 124, 142n.46, 178n.49,
194, 227n.129
Daily Mail [Hull] 208
Daily News (also *Daily News*
and Leader) 206, 209,
224n.92, 236
Dame Europa's School [Pullen] 29
Danger! (Conan Doyle) 163
Dangerfield, George 165, 200
Dawson, A.J. 191
Decline and Fall of the
British Empire, The
('Lang-Tung') 171
declinism 187n.123
'Defeat of the Navy at the "Battle
of Dorking," The' 67
Defence of the Realm Act (1914)
(DORA) 248
defence planning and expertise,
limits of public opinion
129–131
defenceless woman, image of 165
Demm, Eberhard 259n.50, 260n.74
democracy and democratic system
12n.18, 56, 96, 128, 137,
264–266
see also public opinion
governors and masses, tension
between 10
gradual democratisation 5
hyperdemocracy thesis 95
political system 4, 5
and power of press 93
see also public opinion
Denmark 72
Der Tauchbootkrieg: Wie Kapitän
Sirius England Niederzwang
(Conan Doyle, transl.
Schanzer) 176n.24
Devon, Earl of 102

Index

Devonshire, Duke of 84
Dickens, Charles 194
Dilke letter, the 85–86, 87, 103, 104, 131
Dilke, Sir Charles 84, 85, 99, 120, 139n.21, 175n.20
Dilkiad, The ('Jackdaw') 175n.20
directed navalism 105n.18
'Discovery of the Future, The' (Wells) 189
Disraeli, Benjamin, Lord Beaconsfield 61, 70
Doom of the County Council of London, The (Anon.) 153
Dover Castle 198
Doyle, Conan 115n.111, 176n.24
Dracula (Stoker) 170
drawings and caricatures 197
du Maurier, Gerald 125, 142n.46
du Maurier, Guy 125
Dunsany, Lord 99, 101, 114n.96, 114n.108
Dynamite Ship, The (MacKay) 113n.84

Eardley-Wilmot, Sydney 199
Eastern Question 70, 71
Eby, Cecil D. 7, 123, 202
Echevarria II, Antulio J. 58, 221n.69
Eckroyd, William 102
'Edge of the Evening, The (Kipling)' 213
Edgerton, David 58
Edinburgh, Duke of 119
Education Bill (1870) 62
education, role in mass reading 62
Edwardians 9, 56
Eksteins, Modris 160
Elcho, Lord 43
empire and navy, link between 110n.69
Endymion (Keats) 21

Enemy in Our Midst, The (Wood) 129, 156, 161, 162, 163, 165, 169, 179n.52
Enemy of the People, An (Ibsen) 55, 57–58, 144n.68
England in Gefahr (Conan Doyle, transl. Schütze) 176n.24
England's Downfall: or, the Last Great Revolution ('An Ex-Revolutionist') 153, 156, 159, 162, 196
Englishman's Home, An (du Maurier) 125, 127, 164, 165, 166, 196, 200, 214, 219n.47, 236, 237, 241, 242, 243, 245, 269
Ensor, R.C.K. 167
Entente Cordiale 92
Era, The 225n.107
escapism 260n.50
Evans, Arthur J. 72
Evans, Will 208, 225n.107
Evening Gazette, The 27
Evening News 232, 238
expert writers, agitation between 123–129
expertise and expert opinion 67
from 1890s to 1914 118–120
and public pressure 131–137
public role of 59–61
unclear nature of 74n.13
Victorian idea of 57–59
extension of the parliamentary franchise 4, 97

Fabian Society 144n.68, 235
Fears in Solitude (Coleridge) 3
female nature of crowds 164
female role in invasion-scare fiction 163–166
Ferguson, Niall 13n.28
'Fifty Years Ago' (Anon.) 64, 65, 66
Fifty Years Hence (Anon.) 71
film adaptations
Englishman's Home, An 241

Index

Invasion of 1910, The 240
"*Wake Up!*" *A Dream of To-Morrow* 241–243
Final War, The (Tracy) 168, 169, 170
Finkelstein, David 38, 41, 48n.65
Fisher, John 5, 88, 89, 134
food supply threats 156–159
  Corn Laws (1846) 157
  and imports 157–158
  psychological rise in prices 158
  starvation 157
For England's Sake (Cromie) 82n.79, 138n.13
Forster, W.E. 62, 84
Fortnightly Review 60, 135, 189, 190
Four Average Englishmen group 132, 133
four-plus-four Dreadnought building programme 134
France 3, 72, 92, 102, 103, 121, 122, 168, 169, 198, 199, 202, 266
Franco-German war (305–307) 139n.21
Franco-Prussian war (1870–1871) 23, 28, 29, 95, 154, 234
Franklin, Alexandra 3
Franklin, H. Bruce 16n.34
free trade 157
Free Trade 155, 156
Freedman, Lawrence 221n.69
Freeman, Edward 28, 29
French Revolution 4, 163, 164
Fun (magazine) 37, 45n.20
Fussell, Paul 166, 239

Gannon, Charles E. 129, 141n.42
Gasset, José Ortega Y 95
Gaumont Cinematograph Company 240
gender roles 163–166
general election (1895) 117–118, 119, 123
Geppert, Dominik 212

germ theory 155
German Spies in England (Le Queux) 250
Germans in Cork, The (Kartoffel) 251
Germany and the Next War (Bernhardi) 11, 256n.11
Gibbs, Philip 87
Gillray, James 3
Gladstone, Herbert 206
Gladstone, William 23, 24, 27, 34, 38, 39, 43, 61, 70, 84, 97, 100, 153, 159, 198
Gleig, Charles 156, 157
Globe, The (newspaper) 237, 252
Glossop, Reginald 208
Glover, David 188n.124
Gollin, Alfred M. 227n.129
Gooch, John 14n.29, 32
Good Words 217n.31
Gordon, Charles 84
Gortschakoff and Bismarck, or Europe in 1940. A Dream (Anon.) 72, 180n.64
government by journalism 93, 95, 131
government control of the press 248
Gramsci, Antonio 203, 223n.85
Grand Empire Pageant 267
Graves, Robert 257n.29
'Great Britain v. France and Russia' (Hampson) 211
'Great Day in 1920, The' (Beeman) 213
Great Naval War of 1887, The (Clowes) 82n.79, 96
Great Peril, The (Clowes) 190–191
Great Power politics 267
Great War in England in 1897, The (Le Queux) 61, 162, 167, 169, 195, 209, 219n.42
'Great War of 1892, The' (also *Great War of 189-, The* (Colomb)) 120, 121, 139n.21, 195, 197

316 *Index*

Green, Frank W. 37, 270
Greenwich Park explosion 153
Greer, Tom 112n.82
Greg, William Rathbone 31, 47n.59
Gregory, Adrian 204, 178n.49,
    179n.59
Griffith, D.W. 244
Griffith, George 158, 190,
    196, 197
Griffiths, Robert J. 101
Gubbins, Sir Lancelot 255n.7
Guildford 22, 83, 199
Gullickson, Gay 164

Habermas, Jürgen 4
Haines, Donal Hamilton 213
Halkett, George 227n.128
Hamilton, F.T. 216n.16
Hamilton, W. Mark 105, 147n.102
Hamley, Edward Bruce 60, 62
Hampshire Advertiser 42
Hampson, J.N. 211
Happygoland question 80n.64
Harcourt, William Vernon 29, 34,
    47n.48, 48n.69, 68–69, 199
Hardy, Gathorne 45n.13
Hardy, Thomas 245
Harmsworth, Alfred, Lord
    Northcliffe 5, 104, 117,
    122, 123, 137n.2, 140n.36,
    141n.41, 162, 193, 194,
    205, 235
Harmsworth's Magazine 194
Hawkins, Angus 12n.18
Hay, Sir John 89, 92
Hearts of the World (film) 244
heavy-handed symbolism 162, 166,
    213, 244
Hens Who Tried to Crow, The
    (Anon.) 79n.61
Herald 235
Hermon-Hodge, Sir Robert 134
Hernaman-Johnson, Francis 208
Herodotus 2
'Hibernicus' 60
Hicks-Beach, Sir Michael 99

*Hindrances to Good Citizenship,
    The* (Bryce) 265
Hippler, Thomas 154
Hirst, F.W. 211, 270
historians 219n.43
Hitchcock, Alfred 261n.80
HMS *Captain* 67
Hobhouse, L.T. 272n.13
Hohenzollern dynasty 252
Holman, Brett 220n.51
Houghton, Walter E. 129
House of Commons 1, 43, 98, 204
How John Bull lost London
    ('Grip') 102
How the Germans took London
    (Offin) 234
Howkins, Alun 167
Hozier, H.M. 61
Hume-Williams, Ellis 1
Huntington, Samuel 75n.17
Hurd, Archibald 135
Hynes, Samuel 7, 141n.40, 160,
    200, 205
hyperdemocracy 95

Ibsen, Henrik 57–58, 62, 144n.68
If England Were Invaded (film) 240
Imperial Federation League
    conference 110n.69
Imperial Maritime League 133,
    191, 211
imperialism 155, 201–203, 223n.77
imperialism in reverse 170–171
In a Conning Tower
    (Arnold-Forster) 88, 97, 106,
    119, 138, 139, 195
*In the Year One (A.D. 1888)
    of Home Rule de Jure*
    (Anon.) 113n.84
inclusive public sphere 11n.14
Independent Labour Party 153
industrial society 201
*Intellectual Life of the British
    Working Classes, The*
    (Rose) 9
Internationalists 155

Index

'Invaders, The' 209
Invasion (game) 196
Invasion: Its Possibilities (film)
  220n.51
Invasion of 1883, The (Anon.)
  71, 169
Invasion of 1910, The (Le Queux)
  124, 125, 127–128, 129,
  136, 140n.36, 141n.39, 162,
  163, 164, 167, 171, 194,
  196, 208, 210, 225n.104,
  250, 257n.33, 267, 269
  film adaptation 240
  public engagement with and its
    publications 205–209
  reception of 204–205
Invasion of England, The (Butler)
  97, 112n.81, 171
invasion-scare fiction, in
  brief 7
invasion-scare genre
  modernisation about 263
  politics and culture in
    268–269
  popularity and success of
    264–266, 268, 269–270
  power conflicts 266
  security against enemies
    267–268
  spatial fluidity and timelessness
    to 263–264
Ireland 97, 155, 169–170
Irish Home Rule 97
Irish-American involvement in Irish
  affairs 97
'Iron Pirate, The' (Pemberton) 120,
  195

Jackson, Louis 199
James, H. 112n.82
Jane, Fred T. 176n.24, 191, 197,
  216n.13, 216n.14
Japan 188n.124, 188n.126
Jeune École 154
Jingoism 99
John Bull (magazine) 39

Johnson, Matthew 81n.67,
  148n.103
Jones, Heather 200
Jones, Kennedy 140n.36
'Journeyman Engineer' 217n.31
juvenile fiction 7, 202, 212, 269

*Kaiser's Kalendar for 1915,
  The* 259n.61
Kartoffel, Baron von 251
Keats, John 21
Kebbel, Thomas 153
Keep, C.J. 203
Kennedy, David 74n.13
Kennedy, Paul 93, 94, 159, 267
Key, Sir Cooper 99
*Kinematograph and Lantern
  Weekly* 241, 244
Kingdom United, A (Pennell) 14n.30
Kipling, Rudyard 213, 245
Koss, Stephen 5, 94, 211
Krever, Tor 74n.13
Kumar, Krishan 167

Labour movement 265
Lambert, Andrew 76n.24
Laski, Harold 235
Law, Graham 194
Le Bon, Gustave 4, 5, 163, 180n.62
Le Queux, William 8, 61, 51n.120,
  123, 140n.38, 141n.39,
  141n.40, 162, 167, 179n.52,
  181n.69, 194, 195, 196,
  204–210, 214, 226n.114,
  241n.42, 243, 249, 250,
  253, 258n.35, 260n.69,
  261n.75, 269
League of Defenders 128
Leersen, Joep 8
Lehmann, Rudolph 204, 206, 208
Lehmann, John 224n.92
Leith Hill 254
Lester, Edward 184n.104
Lester, H.F. 115n.111
Lewin, Christopher
  George 220n.51

318   *Index*

Liberal government 22, 23, 84, 109n.51, 117, 153
Lincolnshire 267
Linney, Derek 79n.60
'Little Englanders' 191
'Little Englandism' 170
Liverpool Mercury 27
Local Government Act (1888) 174n.5
London County Council (LCC) 174n.5
Longmate, Norman 101

Macaulay, Thomas 186n.113
McClintock, F.L. 107
Machen, Arthur 232, 238, 256n.23
MacKay, Charles 3
MacKay, Donald 113n.84
MacKenzie, John 202, 203
Mackinder, Sir Halford 172–173, 188n.126
MacLeod, Roy 130
Macmillan's Magazine 28
'*Made in Germany*' (Williams) 156
Mahan, Alfred 86, 211
Mail (Portsmouth) 117, 118, 121, 122
'man in the street, the' 2, 4, 5, 58, 86, 131, 136, 267
'*Man Who Stopped a War, The*' (Vaux) 172
Manchester Guardian 85
Mandler, Peter 8
Marder, Arthur 93, 157
Martel, Gordon 268
Mason, A.E.W. 224n.92
mass media 110n.70
mass press, foundation for 4–5
mass readership 5, 69, 121, 211, 249, 266
mass reading public 62
mass-market publishing 211–215
Masterman, Charles 249
Matin, A. Michael 7, 8, 16n.35, 28, 68, 199, 249, 260n.73
Matos, T. Carlo 57

Maude, Frederic Natusch 124
Maurice, John Frederic 76n.28
Maxse, Leo 209, 211, 212
McClintock, F.L.; Macclintock 107n.40
Meisel, Joseph S. 17n.39
Meredith, George 166, 167
Message, The (Dawson) 143n.58, 191
Meyer, Jessica 165
middle-class people 26, 42, 94, 194
Middleton, Alex 47, 47n.59, 74n.12
militant nationalism 7
militant society 201
militarism 201–203
military planning, and invasion-scare fiction 199–200
military unpreparedness, of British state 23–24
'mob-law' 31, 59, 60, 159
Modern Dædalus (Greer) 113n.86
Monthly Review 197
Moore, G.H. 112n.82
Morgan-Owen, David 6
Morley, John 9
Morning Post, The 26–27, 57, 85, 108n.48
Morris, A.J.A. 18n.44
Morris, William 167
Moskowitz, Sam 177n.31, 194, 196
Moss, Eloise 181n.78
'Motly Ranke McCauley' 37
Mr Britling Sees It Through (Wells) 231, 260n.69
'Mr Punch's Naval Novel'; Mr. Punch (Anon.) 138n.14
'Mrs Brown' (Sketchley) 35–37
Mrs Brown on the Battle of Dorking (Sketchley) 36, 42–43
Munro, Hector Hugh 168
Murray's Magazine 88, 195
'My Volunteer'; my volunteer (poem) 45n.20
myths and legends 238–239

Index

Napier, Sir Charles 3
Napoleonic Wars 193
Nash, Eveleigh 225n.104
national defence
  Dilke letter, the 85–86
  naval scare, 1884 87–92
  policy 103
  public opinion on 86–87, 95–96
  scaremongers,
    unintentional 92–95
  signatories plea on 84–85
National Film, The 244, 250, 253
National Review 153, 209, 211,
  212, 213, 226n.120
National Rifle Association 83
National Service League 71,
  131, 135
'Nauticus' 190
naval campaign 89, 93
Naval Defence Act (1889) 86, 121
naval experts 176n.24
'Naval Moltke' 132, 133
naval scare, 1884 87–92, 132
  funding for naval
    expenditure 90–92
  naval agitation and
    debate 89–90
naval war stories 157, 190–192
naval wars 96–97
navy
  1888 naval scare 86
  1884 naval scare 86, 87–92,
    268, 270
  strengthening, versus army
    strengthening 58
Navy League 71, 131, 147n.102,
  148n.103, 211
Neilson, Keith 270
New Battle of Dorking, The
  (Maude) 124, 191
New Grub Street (Gissing) 120
New Journalism 93, 109n.63
New London Journal 208
New Ordeal, The (Chesney) 70,
  80n.64
New Statesman 235

Newnes, George 193, 194, 204,
  240, 250, 253
Newnes Trench Library 240
Newry Bridge (Anon.) 112n.82
News from Nowhere (Morris) 167
newspapers 209–215
  campaigns 86, 93
  and parliament 92
  political scandals in 110n.70
Newton, W. Douglas 184n.104
Next Crusade, The (Cromie)
  138n.13
Nihilists 155
Nineteenth Century 89, 90, 99,
  100, 101, 109n.63, 197
No More War! (Stead) 252
*North Afire, The: A Picture
  of What May Be* (Newton)
  185n.104
Northbrook, Earl of 90, 91
Northcliffe, 227n.129
Number 70, Berlin (Le Queux) 251
nursing women 165

'Octogenarian, An' 72
Odger, George 175n.20
Offer, Avner 157, 158
Official British propaganda
  factual film production 243–245
  invasion-scare literature in
    248–249
  posters 245–248
Offin, T.W. 234–235
'Old Harrovian, An' 95
'Old Soldier, An' 97
'One Who Knows the Facts'; one
  who knows 89, 90, 91,
  108n.48, 109n.53
  see also 'Truth about the
    Navy, The'
Otis, Laura 155
Ottoman Empire 70, 72
Our Hero!! ('Blower, Sergt' and
  'Cheeks the Marine') 36–37
Outlaws of the Air, The
  (Griffith) 190

320 *Index*

Paddock, Troy 264
Pall Mall Gazette, The 27, 30, 35,
 39, 88, 89, 90, 91, 92, 93,
 94, 131, 132, 146n.86, 208,
 212, 213, 227n.129
Pall Mall Magazine 213, 214,
 227n.128
panicmongers 34–35
Parallel Case, A (Anon.) 72
Paris Commune (1871) 31,
 154, 164
Paris, Michael 7, 202, 213,
 220n.51
Parnell, Charles Stewart 97
Parrinder, Patrick 167
Parry, Jonathan 267
patriotic films 240, 241, 249
Patton, Robert L. 194
Pearson, Arthur 193, 194
Pearson's Magazine 194
Peddie, James 102
Pelling, Henry 137n.6
Pemberton, Max 119, 140n.36, 195
Pennell, Catriona 14n.30, 237,
 259n.50
Penny Illustrated Paper 165, 214
Perkin, Harold 178n.49
pétroleuse 164
Phantom Army, The
 (Pemberton) 139n.15
Philp, Mark 3
Phrynicus 2
Pick, Daniel 7, 103, 155, 166, 239
Pictures and the Picturegoer 241
 *see also Great War in England
 in 1897, The* (Le Queux)
'Poisoned Bullet, The' (Le Queux)
 *see also Great War in England in
 1897, The* (Le Queux) 195
political conservatism 7
Polyphemes, The (Hernaman-
 Johnson) 208
Ponsonby, Arthur 205, 206
Posteritas 164
posters, for propaganda 245–248
Potter, George 100–101, 114n.101,
 166

Powell, G.H. 192, 232
press
 expansion of 60
 influencing public opinion
 145n.73
 power of 265
 in Victorian Britain 94
pressure groups
 Imperial Maritime League 133
 National Service League
 135–136
 Navy League 131–134
pre-war British militarism
 200–201
pre-war literature 155, 231, 234,
 251, 253
Prince of Wales 30, 41
'Promis'd Horrors of the French
 Invasion' (Gillray) 3
Propaganda and Empire
 (MacKenzie) 202
psychological rise in prices, of food
 supply 158
public 6–8, 9, 42, 67, 237
 see also crowds
 and Channel Tunnel *see*
 Channel Tunnel
 elusiveness 95–96
 ignorance 204–205, 206
 influence of journalism
 on 88
 interference in military
 planning 69
 mass readership 62, 89, 267
 and newspapers 266
 perception on Crimean War
 outcome 67
 readership 192–195
 role of expertise 57–61
 see also crowds
public, as audience and consumers
 189–192
 authorial intent and popular
 reaction 198–199
 fiction and reading public
 192–195
 and newspapers 209–215

Index

reactions to *The Invasion of 1910* 204–205
public, in invasion-scare fiction 154–155
  food supply threats 156–159
  gender roles 163–166
  nation and nationalities 167–170
  people's class 159–163
  race and empire 170–173
  threats, external and internal 155–156
public mind 42, 69, 94
public opinion 9, 85, 86–87, 91, 98, 119, 137, 145n.73, 268
  on *Battle of Dorking, The* 31–32
  and censorship 248
  changing idea of 3–5
  limits of 129–131
  on national defence 95–96
  and Navy League 134
  and press 93, 121
  see also democracy and democratic system
public pressure 94, 268
Punch 27, 34, 119, 120, 138n.14, 194, 209, 211, 231, 238, 251, 254
Purple Cloud, The (Shiel) 190

Ramsden, John 14n.30, 142n.50, 196
Raphael, J.E. 134
Reader, W.J. 202
reading public, and fiction
  journalism tools 195
  magazines 194
  newspapers 193–194
  texts 194–195
Readman, Paul 123, 158
Recent Publications of Military Interest 199
Redford, Duncan 103
Redford, Paul 116n.116
Redmond-Howard, L.G. 261n.81

Reeves, Nicholas 244
Reform Act (1867) 4, 9, 94, 154, 159, 265
  see also Second Reform Act
Reform Act (1884) 5, 93, 95, 96, 265
  see also Third Reform Act
Reign of George VI, The (Anon.) 234, 255n.9
'Reign of the Engineer' 60
revolution fiction in the 1890s 153
Reynold's Newspaper 34–35
Richards, Grant 124, 191, 232
Riddle of the Sands, The (Childers) 125–127, 129, 168, 200
Ridley, Matthew White 158
Rise of Professional Society: England since 1880, The (Perkin) 178n.49
Roberts, Lord 123, 124, 128, 135, 136, 141n.39, 240, 242
Robinson, Charles Napier 96
Robinson, Sir R. Spencer 107n.46
Rose, George ('Arthur Sketchley') 35–37, 39, 42–43, 166
Rose, Jonathan 9
Rosebery, Earl of 84, 268
Row in Dame Europa's School, The (music) 37
Royal Commission on Supply of Food and Raw Material in Time of War 1, 157, 158, 159
Royal Military Academy, Woolwich 59
Royal Navy 71, 86, 88, 91, 134, 172, 190, 211
Royal United Service Institution (RUSI) 48n.65, 48n.69, 55–56, 64, 68–69, 74n.3, 107n.46, 199
Russell, Lord John 59
Russia 65, 71, 72, 92, 99, 121, 122, 168, 266

Index

Russia's Hope, The (Anon.)
82n.79, 97
Ryan, W. Michael 14n.29

Saki (H.H. Munro) 179n.51
Salisbury, Lord 84, 178n.49
Sanders, M.L. 249
Saturday Review 87, 177n.37
Scandinavian invasion-scare
fiction 263
Scarborough 183n.91
*Schedule of Wellington House
Literature* 249, 260n.73
science fiction 6, 7, 97, 160, 193
scientific romance 193
Scientific Romance
(Stableford) 219n.42
Scott, C.P. 85
Scully, Richard 168
Searle, G.R. 5, 200
'Second Armada, The' 30,
41, 42, 64
Second Reform Act 4, 9, 94, 154,
159, 265
see also Reform Act (1867)
Secord, James A. 180n.64
Secret Agent, The (Conrad) 263
'Seizure of the Channel Tunnel,
The' (F.A.) 102
service authors 56–57, 58, 60,
62–64, 96, 121
service journals 57, 63, 66–67
service writers *see* service authors
Shaw, George Bernard 57,
58, 124, 129, 142n.43,
145n.68, 235
Shaylor, Joseph 47n.49
Sheffield Daily Telegraph 232
Shiel, M.P. 172, 190
*Siege of Bodike: A Prophecy
of Ireland's Future, The*
(Lester) 184n.104
Siege of London, The (J.W.M.) 160
Siege of London, The (Posteritas)
35, 113n.86, 154, 159,
164, 169

'Siege of Portsmouth, The' (Beccles
and Clowes) 118–123, 127,
128, 136, 168, 190
Smallways, Bert 190, 215n.7
Smith, F.E. 248
Smith, Steven R.B. 94, 110n.69
social control 203–204
South African War 125, 129,
200, 265
see also Boer War
Spain 211
Spectator 32, 38
speculative fiction 103, 193, 214
speculative non-fiction 195
Spencer, Herbert 201, 202, 223n.77
Sphere (magazine) 206
Spiers, Edward M. 75n.17
St James's Gazette 112n.82
Stableford, Brian 193, 195,
218n.40
Staff College 59, 60
Staircase of Death, The
(film) 258n.35
Stamp Act (1819) 193
Standard 83, 198
'starvation-leading-to-revolution'
trope 157
starvation theory 157, 176n.28
Starved into Surrender (Clarke)
156, 161
Statist (magazine) 110n.69
Stead, F. Herbert 252
Stead, W.T. 88–89, 92, 93, 94, 95,
106n.25, 107n.36, 109n.51,
109n.63, 119, 131, 194
Stedman Jones, Gareth 196
Steel, John 156, 161
Steiner, Zara 270
Stone, Charles 29–30, 161, 168
Strand Magazine 176n.24,
186n.113, 194
*Strange Death of Liberal England,
The* (Dangerfield) 200
strategic thinking 86
Straus, Ralph 234
Summers, Anne 135, 201, 219n.47

Index

Sunday Times, The 155, 156
Suvin, Darko 7, 38, 79n.60, 97, 154, 160, 193, 205, 206
Sweden 72
Swoop! The (Wodehouse) 167
Swoop of the Eagles, The (V.) 161, 178n.49, 185n.109
Swoop of the Vulture, The (Blyth) 127, 143n.56
Symonds, Sir Thomas 110n.69

Taking of Dover, The (Lester) 82n.79, 115n.111
Tariff Reform campaign 155–156, 158
Tatler (journal) 209
Taylor, Philip M. 249
Thames Valley 167
Thanet 182n.86
theatrical invasion-scare 35, 57, 125, 196, 197, 210, 214, 219n.47, 241, 242, 253, 268, 269, 270
Things I know of Kings, Celebrities, and Crooks (Le Queux) 140n.38
Third Reform Act 5, 93, 95, 96, 265
see also Reform Act (1884)
Thirty-Nine Steps, The (Buchan) 251, 261n.80
Thomas, Elwin 122
Thompson, F.M.L. 203
Thompson, J. Lee 138n.10
Thompson, James 9, 95, 96
'three panics' (Cobden) 3
Through Bosnia and the Herzegóvina on Foot (Evans) 72
Time Machine, The (Wells) 189
Times, The 27, 28, 30, 34, 41, 42, 68, 114n.108, 130, 135, 205, 224n.92, 237, 248, 257n.29
Tit-Bits (magazine) 194
To Venus in Five Seconds (Jane) 216n.14
Tower Publishing Company 197
Tracy, Louis 140n.36, 168

Tredrey, F.D. 44
True Reformer, A (Chesney) 38, 84
'Truth about the Navy, The' series; truth about 89, 90, 91, 92, 94, 95, 98, 108n.48, 110n.69, 131
see also 'One Who Knows [the Facts]'
Truth About Russia, The (Stead) 106n.25
Tsushima, Russian defeat at 92
Tucker, Albert 66

uncivilized public violence 31
United States 66, 97, 171, 188n.125, 211, 249
democracy of 264–265
and invasion panics 29
support to Britain 171, 249

Vaux, Patrick 172, 188n.125
Verne, Jules 1, 210, 215
Versailles (1871), Treaty of 23
Victoria, Queen 161, 200
Victoria-Esquimalt branch, Navy League 133
Victorian science fiction 97, 160, 193
Victorian Science Fiction (Suvin) 79n.60, 97
Victorians 2, 3, 9, 12n.18, 42, 94, 98, 129, 201
Violet Flame, The (Jane) 216
visual culture 196–197, 243–245
visual propaganda 245
Vivian, Captain 43
Voices Prophesying War (Clarke) 6, 255n.3
voluntary enlistment 243
Volunteer(s) 22, 24, 25, 26, 32, 45n.20, 62, 64, 65, 83
City Imperial Volunteers 125
corps, permanence to 83
movement 3, 201
recruitment 32
Surrey Brigade of the Metropolitan Volunteers 83

Index

'Wake, England wake!' (poem) 23
"*Wake Up!*" *A Dream of To-Morrow* (Cowen) 241–243; wake up! A dream 258n.48
Wallace, Brian 219n.47
Wallace, Edgar 252–253
Wallas, Graham 264–265
Waller, Philip 195, 197
War (Newton) 128
'War and a Woman' (Vaux): war and a woman 188n.125
War and the Arme Blanche (Childers) 143n.52
war enthusiasm 6
'War Hawks, The' (Bramah) 212
War in the Air, The (Wells) 190, 212
War Inevitable, The (Burgoyne) 128, 182n.86, 234
war literature 249–251, 269
War Machine (Pick) 182n.81
War of 1886, The (Anon.) 57–58
War of the Nations, The (Le Queux) 250
War of the Worlds, The (Wells) 167, 170
War Office 43, 99, 127, 129, 130, 199, 241
War Office library 82n.80
War Pictorial (magazine) 260n.74
war propaganda 10, 239
War Propaganda Bureau 249
War Tactics: or Can Great Britain be Invaded? (game) 197
wartime invasion literature 251–252
Was England Erwartet (Peuckert) 254
Watkin, Edward 100
Webb, Beatrice 144n.68
Webb, Sidney 144n.68
Weedon, Alexis 194
Weekly Dispatch 235
Weinrich, Arndt 200

Wellesley, Sir Arthur, Duke of Wellington 3, 76n.28
Wellington House literature propaganda 248–249
Wells, H.G. 167, 170, 189–190, 196, 212, 215n.6, 231, 249, 254, 264
What Happened After the Battle of Dorking (Stone) 29–30, 64, 161, 168
When All Men Starve (Gleig) 156
When War Breaks Out (Wilson and White) 162, 219n.41
When William Came (Munro) 168, 171
white and yellow civilization clashes 172–173
White Lie, The (film) 258n.35
White, Arnold 5, 162, 176n.24, 219n.41
Wilhelm, Kaiser 259n.61
William II (German Emperor) 260
William, Emperor 259n.61
Wilkinson, Glenn R. 212
Wilkinson, Spenser 84–85, 131–134, 136, 144n.68, 146n.81
Williams, Ernest Edwin 156
Wilson, Beccles 118
Wilson, H.W. 124, 162, 219n.41
Wilson, Keith M. 99–100, 268
Winter, Jay 160, 245
'With the Nightmail' (Kipling) 213
Wodehouse, P.G. 167
Wolseley, Sir Garnet 98–100, 101, 103, 113n.88, 114n.108, 115n.111, 119, 128, 136, 198
women, resistance against invaders 164–165
Women's Unionist and Tariff Reform Association (WUTRA) 156
Wood, Harry 177n.45

Wood, Walter 156
working class 158, 164, 194
World War, First 4, 6, 9, 10, 56, 58, 60, 87, 137, 158, 160, 176n.26, 192, 199, 204, 231, 232, 239, 243, 245, 249, 252, 253, 254, 268
Wyatt-Tilby, A. 59, 61

xenophobia 7, 161

Yate, Charles 158
Yellow Danger, The (Shiel) 172, 173
'yellow patriots' 209
'Yellow Peril' stories 172; yellow peril 188n.124
yellow press 209, 211–215
Yorkshire Post 234

Zeppelin Destroyer, The (Le Queux) 251